The Aarhus Convention

A Guide for UK Lawyers

Edited by Charles Banner

• HART •
OXFORD • LONDON • NEW YORK • NEW DELHI • SYDNEY

HART PUBLISHING

Bloomsbury Publishing Plc

Kemp House, Chawley Park, Cumnor Hill, Oxford, OX2 9PH, UK

1385 Broadway, New York, NY 10018, USA

29 Earlsfort Terrace, Dublin 2, Ireland

HART PUBLISHING, the Hart/Stag logo, BLOOMSBURY and the Diana logo are trademarks of Bloomsbury Publishing Plc

First published in Great Britain 2015

A catalogue record for this book is available from the British Library.

Library of Congress Cataloging-in-Publication data

ISBN: 978-1-84946-571-7

Typeset by Compuscript Ltd, Shannon

THE AARHUS CONVENTION

The UNECE Convention on Access to Information, Public Participation in Decision-Making and Access to Justice in Environmental Matters—known ubiquitously as the Aarhus Convention—is having an ever increasing influence on domestic and EU environmental law and procedure. Recent years have seen a steady flow of case-law from the UK Courts, CJEU and Aarhus Convention Compliance Committee, a raft of civil procedure reforms in response to concerns about whether the costs rules in domestic environmental litigation are compatible with the Convention, and an infraction by the European Commission against the UK alleging various systemic breaches. Even the EU itself has been the subject of a ruling by the Compliance Committee that the CJEU's rules on standing for judicial review of EU legislation are too narrow to comply with the Convention. This book, written by several of the leading experts in the field, provides a comprehensive guide to the implementation of the Convention in each of the UK's jurisdictions, the three pillars of the Convention (access to information, public participation and access to justice) and the mechanisms by which the rights by the Convention can be enforced.

FOREWORD BY LORD CARNWATH OF NOTTING HILL, JUSTICE OF THE SUPREME COURT OF THE UNITED KINGDOM

As the tenth anniversary of the United Kingdom's ratification of the Aarhus Convention approaches, its prominence in domestic litigation continues to increase. The procedural rules for judicial review in England and Wales, Scotland and Northern Ireland all now include provision for costs capping in challenges to decisions within the scope of the Convention. However, the influence of the Convention goes beyond procedure. It has also helped to shape the substantive grounds of challenge, for example in cases such as the judicial review of the Command Paper on the proposed HS2 railway, and the challenge to the Attorney-General's veto of the disclosure of correspondence between the Prince of Wales and Government ministers. At the same time, the United Kingdom remains one of the most frequent 'customers' of the Aarhus Convention Compliance Committee—perhaps itself a reflection of the awareness within the country of individual's rights under the Convention. It has also contributed to the evolving thinking of the European Court of Justice on the EU Directives which implement parts of the Convention. Many of the recent cases have either originated from this jurisdiction or have featured the United Kingdom as interveners.

Because of the piecemeal, incremental way in which the Convention has found its way into domestic law, access to the relevant legal materials has not always been straightforward. Similarly, the decisions of the Compliance Committee, while not binding in law and not to be found in the conventional law reports, have been gradually acknowledged as having considerable persuasive authority. Against this background, I strongly welcome the provision of a book looking at all aspects of the Convention's application within the United Kingdom, bringing together and analysing the case-law and legislation at domestic, EU and Aarhus levels. We are also fortunate to have the guidance of such a distinguished and expert team of authors.

I congratulate all those involved in this important project.

Robert Carnwath 13 January 2015

CONTENTS

Foreword by Lord Carnwath of Notting Hill, Justice of the Supreme Court of the United Kingdom v
Editor's Introduction ix
Table of Cases xi
Table of Legislation xvii

1. The Aarhus Convention: An Overview 1
Charles Banner

The Implementation of the Aarhus Convention in the UK

2. The Aarhus Convention in England and Wales 13
Brian KA Ruddie

3. The Aarhus Convention in Scotland 41
Lorna Drummond QC

4. The Aarhus Convention in Northern Ireland—A Tale of Two Polities.....73
William Orbinson QC

5. The Aarhus Convention and the European Union.....79
Professor Ludwig Krämer

The Substantive Rights

6. Access to and Collection of Environmental Information 99
David Blundell

7. Public Participation in Environmental Decision-Making, Plan-Making and Executive Regulations—Articles 6, 7 and 8 of the Aarhus Convention 121
Simon Ricketts and Juliet Munn

8. Access to Justice: Review Procedures and Costs.....141
James Maurici QC

9. The Aarhus Convention and NGOs 181
Carol Day

Review of Parties' Compliance with the Aarhus Convention

10. The Aarhus Convention Compliance Mechanism and Proceedings before its Compliance Committee 201
Veit Koester

Appendices

1. The Aarhus Convention 217
2. Decision I/7 of the Meeting of the Parties to the Aarhus Convention 243
3. Format for Communications to the Aarhus Convention Compliance Committee 251
4. Regulation 1049/2001/EC *on public access to Parliament, Council and Commission documents* 255
5. Regulation 1367/2006 *on the application of the Aarhus Convention to Community institutions and bodies* 261
6. Directive 2003/4 (the Environmental Information Directive) 269
7. Directive 2003/35/EC (the Public Participation Directive) 277
8. Directive 2011/92/EU (the Codified Environmental Impact Assessment Directive) 285
9. Directive 2001/42/EC (the Strategic Environmental Assessment Directive) 307
10. Civil Procedure Rules, Rule 45 Section VII, Practice Direction 45 Section VII, and rule 52.9A 315
11. Rules of the Court of Session, Chapter 58A 319
12. The Costs Protection (Aarhus Convention) Regulations (Northern Ireland) 2013 323
13. Tabular analysis of the Meeting of the Parties' Consideration of the Compliance Committee's Findings in Communications and Referrals Concerning the Parties' Compliance 327
14. List of Useful Weblinks Relating to the Aarhus Convention 331

Index 333

EDITOR'S INTRODUCTION

Despite the decade that has passed since the United Kingdom ratified the Aarhus Convention, there is a surprising lack of literature about its application in this jurisdiction. This book seeks to fill that gap, by exploring the implementation of the Convention in the three constituent jurisdictions of the United Kingdom and the European Union, the substantive rights conferred by the 'three pillars' of the Convention, and the mechanism for the review of Parties' compliance with the Convention by the Aarhus Convention Compliance Committee. Each chapter is intended to be capable of being read either on its own or cumulatively with the other chapters. It is expected that the former is most likely to be of use to practitioners seeking to research particular aspects of the Convention and its application within the United Kingdom, and the editing process has been undertaken with that in mind.

There is currently no source, whether in print or online, where the core UNECE, European Union and domestic legislation on the Aarhus Convention is available in one place. Appendices 1–12 to this book therefore include the key provisions at each of these levels. Appendix 13 analyses the responses of the meeting of the Parties to the findings of the Compliance Committee. Appendix 14 sets out a list of useful websites where other materials relating to the Convention can be accessed, including perhaps most significantly a digest of the Compliance Committee's case-law.

A deliberate choice has been made not to extend the scope of this book to the Kiev Protocol on Pollutant Release and Transfer Registers, in order to keep the focus on the core provisions of the Convention itself which are of significantly more regular relevance to legal practice within the United Kingdom and which have been the subject of a great deal more jurisprudence at international, European and domestic levels.

I would like to express my sincere thanks to the various distinguished experts who have gone to considerable trouble contributing to this book and to Rachel Turner and Richard Hart at Hart Publishing (an imprint of Bloomsbury Publishing plc) whose patience and assistance has been greatly appreciated.

This book sets out the law as of 1 October 2014; where possible, subsequent developments until March 2015 have been incorporated.

Charles Banner
Landmark Chambers
180 Fleet Street, London EC4A 2HG
13 March 2015

TABLE OF CASES

Adan v Newham LBC [2001] EWCA Civ 1916, [2002] 1 WLR 2120 186
Air Transport Association of America v Secretary of State for Energy and Climate Change (Case C-366/10) [2012] CMLR 4 80
Alternative A5 Alliance's Application for Judicial Review, Re [2013] NIQB 30, [2014] NI 96 .... 56, 75-76
API (Cases C -514/07P, C-528/07P and 532/07P to 517/07) [2011] 2 AC 359 85
Ashton v Secretary of State for Communities and Local Government [2010] EWCA Civ 600, [2011] 1 P & CR 5 .... 37, 162-63
Associated Provincial Picture Houses Ltd v Wednesbury Corporation [1948] KB 223 .... 14, 39, 44, 60, 106, 166–68, 186, 195–96
Attorney General of the Gambia v N'Jie [1961] AC 617 162
Austin v Miller Argent (South Wales) Ltd [2014] EWCA Civ 1012, [2015] 1 WLR 62 .... 32, 34, 146, 175
AXA General Insurance Ltd v HM Advocate [2011] UKSC 46, [2012] 1 AC 868 61
Bard Campaign and David Bliss v Secretary of State for Communities and Local Government [2009] EWHC 308 (Admin) 121
Bello Fratelli (Case C-268/02) [2004] ECR I-3465 80
Bettati v Safety Hi-Tech (Case C-341/95) [1996] ECR I-3989 .... 9, 80
Birkett v Department for the Environment, Food and Rural Affairs [2011] EWCA Civ 1606, [2012] 2 CMLR 169 20–21
Bova v Highland Council 2011 SCLR 751 .... 59, 63
Brown Bear *see* Lesoochranárske zoskupenie VLK v Ministerstvo životného prostredia Slovenskej republiky (Case C-240/09)
Bund für Umwelt und Naturschutz Deutschland, Landesverband Nordrhein—Westfalen eV v Bezirksregierung Arnsberg (Case C-115/09) [2011] 3 CMLR 15 151–53
Cala Homes (South) Ltd v Secretary of State for Communities and Local Government [2011] 1 P & CR 22 56
Carroll v Scottish Borders Council [2014] CSOH 30, 2014 SLT 659 69
Central Craigavon Ltd v Department for Environment [2011] NICA 17, [2012] NI 60 56
Client Earth v Commission (Case T-111/11) [2014] Env LR 11 86
Coedbach Action Team Ltd v Secretary of State for Energy and Climate Change [2010] EWHC 2312 (Admin), [2010] All ER (D) 60 (Oct) 37
Coedbach Action Team Ltd v Secretary of State for Energy and Climate Change [2010] EWHC 2312 (Admin), [2011] 1 Costs LR 70; upheld [2010] EWCA Civ 1494 163–65

Commission v Belgium (Case 186/85) [1987] ECR 2029 33
Commission v Germany (Case C-61/94) [1996] ECR I-3989 80
Commission v Germany (Case C-217/97) [1999] ECR I-5087 113
Commission v Ireland (Case C-427/07) [2009] ECR I-6277, [2010] Env LR 8 ....37, 59, 67, 158–59
Commission v Ireland (Case C-456/08) [2010] ECR I-859 ....159, 162–63
Commission v Italy (Case C-296/92) [1994] ECR I-1 33
Commission v Stichting Natuur en Milieu (Case C-405/12P), 13 January 2013 94
Commission v United Kingdom (Case C-530/11) [2014] QB 988 ....8–9, 33, 65–66, 141, 149, 159, 171, 174–77, 192
Council and Commission v Milieu-Defensie (Case C-401/12P), 13 January 2015 94
Coventry v Lawrence [2014] UKSC 46, [2014] 3 WLR 555 ....146, 175
Cumming v Secretary of State for Scotland 1992 SC 463, 1993 SLT 228 162
Danielsson v Commission (Case T-219/95R) [1995] ECR II-3051 94
Danmarks Sportfiskerforbund and Lemvig og Omegns Sportfiskerforening v Miljø- & Energiministeriet, Skov- og Naturstyrelsen and Naturklagen æ vnet, U.2001.1594V 157
Davey v Aylesbury Vale DC [2007] EWCA Civ 1166, [2008] 2 All ER 178 31–32
DEB Deutsche Energiehandels- und Beratungsgesellschaft mbH v Bundesrepublik Deutschland (Case C-279/09) [2010] ECR I-13849 173
Deutsche Umwelthilfe eV v Bundesrepublik Deutschland (Case C-515/11) 13 July 2013 ....43, 81
Djurgården-Lilla Värtans Miljöskyddsförening v Stockholms kommun genom dess markn ä mnd (Case C-263/08) [2009] ECR I-09967 ....37, 59, 153–55
Doogan v Greater Glasgow and Clyde Health Board 2012 SLT 1041 67
Dundee Harbour Trustees v D & J Nicol [1915] AC 550 61
Eaton v Natural England [2013] EWCA Civ 628, [2013] Env LR 37 174
Eco-Energy (GB) Ltd v First Secretary of State [2004] EWCA Civ 1566, [2005] 2 P & CR 5 162
Edwards v Environment Agency (Case C-260/11) [2013] 1 WLR 2914 ....8–9, 14, 33, 35–36, 65–67, 159, 171–72, 174, 189, 192
Engel v Netherlands (1976) 1 EHRR 647 110
Fish Legal, Emily Shirley v Information Commissioner, United Utilities, Yorkshire Water and Southern Water (Case C-279/12) [2014] QB 521 ....18–19, 47
Flachglas Torgau GmbH v Germany (C-204/09) [2013] QB 212 ....18, 43, 81
Forbes v Aberdeenshire Council [2010] CSOH 1, [2010] Env LR 36 ....42, 61
Friends of Loch Etive, Petitioner [2014] CSOH 116 70
Genovaitė Valčiukienė v Pakruojo Rajono Savivaldybė [2012] Env LR 283 57
Greenpeace v Commission (Case C-321/95P) [1998] ECR I-1651 94
Guerra v Italy (1998) 26 EHRR 357 115
Harding v Cork CC [2008] IECS 27 159
IATA and ELFA (Case C-344/04) [2006] ECR I-403 80
IFAW v Commission (Case T-362/08), 13 January 2011 84
Inter-Environnement Bruxelles ASBL v Région de Bruxelles-Capitale (Case C-567/10) [2012] 2 CMLR 30 ....54, 56, 124, 126

Inter-Environnement Wallonie ASBL, Terre Wallonne ASBL v Région Wallonne (Case C-41/11) [2012] 2 CMLR 21 57
Inuit Tapiriit Kanatami v European Parliament and Council (Case C-583/11P) [2014] QB 648 ....94, 161
JB Trustees Ltd v Secretary of State for Communities and Local Government [2013] EWHC 3555 (Admin) 163, 165
Khairandish v Secretary of State for the Home Department 2003 SLT 1358 42
Kinnegar Residents' Action Group Application, Re [2007] NIQB 90 74
Lardner v Renfrewshire Council 1997 SCLR 454, 1997 SC 104.... 162–63
Lesoochranárske zoskupenie VLK v Ministerstvo životného prostredia Slovenskej republiky (Case C-240/09) (Brown Bear) [2011] ECR I-1255, [2012] QB 606.... 30, 38, 42, 59, 92, 142, 159–61
Manchester City Council v Secretary of State for the Environment [1988] JPL 774 106
Manchester College v Hazel [2013] EWCA Civ 281....170
Markinson (David) v Information Commissioner, EA/2005/014....113
Marleasing SA v La Comercial Internacional de Alimentacion SA (Case C-106/89) [1990] ECR I-4135 42
McArthur v Lord Advocate 2006 SLT 170....64
McGinty v Scottish Ministers [2013] CSIH 78, 2014 SC 81 ....50, 54, 56, 61–62, 66–67
McHugh's Application, Re [2007] NICA 26 74
Mecklenburg (Case C-321/96) [1999] ECR 1999....82, 88
Minister of Immigration and Ethnic Affairs v Teoh (1995) 183 CLR 273 42
Morbaine Ltd v First Secretary of State [2004] EWHC 1708 (Admin), [2005] JPL 377....162
Morgan v Hinton Organics (Wessex) Ltd [2009] EWCA Civ 107, [2009] Env LR 30 .... 1, 14, 32, 42, 64–65, 169, 175
Musaj v Secretary of State for the Home Department 2004 SLT 623....42
Network Rail Ltd v Information Commissioner, Appeal Nos EA/2006/0061 and EA/2006/0062....47
Newton Mearns Residents Flood Prevention Group for Cheviot Drive v East Renfrewshire Council [2013] CSOH 68; [2013] CSIH 70 ....64, 67
Nomarchiaki Aftodioikisi Aitoloakarnanias v Ipourgos Perivallontos, Khorotaxias kai Dimosion Ergon [2013] Env LR 453 56
Office of Communications v Information Commissioner (Case C-71/10) [2011] ECR I-07205 ....21, 42, 46, 104
Office of Communications v Information Commissioner [2010] UKSC 3, [2010] Env LR 20....104
Plaumann v Commission (Case 25/62) [1963] ECR 199, [1964] CMLR 29 ....94, 161
Port of London Authority v Information Commissioner, Appeal No EA/2006/0083....47
Portobello Park Action Group Association v City of Edinburgh Council [2012] CSIH 69, 2013 SC 184 63
R (Adlard) v Secretary of State for the Environment, Transport and Regions [2002] EWCA Civ 735, [2002] 1 WLR 2515....60

R (An Taisce (The National Trust for Ireland)) v Secretary of State for Energy and Climate Change [2014] EWCA Civ 1111, [2015] Env LR 2 14
R (Berky) v Newport City Council [2012] EWCA Civ 378, [2012] 2 CMLR 44 178–79
R (Botley Parish Action Group) v Eastleigh BC [2014] EWHC 3488 (Admin)....170
R (Buckinghamshire CC) v Secretary of State for Transport [2014] UKSC 3, [2014] 1 WLR 324.... 55–56
R (Buglife) v Medway Council [2011] EWHC 746 (Admin), [2011] 24 EG 108 (CS)....38, 62
R (Burkett) v Hammersmith and Fulham LBC [2004] EWCA Civ 1317, [2004] All ER (D) 186 (Oct)....31, 40
R (Burkett) v Hammersmith and Fulham LBC (Costs) [2004] EWCA Civ 1342, [2005] CP Rep 11 141
R (Compton) v Wiltshire Primary Care Trust [2008] EWCA Civ 749, [2009] 1 WLR 1436....32, 68
R (Corner House Research) v Secretary of State for Trade and Industry [2005] EWCA Civ 192, [2005] 4 All ER 1 ....31–32, 64, 74, 168–70
R (Edwards) v Environment Agency [2010] UKSC 57, [2011] 1 WLR 79.... 7–8
R (Edwards) v Environment Agency (No 2) [2013] UKSC 78, [2014] 1 WLR 55 ....36–37, 65, 69–71, 141, 171–72, 174, 193
R (England) v Tower Hamlets LBC [2006] EWCA Civ 1742, [2006] All ER (D) 314 (Dec)....31
R (Evans) v Attorney General [2013] EWHC 1960 (Admin), [2013] 3 WLR 1631....166–67, 195
R (Evans) v Secretary of State for Communities and Local Government [2013] EWCA Civ 87 60
R (Evans) v Secretary of State for Communities and Local Government [2013] EWCA Civ 114, [2013] JPL 1027.... 14, 39, 167, 167–68, 195
R (Garner) v Elmbridge BC [2010] EWCA Civ 1006, [2011] 3 All ER 418....7, 32, 65–66, 159, 171
R (Greenpeace) v Secretary of State for Trade and Industry [2007] EWHC 311, [2007] Env LR 29 26
R (Halebank Parish Council) v Halton BC, unreported, 30 April 2012....148
R (Hollins) v Cornwall CC [2013] EWCA Civ 1691 179
R (HS2 Action Alliance) v Secretary of State for Transport [2014] UKSC 3, [2014] 1 WLR 324 ....23, 56, 125–27, 138–39, 150
R (HS2 Action Alliance Ltd) v Secretary of State for Transport [2015] EWCA Civ 203 150
R (Lumba) v Secretary of State for the Home Department [2011] UKSC 12, [2012] 1 AC 245.... 106–7
R (Lymington River Association) v Secretary of State for Communities and Local Government [2014] EWCA Civ 1190 179
R (McCaw) v City of Westminster Magistrates' Court [2008] EWHC 1504 (Admin), [2008] All ER (D) 251 (Jun) 31

R (Save Britain's Heritage and the Victorian Society) v Sheffield City Council [2013] EWHC 2456 (Admin) 144
R (Young) v Oxford City Council [2012] EWCA Civ 46 68
R v Lyons [2002] UKHL 44, [2003] 1 AC 976 42
R v North and East Devon Health Authority, ex parte Coughlan [2001] QB 213 121
R v Secretary of State for the Environment, Transport and the Regions and Midland Expressway Ltd, ex parte Alliance Against the Birmingham Northern Relief Road (No 1) [1999] JPL 426 44
R v Secretary of State for the Home Department, ex parte Daly [2001] UKHL 26, [2001] 2 AC 532 195
Rape Crisis Centre v Secretary of State for the Home Department 2000 SC 527 61
Road Sense v Scottish Ministers [2011] CSOH 10, 2011 SLT 889 ....66–67, 159
Scotch Whisky Association, Petitioner [2012] CSOH 156 67
Smartsource Drainage & Water Reports Ltd v Information Commissioner [2010] UKUT 415 (AAC), [2011] JPL 455 ....17–18, 47
Smith and Grady v United Kingdom (1999) 29 EHRR 493 195
Solvay v Région Wallonne (Case C-182/10) [2012] 2 CMLR 19 ....18, 48
Stichting Natuur en Milieu v Commission (Case T-338/08), 14 June 2012 94
Stichting Natuur en Milieu v Commission (Case C-266/09) [2010] ECR I-13119 82
Sustainable Shetland v The Scottish Ministers [2014] CSIH 60 196
Sustainable Shetland v Scottish Ministers [2013] CSOH 158, 2013 SLT 1173 ....51, 67
Sweden and Turco v Council (Cases C-39/05P and C-52/05P), 1 September 2008 86
Terre wallonne ASBL and Inter-Environnement Wallonie ASBL v Région wallonne (Cases C-105/09 and C-110/09) [2010] ECR I-5611 ....54, 56
Thompson's Application, Re [2010] NIJB 356 74
T Mobile (UK) Ltd v Office of Communications [2008] EWCA Civ 1373, [2009] 1 WLR 1565 167
Unibet (Case C-432/05) [2007] ECR I-2271 161
Uniplex (UK) Ltd v NHS Business Services Authority (Case C-406/08) [2010] ECR I-817, [2010] 2 CMLR 47 ....38, 62, 179
Uprichard v Fife Council [2011] CSIH 77 67
Venn v Secretary of State for Communities and Local Government [2014] EWCA Civ 1539, [2015] CP Rep 12 ....1, 34–35, 144, 146–47, 170
Vereniging Milieudefensie v Commission (Case T-396/09), 14 June 2012 94
Walton v Scottish Ministers [2012] CSIH 19 ....50, 52
Walton v Scottish Ministers [2012] UKSC 44, [2013] PTSR 51 ....7, 14, 37–38, 41, 49, 52, 54–56, 61, 163, 165
Zurich Assurance Ltd v Winchester City Council [2014] EWHC 758 (Admin) 165

Compliance Committee Findings

ACCC/S/2004/1 (Romania v Ukraine) 4, 106, 111
ACCC/C/2004/2 (Kazakhstan) 127, 129, 134
ACCC/C/2004/3 (Ukraine) 106, 135
ACCC/C/2004/6 (Kazakhstan) 145, 177
ACCC/C/2004/8 (Armenia) 144, 150
ACCC/C/2005/11 (Belgium) 144–45, 155, 157
ACCC/C/2005/12 (Albania) 122–23, 127, 133
ACCC/C/2005/15 (Romania) 111, 115, 134
ACCC/C/2006/16 (Lithuania) 133
ACCC/C/2006/16 (Lithuania) 50, 122, 125, 127, 129–30, 132–33, 135–36
ACCC/C/2006/17 (European Community) 128, 130, 132, 143
ACCC/C/2006/18 (Denmark) 145–46, 157
ACCC/C/2007/21 (European Community) 103, 109
ACCC/C/2007/22 (France) 127, 130–32
ACCC/C/2008/32 (European Community) 161
ACCC/C/2008/23 (United Kingdom) 32, 169, 177, 214
ACCC/C/2008/24 (Spain) 24, 103–5, 113, 134–35, 171, 177, 329
ACCC/C/2008/26 (Austria) 133, 144
ACCC/C/2008/27 (United Kingdom) 32, 144, 169, 177, 214
ACCC/C/2008/30 (Moldova) 112
ACCC/C/2008/32 (European Union) 95, 161
ACCC/C/2008/33 (United Kingdom) 32–33, 39, 60, 62–63, 145, 165, 168, 170, 177–78, 189, 205, 214
ACCC/C/2009/35 (Georgia) 123
ACCC/C/2009/36 (Spain) 131, 177
ACCC/C/2009/37 (Belarus) 105, 129, 131, 133, 135–36
ACCC/C/2009/38 (United Kingdom) 48, 52, 55, 132
ACCC/C/2009/41 (Slovakia) 137
ACCC/C/2009/43 (Armenia) 130–32, 136
ACCC/C/2010/45 (United Kingdom) 26, 142–43, 214
ACCC/C/2010/48 (Austria) 206, 210
ACCC/C/2010/50 (Czech Republic) 132, 135, 143, 210
ACCC/C/2010/53 (United Kingdom) 107, 188, 208, 210
ACCC/C/2010/54 (European Union) 214
ACCC/C/2010/55 (United Kingdom) 18
ACCC/C/2010/59 (Kazakhstan) 210
ACCC/C/2011/58 (Bulgaria) 213
ACCC/C/2011/61 (United Kingdom) 26, 142–43, 150, 214
ACCC/C/2012/68 (European Union and United Kingdom) 48, 55, 114, 135, 137, 148, 150, 205, 210, 214
ACCC/C/2012/70 (Czech Republic) 329–30
ACCC/C/2012/77 (United Kingdom) 170
ACCC/C/2013/85 (United Kingdom) 32, 145–46
ACCC/C/2013/86 (United Kingdom) 32, 145–46
ACCC/C/2014/1 (Kazakhstan) 102
ACCC/C/2014/100 (United Kingdom) 138
ACCC/C/2014/101 (European Union) 89, 127

TABLE OF LEGISLATION

International Conventions and Treaties

Aarhus Convention 1998 .... 1–215, 217–41
recital 20 27
Art 1 .... 13, 48
Arts 1–3 155
Art 2 .... 2, 114, 149
(2) 43, 112
(b) 114
(c) 114
(d) 29
(3) 16, 43, 114, 146, 186
(4) 24, 149
(5) 24, 58, 151
Art 3 .... 2, 48, 144
(1) 192
(4) 197
(5) 81
(8) 34, 66
Art 4 .... 28, 43, 45, 48, 101–14, 119, 134, 166
(1) 45, 102–3, 111, 188
(b) 102–3
(2) 106, 112
(3) 19, 44–45, 104, 106–7, 113, 119, 188
(a) 105
(b) 102, 106
(c) 112
(4) 19, 44–45, 83, 104, 108–13, 119, 188
(a) 108
(b) 108
(c) 86, 108
(d) 83, 85, 108–9
(e) 108
(f) 108, 111
(g) 108
(h) 108
(5) 105
(6) 112
(7) 112
(8) 113, 116

Arts 4–5 ....2, 15
Art 5 ....21, 43, 45, 82, 101–2, 105, 113–19, 144, 183
(1) 114–15, 117
(a) 114
(b) 114–15
(c) 115, 117, 119
(2) 115–16
(a) 116
(b) 116
(3) 116–17
(4) 116–17
(5) 117
(a) 117
(b) 117
(c) 117
(6) 117–18
(7) 118
(a) 118
(b) 118
(c) 118
(8) 118
(9) 118–19
(10) 119
Art 6 ....22–24, 26, 29, 49–51, 58, 87, 89, 92, 107, 121–23, 127–37, 142–45, 150, 152, 183, 194
(1)(a) 143
(b) 22, 108, 123, 143–44
(c) 22, 123
(2) 24, 49–50, 128, 130, 166–68
(3) 24, 49, 53, 113, 122, 130–31
(4) 24, 49–51, 53, 89, 122, 132, 134
(5) 24, 133
(6) 24, 88, 111, 133–34
(e) 87
(7) 24, 26, 134–35
(8) 24, 49, 122, 135
(9) 24, 49, 136
(10) 136
(11) 27, 137
Art 6 bis 27, 90
Arts 6–8 ....2, 48
Art 7 ....22–24, 26, 49, 52–53, 55, 71, 88–89, 92, 95, 107, 117, 121–27, 137–39, 144, 197
Art 8 ....22, 49, 107, 117, 121–22, 138–39, 144, 197
Art 9 ....2, 7, 32, 39, 59, 69, 76–77, 92, 112, 136, 141–51, 161, 166–67, 169, 174, 190, 205
(1) 20, 28, 58, 142–44, 151, 166
(1)–(3) 30, 175

(2) 28–29, 58–60, 77, 92, 142–45, 150–53, 155, 158, 165–66, 194–95
(3) 7, 29–30, 32, 38, 42, 58–60, 92–94, 142–47, 151, 155–62, 165–66, 194–95, 197–98
(4) 7–8, 30–32, 34–35, 38, 58–60, 62, 74, 94, 142, 144–45, 157, 167, 169, 171, 175, 177–78, 189, 191–92, 195–96, 198
(5) 30, 32, 142, 169, 192
Art 10 ....2, 137
(2) 2
(i) 119
(5) 187
Art 12 5
Art 15 ....3, 48, 187, 189, 202–3
Art 16 ....5, 8–9
Art 19(5) 184
Annex I 22, 49, 122–23, 127, 143
paras 1–19 123
para 20 ....22, 123
para 21 22
Annex I bis 27–28, 90
Annex II 8
Protocol on Pollutant Release and Transfer Registers 2003 204
Convention on Biological Diversity 1992, Cartagena Protocol on Biosafety 2000 27
Convention on Access to Information, Public Participation in Decision-Making and Access to Justice in Environmental Matters 1998 *see* Aarhus Convention 1998
Convention on the Protection and Use of Transboundary Watercourses and International Lakes 1992
Protocol on Water and Health 1999 204
Convention on the Transboundary Effects of Industrial Accidents 1992
Art 9(1) 115
(2) 115
(3) 115
Espoo Convention on Environmental Impact Assessment in a Transboundary Context 1991 115
Art 5(3)(d) 87
Art 6(2)(e) 87
Annex IIb 87
App III, Art 6(1) 115
European Convention on Human Rights 1950 ....77, 95
Art 6 ....60, 110
Art 8 115
Treaty of Amsterdam 1997 84
Treaty on European Union 1992
Art 1(1) 86
Art 9(3) 86
Art 11(2) 86
Art 17 93
Declaration No 17 83

Treaty on the Functioning of the European Union
Art 15 84
(1) 86
Art 216(2) 80
Art 258 86
Art 263 95
(4) 94–95, 161
Art 267 9
Art 298 86
Vienna Convention on the Law of Treaties 1969
Art 26 201
Art 31(3)(a) 205
Arts 31–32 1
Art 33 1
Vienna Convention on Substances that Deplete the Ozone Layer 1985
Montreal Protocol 1987 201

Decisions of the Meeting of the Parties to the Convention

Dec I/1 3
r 22 3
Dec I/6 6
Dec I/7 .... 3, 187, 189, 202–3, **243–50**
Annex 205, 207–9, 213
para 1 3
(2) 4
(8) 4
para 2 204
paras 15–18 4
para 18 148
para 19 209
para 20 209
(a) 210
(b) 210
(d) 210
para 21 .... 18, 210
para 22 209
para 23 .... 211, 329
para 24 211
para 25 213
paras 26–31 213
para 33 205
para 34 .... 205, 212
para 35 207
para 36 4
(a) 205
(b) 205

para 37 ....4–5, 205
(a) 4
(b) 4
(c) 4
(d) 4
para 38 5
Dec I/14 5
Dec II/1 27
Dec II/2 6
para 12 202
para 16 157
Dec II/5 3
Dec II/9 1
Dec III/1 8
Dec III/3 6
Dec IV/1 6
Dec IV/2 6
Dec IV/9i 33
Dec V/9 ....18, 210
para 6(a) 215
Dec V/9a–9o 207
Dec V/9n 33
Dec EMP II/1 6

National Legislation

United Kingdom
Act of Sederunt (Rules of the Court of Session Amendment) (Protective Expenses Orders in Environmental Appeals and Judicial Reviews) 2013, SSI 2013/81 172
r 58A 68–70, 76, **319–21**
r 58A.1(2) 68
r 58A.2 69
(2) 68
(b) 70
(4) 68
(5) 68, 70
r 58A.3(1) 69
(3) 71
r 58A.4 ....68–69, 193
r 58A.5 68
(1) 69
Civil Legal Aid (Scotland) Regulations 2002, SSI 2002/494
reg 15 63
Civil Procedure Rules 1998, SI 1998/3132....30, 32, 193
PD 25A 35
para 5.1A 176
para 5.1B 176

r 44.3(2) ... 168
r 45 ... 76
r 45.41 ... 34–35, **315**
rr 45.41–45.44 ... 148, 150, 170
r 45.42 ... 34, **315**
r 45.43 ... 34, 148, 170, **315**
r 45.44 ... 34, 170, **316**
PD 45 ... 34
paras 5.1–5.2 ... 148, 150, 170, **316**
r 52.9A ... 34, 170, **317**
r 54.5(1) ... 177
(A1) ... 179
(5) ... 179
(6) ... 179
Civil Procedure (Amendment) Rules 2013, SI 2013/262 ... 33
Clean Air Act 1993
s 55(2) ... 147
Control of Pollution Act 1974 ... 44
s 94 ... 47
Costs Protection (Aarhus Convention) Regulations (Northern Ireland) 2013, SI 2013/81 ... 76, **323–26**
Court of Session Act 1988
s 27A ... 63
Crossrail Act 2008 ... 150
Electricity Act 1989 ... 51
Sch 8, para 2 ... 51
para 3 ... 51
Electricity Works (Environmental Impact Assessment) (Scotland) Regulations 2000, SSI 2000/320 ... 51
Environmental Assessment (Scotland) Act 2005 ... 54, 57
s 1(1) ... 54
s 4 ... 54
s 5 ... 54
Environmental Assessment of Plans and Programmes (Scotland) Regulations 2004, SSI 2004/258 ... 54
Environmental Information Regulations 1992, SI 1992/3240 ... 15, 44, 194
Environmental Information Regulations 2004, SI 2004/3391 ... 15–17, 28, 47, 99
Pt 3 ... 19
reg 2(1) ... 16, 47
(2)(c) ... 47
(d) ... 47
reg 4 ... 21
reg 5 ... 19
reg 11 ... 20, 28
reg 12(1)(b) ... 19
(2) ... 19
(4) ... 19
(5) ... 19
reg 18 ... 20, 28

Environmental Information (Scotland) Regulations 2004, SSI 2004/520 ....45–47, 58
reg 5 45
(2) 45
(3) 47
(4) 45
reg 10 45–46
(2)(b) 46
Environmental Impact Assessment (Scotland) Amendment Regulations 2006, SSI 2006/614....................61
Environmental Permitting (England and Wales) Regulations 2010, SI 2010/675
reg 26 25
reg 29 25
reg 46 21
reg 59 25
Sch 5 Pt 1 25
Environmental Protection Act 1990....................44
Pt VI....................27
s 80 147
s 82 147
s 122 27
Freedom of Information Act 2000 15–17
Pt 4....................20
Pt 5....................20, 28
s 3(1)....................17
s 5....................17
Sch 1....................17
Freedom of Information (Scotland) Act 2002....................45–47, 58
Pt 4....................46
s 2....................46
s 5....................47
(1) 47
s 6....................47
s 8(1)(a)....................47
s 21 46
s 39(2)(a)....................46
(b)....................46
ss 47–56 46
Sch 1....................47
Genetically Modified Organisms (Deliberate Release) Regulations 2002, SI 2002/2443
reg 12 27
reg 33 28
Genetically Modified Organisms (Deliberate Release) (Wales) Regulations 2002, SI 2002/3188 (W 304)
reg 13 27
reg 34 28
Human Rights Act 1998....................110, 150

Infrastructure Planning (Environmental Impact Assessment) Regulations 2009, SI 2009/2263 25
Legal Aid Sentencing and Punishment of Offenders Act 2012
s 46 146
Nitrate Pollution Prevention Regulations 2008, SI 2008/2349 24–25
reg 47 25
Noise Act 1996
s 2(4) 147
Planning Act 2008 25
Planning and Compulsory Purchase Act 2004 25
s 19(1A) 147
(2)(a) 147
s 38(6) 147
Pollution Prevention and Control (Public Participation etc) (Scotland) Regulations 2005, SSI 2005/10] 61
Roads (Northern Ireland) Order 1993, SI 1993/3160
art 67BA 75
Roads (Scotland) Act 1984 51–52
Sch 1, para 5 51
para 6 51
para 11 51
para 12 51
Scotland Act 1998 47
Supreme Court Rules 2009, SI 2009/1603
r 46(1) 34
Town and Country Planning Act 1990 25
s 70(2) 147
s 74 138
s 90(2) 164
s 288 ....34, 37, 162–64, 170
s 336 179
Town and Country Planning (Scotland) Act 1997 51
Town and Country Planning (Development Management Procedure) (England) Order 2010, SI 2010/2184 25–26
art 25 138
Town and Country Planning (Environmental Impact Assessment) (England and Wales) Regulations 1999, SI 1999/293 167
reg 6 39
Town and Country Planning (Environmental Impact Assessment) Regulations 2011, SI 2011/1824 ....26, 144
Town and Country Planning (Environmental Impact Assessment) (Scotland) Regulations 1999, SSI 1999/1
Pt III 51
Pt IV 51
Town and Country Planning (Environmental Impact Assessment) (Scotland) Regulations 2011, SSI 2011/139 51
Water Industry Act 1991 18

EU Legislation

Treaties
EC Treaty *see* Treaty on the Functioning of the European Union
European Charter for Fundamental Freedoms 95
Art 47 175
Treaty of Amsterdam 1997 84
Treaty on European Union 1992
Art 1(1) 86
Art 9(3) 86
Art 11(2) 86
Art 17 93
Declaration No 17 83
Treaty on the Functioning of the European Union 2008
Art 15 84
(1) 86
Art 216(2) 80
Art 258 86
Art 263 95
(4) 94–95, 161
Art 267 9
Art 298 86

Regulations
Reg (EEC) 1210/90 on the establishment of the European Environment Agency [1990] OJ L120/1 86
Art 2(vi) 86
Reg (EC) 1049/2001 on public access to European Parliament, Council and Commission documents [2001] OJ L145/43 ....45, 84–86, 95, 101, 109, **255–60**
recital 6 86
Art 2(6) 84
Art 4 ....84, 86
(2) 86
Reg (EC) 1829/2003 on genetically modified food and feed [2003] OJ L268/1 27
Art 6 90
Art 7 90
Art 29s 82–83
Art 30(6) 82
Reg (EC) 1367/2006 on the application of the Aarhus Convention on Community institutions and bodies [2006] OJ L264/13 ....45, 84, 89–91, 93–94, 101, 109, **261–67**
Art 3 84
Art 4 86
(4) 86
Art 9(3)(b) 91
Art 11 93–94
Art 12 93–94
Annex I 89

Reg (EC) 1907/2006 concerning the registration, evaluation, authorisation and restriction of chemicals (REACH) [2006] OJ L396/1
Art 118 82
(2) 83
Reg (EC) 1107/2009 concerning the placing of plant protection products on the market [2009] OJ L309/1
Art 63 82
(2) 83
Reg (EC) 1221/2009 on the voluntary participation by organisations in a Community eco-management and audit scheme (EMAS) [2009] OJ L342/1 117
Reg (EU) 528/2012 concerning the placing on the market of biocidal products [2012] OJ L167/1
Art 63 83
Art 66(2) 83
Reg (EU) 1025/2012 on European standardisation [2012] OJ L316/12
Art 8 91
Reg (EU) 1293/2013 on the establishment of a programme for the environment and climate action (LIFE) [2013] OJ L347/185 91

Directives
Dir 85/337/EEC on the assessment of the effects of certain public and private projects on the environment [1985] OJ L175/40 .... 22–23, 41, 50, 52, 59, 66, 79, 142–43, 152–55, 168, 172–73
Art 1(1) 152–53
(2) 152–54, 165
Art 6(4) 52, 154
Art 10a 142, 152–54, 159, 162, 175–76
Dir 90/313/EEC on freedom of access to information on the environment [1990] OJ L158/56 .... 15, 44–45, 79, 83, 99–101, 113
Art 1 100
Art 5 113
Art 8 100
Dir 91/676/EEC concerning the protection of waters against pollution caused by nitrates from agricultural sources [1991] OJ L375/1 25
Dir 92/43/EEC on the conservation of natural habitats and of wild fauna and flora [1992] OJ L206/7 .... 30, 38, 42, 60, 75, 152, 160–61
Art 6 153
Dir 96/61/EC concerning integrated pollution prevention and control [1996] OJ L16/21 .... 22–23, 79, 142–43, 158–59, 172–73, 175
Art 15a 142, 159, 175–76
Dir 2000/60/EC establishing a framework for Community action in the field of water policy [2000] OJ L327/1 23
Dir 2001/18/EC on the deliberate release into the environment of genetically modified organisms [2001] OJ L106/1 27

Art 24 ... 90
Art 25 ... 83
Dir 2001/42/EC on the assessment of the effects of certain plans and programmes on the environment [2001] OJ L197/30 ... 23, 49, 52–57, 60, 68, 75, 88–89, 92, 123–27, 139, 150, **307–14**
Art 1 ... 124
Art 2(a) ... 53, 55, 89, 124
Art 3 ... 125
(1) ... 53
(2)(a) ... 53, 55, 89
(2)–(4) ... 53
(3) ... 89
(8) ... 89
Art 4 ... 53
Art 5 ... 56–57
Art 6 ... 56
(2) ... 53
(5) ... 57
Art 8 ... 53
Dir 2003/4/EC on public access to environmental information [2003] OJ L41/26 ... 15–19, 21, 45–46, 81–82, 91, 99, 101, 104, **269–75**
Art 2 ... 81
(1) ... 16–17, 45
(b) ... 81
(2)(a) ... 18
(b) ... 18
(c) ... 18
Art 3 ... 45
Art 4(1) ... 45
(2) ... 46
Art 6 ... 28
(2) ... 167
Art 7 ... 82
(3) ... 82
Dir 2003/35/EC on public participation in respect of the drawing up of certain plans and programmes relating to the environment [2003] OJ L156/17 ... 22–23, 32–33, 35, 37, 53, 64–65, 87–89, 92, 125, 142, 158–59, 192, **277–84**
recital 10 ... 23, 53, 125–26
Art 1 ... 23
Art 2 ... 23, 126
(5) ... 23, 53, 125–26
Art 3 ... 23
(7) ... 33, 59, 65, 176
Art 4 ... 23
(4) ... 33, 65, 176

Art 7 ... 194
Annex 1 ... 23, 25, **88–89**
Dir 2004/35/EC on environmental liability with regard to the prevention and remedying of environmental damage [2004] OJ L143/56 ... 93
Art 12 ... 93
Dir 2008/1/EC on integrated pollution prevention and control [2008] OJ L24/8 ... 122, 130, 143
Dir 2009/28/EC on the promotion of the use of energy from renewable sources [2009] OJ L140/16 ... 137
Dir 2009/125/EC establishing a framework for the setting of eco-design requirements for energy related products [2009] OJ L285/10
Art 16 ... 91
Dir 2009/147/EC on the conservation of wild birds [2009] OJ L20/7 ... 60, 196
Dir 2010/75/EU on industrial emissions (integrated pollution prevention and control) [2010] OJ L334/17 ... 23, 50, 59–61, 68, 79, 87–88, 92, 143
Art 3(4) ... 111
Art 24 ... 87
Art 25 ... 59, 92, 143
Art 26 ... 87
Annex IV ... 87
Dir 2011/92/EU on the assessment of the effects of certain public and private projects on the environment [2012] OJ L26/1 ... 23, 41, 49–51, 53,60–61, 65, 67–69, 71, 79, 87–88, 92, 115, 122, 129–30, 285–305
Art 1(2) ... 143
Art 2(1) ... 50
(2) ... 50
Art 4 ... 50
Art 6 ... 59, 87
(1) ... 50
(2) ... 50
(4) ... 50
(5) ... 50
Art 7 ... 87
Art 10a ... 191, 194
Art 11 ... 59, 92, 143
(3) ... 59
(4) ... 59
Annex I ... 122, 143
Annexes I–III ... 50
Annex III ... 115
Annex IV, para 2 ... 88

Dir 2012/18/EU on the control of major-accident hazards involving dangerous substances [2012] OJ L197/1 115
Dir 2014/52/EU on environmental impact assessment [2014] OJ L124/1 87–88

Decisions

Dec 93/731/EC on public access to Council documents [1993] OJ L340/43 84
Dec 94/90/EC on public access to Commission documents [1990] OJ L46/58 84
Dec 2005/370/EC concluding the Aarhus Convention [2005] OJ L124/1 .... 29, 41, 80, 100
Dec 2006/957/EC concluding on behalf of the European Community an amendment to the Aarhus Convention [2006] OJ L386/46 90
recital 4 90

1

The Aarhus Convention: An Overview

CHARLES BANNER[1]

Introduction

The Convention on Access to Information, Public Participation in Decision-Making and Access to Justice in Environmental Matters was signed on 25 June 1998 in the Danish city of Aarhus, its authentic texts being in English, Russian and French.[2]

The Convention was negotiated, and is now overseen by, the United Nations Economic Commission for Europe ('UNECE'), one of the five regional commissions of the United Nations, although non-UNECE states are able to join.[3] As of the date of writing there are 47 parties to the Convention, all of whom are European or CIS countries, the most recent being Switzerland which ratified the Convention on 3 March 2014.

The European Union and the United Kingdom both ratified the Convention in 2005, on 17 February and 23 February respectively. As discussed further in the subsequent chapters of this book, the implementation of the Convention within the United Kingdom has taken place on two levels: first, by the transposition of European Union secondary legislation which itself seeks to implement aspects of the Convention across the European Union Member States, and secondly by the direct transposition of certain aspects of the Convention (in particular on access to justice).[4] Chapters 2–5 below explore how the Convention has been

[1] Barrister, Landmark Chambers, London.

[2] The three authentic texts are equally authoritative, insofar as a comparison discloses a difference of meaning which the principles of interpretation in Articles 31–32 of the Vienna Convention on the Law of Treaties does not remove, the meaning which best reconciles the texts, having regard to the object and purpose of the Aarhus Convention, will be adopted: see Article 33 of the Vienna Convention.

[3] See Decision II/9 of the Meeting of the Parties to the Convention.

[4] The UK constitutional principle that international treaties do not have direct effect in the absence of transposing legislation means that the Convention is not legally binding in domestic proceedings in circumstances where it has not been transposed by EU secondary legislation (which does have direct effect) or domestic legislation. See eg *Morgan v Hinton Organics (Wessex) Ltd* [2009] Env LR 30 per Carnwath LJ at paragraphs 44 & 47 and *Venn v Secretary of State for Communities and Local Government* [2014] EWCA Civ 1539 per Sullivan LJ at paragraph 33.

implemented in each of the constituent jurisdictions of the United Kingdom and by the European Union.

The Three Pillars of the Aarhus Convention

The Convention requires States parties to confer the following rights on the public with regard to the environment:

1) The right to receive environmental information that is held by public authorities ('access to environmental information'): Articles 4–5 (see Chapter 6 below).
2) The right to participate in environmental decision-making ('public participation in environmental decision-making'): Articles 6–8 (see Chapter 7 below).
3) The right to review procedures to challenge certain public decisions that have been made in relation to the environment ('access to justice'): Article 9 (see Chapter 8 below).

These are generally termed as the 'three pillars' of the Convention. There is a degree of inter-relationship between the pillars; in particular, the access to justice provisions of Article 9 seek to ensure that members of the public have legal recourse to challenge decisions which are subject to the requirements of Articles 4–5 and Articles 6–8. Article 2 of the Convention sets out definitions which are common to all of the pillars, and Article 3 sets out general provisions which inform the interpretation and application of the rest of the Convention.

The Institutions of the Aarhus Convention

The Meeting of the Parties

Pursuant to Article 10 of the Convention, at least once every two years (unless otherwise decided by the Parties) there must be a Meeting of the Parties to keep the implementation of the Convention under continuous review. The Meeting of the Parties is the principal governing body of the Convention. Article 10(2) provides that it may:

1) Review the policies for, and legal and methodological approaches to, access to information, public participation and access to justice in environmental matters with a view to improving them.
2) Exchange information regarding experience gained in concluding and implementing agreements or other arrangements relating to the subject matter of the Convention.

3) Seek, where appropriate, the services of relevant UNECE bodies and other competent international bodies in all aspects pertinent to the achievement of the purposes of the Convention.
4) Establish any subsidiary bodies as they deem necessary.
5) Prepare protocols to the Convention.
6) Consider and adopt proposals for amendments to the Convention.

Pursuant to these powers, the Meeting of the Parties has adopted a number of 'Decisions' relating to the governance and application of the Convention. Decision I/1 of October 2002 sets out the rules of procedure for sessions of the Meeting of the Parties.

There have to date been five regular and two extraordinary sessions of the Meeting of the Parties, the most recent being in Maastricht in June–July 2014. The agendas and minutes for each session are available on the UNECE's website.[5]

Rule 22 of Decision I/1 establishes a Bureau of the Meeting of the Parties which comprises of the Chairperson and two Vice Chairperson of the latest ordinary session of the Meeting of the Parties as well as four other members. The Bureau normally meets two to three times per year and its members hold office until the next ordinary session of the Meeting of the Parties. They also comprise the membership of the Working Group of the Parties (see further below).

The Aarhus Convention Compliance Committee

Article 15 of the Convention requires the Meeting of the Parties to:

> … establish, on a consensus basis, optional arrangements of a non-confrontational, non-judicial and consultative nature for reviewing compliance with the provisions of this Convention. These arrangements shall allow for appropriate public involvement and may include the option of considering communications from members of the public on matters related to this Convention.

Pursuant to this obligation, in October 2002, Decision I/7 of the Meeting of the Parties established the Aarhus Convention Compliance Committee to review compliance by the Parties with their obligations under the Convention.[6] The Compliance Committee is required to meet a minimum of once per year, although it normally meets four times per year. It contains nine members all of whom must be nationals of a Party to the Convention (but no more than one from each Party), who are appointed by the Meeting of the Parties and whose term runs until the second session of the Meeting of the Parties thereafter.

[5] See the list of weblinks at Appendix 14 of this book.

[6] Decision I/7 effectively operates as the 'constitution' of the Compliance Committee and is set out in full at Appendix 2 of this book. Note that the provision in Annex I, paragraph 1(1) that the number of members shall be eight was amended by Decision II/5 which increased the number to nine.

Annex I, paragraph 1(2) of Decision I/7 provides that members of the Compliance Committee must be:

> Persons of high moral character and recognised competence in the fields to which the Convention relates, including persons having legal experience.

Paragraph 8 of the same provision further provides that:

> In the election of the Committee, consideration should be given to the geographical distribution of membership and diversity of experience.

The Compliance Committee has a four-fold jurisdiction, covering:[7]

1) Submissions by a Party or Parties alleging non-compliance by another Party with the Convention, of which there has been just one to date: ACCC/S/2004/1 (by Romania about compliance by Ukraine).
2) Submissions by a Party to the effect that, despite its best endeavours, it is or will be unable to comply with the Convention, of which there have been none to date.
3) A referral by the Convention Secretariat about the non-compliance of a Party with the Convention, of which there have been none to date.
4) Communications from members of the public, including NGOs, about the non-compliance of a Party with the Convention. This has been by far the most fertile source of the Compliance Committee's work, with 105 communications as of September 2014, which highlights the importance of the public's role in securing compliance with the Convention.

The operation of the Compliance Committee is the subject of Chapter 10 below.

The Compliance Committee's findings are not legally binding, but are reported to the Meeting of the Parties, whose powers are described in the following terms by paragraph 37 of Decision I/7:[8]

> The Meeting of the Parties may, upon consideration of a report and any recommendations of the Committee, decide upon appropriate measures to bring about full compliance with the Convention. The Meeting of the Parties may, depending on the particular question before it and taking into account the cause, degree and frequency of the non-compliance, decide upon one or more of the following measures:
>
> (a) Provide advice and facilitate assistance to individual Parties regarding the implementation of the Convention;
> (b) Make recommendations to the Party concerned;

[7] See Paragraphs 15–18 of Decision I/7.

[8] The Meeting of the Parties' various decisions on the Compliance Committee's recommendations are set out at www.unece.org/env/pp/ccimplementation.html. See the Tabular Analysis of these decisions at Appendix 13 of this book. It should be noted that pending consideration of its findings by the Meeting of the Parties, the Compliance Committee has power under paragraph 36 of Decision I/7 to take the actions listed in paragraph 37(a) and, with the consent of the Party in question, paragraph 37(b), (c) and (d).

(c) Request the Party concerned to submit a strategy, including a time schedule, to the Compliance Committee regarding the achievement of compliance with the Convention and to report on the implementation of this strategy;
(d) In cases of communications from the public, make recommendations to the Party concerned on specific measures to address the matter raised by the member of the public;
(e) Issue declarations of non-compliance;
(f) Issue cautions;
(g) Suspend, in accordance with the applicable rules of international law concerning the suspension of the operation of a treaty, the special rights and privileges accorded to the Party concerned under the Convention;
(h) Take such other non-confrontational, non-judicial and consultative measures as may be appropriate.

Paragraph 38 of Decision I/7 makes clear that these powers are without prejudice to the provisions of Article 16 of the Convention regarding the settlement of disputes regarding the Convention's interpretation (see further below).

The Secretariat

Article 12 of the Convention provides that the Executive Secretary of the UNECE shall carry out the Secretariat functions of convening and preparing sessions of the Meeting of the Parties as well as the transmitting to the Parties of reports and other information received pursuant to the Convention. As noted above, the Secretariat can also refer the issue of a Party's compliance to the Compliance Committee, although there is no instance to date of it having done so.

The Working Group of the Parties

Decision I/14 of the first Meeting of the Parties in October 2002 established the Working Group of the Parties, whose functions are to oversee the implementation of the work programme for the Convention between sessions of the Meeting of the Parties, to oversee and direct the activities of subsidiary bodies established by the Meeting of the Parties, to keep under review the need for amending the Convention, to make such proposals and recommendations to the Meeting of the Parties as it considers necessary and to perform any other duties requested of it by the Meeting of the Parties. The members of the Bureau of the Meeting of the Parties comprise the officers of the Working Group. Meetings of the Working Group are usually held back-to-back with meetings of the Bureau.

Task Forces

The Meeting of the Parties has established three Task Forces to promote the effective implementation of each of the three pillars of the Convention.

(a) The Task Force on Access to Information

The Task Force on Access to Information was established by Decision IV/1 of the Meeting of the Parties in 2011, replacing the former Task Force on Electronic Information Tools which had been established by Decision I/6 of the Meeting of the Parties in 2002. Its objective is to strengthen the implementation of the Convention's provisions on access to information through promoting the exchange of information, experiences, challenges and good practice concerning public access to environmental information held by the private sector.[9] It is empowered to identify capacity-building needs, barriers and solutions in relation to public access to information, including product information and environmental information held by the private sector. Subject also to the availability of resources, it is also mandated to plan and implement capacity-building activities, including workshops and training; to support the maintenance and further development of the 'Aarhus clearinghouse' online information database about laws and practices relating to the Convention's subject matter, and to promote electronic information tools at the regional level through maintaining online databases (eg, for jurisprudence, national implementation reports and case studies on public participation at the national level and in international forums) and through an interactive online version of the Aarhus Convention Implementation Guide (as to which see below).

(b) The Task Force on Public Participation in Decision-Making

The Public Participation Task Force was established by Decision EMP II/1 of second extraordinary session of the Meeting of the Parties in 2010. Its functions include the documentation and sharing of expertise and good practice relating to public participation in environmental decision-making, the identification of common barriers to public participation, make recommendations for improving implementation of the second pillar of the Convention, and explore possibilities for enhanced public participation in particular fields and/or through innovative methods.

(c) The Task Force on Access to Justice

The Task Force on Access to Justice was established at the first session of the Meeting of the Parties in 2002. Its wide-ranging remit is now governed by Decisions II/2, III/3 and IV/2 and includes:

1) Providing a platform for sharing of information, experiences and good practices related to access to justice (through eg collection and dissemination of relevant practices and establishment of portal for the relevant jurisprudence);
2) Planning and implementing strategic and catalytic capacity-building activities and information exchange, in particular for senior members of the judiciary at the sub-regional level;

[9] See Decision IV/1 of the Meeting of the Parties which sets out the Access to Information Task Force's mandate.

3) Considering means of facilitating the training of trainers on access to justice in environmental matters;
4) Developing training materials on implementation of Article 9 of the Convention that are adaptable to national priorities and the needs of specific groups of legal professionals;
5) Examining the way the issue of remedies is handled in a selection of representative countries;
6) Exchanging information and analytical work on criteria for standing;
7) Exchanging information on practices in the establishment of assistance mechanisms to remove or reduce financial barriers;
8) Considering practical arrangements for increasing support for public interest lawyers and strengthening the capacities of NGOs;
9) Identifying good practice in ensuring that sufficient scientific and technical expertise is available to review bodies dealing with environmental cases;
10) Exploring the potential use of alternative dispute resolution mechanisms as a means to further the objectives of the Convention;
11) Encouraging the involvement of representatives of ministries of justice, the judiciary, other legal professionals, including public interest lawyers and NGOs specialising in litigation and legal advice on environmental matters, in its activities;
12) Carrying out such other tasks related to access to justice as the Working Group of the Parties may assign to it;
13) Presenting the results of its work for consideration and appropriate action by the Working Group of the Parties.

The Task Force made so little progress in its early years that the UNECE Secretariat considered winding it up. Despite that slow start, it has subsequently developed into a productive forum. The role of the chair of the Task Force and some of its expert members in evaluating the implementation of Articles 9(3) and 9(4) of the Convention under contract from the European Commission is one example of its effectiveness.[10]

The Interpretation of the Convention

Although the Compliance Committee's findings are not legally binding (see above), they are of persuasive value in the domestic courts as to the standards required by the Convention. See eg *Walton v Scottish Ministers*:[11]

> Although the Convention is not part of domestic law as such (except where incorporated through European directives) … the decisions of the Committee deserve respect on issues relating to standards of public participation.[12]

[10] See <http://ec.europa.eu/environment/aarhus/studies.htm>.

[11] *Walton v Scottish Ministers* [2013] PTSR 51 per Lord Carnwath at paragraph 100.

[12] See also *R (Edwards) v Environment Agency* [2011] 1 WLR 79 per Lord Hope at paragraph 31 and *R (Garner) v Elmbridge BC* [2011] 3 All ER 418 per Sullivan J at paragraph 43.

A similar approach was taken at the EU level by Advocate General Kokott in *Edwards v Environment Agency*,[13] that in considering the requirements of the Convention, 'reference should be made to the decision-making practice of the Aarhus Convention Compliance Committee.'[14]

It is reasonable to conclude that, where particular findings of the Compliance Committee have been endorsed by the Meeting of the Parties, greater weight should be placed upon those findings than in circumstances where the findings in question have not yet been considered by the Meeting of the Parties or have been considered but not endorsed.[15]

The UNECE has published an Aarhus Convention Implementation Guide (2nd edition, 2014),[16] which is intended to be a 'convenient non-legally binding and user-friendly reference tool to assist policymakers, legislators and public authorities in their daily work of implementing the Convention'.[17] Whilst it is not legally binding as to the interpretation of the Convention, its contents were taken into account by the Court of Justice of the European Union ('CJEU') in *Edwards* (above, at para 34 of the judgment) and by Advocate General Kokott in *Commission v United Kingdom*.[18]

The Meeting of the Parties occasionally issues decisions on the interpretation of the Convention on its own initiative: see for example Decision III/1 on the interpretation of Article 14 regarding the procedure for amending the Convention.

In the event that one or more Parties to the Convention are in dispute as to the Convention's interpretation, Article 16 provides that they 'shall seek a solution by negotiation or by any other means of dispute settlement acceptable to the parties to the Convention' or, failing that arbitration in accordance with the provisions of Annex II to the Convention or submission of the dispute to the International Court of Justice. To date, it has not been necessary for any party to have recourse to this provision.

The decision of the European Union to transpose many of the requirements of the Convention into secondary legislation means that from time to time the CJEU is called upon to rule, in effect, on the interpretation of the Convention since European Union secondary legislation that transposes an international treaty to which the Union is party must be interpreted in accordance with that

[13] Case C-260/11 *Edwards v Environment Agency* [2013] 1 WLR 2914 at paragraph 8.

[14] Advocate General Kokott proceeded at paragraphs 36 and 43–44 to review the Compliance Committee's case-law on the prohibition under Art 9(4) of the Convention of prohibitive expense in environmental litigation, which the EU secondary legislation in issue in that case sought to implement.

[15] As noted above, the Meeting of the Parties' various decisions on the Compliance Committee's recommendations are set out at www.unece.org/env/pp/ccimplementation.html. See the Tabular Analysis of these decisions at Appendix 13 of this Book, The decisions usually contain little if any additional reasoning over and above that given by the Compliance Committee.

[16] See the list of weblinks at Appendix 14 to this book.

[17] Implementation Guide, p 9.

[18] Case C-530/11 *Commission v United Kingdom* [2014] 3 WLR 853 at paragraph 85.

treaty (*Edwards* and *Commission v United Kingdom* are two such examples).[19] As a result, the case-law of the CJEU is a useful resource on the interpretation of the Convention and is discussed in detail in the chapters that follow. It is conceivable that a European Union Member State that disagrees with the CJEU's interpretation of a particular provision of the Convention could invoke the Article 16 procedure to ventilate that dispute, albeit that this may be unlikely to happen in practice in all but the most extreme cases due to the protracted nature of the Article 16 procedure if a dispute cannot be resolved without the matter being referred to the International Court of Justice.[20]

[19] On this principle of interpretation, see eg Case C-341/95 *Bettati v Safety Hi-Tech* [1996] ECR I-3989 at paragraph 20.

[20] The CJEU's ruling would still remain binding for the purposes of EU law. However, the domestic courts might refer the matter back to the CJEU pursuant to Art 267 TFEU to revisit its earlier judgment.

The Implementation of the Aarhus Convention in the UK

2

The Aarhus Convention in England and Wales

BRIAN KA RUDDIE[1]

The influence of the Aarhus Convention on the law in England and Wales has been significant and continues to grow. It is remarkable for a number of reasons.

The main body of the Convention does not contain a single limit value, pollution reduction target or substance ban. Its focus is procedural rather than substantive procedural rights.[2] Yet since the Convention was ratified we have seen developments that have influenced the way in which environmental law is both written and applied in England and Wales. This includes the entrenchment of public rights of access to a wide range of environmental information held by public authorities throughout England and Wales, the cementing of public involvement in environmental decision-making at various levels and the development of a significant body of case law on access to justice, notably in relation to costs.

Drivers for these changes have been both the domestic and European courts, as well as EU legislation adopted to implement aspects of the Convention (the EU is also a Party to the Convention). These drivers are not in themselves surprising. There are plenty of examples of them having a significant impact on the law of England and Wales in other areas, both environmental and non-environmental. What is remarkable is the way in which the Convention has enabled the influence of others, most notably the Aarhus Convention Compliance Committee, environmental non-governmental organisations (NGOs) and individual members of the

[1] Lawyer in the International, EU and Knowledge Team, Defra Legal Advisers, Treasury Solicitor's Department. The views of the author are personal and do not necessarily reflect those of the United Kingdom Government.

[2] Upon signature in 1998 and ratification in 2005, the United Kingdom's declaration confirmed the view that the Convention provides procedural rather than substantive environmental rights: 'The United Kingdom understands the references in article 1 and the seventh preambular paragraph of this Convention to the "right" of every person to "live in an environment adequate to his or her health and well-being" to express an aspiration which motivated the negotiation of this Convention and which is shared fully by the United Kingdom. The legal rights which each Party undertakes to guarantee under article 1 are limited to rights of access to information, public participation in decision-making and access to justice in environmental matters in accordance with the provisions of this Convention.' Depositary notification C.N.124.2005.TREATIES-2(XXVII.13).

public, to also have a significant impact on the ways in which environmental law in England and Wales is shaped.

As the Supreme Court noted in *Walton*,[3] 'the Convention is not part of domestic law as such (except where incorporated through European directives)'.[4] The effect of this, where no directly effective EU law rights are engaged, was explained by the Court of Appeal in *Morgan*:[5]

> For the purposes of domestic law, the Convention has the status of an international treaty, not directly incorporated. Thus its provisions cannot be directly applied by domestic courts, but may be taken into account in resolving ambiguities in legislation intended to give it effect.[6]

The influence of the Compliance Committee's findings is persuasive but not binding, reflecting its non-judicial status. In *Walton*, Lord Reed held that 'the decisions of the Committee deserve respect on issues relating to standards of public participation'; sentiments echoed in the opinion of Advocate-General Kokott in *Edwards*,[7] which drew heavily on the Compliance Committee's findings. More recently, however, the Court of Appeal has appeared reluctant to follow the Compliance Committee unquestioningly. In *Evans*[8] it held:

> The Committee's view and concern is undoubtedly worthy of respect. But, even if it had reached the view that the *Wednesbury* approach does not enable the court to assess the substantive and procedural legality of the Secretary of State's decision, its view would have had no direct legal consequence.[9]

It is also notable that similar views were expressed by the Court of Appeal with regard to another UNECE body, the Espoo Convention Implementation Committee, in *An Taisce*.[10] Sullivan LJ said: 'While I respect the Committee's view, it is not the function of the Committee to give an authoritative legal interpretation of the Convention.'[11]

The most logical way of looking at the legal framework by which the United Kingdom's core obligations under the Convention are met in England and Wales is by reference to the three pillars of the Convention: access to environmental information; public participation in environmental decision-making; and access to justice in environmental matters.

[3] *Walton v Scottish Ministers* [2012] UKSC 44, [2013] 1 CMLR 858.
[4] ibid [100].
[5] *Morgan v Hinton Organics (Wessex) Ltd* [2009] EWCA Civ 107, [2009] 2 P & CR 30.
[6] ibid [22].
[7] Case C-260/11 *Edwards v Environment Agency* [2013] 1 WLR 2914.
[8] *R (Evans) v Secretary of State for Communities and Local Government* [2013] EWCA Civ 114.
[9] ibid [38].
[10] *R (on the application of An Taisce (The National Trust for Ireland)) v Secretary of State for Energy and Climate Change* [2014] EWCA Civ 1111.
[11] ibid [44].

Access to Environmental Information

Introduction

Articles 4 and 5 of the Convention require Parties to provide a system for the provision of environmental information by public authorities to the public. This includes both the provision of information in response to a request and more general requirements to disseminate environmental information. The Convention also allows Parties to refuse requests for environmental information in certain circumstances.

The Environmental Information Directive[12] implemented these requirements in EU law. These, in turn, have been transposed in England and Wales by the Environmental Information Regulations 2004, SI 2004/3391 ('the 2004 Regulations').

Rights of access to environmental information are nothing new in England and Wales. EU legislation (Directive 90/313/EEC),[13] transposed in England and Wales through the Environmental Information Regulations 1992, SI 1992/3240, provided such rights. However, the Convention re-shaped the rights and obligations in this area, leading to wider definitions of 'environmental information' and the 'public authorities' to which the information obligations apply.[14] It also limited the exceptions that could be cited in refusals to disclose environmental information in the revised Environmental Information Directive and domestic implementing legislation.[15]

The 2004 Regulations sit within a wider framework of freedom of information legislation, namely the Freedom of Information Act 2000 ('the 2000 Act'). Despite the subsequent misgivings of the Prime Minister whose government introduced it,[16] this Act has resulted in a cultural change across public authorities throughout England and Wales in terms of how information is recorded and presented, and

[12] Directive 2003/4/EC of the European Parliament and of the Council of 28 January 2003 on public access to environmental information and repealing Council Directive 90/313/EEC [2003] OJ L41/26 (Environmental Information Directive).

[13] Council Directive 90/313/EEC of 7 June 1990 on the freedom of access to information on the environment [1990] OJ L158/56.

[14] The definition of 'information relating to the environment' in Directive 90/313/EEC was considerably shorter than the definition of 'environmental information' in the Convention and less open-ended. For example, it only referred to measures adversely affecting, or likely so to affect, specified aspects of the environment rather than 'activities or measures, including administrative measures, environmental agreements, policies, legislation, plans and programmes, affecting or likely to affect the elements of the environment' mentioned in a non-exhaustive list. The definition of 'public authorities' in Directive 90/313/EEC did not include specific reference to persons performing public administrative functions or those under their or government control providing public services in relation to the environment.

[15] J Macdonald, R Crail and CH Jones (eds), *The Law of Freedom of Information*, 2nd edn (Oxford, Oxford University Press, 2009) 310.

[16] T Blair, *A Journey* (London, Arrow, 2011) 516.

how officials in public authorities interact with the public. A request for information may, for a public authority, also be a warning signal that an administrative or judicial challenge is on its way. This shift is compounded by the explosion of information resulting from the proliferation of electronic information platforms.

Nevertheless, the rights provided by the Convention in respect of environmental information go further than those under the 2000 Act. The 2004 Regulations of course reflect this distinction. The Code of Practice issued by the Information Commissioner's Office (ICO) under regulation 16 lists these differences, which include the wider range of public bodies subject to the environmental information requirements and the application of the public interest test to all exceptions as opposed to the 2000 Act under which certain exemptions are absolute, without regard to the public interest in disclosure.[17] Some have suggested that the existence of these requirements within a larger framework on information provides potential for the Convention's influence to reach beyond the environmental sphere,[18] but the distinction between the environmental and non-environmental regimes remains.

Environmental Information

Given these differences, a crucial issue will often therefore be the question of whether information is 'environmental information' or not.

The Convention (Article 2(3)), Environmental Information Directive (Article 2(1)) and 2004 Regulations (regulation 2(1)) all define 'environmental information' by reference to the different media in which that information may be held (written, visual, aural, electronic or any other material form) and what the information covers. This covers information on: the state of elements of the environment and the interaction of those elements; factors, activities and measures affecting or likely to affect the elements of the environment; reports on the implementation of environmental legislation; the state of cost-benefit and other economic analyses and assumptions used in respect of those activities and measures; and the state of human health and safety, conditions of human life, cultural sites and built structures to the extent that they are or may be affected by the state of the elements or those factors, activities or measures. Examples of elements of the environment, such as air and atmosphere and biological diversity, and of factors affecting or likely to affect the environment, such as energy, noise, radiation and emissions or releases, are also given in the definition.

The Information Commissioner has a duty under the 2000 Act to provide guidance for both the public and public authorities on matters, including the meaning

[17] *Code of Practice on the Discharge of the Obligations of Public Authorities under the Environmental Information Regulations 2004* (February 2005), paragraph 14.

[18] J Macdonald (n 15) 934.

of environmental information.[19] This highlights that the definition of environmental information in the 2004 Regulations is the same as that in Article 2(1) of the Environmental Information Directive. It is of course for the courts, rather than any guidance, to provide a definitive view on the meaning of environmental information, but the Information Commissioner's guidance suggests that 'there is little to be gained from considering the subtle differences between, for example "air and atmosphere" or "discharges and releases". The examples are there to help identify what is environmental information, not to confuse.'

Public Authorities

A second crucial issue around the scope of the 2004 Regulations is the question of who may be required to disclose environmental information; who are 'public authorities' for these purposes? The 2004 Regulations define public authorities as including: government departments; other public authorities set out in line with section 3(1) of the 2000 Act (examples range from police forces to the National Gallery); other bodies or persons carrying out functions of public administration; or a body or person under the control of any of those persons that has public responsibilities relating to the environment, exercises functions of a public nature relating to the environment or provides public services relating to the environment. Notably the exceptions listed in Schedule 1 of the 2000 Act or designated under the section 5 order-making power are disapplied for the purposes of the definition in the 2004 Regulations to ensure that this is wide enough to be in tune with the Convention and Environmental Information Directive. Again, consistent with the Convention and the Environmental Information Directive, regulation 3(3) provides that the 2004 Regulations do not apply to a public authority acting in a legislative or judicial capacity.

In *Smartsource*[20] the question of whether a privatised water company was a 'public authority' under the 2004 Regulations came before the Upper Tribunal. The Information Commissioner was joined by 19 water companies—the bulk which covered England and Wales—as additional parties. The Upper Tribunal found that the water companies were not public authorities for the purposes of the 2004 Regulations. The Tribunal examined the definition in the 2004 Regulations against the background of the Convention and the Environmental Information Directive. In the absence of case law directly on the point the Tribunal considered, among other texts, the wording of the first edition of the Aarhus Implementation Guide (2000), including references to privatised utilities, now reflected in the

[19] www.ico.org.uk/for_organisations/guidance index/~/media/documents/library/Environmental_info_reg/Introductory/EIR_WHAT_IS_ENVIRONMENTAL_INFORMATION.ashx.

[20] *Smartsource Drainage & Water Reports Ltd v Information Commissioner* [2010] UKUT 415 (AAC).

2014 edition of the Guide.[21] The Tribunal's view was that the definition of 'public authority' needed to reflect the context and time in which it was being used, concluding that, within the context of the Water Industry Act 1991, the water companies could not be considered as coming within that definition.

However, in *Fish Legal* the Upper Tribunal decided to make a reference on the question of whether water companies were covered by the definition to the CJEU.[22] The Court judged that it would be necessary to examine whether the water companies are vested, under the applicable national law, with special powers beyond those which result from the normal rules applicable in relations between persons governed by private law. The Court also found that the undertakings in question, providing public services relating to the environment, are under the control of a body or person falling within Article 2(2)(a) or (b) of the Environmental Information Directive. This means that they should be classified as 'public authorities' under Article 2(2)(c), if they do not determine the way in which they provide those services in a genuinely autonomous manner. Classification as a public authority under Article 2(2)(b) or (c) makes a significant difference to how much environmental information is potentially subject to the disclosure obligations. Article 2(2)(b) must, in the Court's judgment, be interpreted as meaning that a person falling within that provision constitutes a 'public authority' in respect of all the environmental information which it holds. A commercial company capable of being considered a 'public authority' under Article 2(2)(c) only in so far as, when they provide public services in the environmental field, they are under the control of a body or person falling within Article 2(2)(a) or (b), would not be required to provide environmental information if the information does not relate to the provision of such services. The question of how these principles should be applied to the circumstances of the water companies in *Fish Legal* was returned to the Upper Tribunal.

The Upper Tribunal's findings in *Smartsource* were also the subject of a communication to the Aarhus Convention Compliance Committee.[23] The Committee—acting consistently with paragraph 21 of the annex to Decision I/7[24]—suspended

[21] *The Aarhus Convention: An Implementation Guide* (2nd edn) (UNECE, 2014) p 46. It should be noted that the Guide does not represent an 'official' view on the interpretation of the Convention by UNECE institutions or Parties and it is not binding. The CJEU has confirmed that it is capable of being taken into consideration, if appropriate, for the purpose of the Convention (Case C-182/10 *Solvay v Regione Wallonne* [2012] 2 CMLR 19 at [27]) but that it is not binding (the CJEU rejected a position set out in the Guide in Case C-204/09 *Flachglas Torgau GmbH v Germany* [2013] QB 212 at [35]).

[22] Case C-279/12 *Fish Legal, Emily Shirley v The Information Commissioner, United Utilities, Yorkshire Water and Southern Water* [2014] QB 521.

[23] ACCC/C/2010/55 (United Kingdom).

[24] Decision I/7 of the Meeting of the Parties (ECE/MP.PP/2/Add.8, 2 April 2004) sets out the procedures for the review of Compliance by the Committee. Paragraph 21 states: 'The Committee should at all relevant stages take into account any available domestic remedy unless the application of the remedy is unreasonably prolonged or obviously does not provide an effective and sufficient means of redress'. This reflects the principle under international law that a complainant must use such institutions as a last resort, having attempted to make use of any domestic remedies first. The 5th Meeting of the Parties in July 2014 reinforced the principle on domestic remedies alongside the need for the Committee to ensure transparency and due process for both communicants and the Parties concerned in respect of communications received from members of the public, in Decision V/9 (ECE/MP.PP/2014/2/Add.1).

its consideration of the issue in 2012, pending a final decision in the case. Although the Committee's activities on this issue were put on hold, its involvement at the direct request of Fish Legal—an NGO representing angling clubs and riparian owners among others—illustrates the way in which the Convention is being used to try and influence the outcome of these sorts of questions.

When Must Information be Disclosed?

Those that are considered public authorities are subject to the core duty in regulation 5 of the 2004 Regulations. This is that if the authority holds environmental information, it must make it available on request, as soon as possible and normally no later than 20 working days after the date of receipt of the request.

There are a number of circumstances in which public authorities may refuse requests for information. These are set out in Part 3 of the 2004 Regulations, and reflect Article 4(3) and (4) of the Convention. Even if one of those specific exceptions applies, each is subject to: (i) a public interest test, whether in all the circumstances of the case, the public interest in maintaining the exception outweighs the public interest in disclosing the information (regulation 12(1)(b)); and (ii) a requirement for the public authority to apply a presumption in favour of disclosure (regulation 12(2)).

As to the exceptions themselves, these again echo the structure and wording of the Convention and the Environmental Information Directive. The Convention recognises that there are circumstances in which it will be in the public interest for environmental information to be withheld by a public authority, for example where relations with another country would be affected by disclosure, or where release of information would have a chilling effect on internal discussions within or between public authorities, depriving them of the space to consider and test ideas before opening them up to wider public scrutiny.

The first group of exceptions, in regulation 12(4), apply where the information falls into one of a number of classes. This covers circumstances in which the public authority does not hold the requested information and where the request is manifestly unreasonable or formulated in too general a manner. It also covers requests relating to material which is still in the course of completion, unfinished documents or incomplete data and requests involving the disclosure of internal communications.

The second group, in regulation 12(5), depend on whether disclosure of the information would have an adverse effect on a number of interests. This includes disclosure having an adverse effect on: international relations; defence; national security; public safety; the course of justice; the ability of a person to receive a fair trial; the ability of a public authority to conduct an inquiry of a criminal or disciplinary nature; intellectual property rights; the confidentiality of the proceedings of that or any other public authority where such confidentiality is provided by law; the confidentiality of commercial or industrial information where such confidentiality is provided by law to protect a legitimate economic interest;

the interests of the person who provided the information where that person was not under a legal obligation to supply it, they did not supply in circumstances in which a public authority is entitled to disclose it and they did not consent to its disclosure; and the protection of the environment to which the information relates.

Challenges to Non-Disclosure

The decision of a public authority to refuse to disclose environmental information on request may be challenged, in accordance with the requirements in Article 9(1) of the Convention. This article states that persons who consider that their request for environmental information has been wrongfully refused have 'access to a review procedure before a court of law or another independent and impartial body established by law'. Where the review is provided by a court, access must also be provided to an 'expeditious procedure established by law that is free of charge or inexpensive for reconsideration by a public authority or review by an independent and impartial body other than a court of law'.

The Convention also requires that an authority can be challenged where it is alleged that the authority has ignored, inadequately answered or otherwise not dealt with the request in accordance with the requirements.

Regulation 11 of the 2004 Regulations provides for a reconsideration by the public authority of its decision upon a request by the applicant within 40 days of the alleged failure to comply.

Regulation 18 incorporates the appeal provisions in Part 5 of the 2000 Act. Broadly, this includes a right to appeal the public authority's decision to the ICO, the independent authority with statutory powers to enforce the 2004 Regulations and duties to provide guidance on it. Its decision notice can include legally binding requirements for the public authority to follow. The ICO's decisions may themselves be appealed to the First-tier Tribunal (Information Rights), with further appeals to the Upper Tribunal, the Court of Appeal and the Supreme Court. Regulation 18 also incorporates the enforcement provisions in Part 4 of the 2000 Act, including enforcement notices against public authorities breaching disclosure duties.

Two cases concerning the application of the exceptions, rooted in these mechanisms, mark the influence of the Convention in relation to the access to environmental information pillar in England and Wales.

The first of these is *Birkett*,[25] in which the Court of Appeal was asked to consider whether a public authority could rely on exceptions it did not initially make use of when withholding requested environmental information. The Court of Appeal rejected the argument that allowing such exceptions to be relied on would

[25] *Birkett v Department for the Environment, Food and Rural Affairs* [2011] EWCA Civ 1606, [2012] 2 CMLR 169 [20].

be at odds with the purpose of the Environmental Information Directive and ultimately the Convention. The Court looked at the timescales for making a decision on whether to release requested environmental information and the requirements for such decisions to be subject to a review process, concluding that there may be complexities around deciding which exceptions applied at the time of the request and that their potential importance to the public interest should not mean that they become unavailable if the public authority does not get it right first time. The need for decisions to be taken quickly and for there to be safeguards through review procedures of those decisions—both key features of the Convention—set the framework for the Court's judgment.

Second, the Supreme Court, following an analysis of the text of the Convention, referred a question to the CJEU in *Office of Communications*[26] as to whether environmental information could still be withheld where exceptions, considered individually, did not provide a sufficient justification for non-disclosure. The CJEU found that it was possible to view the exceptions in a cumulative way because the concept of public interest served by disclosure was one that was broad and overarching, rather than something that needed to be applied in isolation to each exception. The suggestion that this would amount to the introduction of a new exception to the Convention was rejected, having regard to the overall interest represented jointly by the interests served by refusing to disclose.

The requirements in Article 5 of the Convention, concerned with the collection and dissemination of environmental information, are again transposed through the Environmental Information Directive and the 2004 Regulations. An overarching duty on public authorities to progressively make the environmental information it holds available is included in regulation 4. However, reflecting the way in which these requirements impact on different areas of environmental law, measures meeting them are found in a number of places. For example, regulators are placed under a general duty in regulation 46 of the Environmental Permitting (England and Wales) Regulations 2010, SI 2010/675 to maintain a public register of environmental information. This includes information on applications for environmental permits and information obtained from monitoring a permitted operation. One way some of this information is made accessible is through the Environment Agency's 'What's in your backyard?' website,[27] which allows users to find environmental information linked to their location, ranging from air quality, landfills, river basin management plans and flood risks. This includes information risks that may be associated with certain operations, the compliance record of operators and details of overarching plans for dealing with the impact of man-made activities on the environment. Providing such information is one of the means by which the public is given the tools for understanding the activities of both public authorities and those that they regulate, and how they can become involved in the environmental decisions of public authorities.

[26] Case C-71/10 *Office of Communications v Information Commissioner* [2011] ECR I-07205.
[27] www.environment-agency.gov.uk/homeandleisure/37793.aspx.

Public Participation in Environmental Decision-Making

The Convention's second pillar concerns the provision of opportunities for the public to participate in environmental decisions. There are two main aspects to this, dealing with different levels of decision-making.

First, Article 6 requires participation in decisions on specific activities. This includes decisions to permit proposed activities listed in Annex I to the Convention and on other activities not listed there 'which may have a significant effect on the environment'.[28] The sorts of activities listed in Annex I are installations for the provision of energy, the production of minerals, metals and chemicals, waste management, various types of transport infrastructure, water abstraction and treatment and intensive farming operations, among others. Also included are activities not specifically listed but where public participation is provided for under an environmental impact procedure in accordance with national legislation.[29] Exceptions are available in respect of proposed activities serving national defence purposes[30] and for projects undertaken exclusively or mainly for research, development and testing of new methods or projects for less than two years, unless they would be likely to cause a significant adverse effect on the environment or health.[31]

Second, Article 7 requires public participation in the preparation of plans and programmes relating to the environment. It also encourages Parties to provide opportunities for public participation in the preparation of policies relating to the environment, to the extent that this is appropriate.

In addition, under Article 8, Parties must strive to promote public participation during the preparation of 'executive regulations and other generally applicable legally binding rules that may have a significant effect on the environment'. Although the wording of the Convention makes this a weaker obligation than those in Article 6 and the first part of Article 7, public participation in these aspects of decision-making are already established in England and Wales. The Consultation Principles for Government,[32] introduced in July 2012, set out commitments on early and sustained stakeholder engagement, consultation periods and a digital by default consultation process.

Again, the position in England and Wales has had to be aligned with EU legislation adopted to meet the Convention requirements. The Public Participation Directive[33] was adopted in order to contribute to the implementation of the

[28] Aarhus Convention Art 6(1)(b).
[29] ibid Annex I, para 20.
[30] ibid Art 6(1)(c).
[31] ibid Annex I, para 21.
[32] www.gov.uk/government/publications/consultation-principles-guidance.
[33] Directive 2003/35/EC of the European Parliament and of the Council of 26 May 2003 providing for public participation in respect of the drawing up of certain plans and programmes relating to the environment and amending with regard to public participation and access to justice Council Directives 85/337/EEC and 96/61/EC [2003] OJ L156/17 (Public Participation Directive).

obligations arising under the Convention.[34] It did this in two ways in respect of the second pillar: (i) providing requirements for public participation in respect of the drawing up of plans and programmes relating to the environment under certain EU waste, nitrates and air quality legislation;[35] and (ii) amending both the Environmental Impact Assessment (EIA) Directive[36] and the Integrated Pollution Prevention and Control (IPPC) Directive[37] in order to improve the public participation provisions included in this legislation.[38]

Article 2(5) of the Public Participation Directive excludes from its application plans and programmes for which a public participation procedure is carried out under the Strategic Environmental Assessment (SEA) Directive[39] or under the Water Framework Directive.[40] This recognised that existing EU legislation would, other than in those areas addressed by the Public Participation Directive, be sufficient for the purposes of the Convention.[41] The EIA Directive has been codified into a new Directive[42] and the IPPC Directive is being replaced by the Industrial Emissions Directive,[43] and in each case the Convention's public participation principles are being integrated. This all reflects the approach mentioned in the Public Participation Directive's 10th recital.

This approach, drawing on existing arrangements for public participation and integrating anything needed to supplement these into the relevant area (rather than, for example, having separate standalone requirements), means that the provisions giving effect to the Convention's public participation requirements in England and Wales are spread across a wide range of legislative regimes, including those for planning, environmental permitting and environmental assessments.

The public participation requirements under the Convention differ depending on whether they concern specific activities under Article 6 or plans or programmes relating to the environment under Article 7.

[34] ibid Art 1.

[35] ibid Art 2 and Annex 1.

[36] Council Directive 85/337/EEC of 27 June 1985 on the assessment of the effects of certain public and private projects on the environment [1985] OJ L175/40.

[37] Council Directive 96/61/EC of 24 September 1996 concerning integrated pollution prevention and control [1996] OJ L16/21.

[38] Public Participation Directive, Arts 3 and 4, as originally adopted.

[39] Directive 2001/42/EC of the European Parliament and of the Council of 27 June 2001 on the assessment of the effects of certain plans and programmes on the environment [2001] OJ L197/30.

[40] Directive 2000/60/EC of the European Parliament and of the Council of 23 October 2000 establishing a framework for Community action in the field of water policy [2000] OJ L327/1.

[41] In the Supreme Court's dismissal of the appeals brought in respect of a challenge against the HS2 high speed rail link, Lord Carnwath observed, in obiter dicta, that there is no reason to assume that Article 7 and the SEA Directive are intended to cover exactly the same ground, based on his reading of the non-binding *Implementation Guide*, but that this does not invalidate the Directive so far as it goes (*R (HS2 Action Alliance and others) v Secretary of State for Transport and others* [2014] UKSC 3, [2014] 1 WLR 324 [52]).

[42] Directive 2011/92/EU of the European Parliament and of the Council of 13 December 2011 on the assessment of the effects of certain public and private projects on the environment [2012] OJ L26/1. The European Commission published a proposal for a new directive in October 2012.

[43] Directive 2010/75/EU of the European Parliament and of the Council of 24 November 2010 on industrial emissions (integrated pollution prevention and control) [2010] OJ L334/17.

The Article 6 requirements apply to the 'public concerned', who are defined as 'the public affected or likely to be affected by, or having an interest in, the environmental decision-making'.[44] NGOs promoting environmental protection which meet any requirements under national law are deemed to have an interest. The public concerned are to be informed, early on in the decision-making procedure and in an adequate, effective and timely manner, of details such as the proposals, application and nature of any decision, as well as of information on the decision-making procedure, including information on opportunities for public participation, details on any public hearings and how and from whom information can be obtained or to whom comments or questions should be submitted.[45] The procedures are required to include reasonable time-frames so as to allow sufficient time for informing the public and for the public to prepare and participate effectively in the decision-making,[46] and the public participation should be provided 'early … when all options are open and effective public participation can take place'.[47] Article 6 also includes provision for encouraging dialogue between applicants and the public concerned and for public authorities to give the public concerned access to information relevant to the decision-making.[48] The public participation procedures should allow the public to submit comments, information, analyses or opinions relevant to the proposed activity.[49] The decision should take due account of the outcome of public participation,[50] (although as the Compliance Committee has confirmed, this does not amount to the right of the public to veto a decision),[51] and be appropriately publicised.[52]

By contrast, the Article 7 requirements apply to the 'public', defined more widely as 'one or more natural legal persons, and, in accordance with national legislation or practice, their associations, organizations or groups'.[53] The Convention is less prescriptive regarding the public participation procedures for plans and programmes, requiring 'appropriate practical and/or other provisions for the public to participate … within a transparent and fair framework, having provided the necessary information to the public'. The requirements of Article 6(3), (4) and (8), on providing reasonable time-frames, early participation and taking due account of the public participation also apply here.

The public participation requirements of the Convention and the associated EU legislation can be found throughout environmental and planning legislation in England and Wales. For example, the Nitrate Pollution Prevention Regulations

[44] Aarhus Convention Art 2(5).
[45] ibid Art 6(2).
[46] ibid Art 6(3).
[47] ibid Art 6(4).
[48] ibid Art 6(5) and (6).
[49] ibid Art 6(7).
[50] ibid Art 6(8).
[51] ACCC/C/2008/24 (Spain) ECE/MP.PP/C.1/2009/8/Add.1, 8 February 2011, para 98.
[52] Aarhus Convention Art 6(9).
[53] ibid Art 2(4).

2008, SI 2008/2349, implementing in England requirements under the Nitrates Directive[54] (which is one of those listed in Annex I to the Public Participation Directive), sets out public participation duties in regulation 47 concerning the Secretary of State's review of the effectiveness of restrictions in nitrate vulnerable zones. The influence of the Convention is apparent from both the content and structure of the requirements:

> 47.—(1) When carrying out this review the Secretary of State must ensure that the public is given early and effective opportunities to participate.
> (2) The Secretary of State must make adequate arrangements for public participation to enable the public to prepare and participate effectively.
> (3) The Secretary of State must ensure that—
> (a) the public is consulted about any proposals and that relevant information about such proposals is made available to the public, including information about the right to participate in decision-making and about the body to which comments or questions may be submitted; and
> (b) the public is entitled to express comments and opinions when all options are open before decisions on the plans and programmes are made.
> (4) The Secretary of State must identify the public entitled to be consulted, including non-governmental organisations promoting environmental protection.
> (5) Reasonable time must be allowed for consultation.
> (6) Consultation must be taken into account in reaching a decision.
> (7) Following consultation the Secretary of State must inform the public about the decisions taken and the reasons and considerations upon which those decisions are based, including information about the public participation process.

The Environmental Permitting (England and Wales) Regulations 2010, SI 2010/675, which govern the approval processes for a significant number of the specific activities caught by the Convention, set out public participation provisions consistent with the Convention in Part 1 of Schedule 5 (grant, variation, transfer and surrender of environmental permits). Under regulation 59, the Environment Agency for England and the Natural Resources Body for Wales must prepare and publish a statement of their policies for complying with its public participation duties, which include those set out in Schedule 5 regarding handling applications for environmental permits and those in regulations 26 and 29 concerning the use of standard rules for permits.

This integration of public participation principles in both specific and cross-cutting areas of environmental legislation is also reflected in the planning regime. Procedural requirements for decision making under legislation such as the Town and Country Planning Act 1990,[55] the Planning and Compulsory Purchase Act 2004, the Planning Act 2008, the Infrastructure Planning (Environmental Impact Assessment) Regulations 2009, SI 2009/2263, the Town and Country Planning

[54] Council Directive 91/676/EEC of 12 December 1991 concerning the protection of waters against pollution caused by nitrates from agricultural sources [1991] OJ L375/1.
[55] Amended by the Localism Act 2011.

(Development Management Procedure) (England) Order 2010, SI 2010/2184 and the Town and Country Planning (Environmental Impact Assessment) Regulations 2011, SI 2011/1824, include public participation requirements in the form of obligations to publicise and consult on applications, and to take into account views and information provided to decision-making authorities.

This wide range of legislation applying the second pillar in England and Wales reflects its integration in the various decision-making processes that are affected. The legislation listed in the United Kingdom's national implementation report for the Aarhus Convention[56] shows how far-reaching public participation principles are applied.

The influence of the Convention's second pillar has also been seen in the courts. *R (Greenpeace) v Secretary of State for Trade and Industry*[57] concerned the Secretary of State's consultation on future energy production. In considering whether the decision was amenable to judicial review—this concerned a high level strategic policy decision not subject to specific statutory or other established procedural rules that may have made it difficult to establish procedural impropriety—Sullivan J drew on Article 7 of the Convention. In finding that it would have been difficult to see how 'a promise of anything less than "the fullest public consultation" would have been consistent with the Government's obligations under the Aarhus Convention',[58] the Convention became one of the groundings for the case.

Two communications to the Compliance Committee[59] alleged non-compliance with the Convention in respect of Articles 6 and 7. These arose in the context of the proposed construction of a superstore in Kent and various planning applications in London. The Committee examined the communicants' arguments about whether the planning laws and procedures of England and Wales met the standards regarding public participation required in Articles 6 and 7, including whether the fact that oral hearings might not be held at meetings of planning committees breached the Convention. In rejecting these submissions, the Committee found nothing to substantiate the more general allegations about the planning system in England and Wales. It also noted that Article 6(7) of the Convention gives the public the right to submit comments, information, analyses or opinions during public participation procedures, either in writing or, as appropriate, orally at a public hearing or inquiry with the applicant. If local authorities only provide for participation of members of the public at planning meetings via written submissions this would not, according to the Committee, be in non-compliance with Article 6(7).[60]

One issue specifically addressed in the second pillar of the Convention is public participation in decision-making relating to the release of genetically modified

[56] The United Kingdom's 2014 National Implementation Report is available on the UNECE website at www.unece.org/env/pp/reports_trc_implementation_2014.html.

[57] *R (Greenpeace) v Secretary of State for Trade and Industry* [2007] EWHC 311, [2007] Env LR 29.

[58] ibid [51].

[59] Joined communications ACCC/C/2010/45 and ACCC/C/2011/61 (United Kingdom).

[60] Findings adopted by the Compliance Committee on 28 June 2013, para 78.

organisms. The 20th recital to the Convention mentions the need for 'increased transparency and greater public participation in decision-making' in this area. Article 6(11) provides a specific requirement for the Article 6 obligations to be applied 'to the extent feasible and appropriate' to decisions on whether to permit the deliberate release of genetically modified organisms into the environment.

In 2005, at the second Meeting of the Parties to the Convention, an agreement was reached to strengthen these requirements. Amendments to the Convention[61] introduce a new Article 6 bis and annex I bis. These set out requirements for 'early and effective information and public participation prior to making decisions on whether to permit the deliberate release into the environment and placing on the market of genetically modified organisms' and should complement provisions for delivering the objectives of the Cartagena Protocol on Biosafety,[62] to which the United Kingdom is also a Party. The requirements are already reflected in EU law through the Deliberate Release Directive[63] and the GM Food and Feed Regulation.[64]

Annex 1 bis to the Convention prescribes how this is to be achieved, which includes making public information on applications for authorisation to place on the market or deliberately release genetically modified organisms together with any assessment report. The annex specifically states that confidentiality should not be afforded to information on the applicant, the intended use of the genetically modified organism, where it is to be released, methods and plans for monitoring and the environmental risk assessment. Parties must endeavour to ensure that decisions take due account of the outcome of the public participation.

Although the amendment has been ratified by both the United Kingdom and the European Union, it has not yet been brought into force because an insufficient number of Parties that were party to the Convention at the time the amendment was adopted have ratified. However, the transposition of these requirements in EU law, and therefore in England and Wales, provides for compliance with the Convention, both before and after the amendment comes into force.

For example, publicity requirements relating to applications for consent to release genetically modified organisms are included in regulation 12 of the Genetically Modified Organisms (Deliberate Release) Regulations 2002, SI 2002/2443 in respect of England (in Wales this is in regulation 13 of the Genetically Modified Organisms (Deliberate Release) (Wales) Regulations 2002, SI 2002/3188 (W 304)). Part VI of the Environmental Protection Act 1990 provides the wider framework for the regulation of genetically modified organisms in England and Wales. Under section 122, the Secretary of State and Welsh Ministers

61 Decision II/1 of the Meeting of the Parties (ECE/MP.PP/2005/2/Add.2, 20 June 2005).

62 Cartagena Protocol on Biosafety to the Convention on Biological Diversity.

63 Directive 2001/18/EC of the European Parliament and of the Council of 12 March 2001 on the deliberate release into the environment of genetically modified organisms and repealing Council Directive 90/220/EEC [2001] OJ L106/1.

64 Regulation (EC) 1829/2003 of the European Parliament and of the Council of 22 September 2003 on genetically modified food and feed [2003] OJ L268/1.

must maintain a public register that includes information such as applications for consents and any advice given by the Advisory Committee on Releases to the Environment as well as 'any other information obtained or furnished under any provision of this Part'. Reflecting annex I bis to the Convention, regulation 33 of the 2002 Regulations (regulation 34 of the Welsh 2002 Regulations) lists the information for which the public interest requires it to be included in the register notwithstanding that it may be commercially confidential. Part IV of the 2002 Regulations imposes duties on the decision-maker, be it the Secretary of State or Welsh Ministers, in respect of consents, to allow representations to be made on applications and for these to be taken into account when making a decision.

Access to Justice in Environmental Matters

Overview

Access to justice requirements under the environmental information and public participation pillars of the Convention—set out in Article 9, paragraphs (1) and (2) respectively—have been incorporated into the EU legislation used to implement those pillars.

Article 9(1) requires that those who consider their request for environmental information under Article 4 to have been ignored, wrongfully refused, inadequately answered or otherwise not dealt with in accordance with the Article to have access to a 'review procedure before a court of law or another independent and impartial body established by law'. The provision of such a review by a court of law needs to be accompanied by access to an 'expeditious procedure established by law that is free of charge or inexpensive for reconsideration by a public authority or review by an independent and impartial body other than a court of law'. The decisions made in these procedures must be binding on the public authority and be accompanied by reasons where access to the information is refused.

As with the other requirements of the first pillar, the Environmental Information Directive incorporates them into EU law.[65] The Environmental Information Regulations 2004 provide, in turn, for the transposition of these requirements in England and Wales. Regulation 11 provides for a reconsideration by the public authority of its decision upon a request by the applicant within 40 days of the alleged failure to comply. Regulation 18 incorporates the appeal provisions in Part 5 of the 2000 Act. Broadly, this includes a right to appeal the public authority's decision to ICO, an independent authority with statutory powers to enforce the 2004 Regulations and duties to provide guidance on it. Its decision notice can

[65] Environmental Information Directive, Art 6.

include legally binding requirements for the public authority to follow. The ICO's decisions may themselves be appealed to the First-tier Tribunal (Information Rights), with further appeals to the Upper Tribunal, the Court of Appeal and the Supreme Court.

In respect of the public participation pillar, Article 9(2) requires Parties to ensure that the 'public concerned' with a sufficient interest or maintaining impairment of a right have access to 'a review procedure before a court of law and/or another independent or impartial body established by law, to challenge the substantive and procedural legality of any decision, act or omission subject to the provisions of article 6' and other provisions of the Convention where provided under national law. What constitutes a sufficient interest and impairment of a right is left to be determined by requirements under national law, but needs to be consistent with the objective of giving the public concerned wide access to justice and includes NGOs promoting environmental protection. The Public Participation Directive incorporated these requirements into the EU's EIA and IPPC regimes and the rules on judicial reviews available in England and Wales were used to deliver them.

Beyond the access to justice provisions associated with the first two pillars there is no EU legislation addressed to Member States on the more general requirements on access to justice, set out in Article 9(3). This Article requires Parties to ensure that members of the public meeting any criteria in national law 'have access to administrative or judicial procedures to challenge acts and omissions by private persons and public authorities which contravene provisions of its national law relating to the environment'.

The position reflects the wide variation in legal systems both across and within the 28 Member States of the EU. A 2003 Commission proposal for an access to justice directive was rejected by Member States, with the principle of subsidiarity and the practicalities of having an EU framework in this area among the concerns.[66] Upon approval of the Convention, the EU position was confirmed in a declaration:

> [T]he European [Union] also declares that the legal instruments in force do not cover fully the implementation of the obligations resulting from Article 9(3) of the Convention as they relate to administrative and judicial procedures to challenge acts and omissions by private persons and public authorities other than the institutions of the European [Union] as covered by Article 2(2)(d) of the Convention, and that, consequently, its Member States are responsible for the performance of these obligations at the time of approval of the Convention by the European [Union] and will remain so unless and until the [Union], in the exercise of its powers under the EC Treaty, adopts provisions of [Union] law covering the implementation of these obligations.[67]

[66] The Commission withdrew the 2003 proposal on 21 May 2014 as part of its REFIT (Regulatory Fitness and Performance) Programme.

[67] Council Decision of 17 February 2005 on the conclusion, on behalf of the European Community, of the Convention on access to information, public participation in decision-making and access to justice in environmental matters (2005/370/EC) [2005] OJ L124/1.

It is certainly not necessary, even where the EU is also a Party to that agreement, for there to be EU legislation addressed to the Member States in place. The United Kingdom takes the position that everything needed to comply with a signed international agreement will be in place before that agreement is ratified. The existing legal framework in England and Wales, including that underpinning the Civil Procedure Rules (CPR), was considered sufficient for the purposes of the access to justice requirements of the Convention at the time of its ratification in 2005. The availability of procedures for access to justice in environmental matters in the United Kingdom is long-standing.[68] The position taken on ratification has, however, been the subject of challenges both in the courts and through communications to the Compliance Committee, which are examined in more detail below.

As to the status of Article 9(3) under EU law, the question came before the EU in the context of a case on standing regarding the protection of bears in Slovakia (commonly known as the 'Brown Bear case').[69] The CJEU found that it had jurisdiction to decide on the question of whether Article 9(3) has direct effect in the absence of specific EU legislation because the specific issue before it related to a field covered in large measure by it;[70] the protection of a species mentioned in the Habitats Directive.[71] The CJEU stated that it was 'seeking to forestall future differences of interpretation' by applying a uniform interpretation.[72] Article 9(3) was not considered sufficiently clear and precise for it to have direct effect since it was contingent on provisions laid down in national law,[73] and it falls to the domestic legal system of each Member State to lay down detailed procedural rules for safeguarding rights derived from EU law.[74] In the context of species protected under EU law, the national court must, in order to provide the effective judicial protection in respect of EU environmental law, 'interpret its national law in a way which, to the fullest extent possible, is consistent with the objectives laid down in Article 9(3) of the Aarhus Convention'.[75]

Article 9(4), which applies in respect of the access to justice requirements in paragraphs (1) to (3) requires that the associated procedures provide 'adequate and effective remedies, including injunctive relief as appropriate, and be fair, equitable, timely and not prohibitively expensive'. These requirements are often considered alongside the provisions in Article 9(5), for Parties to ensure that 'information is provided to the public on access to administrative and judicial

[68] See, eg T Jewell and B Pontin, 'United Kingdom' in J Ebbesson (ed), *Access to Justice in Environmental Matters in the EU* (The Hague, Kluwer Law International, 2002) 471.

[69] Case C-240/09 *Lesoochranárske zoskupenie VLK v Ministerstvo životného prostredia Slovenskej republiky ('Brown Bear case')* [2011] ECR I-01255.

[70] ibid [40].

[71] Council Directive 92/43/EEC of 21 May 1992 on the conservation of natural habitats and of wild fauna and flora [1992] OJ L206/7 (Habitats Directive).

[72] *'Brown Bear case'* (n 69) [42].

[73] ibid [45].

[74] ibid [47].

[75] ibid [50].

review procedures' and to 'consider the establishment of appropriate assistance mechanisms to remove or reduce financial and other barriers to access to justice'.

Avoiding Prohibitively Expensive Costs

One issue to have generated debate on the implementation of Convention requirements has been the costs associated with bringing a judicial review, notably in the Environmental Justice Project Report,[76] the Sullivan Report[77] and the Jackson Report.[78] The first judicial reference to the Convention, by the Court of Appeal in *Burkett*,[79] mentioned the Environmental Justice Project Report and suggested further study of the 'difficult issue' of costs and their effects on potential environmental litigants. These sentiments were echoed in the Court of Appeal in *England*.[80]

Shortly after the Convention was ratified by the United Kingdom in February 2005, the Court of Appeal decided a case (*Corner House Research*)[81] in which it set out guidance to be used when considering whether to award a protective costs order (PCO) in public interest litigation. The court should be satisfied that: the issues raised are of general public importance; the public interest requires those issues to be resolved; the claimant has no private interest in the outcome of the case; having regard to the financial resources of the parties and the likely costs of the case, it is fair and just to make the order; and if the order is not made the claimant will, acting reasonably, probably discontinue the proceedings.[82] Although this was not a case concerning the Convention, it would become the basis for the courts' approach to PCOs and their use in helping to meet the requirements of Article 9(4) of the Convention in England and Wales. This was seen in *McCaw*,[83] where the High Court confirmed that it must apply the *Corner House* principles flexibly, and in the context of environmental cases, in the light of the Aarhus Convention.

Having recognised its relevance to the question of costs in environmental cases in England and Wales, the Convention would be cited more frequently by parties in their arguments and courts in their judgments on issues of costs. In *Davey*,[84]

[76] *A Report by the Environmental Justice Project* (March 2004).

[77] *Ensuring Access to Environmental Justice in England and Wales: Report of the Working Group on Access to Environmental Justice* (May 2008).

[78] *Review of Civil Litigation Costs: Final Report* (December 2009).

[79] *R (Burkett) v Hammersmith and Fulham London Borough Council* [2004] EWCA Civ 1317, [2004] All ER (D) 186 (Oct).

[80] *R (England) v Tower Hamlets London Borough Council and others* [2006] EWCA Civ 1742, [2006] All ER (D) 314 (Dec) [15].

[81] *R (Corner House Research) v Secretary of State for Trade and Industry* [2005] EWCA Civ 192, [2005] 4 All ER 1.

[82] ibid [74].

[83] *R (McCaw) v City of Westminster Magistrates' Court* [2008] EWHC 1504 (Admin), [2008] All ER (D) 251 (Jun).

[84] *Davey v Aylesbury Vale District Council* [2007] EWCA Civ 1166, [2008] 2 All ER 178.

the Court of Appeal considered Article 9(3) and (4) of the Convention alongside principles the courts had developed for the purposes of awarding costs at the permission stage in a judicial review. The influence of the Convention was even felt beyond environmental cases. In *Compton*[85] the Court of Appeal considered principles applicable to PCOs arising from the need to comply with the Convention in the context of other serious non-environmental issues. The limits of that direct influence on the courts was, however, demonstrated in *Morgan*.[86] The Court of Appeal found that, outside those areas incorporated into EU law and given direct effect, the principles of the Convention were 'at most a matter to which the court may have regard in exercising its discretion' under the CPR, with the *Corner House* criteria taking the principles governing the grant of PCOs settled as far as the Court was concerned.[87]

The Court of Appeal did however return to the *Corner House* principles in *Garner*.[88] These were modified in order to comply with the access to justice requirements originally implemented through the Public Participation Directive. The Court defined cases that fell within the scope of the Directive as being automatically within the public interest, meaning that effectively no public interest test needed to be met in these cases. The Court also rejected a wholly subjective approach to assessing the means of the parties.

The issue of costs has been raised with the Compliance Committee, which accepted three communications regarding compliance with Article 9 of the Convention in 2008,[89] two of which concerned England and Wales. In communication 23, the issue of costs in private nuisance proceedings—complaints brought directly against those who are alleged to have caused or be causing a nuisance by an injured party, rather than against a public authority—was raised by the claimants in *Morgan*. The Committee made a finding of *stricto sensu* non-compliance with Article 9(4) in this area, but found nothing to substantiate a systemic breach and made no recommendations.[90] In communication 33, the Committee found, after an analysis of costs in environmental claims focused on judicial reviews, that the United Kingdom was in non-compliance with Article 9(4) and (5) by

85 *R (Compton) v Wiltshire Primary Care Trust* [2008] EWCA Civ 749, [2009] 1 All ER 978.
86 *Morgan* (n 5).
87 ibid [47].
88 *R (Garner) v Elmbridge Borough Council* [2010] EWCA Civ 1006, [2012] PTSR D7.
89 ACCC/C/2008/23, ACCC/C/2008/27, ACCC/C/2008/33 (United Kingdom).
90 ACCC/C/2008/23 (United Kingdom) ECE/MP.PP/C.1/2010/6/Add.1, 24 August 2011, paras 58 and 59. The issue of costs in private nuisance proceedings was again raised with the Committee in communications ACCC/C/2013/85 and ACCC/C/2013/86 (United Kingdom), discussing the matter at its 44th meeting in March 2014. In a domestic case brought by the communicant in ACCC/C/2013/86, the Court of Appeal found that private nuisance actions would only be capable of falling within the scope of Article 9(3) of the Convention where the nature of the complaint has a close link with the particular environmental matters regulated by the Convention, and where the claim, if successful, confers significant public environmental benefits. The Court's judgment was that 'if on the particular facts the court were to conclude that the purpose of the claim was principally to protect private property interests and any public benefit was limited and incidental, it ought not to attract the procedural costs protections afforded by art 9.4' (*Austin v Miller Argent (South Wales) Limited* [2014] EWCA Civ 1012 [22]).

'failing to ensure that the costs for all court procedures subject to article 9 were not prohibitively expensive, and in particular by the absence of any clear legally binding directions from the legislature or judiciary to this effect' and because the system as a whole 'is not such as "to remove or reduce financial [...] barriers to access to justice"'.[91] It recommended a review of the system for allocating costs in environmental cases to ensure that they are fair and equitable and not prohibitively expensive and provide a clear and transparent framework. Although the Committee's findings are not themselves directly binding in law, as discussed above, they were endorsed in Decision IV/9i[92] of the 4th Meeting of the Parties to the Convention. A recommendation by the Committee for a further review of the system, following its consideration of the revisions to the CPR in 2013 (discussed below), was also endorsed by the 5th Meeting of the Parties to the Convention.[93]

The CJEU has also considered the issue of costs in judicial reviews in England and Wales. In 2011 the Commission formally commenced infraction proceedings against the United Kingdom in respect of the application of the 'prohibitively expensive' provisions in Articles 3(7) and 4(4) of the Public Participation Directive applying the access to justice requirements to the EIA and IPPC regimes.[94] In accordance with EU case law,[95] the scope of the judicial proceedings before the CJEU is defined by the Commission's reasoned opinion on the alleged infringement. As this was submitted in March 2010, the CJEU's judgment, given in February 2014, focused on the position as it stood in the United Kingdom at that date, so did not take account of the subsequent legislative developments in England and Wales. The CJEU found, based on its consideration of the position as it stood at the time of the Commission's reasoned opinion, that the United Kingdom had failed to correctly transpose Articles 3(7) and 4(4) of the Public Participation Directive, inasmuch as they provide that the judicial proceedings referred to must not be prohibitively expensive.

The CJEU was also asked to consider the meaning of 'prohibitively expensive' with particular regard to the means of the claimant in a reference from the Supreme Court in *Edwards*,[96] a case concerning the costs associated with an unsuccessful claim within the scope of the Public Participation Directive.

Following a consultation in 2011/2012,[97] the Ministry of Justice introduced amendments to the CPR in England and Wales in April 2013.[98] In the case of

[91] ACCC/C/2008/33 (United Kingdom) ECE/MP.PP/C.1/2010/6/Add.3, 24 August 2011, paras 141 and 142.

[92] Decision IV/9i of the Meeting of the Parties (ECE/MP.PP/2011/2/Add.1, 19 August 2011).

[93] Decision V/9n of the Meeting of the Parties (ECE/MP.PP/2014/2/Add.1).

[94] Case C-530/11 *Commission v United Kingdom* [2014] QB 988.

[95] Case 186/85 *Commission v Belgium* [1987] ECR 2029; Case C-296/92 *Commission v Italy* [1994] ECR I-1.

[96] *Edwards* (n 7).

[97] *Cost Protection for Litigants in Environmental Judicial Review Claims*, Ministry of Justice (October 2011).

[98] The Civil Procedure (Amendment) Rules 2013, SI 2013/262. The relevant new rules are included at Appendix 10 to this book.

an 'Aarhus Convention claim'—defined as a claim for judicial review of a decision, act or omission all or part of which is subject to the provisions of the Convention[99]—a claimant will not be ordered to pay costs of more than £5,000 as an individual, or £10,000 in other cases.[100] The Convention does not require a total bar on costs. Article 9(4) refers to the need for procedures not to be 'prohibitively expensive' rather than for them to be free and Article 3(8) makes specific reference to the awarding of 'reasonable costs' in judicial proceedings.

A defendant's liability for costs is also limited, but at a higher level of £35,000. A claimant can opt to exclude their claim from these rules[101] and a defendant may contest whether it is an 'Aarhus Convention claim'.[102] These changes were made so that applicants in environmental judicial review cases would be provided with greater clarity about the level of costs through a codification of the rules on PCOs concerning when they will be granted and at which level they will be made. The rules apply to claims at first instance. On appeal, Rule 52.9A, adopted as part of the wider Jackson reforms on costs,[103] will apply. In cases where costs recovery is normally limited at first instance the court may make an order that the recoverable costs of an appeal will be limited to the extent which the court specifies, having regard to the means of both parties, the circumstances of the case and the need to facilitate access to justice. For cases that make it to the Supreme Court, rule 46(1) of the Supreme Court Rules 2009 allows the Court to make such orders as it considers just in respect of the costs of any appeal.

The 2013 amendments to the CPR applied only to judicial reviews. Statutory reviews potentially within the scope of the Convention, such as section 288 of the Town and Country Planning Act 1990, are subject instead to the principles established in the case law on PCOs. The courts have considered the application of the Convention outside judicial reviews. In *Venn v Secretary of State for Communities and Local Government and others*,[104] at paragraph 36, Lang J considered that 'the *Corner House* criteria should be relaxed to give effect to the requirements of the Aarhus Convention'. However, the Court of Appeal in *Austin v Miller Argent (South Wales) Limited*[105] did not accept 'the principle that UK law should be interpreted and applied in harmony with international obligations'. This included the observations of Lang J in *Venn* 'which suggested that this principle would require a PCO to be granted where the failure to do so would involve a Convention breach', with the Court of Appeal stating that it did not accept that 'the principle extends to requiring domestic courts to exercise discretions so as to give effect to

[99] CPR 45.41.

[100] CPR 45.43 PD 45.

[101] CPR 45.42.

[102] CPR 45.44.

[103] *Review of Civil Litigation Costs: Final Report*. Jackson LJ was asked by the then Master of the Rolls, Lord Clarke of Stone-cum-Ebony, to review and report on the costs on civil litigation.

[104] *Venn v Secretary of State for Communities and Local Government and others* [2013] EWHC 3546 (Admin).

[105] *Austin v Miller* (n 90) [36], [37].

those obligations'. Subsequently, the Court of Appeal reversed Lang J in *Venn*,[106] holding that the exclusion of statutory appeals and applications from CPR 45.41 'was not an oversight, but a deliberate expression of legislative intent' and that

> it necessarily follows that it would not be appropriate to exercise a judicial discretion so as to side-step the limitation (to applications for judicial review) that has been deliberately imposed by secondary legislation. It would be doubly appropriate to exercise the discretion for the purpose of giving effect under domestic law to the requirements of an international Convention which, while it is an integral part of the legal order of the EU, is not directly effective ... and which has not been incorporated into UK domestic law.[107]

The rules on cross-undertakings in cases involving interim injunctions were also amended in April 2013. The Convention is not prescriptive in respect of remedies such as injunctive relief.[108] When an interim injunction is granted the applicant is often required to give an undertaking in damages reflecting the risk to the respondent. Amendments to Practice Direction 25A[109] provide that where, in an 'Aarhus Convention claim', the court is satisfied that an injunction is necessary to prevent significant environmental damage and to preserve the factual basis of the proceedings, the court will, in considering whether to require an undertaking by the applicant to pay any damages which the respondent or any other person may sustain as a result and the terms of any such undertaking, have particular regard to the need for the terms of the order overall not to be such as would make continuing with the claim prohibitively expensive for the applicant and ensure that the case is heard promptly.

The CJEU's judgment in *Edwards* was given shortly after the CPR revisions came into force. The Supreme Court asked the CJEU if the question whether the cost of litigation is or is not 'prohibitively expensive' within the meaning of Article 9(4) of the Convention and the Public Participation Directive should be decided on an objective basis (eg the ability of an 'ordinary' member of the public to meet the potential liability for costs), a subjective basis (by reference to the means of the particular claimant) or a combination of these. The CJEU rejected the necessity of a purely objective approach, finding that a court carrying out this assessment

> cannot act solely on the basis of the claimant's financial situation but must also carry out an objective analysis of the amount of the costs. It may also take into account the situation of the parties concerned, whether the claimant has a reasonable prospect of success, the importance of what is at stake for the claimant and for the protection of the environment, the complexity of the relevant law and procedure, the potentially frivolous nature of the claim at its various stages, and the existence of a national legal aid scheme or a costs protection regime.[110]

106 [2014] EWCA Civ 1539.
107 Per Sullivan LJ at paragraph 33.
108 J Ebbesson, 'Comparative Introduction' in J Ebbesson (ed), *Access to Justice in Environmental Matters in the EU* (The Hague, Kluwer Law International, 2002) 14.
109 Para 5.1A.
110 *Edwards* (n 7) [46].

Alongside the need to ensure that the costs of proceedings is not 'objectively unreasonable',[111] the CJEU acknowledged the need to make a subjective assessment of the situation of the parties.[112] Although the CJEU did not refer to the findings of the Compliance Committee in communication 33 in its judgment, it is notable that the Advocate General did.[113]

The Supreme Court applied these principles to this case when the reference returned from the CJEU.[114] Lord Carnwath SCJ gave guidance on the principles which are worth setting out in full:

> i) *A reasonable prospect of success* Lack of a reasonable prospect of success in the claim may, it seems, be a reason for allowing the respondents to recover a higher proportion of their costs. The fact that 'frivolity' is mentioned separately (see below), suggests that something more demanding is envisaged than, for example, the threshold test of reasonable arguability.
> ii) *The importance of what is at stake for the claimant* As indicated by Advocate General Kokott, this is likely to be a factor increasing the proportion of costs fairly recoverable. As she said, a person with 'extensive individual economic interests' at stake in the proceedings may reasonably be expected to bear higher risks in terms of costs.
> iii) *The importance of what is at stake for the protection of the environment* Conversely, and again following the Advocate General's approach, this is likely to be a factor reducing the proportion of costs recoverable, or eliminating recovery altogether. As she said, the environment cannot defend itself, but needs to be represented by concerned citizens or organisations acting in the public interest.
> iv) *The complexity of the relevant law and procedure* This factor is not further explained. Its relevance seems to be that a complex case is likely to require higher expenditure by the respondents, and thus, objectively, to justify a higher award of costs. Although mention is only made of complexity of law or procedure, the same presumably should apply to technical or factual complexity.
> v) *The potentially frivolous nature of the claim at its various stages* The respondents should not have to bear the costs of meeting a frivolous claim. In domestic judicial review procedures, whether at first instance or on appeal, this issue is likely to be resolved in favour of the claimant by the grant of permission.[115]

The Supreme Court, recognising that the changes to the CPR only applied to proceedings commenced after they came into force, also found that the factors affecting the judgment of what is subjectively or objectively reasonable may be changed on appeal.[116] This line of reasoning is given in more force where the case is subject to a second appeal and needs special justification. The factors justifying a relatively low figure for a cap, such as avoiding satellite litigation prior to a hearing on the merits, would not have the same force after the merits have been

[111] ibid [40].
[112] ibid [42].
[113] ibid, Opinion of Advocate General Kokott, 18 October 2012 [36].
[114] *R (on the application of Edwards and another) v Environment Agency and others (No 2)* [2013] UKSC 78, [2014] 1 WLR 55 [28].
[115] ibid [28].
[116] ibid [33].

considered. The courts are considering the principles laid down by the CJEU in a different context when the case is on appeal (or on a second appeal). In this case, the Supreme Court found the figure of £25,000, claimed by the respondents, to be 'neither subjectively nor objectively excessive'.[117]

Standing

Costs have been one of the most significant areas which the Convention has influenced, but this is not the only issue to have been considered under the access to justice pillar. The Convention has also influenced cases relating to standing, which has, to date, generally been interpreted widely in England and Wales. The access to justice requirements of the Public Participation Directive applying to the EIA regime were considered in the Court of Appeal in *Ashton.*[118] The Court drew together analyses of cases including *Djurgården-Lilla Värtans Miljoskyddsförening*[119] and *Commission v Ireland.*[120] In this case, a statutory planning challenge under section 288 of the Town and Country Planning Act 1990 in which a 'person aggrieved' test applies, the Court considered that while wide access is required, the appellant's lack of involvement in the earlier stages of the planning process meant that, despite having an interest in the proposals, he did not play a sufficiently active role in the planning process properly to be described as 'aggrieved'. In *Coedbach*[121] the Court found that the claimant, this time for a judicial review, did not have standing because they were not a member of the 'public concerned', again having regard to the level of their involvement in the decision-making process.

The Supreme Court, in *Walton,*[122] examined the 'person aggrieved' standing test in the context of the Convention. Lord Hope also provided, in obiter dicta, some more general comments on the question of standing in environmental law and who may be considered to have an interest for these purposes, which appear to echo some aspects of the Convention:

> An individual may be personally affected in his private interests by the environmental issues to which an application for planning permission may give rise ... But some environmental issues that can properly be raised by an individual are not of that character. Take, for example, the risk that a route used by an osprey as it moves to and from a favourite fishing loch will be impeded by the proposed erection across it of a cluster of wind turbines. Does the fact that this proposal cannot reasonably be said to affect

[117] ibid [39].

[118] *Ashton v Secretary of State for Communities and Local Government* [2010] EWCA Civ 600 [2011] 1 P & CR 117.

[119] Case C-263/08 *Djurgården-Lilla Värtans Miljöskyddsförening v Stockholms kommun genom dess marknämnd* [2009] ECR 2009 I-09967.

[120] Case C-427/07 *Commission v Ireland* [2009] ECR I-06277.

[121] Coedbach Action Team Ltd v Secretary of State for Energy and Climate Change [2010] EWHC 2312 (Admin), [2010] All ER (D) 60 (Oct).

[122] *Walton* (n 3).

> any individual's property rights or interests mean that it is not open to an individual to challenge the proposed development on this ground? That would seem to be contrary to the purpose of environmental law, which proceeds on the basis that the quality of the natural environment is of legitimate concern to everyone. The osprey has no means of taking that step on its own behalf, any more than any other wild creature. If its interests are to be protected someone has to be allowed to speak up on its behalf ... Of course, this must not be seen as an invitation to the busybody to question the validity of a scheme or order under the statute just because he objects to the scheme of the development. Individuals who wish to do this on environmental grounds will have to demonstrate that they have a genuine interest in the aspects of the environment that they seek to protect, and that they have sufficient knowledge of the subject to qualify them to act in the public interest in what is, in essence, a representative capacity. There is, after all, no shortage of well-informed bodies that are equipped to raise issues of this kind ... But it is well-known they do not have the resources to object to every development that might have adverse consequences for the environment. So there has to be some room for individuals who are sufficiently concerned, and sufficiently well-informed, to do this too. It will be for the court to judge in each case whether these requirements are satisfied.[123]

As has already been mentioned, in the 'Brown Bear case'[124] the CJEU framed the Convention requirements by reference to giving full effect to EU law, even where the Convention is not directly implemented in EU law, as is the case with Article 9(3). In the context of standing to bring a challenge within the framework of the Habitats Directive, the CJEU found that the need for domestic courts to interpret procedural rules in accordance with the objectives of Article 9(3) 'so as to enable an environmental protection organisation, such as the zoskupenie, to challenge before a court a decision taken following administrative proceedings liable to be contrary to EU environmental law'.[125]

Other Aspects of Access to Justice

Other aspects of compliance in England and Wales with the requirements of the access to justice pillar were also mentioned by the Compliance Committee in communication 33. With regard to the requirement that a judicial review claim be filed '(a) promptly and (b) in any event not later than 3 months after the grounds to make the claim first arose',[126] the Committee found that, while the three month limit was not problematic, the 'promptly' requirement was insufficiently clear for the purposes of Article 9(4). In practice, however, the effects of the CJEU's judgment in *Uniplex*[127] and its application in environmental cases including the *Buglife*[128] reference suggests that in cases involving EU environmental law the

123 ibid [152], [153].
124 '*Brown Bear* case' (n 69).
125 ibid [51].
126 CPR 54.5.
127 Case C-406/08 *Uniplex (UK) Ltd v NHS Business Services Authority* [2010] ECR I-00817.
128 *R (Buglife) v Medway Council* [2011] EWHC 746 (Admin), [2011] 24 EG 108 (CS).

'promptness' requirement would not be applied. Following further changes to the CPR in July 2013, in cases where the application for judicial review relates to a planning decision, the 'promptness' requirement has been removed and the claim form must be filed within six weeks of the grounds for making the claim first arising.

The Compliance Committee expressed concerns about the adequacy of judicial review procedures for the purposes of delivering the Article 9 requirements for reviewing procedural and substantive legality,[129] but has made no finding of non-compliance. The Court of Appeal rejected these concerns when they were cited in *Evans*.[130] The case concerned a challenge to a screening direction by the Secretary of State under regulation 6 of the Town and Country Planning (Environmental Impact Assessment) (England and Wales) Regulations 1999, SI 1999/293. At paragraph 37 Beatson LJ said:

> [T]he Compliance Committee has reached no concluded view that the *Wednesbury* approach is impermissible. Moreover, its expression of concern is general and unparticularised. For example, it only refers to *Wednesbury* and does not refer to the other established heads of public law review; error of law, error of fact, and the principles of relevance and of propriety or purpose which are sometimes insufficiently distinguished from Lord Greene's residual category, which Lord Diplock termed 'irrationality'. It also does not identify the variations in the intensity of *Wednesbury* review that reflect the nature of the interest affected.

Conclusions

Together the three pillars have helped to provide the public in England and Wales with the tools to help hold decision-makers to account and to involve the public in decisions about the environment, with the potential to help bring about benefits for the protection of the environment. In some respects this has been achieved through refocusing or adapting existing legislation or practice, and in others through the adoption of new requirements. The influence of EU law is apparent throughout, including in the third pillar where there remains greater responsibility on individual Member States for meeting the Convention's requirements. That members of the public and environmental NGOs can, after exhausting domestic remedies (in keeping with international law), take their allegations of non-compliance directly to the Compliance Committee in Geneva, has provided an additional dimension to environmental cases in England and Wales. The Convention's influence has also been driven by its increasing prominence in the courts.

[129] ACCC/C/2008/33 (United Kingdom) ECE/MP.PP/C.1/2010/6/Add.3, 24 August 2011, paras 123 to 127.

[130] *Evans* (n 8).

In the time since the *Burkett* case,[131] the citation of the Convention in environmental cases has become more frequent, and although in many cases the limitations of the influence of the Convention and its Compliance Committee have been found, it is becoming less unusual for this international agreement to be called upon by the courts when grappling with issues of EU law and the law of England and Wales.

131 *Burkett* (n 79).

3

The Aarhus Convention in Scotland

LORNA DRUMMOND QC[1]

Introduction

The Aarhus Convention gives high priority to protection of the environment in international law, recognising that adequate protection of the environment is essential to human well-being and essential to the right to life itself.[2] It also recognises a duty, both individually and in association with others, to protect and improve the environment for the benefit of present and future generations. By ratifying the Aarhus Convention, the UK has bound itself to abide by its provisions. But how well is Scotland, as a separate jurisdiction within the UK, implementing these international obligations, through the operation of EU law and through development of its own case law and legislation?

The Status of the Aarhus Convention in Scots Law

As an international treaty, the Aarhus Convention does not form part of domestic Scots law, except where it has been incorporated by EU Directives and can be directly relied upon by individuals in the domestic courts.[3] The EU, itself a party to the Convention, has enacted a number of Directives in implementation of the Convention which have been held to be of direct effect.[4] In cases which do not

[1] Sheriff of Tayside, Central and Fife.

[2] The Aarhus Convention was adopted under the UN Economic Commission for Europe (UNECE) and signed in 1998 by 39 of the UNECE Member States including the UK and the European Community. The UK ratified it on 23 February 2005 and the EC by Council decision 17 February 2005. It entered into force for the UK on 24 May 2005. The Convention was described by the UN Secretary General as the most impressive elaboration of 'Principle 10 of the Rio Declaration': it fleshes out the rights identified in Principle 10 and gives them legal substance.

[3] *Walton v Scottish Ministers* [2013] PTSR 51 at paragraph 100.

[4] Eg Directive 85/337/EEC on the assessment of the effects of certain public and private projects on the environment [1985] OJ L175/40 (as amended by various subsequent directives and codified in Directive 2011/92/EU [2012] OJ L26/1. Since the EU has ratified Aarhus, the Convention, like all other international conventions concluded by the European Union, prevails over provisions of secondary

fall within the EU Directives, the Convention still has relevance. In the field of EU law, the Court of Justice of the European Union has held that Member States should interpret their national laws in a way which, to the fullest extent possible, is consistent with the objectives laid down in the Convention.[5] The domestic courts have recognised that there is a strong presumption in favour of interpreting statute and common law in a manner which does not place the UK Government in breach of its international obligations, including provisions under the Aarhus Convention[6] and that the Convention may be taken into account in exercising judicial discretion.[7] In the context of some international treaties, the courts have held that a legitimate expectation can arise that a state will act in accordance with obligations in an international treaty notwithstanding that it has not been incorporated into domestic law.[8]

The Aarhus Convention

The Aarhus Convention objective provides that in order to contribute to the protection of the right of every person of present and future generations to live in an environment adequate to his or her health and well-being, Parties shall guarantee rights in accordance with the Convention:

(i) of access to environmental information (Pillar I),
(ii) to participate in environmental decision-making (Pillar II), and
(iii) to have access to justice in environmental matters (Pillar III).

The Convention acknowledges that the public may need assistance in order to exercise their rights; that improved access to environmental information and

Union legislation. Because of that primacy, secondary Community legislation is to be interpreted as far as possible consistently with the Union's obligations under international law (see *Office of Communications v Information Commissioner* [2012] 1 CMLR 7 Advocate General Kokott's Opinion at paragraph 47). The European Court has also stated that when a national court is applying national law implementing a Directive, the court must interpret the national law, as far as possible, in light of the wording and the purpose of the Directive: Case C-106/89 *Marleasing SA v La Comercial Internacional de Alimentacion SA* [1990] ECR I-4135.

[5] Case C-240/09 *Lesoochranárske zoskupenie VLK v Ministerstvo životného prostredia Slovenskej republiky* [2011] 2 CMLR 43 at paragraphs 50 and 51. The case concerned Directive 92/42/EEC on the conservation of natural habitats and of wild fauna and flora [1992] OJ L206/7 and the effect of Article 9(3) of the Aarhus Convention, but in principle it is suggested it should also apply in other EU environmental contexts and in respect of other provisions of Aarhus.

[6] *R v Lyons* [2003] AC 976 at paragraph 51 per Lord Hoffman and *Forbes v Aberdeenshire Council* [2010] Env LR 36, per Lady Smith at paragraph 11.

[7] *Morgan and Baker v Hinton Organics (Wessex) Limited* [2009] Env LR 30; *Forbes v Aberdeenshire Council* [2010] Env LR 36.

[8] *Minister of Immigration and Ethnic Affairs v Teoh* (1995) 183 CLR 273; *Musaj v Secretary of State for the Home Department* 2004 SLT 623 at paragraphs 20–22; *Khairandish v Secretary of State for the Home Department* 2003 SLT 1358; De Smith's, *Judicial Review*, 7th edn (London, Sweet & Maxwell, 2013) paragraph 12–028.

public participation in decision-making enhance the quality and the implementation of decisions, contribute to public awareness of environmental issues, give the public the opportunity to express its concerns and enable public authorities to take due account of such concerns. The aim is to further the accountability of and transparency in decision-making and to strengthen public support for decisions on the environment recognising also that the public needs to be aware of the procedures for participation in environmental decision-making, have free access to them and know how to use them.

Pillar I: Access to and Collection of Environmental Information

Aarhus

Articles 4 and 5 of the Convention address access to and collection of environmental information under Pillar I. These Articles have a clear link to the right to public participation under Pillar II: for the public to participate in environmental decision-making in any meaningful way, the public needs access to environmental information collected by public authorities. Parties are required to ensure that public authorities, in response to a request for environmental information, make such information available to the public, without an interest having to be stated, as soon as possible and at the latest within one month of the request being submitted.

Article 2(2) and (3) provides definitions of 'public authority' and 'environmental information'. The definition of 'public authority' includes (a) government at national, regional and other level; (b) natural or legal persons performing public administrative functions under national law, including specific duties, activities or services in relation to the environment; and (c) any other natural or legal persons having public responsibilities or functions, or providing public services, in relation to the environment, under the control of a body or person falling within subparagraphs (a) or (b). The definition expressly excludes bodies or institutions acting in a judicial or legislative capacity.[9] A broad definition of 'environmental information' is provided in Article 2(3) which extends to any information in written, visual, aural, electronic or any other material form on the state of the elements of the environment, factors such as substances, energy, noise and radiation and the state of human health and safety.

[9] For the Court of Justice's interpretation on bodies or institutions acting in a judicial or legislative capacity see Case C-515/11 *Deutsche Umwelthilfe eV v Bundesrepublik Deutschland* 13 July 2013; Case C-204/09 *Flachglas Torgau GmbH v Germany* [2013] QB 212.

The right to environmental information is subject to exceptions stated in Article 4(3) and (4). The grounds on which requests may be refused include that the public authority does not hold the information, that the request is manifestly unreasonable or the request is formulated in too general a manner. Under Article 4(4) a request may be refused if the release of information would adversely affect: the confidentiality of the proceedings of public authorities; international relations, national defence or public security; the course of justice; the confidentiality of commercial or industrial information in certain circumstances; intellectual property rights; the confidentiality of personal data; the interests of a third party who has supplied the information in certain circumstances, or the environment to which the information relates. Article 4(4) provides that the grounds for refusal must be interpreted in a restrictive way, taking into account the public interest served by disclosure and whether the information requested relates to emissions into the environment.

EU Transposition

The EU transposed the access to environmental information provisions of the Convention by Council Directive 90/313/EEC *on the freedom of access to information on the environment* ('the 1990 Directive').[10] The 1990 Directive provided for rights of access to environmental information subject to certain exceptions but left it to Member States to define their own procedural rules. The UK implemented the 1990 Directive by the Environmental Information Regulations 1992 ('the 1992 Regulations').[11] Although existing rights to environmental information were provided through a system of public registers,[12] the 1992 Regulations provided a more general right of public access to environmental information held by 'relevant persons' which included the Scottish administration and planning authorities. The 1992 Regulations contained relatively narrow definitions of 'environmental information' and 'public authority' and broadly cast exemptions which were not subject to the public interest test. The only means of enforcing the regulations was by way of judicial review.[13] The confidentiality exception in particular allowed for broad exclusion of information and there was some concern that public authorities were taking an overly restrictive approach to the supply of information.[14]

[10] [1990] OJ L158/56.

[11] SI 3240/1992.

[12] Under the Control of Pollution Act 1974 and the Environmental Protection Act 1990.

[13] *R v Secretary of State for the Environment, Transport and the Regions and Midland Expressway Ltd, ex parte Alliance Against the Birmingham Northern Relief Road (No 1)* [1999] JPL 426 per Sullivan J at 467 who held that the issues of whether information related to the environment and, if it did, whether any of the exceptions to the duty to disclose were applicable, were to be decided objectively and were primary questions of fact to be decided by the Court but that the decision to disclose confidential information was a discretionary one subject to review on *Wednesbury* grounds only.

[14] Legislative Comment, 'The Environmental Information Regulations 1992' (M Poustie) SPEL 1993, 39, 43–44.

Following signature by the UK and the EU of the Aarhus Convention in 1998 and review of the 1990 Directive by the European Commission, the 1990 Directive was repealed and replaced by the European Parliament and European Council Directive 2003/4/EC *on public access to environmental information* ('the 2003 Directive').[15] The 2003 Directive improved upon the 1990 Directive: it provided wider definitions, increased the obligations on public authorities to assist those requesting information and improved the remedies available where a request for information is refused.

Article 2(1) of the 2003 Directive adopts similar definitions of 'environmental information' and 'public authority' as in the Aarhus Convention. Article 3 reflects Article 4(1) of the Convention and provides that public authorities are required to make available environmental information held by or for them to any applicant at his request and without his having to state an interest, as soon as possible or, within one or two months, depending on the volume and complexity of the information. The grounds for refusing requests for environmental information in Article 4 of the 2003 Directive reflect Article 4(3) and (4) of the Convention and the public interest test.

Domestic Transposition

Scotland transposed the provisions of the 2003 Directive into domestic law by enactment of the Environmental Information (Scotland) Regulations 2004 ('the 2004 Regulations'),[16] which came into force on 1 January 2005, the same day that the Freedom of Information (Scotland) Act 2002 (the FOISA) came into force. The 2004 Regulations to a large extent mirror the provisions in the 2003 Directive (and Articles 4 and 5 of the Convention), adopting the same definition of environmental information under Article 2(1). Under regulation 5, a Scottish public authority that holds environmental information has a duty to make it available when requested to do so by an applicant. Requests must be complied with as soon as possible and not later than 20 working days after receipt.[17] In making information compiled by it available, a Scottish public authority must, so far as practicable, ensure that it is up to date, accurate and comparable.[18] A Scottish public authority may refuse a request for information under regulation 10 if an exception applies under paragraph (4) or (5) (which broadly follow the exceptions in the 2003 Directive), and,

[15] [2003] OJ L41/26. The application of the law on environmental information to EU institutions and bodies is governed by European Parliament and Council Regulation (EC) No 1049/2001 of 30 May 2001 regarding public access to European Parliament, Council and Commission documents [2001] OJ L145/43 and the Parliament and Council Regulation (EC) No 1367/2006 of 6 September 2006 on the application of the provisions of the Aarhus Convention on access to information, public participation in decision-making and access to justice in environmental matters to Community institutions and bodies [2006] OJ L264/13.

[16] SSI 2004/520.

[17] Regulation 5(2).

[18] Regulation 5(4).

in all the circumstances, the public interest in making the information available is outweighed by maintaining the exception.[19] Reflecting both the Convention and the 2003 Directive, the regulations provide that the authority must interpret the exceptions in a restrictive way.[20] Under regulation 10(2)(b), the authority must apply a presumption in favour of disclosure.

As under the 2003 Directive, the exceptions in regulation 10 are discretionary, so that a Scottish public authority may decide that it would be acting lawfully not to disclose the information under an exception but may still decide to disclose it.[21] Regulation 17 applies the system of enforcement in Part 4 of the FOISA to the 2004 Regulations. Enforcement involves an internal review followed by an appeal on the merits of the application to the Scottish Information Commission and thereafter to the Court of Session on a point of law.[22]

Although the 2004 Regulations specifically concern the provision of environmental information, most requests for environmental information are made under the FOISA without any reference to the 2004 Regulations. Nonetheless, Scottish public authorities are bound to consider whether the request is for environmental information under the 2004 Regulations, since authorities have a duty to disclose the information under those Regulations unless an exception applies.[23] Section 39(2)(a) of the FOISA allows an authority to exempt information from disclosure under that Act if it is environmental information which Scottish public authorities are obliged, under the 2004 Regulations, to make available to the public. Section 39(2)(b) provides that if the information is subject to one of the exceptions under the 2004 Regulations, it is exempt information. If a Scottish public authority claims the exemption under section 39(2), it also needs to consider the public interest test under section 2 of the FOISA. The Scottish Information Commissioner has decided that, as there is a separate statutory right of access to environmental information under the 2004 Regulations, the public interest in maintaining this exemption and allowing access in line with the requirements of the 2004 Regulations, will generally outweigh the public interest in the disclosure of information under the FOISA.[24]

[19] See Case C-71/10 *Communciations v IC* [2012] 1 CMLR 7, where the Supreme Court considered that the requirements of the Directive on the weighing of interests were not clear and sought a preliminary ruling from the Court of Justice. The Court of Justice found that when assessing a request for environmental information, a public authority could cumulatively, rather than separately, weigh the grounds for refusal listed in Directive 2003/4/EC Article 4(2) against the public interest in disclosure.

[20] Regulation 10(2)(a).

[21] The Scottish Ministers are required to issue a code of practice as to desirable practice by Scottish public authorities in connection with the discharge of their functions under the Regulations: the Scottish Ministers Code of Practice on the Discharge of Functions by Scottish Public Authorities under the Freedom of Information (Scotland) Act 2002 and the Environmental Information (Scotland) Regulations 2004 (December 2010).

[22] Sections 21 and 47–56 of the FOISA.

[23] The Scottish Information Commissioner considered the relationship between the FOISA and the 2004 Regulations in *Decision 218/2007: Professor A D Hawkins and Transport Scotland.*

[24] Scottish Information Commissioner's *Decision 120/2008: Mr Rob Edwards and the Scottish Ministers.*

There are some notable differences between the two regimes: the 2004 Regulations contain an express presumption in favour of disclosure which is not contained in the FOISA. Verbal requests are valid under the 2004 Regulations but the FOISA requires requests in writing or some other format capable of having some permanency.[25] Under the FOISA a public authority is prohibited from disclosing information which is subject to a statutory bar[26] but under the 2004 Regulations any statutory bar on disclosing information does not apply under regulation 5(3) and may not be used to refuse a request for environmental information, although it may be relevant to the operation of the exceptions under the 2004 Regulations.[27] The definition of a Scottish public authority is wider under the 2004 Regulations than it is under the FOISA.[28]

The definition of 'Scottish public authority' in the 2004 Regulations, does not precisely reflect the Aarhus Convention insofar as it does not include in its definition a requirement that the body or person performs '*public administrative functions*' under national law.[29] Instead the definition includes (a) any body listed in Schedule 1 to the FOISA or designated under section 5(1) of the FOISA; (b) a publically owned company as defined by section 6 of the FOISA; (c) any other Scottish public authority with mixed functions or no reserved functions within the meaning of the Scotland Act 1998 and (d) any other person who is under the control of a person within paragraphs (a) to (c) and has public responsibilities, exercises functions of a public nature or provides public services, relating to the environment.[30] Paragraph (c) is intended to operate so that those bodies which carry out reserved functions are subject to the UK wide Environmental Information Regulations 2004 and not the Scottish 2004 Regulations. The Scottish Information Commissioner's Guidance[31] suggests that bodies such as public utility companies might fall within the definition of a Scottish public authority and that a private organisation under the control of a Scottish public authority may have responsibilities under the 2004 Regulations which could include private contractors.[32]

[25] Section 8(1)(a).

[26] Eg under section 94 of the Control of Pollution Act 1974.

[27] Key differences between the FOISA and the 2004 Regulations are set out in the Scottish Information Commissioner's Guidance (November 2012) (page 55).

[28] The FOISA only applies to bodies listed in Schedule 1 of the FOISA, designated by order under section 5 or publicly-owned companies defined by section 6 of the FOISA.

[29] This part of the definition has been the subject of case law in England: See *Port of London Authority v The Information Commissioner Appeal No EA/2006/0083*, *Network Rail Ltd v The Information Commissioner Appeal Nos EA/2006/0061 and EA/2006/0062*. In *Smartsource Drainage & Water Reports Ltd v Information Commissioner* [2011] JPL 455, the Upper Tribunal decided that water companies were not a body or person carrying out the functions of public administration under regulation 2(2)(c) and were not under the control of a person with public responsibilities within regulation 2(2)(d) either but this needs to be read in the context of CJEU's subsequent judgment in Case C-279/12 *Fish Legal v Information Commissioner* [2014] QB 521.

[30] Regulation 2(1).

[31] November 2012.

[32] *The Aarhus Convention: An Implementation Guide*, 2nd edn (UNECE, 2013) indicates that privatisation should not take such bodies outside the definition of public authority: pages 35–37. The European Court of Justice has held that the Implementation Guide is to be regarded as an explanatory

Decisions of the Scottish Information Commissioner illustrate the breadth of information caught by the regulation and how widely it is applied in practice. Information which in isolation may not be regarded as environmental can and should be regarded as having the quality of environmental information when read in context.[33] Such an approach is consistent with the provisions of the Aarhus Convention. The Aarhus Convention Compliance Committee[34] was satisfied that the Scottish authorities had complied with their obligations in a Scottish case where it was claimed that information which had been withheld ought to have been disclosed. The Committee considered that even though the exemptions in the Convention were to be interpreted restrictively, disclosure which would result in adverse effects to protected species could be reasonably denied.[35]

Pillar II: Public Participation in Environmental Decision-Making

Aarhus

Articles 6 to 8 of the Aarhus Convention address the right of the public to participate in decisions on specific activities, during the preparation of plans and programmes and the preparation of executive regulations/normative instruments.

document, capable of being taken into consideration if appropriate among other relevant material for the purpose of interpreting the Convention but not of binding force and not of the normative effect of the provisions of the Aarhus Convention (Case C-182/10 *Solvay and others v Region Wallonne* [2012] 2 CMLR 19).

[33] *Decision 056/2008: Mr Rob Edwards and the Scottish Ministers*; information about the transfer of giant pandas to Edinburgh zoo is environmental information: *Decision 051/2009 Advocates for Animals and the Scottish Ministers*; a loss adjuster's report was environmental information because it related to the interaction of water with an infrastructure potentially causing flood damage and erosion to further built structures *Decision 096/2006: Mr George Waddell and South Lanarkshire Council*; information about the costs and financing of a road building project was environmental information *Decision 218/2007 Professor A D Hawkins and Transport Scotland*; a Local Plan and officers' observations on the comments/objections of Councillors and others on the Local Plan proposals (with supporting information such as maps), together with Councillors' requests for advice on these were also environmental information: *Decision 102/2009: Councillor David Alexander and Falkirk Council.*

[34] Established under Article 15 of the Aarhus Convention.

[35] See communication *ACCC/C/2009/38*: the communicant, Road Sense, claimed that Scottish Natural Heritage breached Articles 1, 3 and 4 of Aarhus by failing to disclose a report relating to the site conditions of freshwater pearl mussels on the River Dee which had been subject to illegal fishing. The Committee considered that the refusal to disclose information on the breeding sites of pearl mussels was justified on the grounds that, while the communicant may not personally represent a threat to the pearl mussels, releasing the information would mean that the public in general (including those with ulterior motives) would be entitled to seek release of the information. In another Scottish case a communicant alleged failure to provide information regarding implementation of the renewable energy programme under the first pillar of Aarhus. In its findings, the Committee did not find any failure to comply with the first pillar: *ACCC/C/2012/68.*

To ensure adequate involvement the Convention provides for early release of information before decisions are made and obliges Member States to take due account of the outcome of public participation. A key method of securing public participation is through the environmental assessment process.

Article 6 applies to all activities listed in Annex I to the Convention and also, in accordance with national law, to other activities not listed in Annex I, which may have a significant effect on the environment. Under Article 6(2), the public concerned shall be informed, either by public notice or individually as appropriate, early in the environmental decision-making procedure, and in an adequate, timely and effective manner, *inter alia* of the proposed activity, the application on which a decision will be taken and the envisaged procedure including the opportunities for the public to participate and an indication of what environmental information is available. Article 6(3) provides that the procedures shall include reasonable time-frames for the different phases, allowing sufficient time frames for informing the public in accordance with Article 6(2) and for the public to prepare and participate effectively during the environmental decision-making process. Under Article 6(4), each Party is obliged to provide '*for early public participation, when all options are open and effective public participation can take place*'. Article 6(8) requires each Party to ensure that in the decision due account is taken of the outcome of the public participation. The public must be informed promptly of the decision. The decision, the reasons for it and any considerations on which it is based must be made accessible to the public.[36]

Article 7 requires parties to make appropriate practical and/or other provisions for the public to participate during the preparation of plans and programmes relating to the environment, within a transparent and fair framework, having provided the necessary information to the public. Within this framework Article 6(3) (sufficient time frames for informing the public), 6(4) (early public participation when all options are open) and 6(8) (due account taken of the outcome of public participation) shall be applied. Under Article 8, each party must strive to promote effective participation at an appropriate stage, and while options are still open, during the preparation by public authorities of executive regulations and other generally applicable legally binding rules that may have a significant effect on the environment.

As is evident from this structure, the Convention distinguishes between 'plans and programmes' in Article 7 and 'activities' or 'projects' in Article 6 (sometimes referred to as the 'upstream' or 'upper tier' and 'downstream' or 'lower tier' respectively).[37] The Compliance Committee and the courts have considered that the Article 6(4) requirement for early participation when all options are open must

[36] Article 6(9).

[37] See the European Commission's Report on the Effectiveness of the Directive on Strategic Environmental Assessment (COM 2009 469 final) which observed that the SEA Directive and the EIA Directive are to a large extent complementary: the SEA is 'up-stream' and identifies the best options at an early planning stage, and the EIA is 'down-stream' and refers to the projects that are coming through at a later stage (paragraph 4.1). Referred to by Lord Reed in *Walton v Scottish Ministers* (n 3) at paragraph 14.

be seen within this tiered framework with each stage of decision-making, needing only to address the options available within that stage:

> The requirement for 'early public participation when all options are open' should be seen first of all within a concept of tiered decision-making, whereby at each stage of decision-making certain options are discussed and selected with the participation of the public and each consecutive stage of decision-making addresses only the issues within the option already selected at the preceding stage.[38]

EU Transposition at the Project Level

Article 6 of the Aarhus Convention is implemented at the EU level by Directive 2011/92/EU *on the assessment of the effects of certain public and private projects on the environment* ('the EIA Directive')[39] and by Directive 2010/75/EU *on industrial emissions (integrated pollution prevention and control)* ('the Industrial Emissions Directive').[40] Article 2(1) of the EIA Directive requires Member States to adopt all measures necessary to ensure that, before consent is given, projects likely to have a significant effect on the environment by virtue *inter alia* of their nature, size or location are made subject to an assessment with regard to their effects.[41] Article 4 and Annexes I to III determine which projects shall be subject to environmental assessment. Article 6(1) requires Member States to take measures to ensure that authorities concerned in a project by reason of their specific environmental responsibilities are given the opportunity to participate in the decision-making. Article 6(2) (reflecting Article 6(2) of the Convention) requires the public to be informed of the environmental decision-making procedures and availability of information. Article 6(4) (reflecting Article 6(4) of the Convention) requires the public concerned to be given early and effective opportunities to participate in the environmental decision-making procedures and for that purpose, to be entitled to express comments and opinions when all options are open to the competent authority before the decision on the request for development consent is taken. Article 6(5) provides that the detailed arrangements for informing the public (for example by bill posting within a certain radius or publication in local newspapers) and for consulting the public concerned (for example by written submissions or by way of public inquiry) shall be determined by the Member States.

[38] From the Findings of the Aarhus Convention Compliance Committee dated 4 April 2008 into compliance by Lithuania with its obligations under Aarhus ACCC/C/2006/16 (Lithuania) at paragraph 71. This passage was approved by the Inner House in *Walton v Scottish Ministers* [2012] CSIH 19 at paragraph 18, and *McGinty v Scottish Ministers* 2014 SC 81 at paragraph 44.

[39] The EIA Directive codified Directive EC 85/337/EEC (as amended by Directive 97/11/EC and Directive 2003/35/EC providing for public participation in respect of the drawing up of certain plans and programmes).

[40] [2010] OJ L334/17. The Industrial Emissions Directive recasts Directive 2008/1/EC concerning integrated pollution prevention and control.

[41] Under Article 2(2) the environmental impact assessment may be integrated into the existing procedures for project consent.

Domestic Transposition at the Project Level

In Scotland the projects to which environmental assessment is applicable are subject to a variety of different consenting regimes, involving different consenting authorities and resulting in a multi-regime approach to transposition of the EIA Directive. There are at least 11 discrete sets of environmental impact assessment regulations for which the Scottish Parliament has legislative competence.[42] Consistent with the Aarhus Convention and the EIA Directive, there are three broad stages to the procedures:

(i) the developer must compile detailed information about the likely significant environmental effects in an environmental statement;
(ii) the environmental statement (and the application to which it relates) must be publicised and the public and statutory bodies given an opportunity to give their views about the development and environmental statement; and
(iii) the environmental statement, together with any other information, comments and representations made on it, must be taken into account by the competent authority in deciding whether or not to give consent for the development. The public must be informed of the decision and the main reasons for it.

The three stages reflect the provisions in the Convention and the EIA Directive to allow the public to participate under Article 6. It is important that the EIA Directive leaves it to Member States to determine the detailed arrangements for consulting the public whether by written submissions or by public local inquiry. The Scottish procedures reflect that by providing that in some circumstances a local inquiry is required (for example where certain persons object) but in other circumstances there is a discretion to hold an inquiry.[43]

What is meant under Article 6(4) by opportunities for early public participation at the project level when all options are open and effective participation can

[42] Ie town and country planning, trunk roads, land drainage, marine works, infrastructure projects, energy consents, agriculture, controlled activities (water), flooding, ports and harbours and forestry. A large-scale onshore electricity generating project, is subject to consent under the Electricity Act 1989, and procedures in the Electricity Works (Environmental Impact Assessment) (Scotland) Regulations 2000 (SI 2000/320). An application for planning permission under the Town and Country Planning (Scotland) Act 1997 is subject to the Town and Country Planning (Environmental Impact Assessment) (Scotland) Regulations 2011 (SI 2011/139). The 2011 Regulations consolidate, update, and replace Part II of the Environmental Impact Assessment (Scotland) Regulations 1999 (SI 1999/1), with effect from 1st June 2011. Parts III and IV of the 1999 Regulations, concerning Roads and Bridges, and Land Drainage, remain in force. See the Review of Transposition of the Environmental Impact Assessment Directive in Scotland 2012 commissioned by the Scottish Government (www.scotland.gov.uk/Resource/0042/00422499.pdf) which concluded that the multi-regime approach caused no real difficulty in practice

[43] Eg paragraphs 5, 6, 11 and 12 of Schedule 1 to the Roads (Scotland) Act 1984 and paragraphs 2 and 3 of Schedule 8 to the Electricity Act 1989. Although not argued under the EIA Directive, arguments were made in *Sustainable Shetland v Scottish Ministers* 2013 CSOH 158 that a public local inquiry required to be held.

take place was considered by the Scottish courts in *Walton v Scottish Ministers*.[44] The appellant argued that in making certain orders under the Roads (Scotland) Act 1984 for construction of the Aberdeen Western Peripheral Route, the Scottish Ministers acted in a manner incompatible with Article 6(4) of Directive 85/337/EC.[45] The appellant claimed he had not been given an adequate opportunity to express his opinions on the Ministers' preferred route option, which included a dual carriageway known as the Fastlink, either through consultation or subsequently at the public local inquiry which had a restricted remit to exclude inquiry into the need for the road. Lord Tyre held that there was nothing in Directive 85/337/EEC which required the Ministers to seek or take account of further public opinion in relation to the Fastlink or to hold a public inquiry into the need for it. The Ministers had conducted a public consultation which had included the Fastlink as a route, and the public, including the appellant, had the opportunity then to express opinions on all the alternative routes at a time when all options had been open. Consistently with the concept of tiered decision-making underlying the European Directives, the Ministers were entitled, by the time of the public inquiry, to take the view that the focus should be on environmental and technical issues affecting the route. The Inner House upheld the Lord Ordinary's Opinion.[46] The Court's conclusion is consistent with the findings of the Aarhus Convention Compliance Committee when it considered complaints into the same orders on the same grounds.[47] Both the Lord Ordinary and the Extra Division drew support from the reasoning of the Committee.[48]

Public Participation at the Plan or Programme Level

EU Transposition at the Plan or Programme Level

Article 7 of the Aarhus Convention, public participation at the strategic level or upper tier, is given effect to by Directive 2001/42/EC *on the assessment of the*

[44] 2011 SCLR 686.

[45] The appellant also argued that the environmental impact regulations failed to properly transpose Directive 85/337/EEC following its amendment by Directive 2003/35/EC on public participation. It was a matter of dispute but since it was conceded that Article 6(4) of Directive 85/337/EEC had direct effect, the point became academic (see paragraph 32). Breach of Directive 85/337/EEC was not argued in the Supreme Court.

[46] See *Walton v Scottish Ministers* [2012] CSIH 19.

[47] *ACCC/C/2009/38* adopted on 25 February 2011 in communication by Road Sense (of which Mr Walton was chairman). Although the Committee had some concerns that the route finally selected and the dual carriageway nature of the Fastlink were not subject to formal consultation, it found that these aspects were ultimately subject to public participation through the statutory authorisation process following the publication of the draft schemes and orders under the environmental impact regulations. On appeal to the Supreme Court in *Walton*, Lord Reed observed that, although Aarhus was no longer being relied upon, the decisions of the Committee deserve respect on issues relating to standards of public participation (paragraph 100).

[48] *Walton v Scottish Ministers* 2011 SCLR 686 paragraph 43; [2012] CSIH 19, at paragraph 22. This issue was not the subject of the further appeal to the Supreme Court in the case.

effects of certain plans and programmes on the environment ('the SEA Directive') which required to be transposed into domestic law by 21 July 2004.[49] Article 2(a) provides that:

> 'plans and programmes' shall mean plans and programmes including those co-financed by the European Community as well as any modifications to them:
>
> which are subject to preparation and/or adoption by an authority at national, regional or local level or which are prepared by an authority for adoption, through a legislative procedure by Parliament or Government and
>
> which are required by legislative, regulatory or administrative provisions.

Article 3(1) requires an environmental assessment to be carried out for plans and programmes, referred to in paragraphs 2 to 4, which are likely to have significant environmental effects. Paragraph 2(a) requires an environmental assessment to be carried out for plans and programmes prepared for certain purposes including energy and town and country planning or land use and '*which set the framework for future development consent*' of projects under the EIA Directive. Article 4 requires the assessment to be carried out during the preparation of the plan or programme and before its adoption or submission to the legislative procedure. An environmental report must be prepared in which the likely significant effects on the environment of implementing the plan or programme and reasonable alternatives are identified.[50]

Article 6(2), (reflecting Articles 6(3) and (4) of the Convention) provides that the public must be given an early and effective opportunity within appropriate time frames to express their opinion on the draft plan or programme and the accompanying environmental report before the adoption of the plan or programme. Member States shall identify the authorities and the public to be consulted, including the public affected or likely to be affected by, or having an interest in, the decision-making subject to the Directive.[51] Article 8 requires that the environmental report and the opinions expressed pursuant to it shall be taken into account during the preparation of the plan or programme.

The European Commission Guidance indicates that in identifying whether a proposal constitutes a '*plan or programme*' for the purposes of the SEA Directive, a broad approach should be used in light of the wide scope of the SEA Directive: '*the terms should be taken to cover any formal statement which goes beyond aspirations and sets out an intended course of future action*'.[52] The Court of Justice has held that the need for the plan or programme to be '*required by legislative, regulatory*

[49] [2001] OJ L197/30. The Public Participation Directive 2003/35/EC ('the PPD') amended EU environmental legislation in order to comply with Aarhus before the EU's accession, but did not amend the SEA Directive because it was already considered to be compliant with Article 7 of Aarhus (see Recital 10 and Article 2(5) of the PPD). The PPD introduced provisions for public participation into the preparation of environmental plans and programmes to six Directives on waste, air pollution, and protection of waters against nitrate pollution.

[50] Article 5.

[51] Article 6(4).

[52] Implementation of Directive 2001/42 on the Assessment of the Effects of Certain Plans and Programmes on the Environment, sections 3.3–3.4.

or administrative provision' is not to be understood as excluding from the scope of the Directive plans or programmes whose adoption is not compulsory.[53] Furthermore, the repeal of a plan or programme can amount to modification of a plan or programme where such a measure necessarily entails a change in the framework for development consent of projects, and might therefore be likely to have significant effects on the environment.[54]

Whether a plan or programme sets the framework for development consent was considered in *Terre wallonne ASBL and Inter-Environnement Wallonie ASBL v Region wallonne*.[55] The Advocate General considered that plans or programmes may influence the development consent of individual projects in very different ways and, in so doing, prevent appropriate account from being taken of environmental effects. Consequently the SEA Directive is based on a very broad concept of 'framework' which must be construed flexibly. The plan or programme need not be determinative. The framework covers forms of influence that leave room for some discretion and need not be determinative. A plan or programme sets a framework insofar as decisions are taken which influence any subsequent development consent or projects, in particular with regard to location, nature, size and operating conditions or by allocating resources.[56]

Domestic Transposition at the Plan or Programme Level

The SEA Directive was transposed into Scots law by the Environmental Assessment of Plans and Programmes (Scotland) Regulations 2004, which were subsequently repealed by the Environmental Assessment (Scotland) Act 2005 which came into force with effect from 20 February 2006.[57] It has been accepted that the 2005 Act adequately transposed the requirements of the SEA Directive into Scots law and in any event that the terms of the SEA Directive can be relied on directly in Scots law.[58]

[53] *Inter-Environnement Bruxelles ASBL and others v Region de Bruxelles-Capitale* [2012] 2 CMLR 30 at paragraph 31.

[54] *Inter Environnement Bruxelles*, per Advocate General Kokott's Opinion, paragraphs 36–41.

[55] C-105/09 and C-110/09 [2010] ECR I-5611.

[56] Paragraphs 64–67 of Advocate General Kokott's Opinion (n 54 above).

[57] The Scottish Government hosts an SEA Database, which provides information about all SEA activity in Scotland, www.scotland.gov.uk/Topics/Environment/environmental-assessment/sea/SEAG. The Scottish Government has also produced a basic introduction to SEA explaining the purpose of the assessment process: www.scotland.gov.uk/Topics/Environment/environmental-assessment/sea/guidance/SEAGuidance/basicguidance.

[58] *McGinty v Scottish Ministers* (n 38) at paragraph 19 and *Walton v Scottish Ministers* (n 3) at paragraph 30 where the Court did not consider the domestic law since it was common ground that the appellant could directly rely on the SEA Directive. Section 1(1) of the 2005 Act requires the responsible authority, during the preparation of a qualifying plan or programme, to secure the carrying out of an environmental assessment in relation to the plan or programme; and do so either before its adoption or submission to legislative procedure. Section 4 provides that any references to plans or programmes, includes reference to modification of plans or programmes. Section 5 includes within the definition of qualifying plans or programmes, a plan or programme which is required by legislative, regulatory or administrative provision and which, under paragraph (a)(ii) or (c) sets the framework for future development consent of projects.

To date two cases have reached the Supreme Court where appellants have placed reliance on provisions in the SEA Directive, but in each case without success. The Supreme Court considered the meaning of modification of a plan or programme under the SEA Directive in *Walton v Scottish Ministers*.[59] The appellant argued that the Scottish Ministers had modified a plan or programme when adopting the Fastlink as part of its preferred route and in adding a new objective to a transport strategy (the Modern Transport System). Lord Reed observed that the SEA Directive does not provide a definition of plan or programme, which is a concept of EU law and much wider than development plans in domestic law. Under reference to the European case law, Lord Reed concluded that the decision to construct the Fastlink did not alter the framework for future development consents of projects, but instead altered a particular project. The decision to incorporate the Fastlink did not modify the legal or administrative framework which had been set for future development consent of projects. The SEA Directive was not therefore applicable.[60] It was arguable that the adoption of the Modern Transport System was within the scope of Article 2(a) and 3(2)(a) of the SEA Directive but the Court did not require to decide the point.[61] The Aarhus Convention Compliance Committee reached a similar conclusion when it considered the same argument.

The Supreme Court more recently considered the application of the SEA Directive in *R (on the application of Buckinghamshire CC) v Secretary of State for Transport*[62] where the appellant unsuccessfully argued that the Government's proposals for the HS2 high speed rail line published in a command paper ('the DNS') should have been subject to a strategic environmental assessment. Although the Supreme Court held that the consultation leading to the DNS had not provided the public with sufficient information about the environmental impacts of the rail line and the reasonable alternatives to it so as to amount to a strategic environmental assessment, it concluded that the lack of information did not render the DNS unlawful. The DNS did not 'set the framework for development consent', which was a necessary precondition for the applicability of the Directive, and the Directive therefore did not apply.[63] Whilst the DNS might be seen as helping to set the framework for a subsequent debate, and was intended to influence its result, it did not in any way constrain the decision-making of Parliament which ultimately

[59] *Walton v Scottish Ministers* (n 3).

[60] The Aarhus Convention Compliance Committee reached the same conclusion and found there to be no breach of Article 7, concluding that there had been no modification of a plan or programme: *ACCC/C/2009/38* at paragraph 87. The Committee subsequently made findings under Article 7 of Aarhus in relation to another communication about UK renewable energy policy. In its draft findings the Committee found that there was public participation in plans, programmes and policies in Scotland, but that the UK National Renewable Energy Plan was not subject to public participation in accordance with Article 7: *ACCC/C/2012/68*.

[61] *Walton v Scottish Ministers* (n 3) paragraph 62, 69, 70 per Lord Reed.

[62] [2014] 1 WLR 324 (SC).

[63] The Aarhus Convention Compliance Committee made a preliminary ruling on 10 July 2014 that the two complaints against the UK and the EU arising out of the legal challenge to the UK Government's proposals for the High Speed 2 railway are admissible and will proceed to a full hearing.

had the power to decide whether to grant consent under hybrid bill procedures, without being bound by 'criteria' contained in earlier government statements.[64] The Supreme Court interpreted the European case law as indicating that 'setting the framework' means more than mere influence.[65]

Assuming the SEA Directive is applicable, the Supreme Court also considered in *Walton* what remedy might be available had an applicant been able to establish that there had been a failure to comply with its provisions. Lord Carnwath, with whom the others agreed, considered that if the Court was satisfied that the applicant has been able in practice to enjoy the rights conferred by the European legislation, and that a challenge would fail under domestic law because the breach has caused no substantial prejudice, there was nothing in principle or authority to require the Court to adopt a different approach merely because the procedural requirement arose from a European rather than a domestic source.[66]

The Supreme Court's approach was followed in another Scottish challenge, *McGinty v Scottish Ministers*,[67] which reached the Inner House of the Court of Session. The petitioner argued under Articles 5 and 6 of the SEA Directive that he had not been provided with an effective opportunity to participate in the preparation of the Second National Planning Framework (NPF2) which designated Hunterston as a national development power station and transshipment hub. The Court recognised that the designation of Hunterston would be a material consideration in determination of a subsequent application for consent. The Hunterston project had emerged as a candidate for designation in a Supplementary Assessment and notice of opportunity to consult was provided by an e-newsletter sent to 7000 subscribers, and by notices in the Edinburgh Gazette. No notice was published in the local paper and the local community council, including the petitioner, was unaware of the right to comment. The petitioner argued that the Ministers had failed to comply with requirements for publication of notices since the means used did not ensure that the contents of the notice were likely to come to the attention of the public affected, or likely to be affected, or having an interest. The Edinburgh Gazette was not of wide publication and not readily available to, or even known by, members of the general public. However,

[64] Per Lord Carnwath (with whom Lord Neuberger of Abbotsbury, Lord Mance, Lord Kerr of Tonaghmore, Lord Sumption and Lord Reed agreed) at paragraph 38. A number of other English cases have considered when a plan or programme is 'required' or 'set the framework for development consent': see *Central Craigavon Ltd v Department for Environment* [2011] NICA 17 per Girvan LJ at §§34–43; *(Cala Homes (South) Limited) v Secretary of State for Communities and Local Government and another* [2011] 1 P&CR 22 per Lindblom J at paragraphs 92–100; *R (Buckinghamshire County Council and others) v Secretary of State for Transport and another* [2014] 1 WLR 324 (SC); *R (HS2 Action Alliance Ltd & others) v Secretary of State for Transport* [2014] EWHC 2759 (Admin); *A5 Alliance application for judicial review* [2013] NIQB 30.

[65] *Terre Wallonne ASBL and Inter-Environnement Wallonie ASBL v Region Wallonne* C-105/09 and C-110/09; Case C-567/10 *Inter-Environnement Bruxelles ASBL v Région de Bruxelles-Capitale* [2012] 2 CMLR 909; Case C-43/10 *Nomarchiaki Aftodioikisi Aitoloakarnanias and Others v Ypourgos Perivallontos, Chorotaxias kai Dimosion ergon* [2013] Env LR 453.

[66] *Walton v Scottish Ministers* (n 3) paragraph 139.

[67] *McGinty v Scottish Ministers* (n 38).

the Inner House held that since the NPF2 was a national plan or programme and the Gazette a national paper designed to perform the function of disseminating official, regulatory and legal information, it was 'circulating in the area' within the meaning of the 2005 Act. The Court observed that Article 6(5) of the SEA Directive leaves the means whereby early and effective participation is given to the public, to be determined by Member States, and the Court should be very slow to substitute its own view on what is a matter of public administration for that of the responsible authority.[68]

In the same case, the petitioner more successfully argued that the consultation documents did not obtain the requisite information, particularly consideration of reasonable alternatives, and did not therefore comply with the 2005 Act or Article 5 of the SEA Directive. However, whilst the Court held that there may have been some force in those submissions, it ultimately concluded that since the NPF2 had left the project open to the full rigour of a specific environmental assessment at a later stage, there would be less need for a comprehensive report at the initial stage, and the complaint was therefore technical rather than material. On remedy, the Court held that the petitioner could not claim to be disenfranchised by any flaw in the consultation process since the Ministers had given an undertaking that all of the issues of concern to him would be considered by the reporter appointed to conduct any inquiry relative to development consent, when there would be a full environmental impact assessment. Through these means, the appellant was guaranteed the opportunity to put precisely the same objections to an inquiry as he would have made as part of an earlier consultation. In those circumstances, the Court concluded that it need not provide a remedy where the appellant had suffered no prejudice.[69]

[68] ibid paragraph 51. Although Article 6(5), under the principle of procedural autonomy, leaves the detailed arrangements to Member States to set the appropriate arrangements for information and consultation of the public, EU law requires that these procedures are not less favourable than those governing similar domestic situations ('the principle of equivalence') and that they do not render impossible in practice or excessively difficult the exercise of rights conferred by the European Legal Order ('the principle of effectiveness') (see paragraph 45 of C-41/11 *Inter-Environnement Wallonie ASBL, Terre Wallonne ASBL v Region Wallonne* [2012] 2 CMLR 21. Mr McGinty had pointed to the fact that at the project level the domestic requirement was for publication in both a local and national paper unlike at the SEA level which only required publication of notice 'circulating in the area' and that the procedures had made it excessively difficult for him and others to exercise his rights.

[69] Whether or not assessment at the project level and the programme level is required was considered in *Genovaite Valčiukienė and ors v Pakruojo Rajono Savivaldybė and ors* [2012] Env LR 283 where the European Court of Justice held that an EIA assessment cannot dispense with the obligation to carry out an assessment under the SEA Directive and is additional to any such assessment, although where an assessment has been carried out under a co-ordinated or joint procedure a second assessment may not be appropriate (paragraphs 57–60). At the EU level, the Court of Justice requires competent authorities to take '*all general or particular measures for remedying the failure to carry out such an assessment*' (paragraph 44 of *Inter-Environment Wallonie ASBL, Terre wallonne ASBL v Region Wallonne* (n 68)).

Pillar III: Access to Justice

Aarhus

Pillar III guarantees access to justice in three contexts:

(i) the right of access to review procedures with respect to information requests (Article 9(1));
(ii) the right of access to review procedures with respect to environmental decision making subject to public participation under Article 6 (Article 9(2)); and
(iii) the right of access to administrative or judicial procedures to challenge breaches of environmental law in general (Article 9(3)).

The right of access to a review procedure for information requests under Article 9(1) is implemented through the 2004 Regulations and the FOISA. Article 9(2) concerns challenges to the legality of a decision, act or omissions subject to the public participation provisions of Article 6. Each Party shall, within the framework of its national legislation, ensure that members of the public concerned:

a. having a sufficient interest or, alternatively,
b. maintaining impairment of a right, where the administrative procedural law of a Party requires this as a precondition,

have access to a review procedure before a court of law and/or another independent and impartial body established by law, to challenge the substantive and procedural legality of any such decision, act or omission and, where so provided for under national law, and without prejudice to Article 9(3), of other relevant provisions of the Convention. What constitutes a sufficient interest and impairment of a right shall be determined in accordance with national law and consistently with the objective of giving the public concerned wide access to justice within the scope of the Convention. The interests of non-governmental organisations (NGOs) meeting the requirements of Article 2(5) shall be deemed sufficient.

Without prejudice to the review procedures under Article 9(1) and (2), Article 9(3) provides that each Party shall ensure that, where they meet the criteria, if any, laid down in its national law, members of the public have access to administrative or judicial procedures to challenge acts and omissions by private persons and public authorities which contravene provisions of its national law relating to the environment. Article 9(3) extends to environmental cases in general and to challenges to acts or omissions of private persons as well as public authorities, provided that members of the public meet any criteria laid down in domestic law. Article 9(4) regulates the terms on which access to justice shall be made: the procedures referred to in Article 9(1), (2) and (3) shall provide adequate and effective remedies, including injunctive relief as appropriate, and be fair, equitable, timely and not prohibitively expensive.

The Court of Justice has ruled that although Article 9(3) does not have direct effect, in the field of EU law, it is for the national court to interpret, to the fullest extent possible, the procedural rules relating to the conditions to be met in order to bring administrative or judicial proceedings in accordance with the objectives of Article 9(3) and the objective of effective judicial protection of the rights conferred by EU law.[70] The principle was applied, *obiter*, in a Scottish judicial review of a grant of planning permission, where the Court upheld an argument that it would run counter to Article 9(3) of maximizing citizens' rights of access to the courts in environmental cases, to have a domestic rule to the effect that unless a petitioner challenged a conditional resolution of a planning authority, he was precluded from challenging the substantive grant of planning permission.[71]

EU Transposition

At the EU level, the provisions on access to justice in Article 9(2), (3) and (4) of the Aarhus Convention were implemented by Article 3(7) of Directive 2003/35/EC (the Public Participation Directive) which inserted Article 10a into Directive 85/337/EEC and Article 15a into Directive 2008/1/EC.[72] Article 10a was subsequently codified by Article 11 of the EIA Directive which provides that Member States shall ensure that, in accordance with the relevant national legal system, members of the public concerned (a) having a sufficient interest or alternatively (b) maintaining the impairment of a right, where administrative procedural law of a Member State required that as a precondition, have access to a review procedure before a court of law or another independent and impartial body to challenge the substantive and procedural legality of decisions, acts or omissions subject to the public participation provisions of the EIA Directive. Under Article 11(3) what constitutes a sufficient interest and impairment of a right shall be determined by Member States consistently with the objective concerned of giving the public concerned wide access to justice.[73] NGOs are deemed to have a sufficient interest. Under Article 11(4) any such procedure shall be fair, equitable, timely and not prohibitively expensive.

Article 11 applies only to the public participation provisions in Article 6 of the EIA Directive. It has no application as regards broader environmental decision-

[70] *Lesoochranárske zoskupenie VLK* (n 5) at paragraphs 50 and 51.

[71] *Bova v Highland Council* 2011 SCLR 751 per Lord Pentland at paragraph 54.

[72] The 2008 Directive was recast by the IPPC Directive. Article 9 of the Aarhus Convention is given effect by Article 25 of the IPPC Directive.

[73] See: C-263/08 *Djurgarden-Lilla V*artans Miljoskyddsforening *v Stockholms Kommun genom dess Marknamnd* [2010] 1 CMLR 36 where the CJEU held that Directive 85/337/EEC precluded national laws which reserved the right of appeal solely to environmental protection associations with at least 2,000 members as that would run counter to the objective; C-427/07*Commission v Ireland* [2011] 3 CMLR 46 where Advocate General Kokott noted that in order to determine what constitutes sufficient interest to bring an action, a balance had to be struck between the objective of wide access and the need to avoid undue delays to projects and unnecessarily burdening the courts with unmerited actions (paragraph 69).

making, eg under the SEA Directive, the Habitats Directive[74] or Wild Birds Directive.[75] Except for the public participation provisions of the EIA Directive and the IPPC Directive, Article 9(2), (3) and (4) of the Aarhus Convention is not the subject of directly effective EU legislation.

Domestic Transposition

Domestic implementation of the rights of access to review procedures under Articles 9(2) and (3) and in particular to the requirements under Article 9(4) (that the procedures must provide adequate and effective remedies and be fair, equitable, timely and not prohibitively expensive) has been controversial and the subject of scrutiny by the European and domestic courts in recent years.

(i) Access to Review Procedures: Wednesbury and Standing

Although domestic law provides for acts and decisions to be subject to review procedures, the Aarhus Convention Compliance Committee has expressed concern regarding the availability of appropriate procedures in which the substantive legality of decisions, acts or omissions within the scope of the Convention can be subjected to review under the law of England and Wales.[76] The Committee did not go so far as to find the UK to be in non-compliance, but it noted the very high threshold for review imposed by the *Wednesbury* test and considered that the application of a 'proportionality principle' could provide an adequate standard of review in cases within the scope of the Aarhus Convention. However, the domestic authorities do not appear to share those concerns: the Court of Appeal rejected a proportionality test and an argument that *Wednesbury* review was insufficient for the purposes of the Convention.[77] The Court observed that the views of the Committee were not part of domestic law and were not in any event conclusive.[78]

Traditionally the courts in Scotland applied a strict interpretation as to who was entitled to bring judicial review proceedings, borrowing rules from private law that a person required to show both title and interest. As a result, individuals could

[74] Council Directive 92/43/EEC of 21 May 1992 on the conservation of natural habitats and of wild fauna and flora [1992] OJ L206/7.

[75] Directive 2009/147/EC of the European Parliament and of the Council on the conservation of wild birds [2009] OJ L20/7.

[76] *ACCC/C/2008/33*: paragraphs 125 to 126.

[77] *R (on the application of Evans) v Secretary of State for the Communities and Local Government and others* [2013] EWCA Civ 87.

[78] The leading case in England suggests that a lack of third party rights of appeal in planning cases is compatible with Article 6 of the European Convention on Human Rights (*R (Adlard) v Secretary of State for the Environment, Transport and Regions* [2002] 1 WLR 2515 (paragraphs 13–32)). The Scottish Executive rejected a third party right of appeal in its White Paper 'Modernising the Planning System' (2005) on the grounds that 'adding a new right of appeal against decisions to grant planning permission would inevitably build new delays and unpredictability into the system' and that the government 'want to strengthen the participation of local people at an earlier stage in the process', paragraph 5.3.4.

not bring proceedings unless they had a strong private interest.[79] In its landmark decision in *AXA General Insurance Ltd and others v HM Advocate and others*[80] the Supreme Court swept away the strict common law rules which it held had no place in applications to the court's supervisory jurisdiction which lay in the field of public law. In doing so it intended to put an end to an unduly restrictive approach which had too often obstructed the proper administration of justice. The Court ruled that standing to take part in judicial review proceedings, depended instead on demonstrating a sufficient interest in the issues raised by the application. The Court distinguished between mere busybodies and those with a legitimate interest. A personal interest need not be shown if the individual is acting in the public interest and can genuinely say that the issue directly affects the section of the public that he seeks to represent.[81] The type of interest which is relevant, and therefore required in order to have standing, will depend upon the particular context and in particular upon what will best serve the purposes of judicial review in that context.[82]

In *Walton*, the Supreme Court in addressing, *obiter*, the question of whether the appellant was a statutory 'person aggrieved', expanded on the concept of standing. The Court held that the appellant was a 'person aggrieved' since he had made representations in accordance with the statutory procedures, had taken part in the local inquiry, lived in the vicinity of the route and was an active member of various local environmental organisations. As a participant in the procedure, he was entitled to be concerned about a perceived failure to follow a fair procedure.[83] Those same factors would also have given him standing to bring an application for judicial review. The Court accepted that a 'person aggrieved' or having a 'sufficient interest' might include those who are not themselves directly affected but who are legitimately concerned about damage to wider public interests such as the damage to the environment.[84] The Court added that the interest of the appellant is not merely a threshold issue, it may also bear upon the Court's exercise as to the remedy if any, which it should grant in the event that the challenge is well founded.[85]

As the Extra Division subsequently observed in *McGinty*,[86] what is perhaps left unclear is exactly how one distinguishes between the mere busybody and the individual who has a genuine interest sufficient to be accorded standing to challenge a decision with environmental consequences which do not impact on the

[79] *Rape Crisis Centre v Secretary of State for the Home Department* 2000 SC 527; *Dundee Harbour Trustees v D & J Nicol* [1915] AC 550; *Forbes v Aberdeenshire Council* [2010] Env LR 36. Specific legislation was enacted providing that NGOs had sufficient interest for the purposes of the public participation provisions of the EIA and IPPC Directives: The Environmental Impact Assessment (Scotland) Amendment Regulations 2006 and the Pollution Prevention and Control (Public Participation etc) (Scotland) Regulations 2006.

[80] [2012] 1 AC 868. Friends of the Earth intervened by written submission and made detailed submissions on the question of standing.

[81] ibid per Lord Hope, paragraphs 62–63.

[82] ibid per Lord Reed, paragraph 170.

[83] *Walton v Scottish Ministers* (n 3) paragraphs 83–88, 103 and 151–56.

[84] ibid per Lord Carnwath at paragraph 103.

[85] ibid per Lord Reed at paragraph 89–96; Lord Hope paragraphs 151–54.

[86] *McGinty v Scottish Ministers* (n 38).

individual's private interest.[87] Ultimately the Court held that Mr McGinty did have standing since he complained that the statute imposed an obligation to give him an opportunity to participate in decision-making which he would have taken up had he been aware of it. The Court considered that there is a public interest in ensuring that statutory obligations owed to members of the public are fulfilled and that there is also a public interest in protecting the environment. Although these were different sorts of public interests, both were relevant to the question of standing. The fact that as matters of public interest Mr McGinty shared them with a large number of other residents of the Hunterston area and beyond, did not mean that he could not rely on them as giving him, as an individual, standing to complain when these interests had been adversely affected. Although not representing the general public in a strict sense, Mr McGinty was entitled to rely on his objective of protecting the interest of the general public as a basis for bringing proceedings.[88] There can be no doubt that this case law represents a shift in thinking consistent with the need to recognise a wider category of person that have rights to access to justice under the EU Directives and the Aarhus Convention. In considering whether an individual has standing it is relevant to consider not only their interest in the decision-making but also the public interest in protecting the environment.

(ii) Timing

Judicial review procedure in Scotland currently differs from England and Wales in having no permission stage, nor any fixed time limit within which to bring an application. However a party who does not act quickly may well face a plea of *mora, taciturnity and acquiescence* at common law. The plea has been taken relatively frequently in recent judicial review petitions, resulting in additional court time and expense and added uncertainty for parties bringing proceedings. The Scottish Civil Courts Review in 2009 took the view that the plea was undesirably vague and not well suited to a procedure designed to provide a speedy and effective remedy. It recommended that petitions for judicial review be brought promptly and within a period of three months, subject to the court's discretion to permit a petition to be presented outwith that period.

In September 2010 the Aarhus Compliance Committee found the UK to be failing to live up to its full obligations under Article 9(4) of the Convention by failing to provide clear time limits, particularly given the wide discretion available to the Courts in England and Wales in interpreting the requirement to bring proceedings 'promptly' and resulting uncertainty.[89] The CJEU also considered the requirement that proceedings be brought 'promptly' was too uncertain.[90] In light

[87] ibid paragraph 48: 'All that can be said so far, it seems, is that the question is fact sensitive and it will depend on all the circumstances of the challenge under consideration.'

[88] Ibid paragraph 46.

[89] *ACCC/C/2008/33:* paragraphs 138–39.

[90] C-406/08 *Uniplex (UK) Ltd v NHS Business Services Authority* [2010] 2 CMLR 47; *R (on the application of Buglife: The Invertebrate Conservation Trust) v Medway Council (National Grid Property Holdings Ltd and another, intervening)* [2011] 3 CMLR 39.

of that decision, the Scottish Government decided not to include any overriding requirement that proceedings should be brought promptly in the Courts Reform (Scotland) Bill.[91] Instead the Bill proposes a time limit in all applications to the supervisory jurisdiction, requiring proceedings to be brought within a period of three months starting from the date that the grounds giving rise to the application for judicial review arose, or such longer period as the Court considers equitable having regard to all the circumstances.[92]

Although the Bill might be thought to provide more certainty insofar as it sets a time limit, it may well result in arguments as to whether the time limit has been met, when time starts to run[93] and whether it is equitable to allow a longer period in all the circumstances. If, as the Scottish Legal Aid Board suggests in its response to the consultation on the draft Bill, petitions brought after three months are unlikely to obtain legal aid, the enactment of the time limit may even reduce access to justice in some cases.

(iii) Avoiding Prohibitive Expense

In times of restricted public expenditure and limited legal aid,[94] the approach that the courts should take to widening access to justice and limiting expenses is highly contentious. When compared to other countries, the cost of litigating in the UK is amongst the highest,[95] with lawyers' fees comprising the major element in total costs. In September 2010 the Aarhus Convention Compliance Committee found the UK to be failing to live up to its full obligations under the Convention in terms of litigation costs.[96] The European Court of Justice made it clear that the Court's

[91] Making Justice Work, Courts Reform (Scotland) Bill—A Consultation Paper, February 2013.

[92] Following amendment at Stage 2, the provision appears in section 85 of the Bill, inserting new section 27A into the Court of Session Act 1988.

[93] See *Portobello Park Action Group Association v City of Edinburgh Council* 2013 SC 184; *Bova v Highland Council* (n 71).

[94] In Scotland, it is still relatively rare for an environmental challenge to be funded by legal aid: Friends of the Earth, 'Tipping the Scales, Complying with the Aarhus Convention on Access to Environmental Justice', by Mary Church, edited by Frances McCartney and Emma Quinn (2013) p14. Some applications have been refused under Regulation 15 of the Civil Legal Aid (Scotland) Regulations 2002, which suggest that it is not only necessary to have a private interest to qualify for legal aid but that a wider public interest, where there are other persons having the same interest in the matter may disqualify the applicant, see Frances McCartney, 'Public Interest and Legal Aid' (2010) *Scots Law Times* 37, 201–04.

[95] See Christopher Hodges, Stefan Vogenaur and Magdalena Tulibacka (eds), 'Costs and Funding of Civil Litigation: A Comparative Study' *Oxford Legal Studies Research Paper No 55 2009*, founded on by the 'Review of Civil Litigation Costs: Final Report' December 2009, by Jackson LJ, paragraph 5.15. In the comparative study, England and Wales was amongst the highest in lawyers' fees alongside Australia and Denmark.

[96] *ACCC/C/2008/33:* The Committee was considering costs in England and Wales alone and identified 'at least four problems' with the legal system of England and Wales, namely (i) the very limited circumstances in which protective costs orders were granted under the Corner House rules, (ii) the limiting effect on the claimant's recoverable costs if a PCO was granted (leading to lack of equality of arms), (iii) the potential effect of cross undertakings on a Claimant's damages, and (iv) the fact that the public interest of the environmental claims is not 'in and of itself given sufficient consideration' (paragraph 129).

discretion, after the event, to modify the amount of expenses payable, was not compliant with Directive 2003/35/EU since it did not have the specificity, precision and clarity required to satisfy the need for legal certainty and did not satisfy the requirement that proceedings are not prohibitively expensive.[97]

Over the last few years the Scottish courts have afforded some protection against prohibitive expense by awarding litigants protective expenses orders ('PEO') in advance of the substantive hearing. The courts have made these orders in the exercise of its wide discretion at common law providing litigants with protection from adverse expenses awards at an early stage in proceedings.[98] In making PEOs, Scottish courts have adopted the principles from the leading English case *R (on the application of Corner House Research) v Secretary of State for Trade and Industry*[99] in which the Court of Appeal laid down guidelines which should be taken into account in deciding whether to make a protective costs order ('a PCO'). These are:

(1) A PCO may be made at any stage of the proceedings, on such conditions as the court thinks fit, provided that the court is satisfied that: (i) the issues raised are of genuine public importance; (ii) the public interest requires that those issues be resolved; (iii) the applicant has no private interest in the outcome of the case; (iv) having regard to the financial resources of the applicant and the respondent(s) and to the amount of costs that are likely to be involved, it is fair and just to make the order; (v) if the order is not made the applicant will probably discontinue the proceedings and will be acting reasonably in doing so.
(2) If those acting for the applicant are doing so *pro bono*, this will be likely to enhance the merits of the application for a PCO.
(3) It is for the court, at its discretion, to decide whether it is fair and just to make the order in light of the considerations set out above.

The English courts subsequently modified the Corner House principles distinguishing between environmental cases where the EU Directives are applicable and those where they are not. In *Morgan and Baker v Hinton Organics (Wessex) Ltd*[100] the Court of Appeal held that in cases where the EU Directives were in play, the Court's discretion may not be regarded as adequate implementation of the rule against prohibitive costs and more modification of the rules may need to be considered. In other cases, the principles applying to PCOs apply alike to environmental and other public interest cases, although the principles had to be applied flexibly, in particular the requirement that the claimant should have no private

[97] *Commission v Ireland* (n 73).

[98] In *McArthur v Lord Advocate* 2006 SLT 170, not an environmental case, Lord Glennie held that it was competent to make protective expenses orders, pointing to the width of the discretion of the Court in the matter of awards of expenses. Lord Glennie's reasoning was subsequently approved by the Inner House, in *The Newton Mearns Residents Flood Prevention Group for Cheviot Drive v East Renfrewshire Council* [2013] CSIH 70 at paragraph 31.

[99] [2005] 1 WLR 2600.

[100] *Morgan and Baker v Hinton Organics (Wessex) Ltd* (n 7).

interests in the case.[101] In *R (on the application of Garner) v Elmbridge BC*,[102] Sullivan LJ held that if the public participation provisions of the EIA Directive were applicable, the courts should disapply the requirement to show that the issues raised are of general public importance and/or that the public interest requires that those issues should be resolved since the Directive is based on the principle that it is in the public interest that there should be effective participation in the decision-making process.

In *Garner*, the question arose as to what approach the Court should take to an applicant's resources when considering prohibitive expense. Should it be decided on an 'objective' basis by reference to the ability of an 'ordinary' member of the public to meet the potential liability for costs, or should it be decided on a 'subjective' basis by reference to the means of the particular claimant, or upon some combination of the two bases? The question was referred to the Court of Justice by the Supreme Court in *R (on the application of Edwards v Environment Agency and others)*.[103] When the case was referred back to the Supreme Court, Lord Carnwath extracted the following significant points from the judgment of the CJEU: the test of prohibitive expense is not purely subjective; the cost of proceedings must not exceed the financial resources of the person concerned nor appear to be objectively unreasonable, at least in certain cases; the CJEU did not give definitive guidance as to how to assess what is objectively unreasonable; the Court could take into account the merits of the case, that is 'whether the claimant has a reasonable prospect of success,[104] the importance of what is at stake for the claimant and for the protection of the environment, the complexity of the relevant law and procedure, the potentially frivolous nature of the claim at its various stages'; the fact that the claimant has not been deterred from carrying on the proceedings is not itself determinative; the same criteria are to be applied on appeal as at first instance although there may be different considerations at each level and an appellate court should bear in mind what has already been spent on the case. Applying the CJEU's judgment in *Edwards*, the Supreme Court held that since the claimant had already paid into court the amount sought in costs there was no evidence that an order for payment of that sum would be beyond her means and it was impossible to say that an award of such a figure would be subjectively unreasonable. Further, having regard to the unusual circumstances of the case and all the facts, it could not be said such a figure would be objectively unreasonable.

The Court of Justice recently scrutinised the approach of the UK Government to prohibitive expense in the infraction proceedings against the UK for failure to transpose Articles 3(7) and 4(4) of Directive 2003/35/EC.[105] It is important to recognise that the Court's judgment, delivered on 13 February 2014, is an assessment

[101] ibid per Carnwath LJ at paragraphs 28–40 and 47.

[102] [2011] Env LR 10.

[103] Case C-260/11 [2013] 3 CMLR 18; [2014] 1 WLR 55.

[104] Lord Carnwath's observations on how the merits of the case might affect an order for costs are at paragraphs 27–28.

[105] C-580/11 *Commission v United Kingdom* [2014] 3 WLR 853.

of domestic law as at 22 May 2010 (which was the date for complying with the Reasoned Opinion) and not at any later date. One of the arguments made by the Commission was that the UK Government had not, by 22 May 2010, properly transposed the Directive because it had not enacted its precise terms into domestic law. The Court held that enactment was not necessary and that the UK could rely on the general legal context in the UK provided it actually ensured the full application of the Directive in a sufficiently clear and precise manner.[106] On prohibitive expense, the Court held that the possibility for the domestic court hearing a case to grant a PCO ensures greater predictability as to the cost of the proceedings and contributes to compliance with the requirement that proceedings are not prohibitively expensive.[107] However, the mere fact that in order to determine whether national law meets the objectives of the Directive, the Court is obliged to analyse and debate a body of case law, lead the Court to conclude that the transposition relied on by the UK was not sufficiently clear and precise.[108] The Court considered that the condition under domestic case law (pre *Garner*) that the issues to be resolved must be of public interest was not appropriate.[109] Even assuming that the public interest requirement had been removed by *Garner*, the domestic courts did not appear to be obliged by a rule of law to ensure that proceedings are not prohibitively expensive, or to grant protection where the cost of the proceedings is objectively unreasonable. Nor did the domestic courts appear to provide protection where only the particular interest of the claimant is involved.[110] The regime laid down by case law does not ensure the claimant reasonable predictability as regards both whether the costs of the proceedings are payable by him and their amount, although such predictability appears particularly necessary because proceedings in the UK entail high lawyers' fees.[111]

The first Scottish PEO was awarded in *McGinty v Scottish Ministers*[112] on Corner House principles, and was shortly followed by a PEO in *Road Sense v Scottish Ministers*.[113] Both cases predated the CJEU judgments in *Edwards* and in the infraction proceedings. *Road Sense* was a case falling within Directive 85/337/EEC, where it was argued that uncertainty as to the expenses outcome is in itself a powerful disincentive to participation, a state of affairs which is not consistent with the purposes of the EU legislation. Lord Stewart recognised that the Aarhus Convention, by the terms of Article 3(8), expressly contemplates that national courts can, acting within the Convention, award 'reasonable costs' against

[106] ibid paragraph 33.
[107] ibid paragraph 54.
[108] ibid paragraph 56.
[109] ibid paragraph 57.
[110] ibid paragraphs 55 and 57.
[111] ibid paragraph 58. The Commission's arguments on the unlawfulness of the reciprocal cap in PCOs was held not to be fully supported and is therefore left to argue on another occasion.
[112] [2010] CSOH 5. Mr McGinty's liability was restricted to £30,000 which was not overturned in the reclaiming motion to the Inner House notwithstanding the £5,000 limit for other cases had by then been introduced by new rules of court (discussed below).
[113] 2011 SLT 889.

claimants,[114] but held that the court was bound to make a PEO since the court's discretionary power, after the event, to modify the amount of expenses payable by the unsuccessful party, including the power to modify to nil, was not compliant with EU law.[115] As regards the approach to resources, the courts considered both the applicant's resources and the overall expenses of proceedings,[116] as well as other factors such as whether or not the applicant had failed to make an application for an order at an earlier stage or been deterred by the absence of any order (although no court ruled that in itself was sufficient) to establish that proceedings were not prohibitively expensive.[117] Following *Edwards*, it seems clear that when considering what is objectively unreasonable the court is entitled to consider all these factors as well as the merits, what is at stake for the parties and the complexity of the case.

Even before *Edwards*, the Scottish courts considered the prospects of success to be relevant. That was one of the reasons why the Lord Ordinary refused to grant an application for a PEO under Corner House principles in *Newton Mearns Residents Flood Prevention Group for Cheviot Drive v East Renfrewshire Council*.[118] The application was made by a group of local residents challenging the grant of planning permission for the construction of houses, without ensuring adequate flood prevention measures. The Lord Ordinary held that the circumstances of the case did not satisfy the requirement of general public importance. No important point of law or of principle was raised where the petitioners' primary objective

[114] At paragraph 40 under reference to Advocate General Kokott's Opinion in *Commission v Ireland* (n 73).

[115] In *Road Sense v Scottish Ministers* (n 113), Lord Stewart set the petitioner's liability at £40,000 with a reciprocal cap allowing the appellants to recover the taxed expenses of a solicitor and senior counsel. In the same case, Mr Walton obtained further PEOs in the Inner House (where liability was capped at nil) and in the Supreme Court where liability was capped at £5,000. In *McGinty v Scottish Ministers* (n 112), Lady Dorrian, applying Corner House rules, restricted the petitioner's liability to £30,000 and the cross cap to recovery of expenses of a solicitor and one senior counsel. PEOs have been granted by agreement in other cases: *Sustainable Shetland v Scottish Ministers* [2013] CSOH 158; 2013 SLT 1173, with the petitioner's liability limited to £5,000 and a cross-cap of £30,000. The cross-cap was later increased of consent to £60,000 when the hearing was extended. Expenses protection has been granted in non-environmental cases in public interest interventions on the basis that parties will bear their own expenses: *Scotch Whisky Association and others, Petitioner* [2012] CSOH 156.

[116] In *Road Sense v Scottish Ministers* (n 113), Lord Stewart ultimately concluded at paragraph 47 that the proceedings as a whole would not be prohibitively expensive for the appellants.

[117] In *Uprichard v Fife Council* [2011] CSIH 77, the unsuccessful appellant was found liable for expenses in the Inner House, the Lord Justice Clerk noting that it is a relevant consideration at the end of proceedings that the threat of an adverse award of expenses did not prevent the applicant from pursuing the appeal. The appellant subsequently obtained a PEO in the Supreme Court limiting her liability in expenses to £6,000. In *Doogan v Greater Glasgow and Clyde Health Board* 2012 SLT 1041, not an environmental case, Lady Smith noted: 'More importantly this is not a case where issues of public importance will be stifled at the outset if the award is not put in place. The petitioners embarked on it knowing that they did not have the protection of such an award. Further, I am advised that the petitioners will not give up this cause even if they are not successful in securing the award of protective expenses.' Ultimately, having regard to the income and assets of the company supporting the petitioners, Lady Smith concluded that it was not, in all the circumstances, in the interests of justice that the PEO be granted (paragraphs 87–88).

[118] [2013] CSOH 68. The case did not fall within the scope of the EIA Directive.

was the safeguarding of their respective private interests and there was a strong indication that they were seeking to challenge the merits of the decisions rather than raise any issue for judicial review and the Court could not be satisfied that the petition had a real prospect of success.[119]

Whilst the infraction proceedings make it clear that the UK was in breach of its obligations under EU law as at 22 May 2010, the question remains whether the latest developments in the case law and rules of procedure have now provided the requisite clarity and precision. In Scotland, new rules were introduced as Chapter 58A of the Rules of the Court of Session to enable PEOs to be obtained in certain statutory appeals and judicial reviews.[120] The rules only apply to cases which include a challenge to a decision, act or omission which is subject to, or said to be subject to, the public participation provisions of the EIA Directive or the IPPC Directive. In contrast to the English procedural rules, the rules do not apply to challenges to decisions, acts or omissions subject to the SEA Directive, eg to challenges to plans or programmes which must rely on Corner House principles as modified.

Under Rule 58A, the applicant must be an individual (which does not include persons who are acting as a representative of an unincorporated body or in a special capacity such as trustee) or a NGO promoting environmental protection.[121] The court must make a PEO where it is satisfied that the proceedings are prohibitively expensive for the applicant, that is the applicant could not reasonably proceed with them in the absence of a PEO.[122] The court may refuse to make the PEO if it considers that the applicant has failed to demonstrate a sufficient interest in the subject matter of the proceedings or the proceedings have no real prospect of success.[123] The limits are fixed with the applicant's liability limited up to £5,000 if unsuccessful and the respondent being liable to a successful applicant up to £30,000. Both figures can be altered in favour of the applicant only, on cause shown.[124]

Rule 58A.5 provides that in deciding the terms of a PEO the court shall take into account all the circumstances including the need to ensure that it is not prohibitively expensive for the applicant to continue with the proceedings, the

[119] The Extra Division upheld the Lord Ordinary's Opinion that the case did not satisfy the requirement of general public importance, (n 96). A similar approach was taken in England in *R (on the application of Young) v Oxford City Council* [2012] EWCA Civ 46. The cases can be compared with *R (application of Compton) v Wiltshire Primary Care Trust)* [2009] 1 WLR 1436 at paragraph 23 where Waller LJ held that someone bringing an action to obtain resolution of issues as to the closure of parts of a hospital which affects a wide community, and where that community has a real interest in the issues that arise being resolved, it is certainly open to a judge to hold that there is a public interest in resolution of the issues and that the issues are ones of general public importance.

[120] Act of Sederunt (Rules of the Court of Session Amendment) (Protective Expenses Orders in Environmental Appeals and Judicial Reviews) 2013, SSI 2013/81. Chapter 58A is included at Appendix 11 to this book.

[121] RCS 58A.1(2) and 58A.2(2).

[122] RCS 58A.2(4) and (5).

[123] ibid.

[124] RCS 58A.4.

extent to which the applicant would benefit (whether financially or otherwise) if successful in the proceedings to which the order would apply, the terms on which the applicant is represented, whether and to what extent the applicant is acting on behalf of another person which would have been able to bring the proceedings and whether and to what extent the applicant is willing to limit the expenses which he or she would be able to recover from another party if successful.

There was a full discussion of the considerations to be given to applications under the new rules, in light of *Edwards*, by Lord Drummond Young in *Carroll v Scottish Borders Council* where the Court also gave some guidance on procedural issues.[125] Lord Drummond Young held that it was clear that Rule 58A had to be interpreted according to its own terms, in light of the EIA Directive, and the case law dealing with the requirements of that Directive. It also had to be given an interpretation that was both purposive and contextual.[126] He granted a PEO as he was satisfied under Rule 58A that: the appellant clearly had an interest in the subject matter of the proceedings and it could not be said that the proceedings had no real prospect of success;[127] the Court had been provided with adequate financial information about the appellant's resources and an apparently realistic estimate of the expenses of the litigation, from which it could be concluded that without the order the proceedings would be prohibitively expensive for the appellant.[128] Following *Edwards,* the Court had to consider the likely expenses of the proposed proceedings and the applicant's financial resources, with a wholly objective approach to be adopted in respect of the former, and a partly subjective and partly objective approach in relation to the latter.[129] On the parties' resources, Lord Drummond Young recognised that although the financial limits specified in Rule 58A could be varied, the figures selected appeared to have been chosen to represent a realistic amount in a 'standard' environmental case. The respondent and the interested party had to be taken together, so that the appellant's liability was to be limited to a cumulative total of £5,000 to both. Similarly, the limit of £30,000 on the appellant's liability should relate to both the respondent and the interested party. As far as the expenses of the hearing itself were concerned, the

[125] 2014 SLT 659. The decision on the merits of the petition is reported at 2014 SCLR 532. At the time of writing, the decision is subject to a reclaiming motion before the Inner House for which a PEO has been granted.

[126] ibid paragraphs 11 and 22.

[127] Lord Drummond Young considered that it was wrong to equate the word 'interest' as used in Rule 58A.2 with 'interest to sue', on the basis that interest to sue is concerned with the very fundamental right to bring proceedings, whereas Chapter 58A is concerned with immunity from the normal rules governing liability in expenses and a more stringent test should therefore be used. However, it is suggested that Article 9 of the Aarhus Convention is indeed concerned with access to justice and the very fundamental right to bring proceedings which are not prohibitively expensive and it is not clear on what basis a more stringent test should therefore be applied under the new rules. Lord Drummond Young also observed that the words in parentheses in the text of the opening part of Rule 58A.5(1), namely 'subject to rule 58A.3(1)', did not appear to make sense and had to be a drafting error, and the words 'rule 58A.4' should be substituted as that was clearly what had been intended (paragraph 8).

[128] *Carroll v Scottish Borders Council* (n 125) paragraphs 28 and 29.

[129] ibid paragraphs 12 to 16.

application for a PEO should be treated as a separate hearing and those expenses would not form part of the £30,000 limit as that sum was clearly designed to relate to the expenses of the substantive challenge to the planning decision.[130]

It is notable that Lord Drummond Young considered that the test of a 'real prospect of success' was a low hurdle, suggesting that if one or more of the standard grounds of judicial review appeared *prima facie* to be stateable, that should suffice.[131] Such a view is perhaps not entirely consistent with Lord Carnwath's view in *Edwards* that something higher than reasonable arguability is required. However if the court is not to conduct 'a stringent and detailed examination of the applicant's case' as Lord Drummond Young suggests, it is difficult to see how much more than reasonable arguability could be required. Otherwise, there is a risk that hearings on PEOs will develop into something akin to full hearings on the merits, something which would not only be 'time-consuming and expensive' but likely to 'defeat the objectives of [Chapter 58A] and the underlying Directive'.[132]

Whilst the courts may not be willing to look too stringently at the merits, it seems they may be more willing to closely examine the nature of the organisation bringing proceedings and the resources available to it. In *Friends of Loch Etive, Petitioner*,[133] Lord Malcolm refused to grant a PEO as he was not satisfied under Rule 58A.2(5) that the petitioner could not reasonably proceed absent a PEO. The petition challenged the grant of planning permission for a fish farm development and was presented by an organisation created, controlled and funded by the owner of an estate opposite the development. Donations in support of proceedings had been sought from supporters of the organisation. The petitioner argued that it was a NGO promoting environmental protection within the meaning of Rule 58A.2(2)(b) and that it had only £4,000 in its bank account. Lord Malcolm considered that it was unrealistic to focus only on the two factors advanced by the organisation, particularly given the estate owner's role as *dominus litis* and that there was no information as to the resources which could realistically be expected from the 250 or so people who had indicated support. Lord Malcolm observed that if it was correct that consideration was limited to the two factors mentioned, it would always be open to an individual, whatever his resources, to obtain a PEO by setting up a charitable organisation in which he controlled its activities and membership.

Insofar as the rules make it clear that a PEO must be granted where one court is satisfied proceedings are prohibitively expensive for the applicant and set fixed limits for a standard environmental case which can be reduced in favour of the applicant only, it might be thought that they provide some of the certainty and precision required by the Court of Justice and reflect the correct approach to resources as explained in *Edwards*. However, some limitations and uncertainties

[130] ibid paragraph 27.
[131] ibid paragraph 26.
[132] ibid paragraph 14.
[133] [2014] CSOH 116.

remain. By only applying to judicial reviews and statutory appeals in cases under the public participation provisions of the EIA and IPPC Directives, the new rules are considerably more restrictive than their English counterparts. The rules are silent on how the court should deal with the expenses of the PEO hearing itself. Any application for a PEO under the rules (and also under Corner House principles), is at risk of becoming involved in lengthy debate and being faced with a substantial adverse expenses award. If the applicant is unsuccessful, there is no presumption that parties will bear their own costs only. The very act of seeking a PEO may therefore expose the applicant to uncertain expense. By contrast, the English rules, applying to all Aarhus cases, make it clear that there will be no adverse costs awards made, each party will bear their own expenses and that lengthy debates are positively discouraged.[134] Although the Scottish rules make it clear an application for a PEO can be made at any time in the reclaiming motion (Rule 58A.3)(3)), whether or not an application was made at first instance, the rules are silent on how the court should assess prohibitive expense on appeal. The Supreme Court in *Edwards* recognised that different considerations may apply and that a court may have to consider the expenses incurred at the lower level when assessing prohibitive expense at the appeal level and it is expected that the Scottish courts will apply that approach too since the rules must be read purposively and in accordance with the EU Directives and relevant case law. However, it is questionable whether the continuing need to read the rules in such a manner provides the precision, certainty and clarity required by the Court of Justice.

Conclusion

It remains to be seen how much protection will be provided under the new rules for PEOs which operate in the EIA and IPPC Directive cases and how much these

[134] By contrast the English rules apply after 1 April 2013 to a judicial review 'all or part of which is subject to the provisions' of the Aarhus Convention. That includes a judicial review under the SEA Directive (since it implements Art 7 Aarhus) as well as under the EIA Directive. The rules include provision to deter expensive arguments about whether a case is an Aarhus case: if the claimant loses, there is normally no order for costs. If the defendant loses, normally the claimant will get his or her costs on an indemnity basis, even if the total is taken beyond the £35,000 fixed limit. Prior to these rules in England, the Jackson, 'Review of Civil Litigation Costs: Final Report' (n 93) Chapter 30, paragraph 4.1, recommended one way cost shifting for all judicial reviews, a regime '*under which the defendant pays the claimant's costs if its claim is successful but the claimant does not pay the defendant's costs if the claim is unsuccessful.*' This was followed by the update report 2010 by Sullivan J: 'Ensuring access to environmental justice in England and Wales' which suggested that an unsuccessful claimant shall not be ordered to pay the costs of any other party except where the Claimant has acted unreasonably in bringing or conducting the proceedings (paragraph 30). The Taylor Review of Funding and Civil Litigation in Scotland, September 2013, recommended that the power to apply for a PEO should be available in all public interest cases and that the decision on whether to award a PEO and at what level ought to be a matter for judicial discretion unless otherwise prescribed under rules of court for specific types of action (which appears to be the current position under Corner House rules). It also recommended PEOs ought to be available in multi-party actions also (paragraphs 33 and 37).

cases might influence those determined under Corner House principles as modified. There is still a risk that considerable time, effort and expense will be incurred in determining expenses protection rather than furthering the resolution of the environmental issues. Some have recommended that an independent working group is established to consider how an environmental court or tribunal could improve access to justice in terms of cost, timing and substantive review to comply with the obligations of the third Pillar.[135] It has been suggested this might lead to increased specialisation and expertise in environmental issues including expert judges, lower cost and non-adversarial techniques such as mediation, as well as greater consistency and clarity in decision-making. As matters stand, although there has been relatively full implementation of the first two Pillars of the Aarhus Convention, it can only be concluded that Scotland is still some way off achieving full implementation of the third Pillar of Aarhus into domestic law.

[135] Access to Justice in Environmental Matters, Friends of the Earth Scotland, June 2013 and 'Tipping the Scales' (n 94) and the RSPB's response to the draft Courts Reform (S) Bill 1 May 2013.

4

The Aarhus Convention in Northern Ireland—A Tale of Two Polities

WILLIAM ORBINSON QC[1]

Introduction

The Northern Ireland experience of the Aarhus Convention has been marked by a stark contrast between the evident desire of the courts to secure compliance, and at best an indifference on the part of the dominant parties in the Executive towards the Convention.

The Response of the Courts

North Down is known in Northern Ireland as the Gold Coast, where the social divide lies between the Haves and the Have Yachts.[2] And the most gilded enclave of the Gold Coast is Cultra. It is therefore not without irony that to date the only Northern Irish costs complaint to be made to the Aarhus Compliance Committee has come from the Cultra Residents' Association ('CRA'). Cultra's only misfortune is to lie under one of the flight paths for Belfast City Airport, one of a very few City Airports in Europe, and for some years CRA has vigorously opposed the Airport's expansion plans on amenity grounds. In 2007, CRA and a number of other residents groups brought a judicial review challenge *inter alia* in relation to certain recommendations made by a panel appointed by the Department of the Environment to conduct an independent examination in public of issues touching upon a planning agreement governing the Airport's operations. The challenge failed, primarily because Girvan LJ concluded that the recommendations under

1 Bar Library, Belfast; Legal Associate, RTPI.
2 For the record, this chapter author and North Down resident is not a Have Yacht (but is taking sailing lessons).

challenge were advisory and not justiciable decisions.[3] Applying the usual approach of costs following the event, CRA was ordered to pay the Department's costs amounting to £39,454. Though the point is unclear from the public record, it appears that CRA may not have applied for a Protective Costs Order ('PCO'). CRA successfully complained to the Compliance Committee that this award by a court of the United Kingdom breached its rights under Article 9(4) of the Convention, which requires that access to justice in the environmental field not be 'prohibitively expensive'. In May 2011, the Compliance Committee agreed,[4] stressing that in allocating costs the fact that a party is pursuing environmental concerns involving the public interest should be taken into account. The Committee went on to recommend that the United Kingdom review its system for allocating costs in judicial review applications falling within the scope of the Convention, and undertake practical and legislative measures to ensure that such allocation would be fair and not prohibitively expensive.

Since the CRA judicial review, the Northern Ireland courts have only occasionally been troubled with how to square costs awards with the Convention, and on those occasions notably have striven to satisfy Convention requirements.

In *Re Thompson's Application*,[5] the Lord Chief Justice granted a PCO to a judicial review applicant, capping her exposure to an adverse award of costs to £10,000. The challenge was to the grant of planning permission for a housing scheme in Bryansford village in County Down, and the applicant was a supporter of a community group that had supported local residents in objecting to the proposed scheme. Though she had only a low income, the applicant was refused legal aid funding because it was considered reasonable and proper for other persons having the same interest in the matter to defray the costs payable from the legal aid fund were legal aid to be granted. Applying the *Corner House*[6] principles as reviewed by the Northern Ireland Court of Appeal in *Re McHugh's Application*,[7] Morgan LCJ found that there was a 'borderline' issue of general public interest which required to be resolved, namely whether it was reasonable for the planning authority to grant planning permission on the basis of a consultation response from the Water Management Unit indicating that it was acceptable for the development to connect to the local waste water systems, when a later email indicated that foul sewer connections would be refused for development proposals affected by capacity problems. Following the observations of the Northern Ireland Court of Appeal in *McHugh* that the fact that an applicant had a personal interest in proceedings did not invariably amount to a complete bar to the making of a PCO, Morgan LCJ concluded that the existence of a personal interest on the part of the

[3] *Re Kinnegar Residents' Action Group & Ors Application* [2007] NIQB 90.

[4] See the Committee's report on communication ACCC/C/2008/27 at www.unece.org/fileadmin/DAM/env/pp/compliance/CC-31/ece_mp.pp_c.1_2011_2_add.9_adv%20edited.pdf.

[5] *Re Thompson's Application* [2010] NIJB 356.

[6] *R (on the application of Corner House Research) v Secretary of State for Trade and Industry* [2005] EWCA Civ 192.

[7] *Re McHugh's Application* [2007] NICA 26.

applicant 'should [not] markedly weigh against her', because although she was clearly supported by a wider community to an undisclosed extent she remained a person of limited means and the evidence indicated that exposure to unlimited costs would make it inevitable that she would not proceed with the challenge.

Re Alternative A5 Alliance[8] was a statutory challenge[9] to the decision of the Department for Regional Development for Northern Ireland ('DRD') to progress the £330M 85 km A5 Western Transport Corridor dual carriageway scheme. The scheme was regarded as economically important for the western counties of Northern Ireland, but provoked a substantial body of opposition by those adversely affected. The Alliance mounted the challenge on a multiplicity of grounds, including non-compliance with the Strategic Environmental Assessment Directive,[10] but ultimately it succeeded on the single ground that the Minister had irrationally concluded that there was no doubt as to the efficacy of mitigation measures proposed in respect of the River Foyle and River Finn Special Areas of Conservation and that an appropriate assessment under the Habitats Directive[11] ought to have been, but was not, carried out. At the outset,[12] the Alliance had applied to Horner J for a PCO capping its exposure to any adverse costs award at £5,000. DRD did not object in principle to a PCO, but said that the appropriate cap should be £50,000, and that there should also be a cross-cap of £30,000 on any costs recoverable from DRD in the event that the Alliance were to succeed. The Alliance resisted the cross-cap, pointing out that the costs it could recover would be limited in any event because its legal team was working at discounted commercial rates. Horner J was not impressed by the Alliance's request for a cap fixed at £5,000, which seemed to him to be 'arbitrary' and unrelated to the means and circumstances of the Alliance, and approached the matter in a 'more nuanced' and relative way—'What may be prohibitively expensive to one person who is in receipt of the minimum wage will not be so to another person who earns a six figure salary'. Adopting that approach, and bearing in mind the public interest in protecting the environment, the private interests of the Alliance members involved in the challenge, the evidence of the members means and of their supporters, the importance of ensuring the Alliance had access to justice, and the fact that DRD was funded by the taxpayer, His Lordship granted a PCO capping the Alliance's costs exposure at £20,000. This, he pointed out, amounted to a contribution of just over £150 from each of the Alliance's 135 members, something that could not be regarded as prohibitively expensive even taking into account the need to fund the Alliance's own costs, and hence an order which satisfied the Convention. Horner J rejected the DRD suggestion of a cross-cap, considering

[8] *Re Alternative A5 Alliance* [2013] NIQB 30.

[9] Under Article 67BA of the Roads (Northern Ireland) Order 1993, as amended.

[10] Directive 2001/42/EC of the European Parliament and of the Council of 27 June 2001 on the assessment of the effects of certain plans and programmes on the environment [2001] OJ L197.

[11] Directive 92/43/EEC of 21 May 1992 on the conservation of natural habitats and of wild fauna and flora [1992] OJ L206/7.

[12] [2012] NIQB 97.

that the Alliance's own costs were to some extent already capped by the discount secured from its lawyers. The suggestion of a cross-cap is an interesting one, and the chapter author knows of one case where an environmental pressure group was deterred from pressing for a PCO because the respondent authority indicated that if a PCO were granted it would seek a cross-cap that would effectively leave the group bearing the bulk of its costs, even if successful.

Following *A5 Action Alliance*, the Costs Protection (Aarhus Convention) Regulations (Northern Ireland) 2013 were made on 25 March 2013, coming into force on 15 April 2013.[13] These Regulations, which were virtually simultaneous with the corresponding amendments to the English Civil Procedure Rules and the insertion of a new Chapter 58A of the Scottish Rules of the Court of Session, put the Court's recognition of the scope for an Aarhus PCO on a statutory footing. The new rules set out in the Regulations are broadly similar to their English counterparts in CPR rule 45 (as to which see chapters 2 and 8 of this book). An applicant in an Aarhus Convention case who is an individual is entitled to a costs cap of £5,000 and all other applicants are entitled to a cap of £10,000. There is a £35,000 reciprocal cap on the applicant's ability to recover costs from the respondent. These values are exclusive of VAT. Greater flexibility exists on appeal, where the Court has discretion to make such order as it considers appropriate having regard to the means of the parties, all the circumstances of the case and the need to facilitate access to justice. Provision is made for a respondent to challenge whether the case is an Aarhus Convention case to which these rules apply, although an unsuccessful challenge will render the respondent liable to pay the applicant's costs of resisting that challenge on the indemnity basis. The Regulations also require that when considering whether to require an applicant to make a cross-undertaking in damages as a condition of an interim injunction in an Aarhus Convention case, the Court must have regard to the need to avoid prohibitive expense contrary to Article 9 of the Convention.

The Response of the 'House on the Hill'

In sharp contrast to the evident desire of the Northern Ireland courts to meet Aarhus requirements, the response of the dominant parties in the Stormont Executive has been to treat Aarhus with at best indifference, and at worst contempt.[14]

At the time of writing, Northern Ireland is about to undergo a seismic shift in development planning, with planning powers being returned to local

[13] See Appendix 12 to this book.

[14] It is reasonably clear that the principal driver for the 2013 Regulations referred to above was the Westminster Government as opposed to the Stormont Executive, given the co-ordinated amendments to the procedural rules in all the jurisdictions of the UK around the same time in spring 2013, each of which introduced broadly similar rules.

government some 40 years after they were removed and given to the Department of the Environment for Northern Ireland. In that context, the Planning Bill was a key enabler for change. Sadly, it imploded because of a hugely controversial, last-minute amendment promoted jointly by the two most powerful parties in the Executive, the Democratic Unionist Party ('DUP') and Sinn Féin. That amendment—vaunted as having been agreed with Downing Street, perhaps as a precursor to a similar manoeuvre in Great Britain—proposed restricting planning judicial reviews to European grounds only. The objective was to expedite preferred major development projects (such as the John Lewis-anchored, out-of-centre major comparison retail development at Sprucefield much favoured by the DUP), a number of which had been delayed because of successful judicial reviews. On the basis of reported advice from David Elvin QC that the amendment was a breach of the European Convention on Human Rights, the Social Democratic and Labour Party Environment Minister Mark H Durkan MLA refused to progress the Bill. It is not known whether and to what extent Mr Elvin QC in his advice also addressed the question of whether the proposed amendment was compatible with the Aarhus Convention, but certainly a number of interest groups had lobbied against the proposed amendment on the basis that it breached the Article 9(2) requirement that signatories ensure that those affected by an environmental decision have access to a review procedure before a court of law and/or another independent and impartial body established by law, to challenge the substantive and procedural legality of any decision, act or omission by a public authority. Those interest groups made the point that, as the UK implementation report on Aarhus confirms,[15] the United Kingdom as a whole has secured compliance with Article 9 by allowing judicial review, so that imposing the radical constraint on access to judicial review proposed would undermine that compliance. Suffice to say that this argument was loftily dismissed by the two dominant parties in the Executive, and that if it were not for the stalwart resistance of Minister Durkan, the change would have been forced through regardless.

A Wider Divergence on the Importance of the Rule of Law?

The Planning Bill debacle should be seen in its proper context—one in which there is an increasing tendency among Northern Ireland politicians to treat their electoral mandate as *carte blanche* to thumb their noses at the rule of law. This was writ large recently when our Lord Chief Justice Sir Declan Morgan felt compelled to take the unprecedented step of releasing to the press a letter he had written to the First and Deputy First Ministers some eight months previously, to which

[15] www.unece.org/env/pp/reports_trc_implementation_2014.html.

he had yet to receive a reply. In that letter, the Lord Chief Justice expressed grave concern at remarks made in the Assembly by the Health Minister Edwin Poots MLA to the effect that he did not believe he would receive a fair hearing from the Court of Appeal if he were to appeal a first instance judgment quashing his decision not to lift a ban on gay men giving blood, and that the judiciary would simply 'circle their wagons'. Sir Declan told the First and Deputy First Ministers that these remarks were not only untrue but also damaging to public confidence in the administration of justice:

> Regrettably, this is not the first time that I have had to raise such concerns, which only adds to the seriousness with which I view the matter. Our system of government depends on mutual respect between the executive, the legislature and the judiciary. That is something which I wish to promote. These comments by Minister Poots, however, are damaging to the constitutional relationships and are not in the public interest.

Tellingly, the DUP chair of the Assembly's Justice Committee, Paul Givan MLA, responded by telling the judiciary to be 'careful that they don't get too precious about their status … Politicians ultimately are the lawmakers which the judiciary then need to enforce through the courts'. That being the attitude, one imagines that the dominant parties in the Northern Ireland Assembly and Executive are not likely to be too precious about securing Aarhus compliance, in any context.

5

The Aarhus Convention and the European Union

PROFESSOR LUDWIG KRÄMER[1]

The Integration of the Convention into EU Law

The European Union (EU), represented by the Commission, participated in the discussions on the elaboration of the international agreement which was later known as the Aarhus Convention, right from its beginnings, without having been given a specific negotiation mandate by the Council. The justification for this was taken from the fact that the discussions originally centered around the questions on access to information and participation in public decision-making in environmental matters; the third 'pillar' on access to justice, was brought into the international discussions at a rather late stage. And for the first two pillars, the EU already had detailed legislation in force: on access to environmental information, a directive of 1990 on the 'freedom of access to information on the environment'[2] had established a fundamental right for each person to have access to environmental information without having an interest to state. The participation in public decision-making was regulated, at EU level, in the Environmental Impact Assessment Directive of 1985[3] and, later, in a directive of 1996 on the permitting of industrial installations.[4]

[1] Director of Client Earth's European Union Aarhus Centre. Previously Head of Environmental Governance, Head of Waste Management Unit and Head of Legal Unit within the European Commission Directorate-General for the Environment (2001–2004, 1994–2001 and 1987–1994 respectively).

[2] Directive 90/313 on the freedom of access to information on the environment [1990] OJ L158/56.

[3] Directive 85/337 on the assessment of the effects of certain public and private projects on the environment [1985] OJ L175/40; since then, this Directive changed the number into Directive 2011/92 [2012] OJ L26/1.

[4] Council Directive concerning integrated pollution prevention and control [1996] OJ L257/26; since then, the Directive was several times amended. The permitting is now regulated under Directive 2010/75 on industrial emissions [2010] OJ L334/17.

This EU legislation very considerably influenced the negotiations of the Aarhus Convention, because of the numeric weight which the 15 EU Member States brought to the negotiations, their experience with the application of the EU legislation and their reluctance to go significantly beyond the status quo of existing EU law.

When the Aarhus Convention was adopted, the EU was relatively eager to initiate the legislative process in order to see the provisions of the Convention applied within the EU Member States. It was much more reluctant to consider an application of the Convention by the EU institutions and bodies themselves. The reason for this was that the EU institutions had, until the end of the twentieth century, reflected little on EU governance, transparency, citizens' rights and the participation of civil society in the European integration process. Since 1979, citizens were asked, every four or five years, to vote in elections to the European Parliament; however, in the opinion of the EU institutions, this exhausted their possibilities of participation.

In 2005, the EU ratified to the Aarhus Convention.[5] Under international law, ratification of an international agreement involves the commitment of the Contracting Party to ensure that the provisions of the agreement are complied with all over the territory of the Contracting Party. Accordingly, Article 216(2) of the Treaty on the Functioning of the European Union ('TFEU') states that an international agreement, to which the EU adhered, is binding 'on the Union and its Member States'.

The relationship between an international agreement which had been ratified by the EU and EU law has been the subject of a number of judgments of the Court of Justice. The Court has held that an international agreement cannot amend the EU Treaties themselves, as its ratification by the EU is based on the Treaty provisions, and as a Treaty amendment would need to be ratified by all EU Member States. By contrast, it has held that international agreements prevail over secondary EU law (regulations, directives and decisions) due to the effect of Art 216(2) TFEU, which provides that international agreements entered into by the EU are 'binding on the institutions of the Union and on Member States'.[6] The consequence of this is two-fold. First, EU legislation must, insofar as possible, be interpreted in a manner which is harmonious with international agreements to which the EU is party.[7] This is the case regardless of whether the legislation was originally intended to implement the international agreement. Secondly, where harmonious interpretation is not possible, the legislation in question may be invalid on account of its inconsistency with the international agreement.[8]

This means that the Aarhus Convention prevails over EU regulations or directives. In case of a conflict, EU law has thus to be amended and aligned to the Convention. However, the Aarhus Convention does not prevent Contracting

[5] Decision 2005/370 [2005] OJ L124/1.

[6] Case C-344/04 *IATA and ELFA* [2006] ECR I-403. See also Case C-61/94 *Commission v Germany* [1996] ECR I-3989; and Case C-268/02 *Bello Fratelli* [2004] ECR I-3465.

[7] Case C-341/95 *Bettati v Safety Hi-Tech* [1996] ECR I-3989 at para 20.

[8] See Case C-366/10 *Air Transport Association of America v Secretary of State for Energy and Climate Change* [2012] CMLR 4 at paras 50–55.

Parties from providing for broader access to information, more extensive participation in decision-making or wider access to justice.[9]

It is appropriate to examine the implementation of the Aarhus Convention separately for each of the three pillars of the Convention and, furthermore, to separate the implementation by directives—which address the EU Member States—and by provisions which apply the Aarhus Convention to the activity of the EU institutions.

EU Law on Access to Information

Access to Information Held by Member State Authorities

The EU transposed the Aarhus Convention provisions on access to information by adopting Directive 2003/4.[10] The Directive tried—and very largely succeeded—to follow the requirements of the Aarhus Convention word by word. In some aspects it goes beyond the Aarhus Convention, thus providing for better access to environmental information.

With regard to the definition of 'public authorities', Article 2 of the Directive clarified that advisory bodies of public authorities are also covered by the Directive. In conformity with the Convention, the Directive allowed Member States to exclude from the term 'public authorities' institutions or bodies acting in a judicial or legislative capacity. And the Court of Justice interpreted this provision as also allowing to exclude governmental departments (ministries) which took part in the legislative process, by giving evidence, submitting drafting proposals, etc. However, this exclusion only applied during the duration of the legislative process. Once the process ended, the departments were no longer exempted.[11] Government departments that elaborated regulatory acts, were covered by the Aarhus Convention and, consequently, by the Directive.[12]

Directive 2003/4 defined 'environmental information' as including (amongst other things) any information on 'emissions, discharges and other releases into the environment',[13] a broader definition than the corresponding provision of the Aarhus Convention.[14] This very broad EU formulation practically means that

[9] Aarhus Convention, Article 3(5): 'The provisions of this Convention shall not affect the right of a Party to maintain or introduce measures providing for broader access to information, more extensive public participation in decision-making and wider access to justice in environmental matters than required by this Convention'.

[10] Directive 2003/4 on public access to environmental information and repealing Council Directive 90/313/EEC [2003] OJ L41/26.

[11] Case C-240/09 *Flachglas Torgau*, judgment of 14 February 2012.

[12] Case C-515/11 *Deutsche Umwelthilfe*, judgment of 12 July 2013.

[13] Art 2(b).

[14] Art 2(3)(b).

anything which—voluntarily or involuntarily—gets out the control of a producer or an economic operator and into the physical environment, must be considered as being put into the environment (and thus information which falls within the Directive's scope). The reason for this understanding is that the environment is everybody's environment and cannot remain at the disposal of only some; in the same way as substances or products which are put on the market cannot be kept 'confidential', information on substances or products which are put into the environment cannot remain confidential.

The Court of Justice appears to support a broad approach to the scope of the Directive: in *Stichting Natuur en Milieu*, the applicants had asked to have access to the data of studies which a company had made in preparation of an authorisation request regarding the maximum permissible levels of pesticide residues in lettuce. The Court held that such data could be relevant for the protection of the environment and human health, as they were to support the decision of the administration on the maximum permissible levels. Therefore, they constituted 'environmental information'.[15]

A narrow approach has, by contrast, been taken to the exemptions pursuant to which access to information may be refused. In *Mecklenburg* the Court of Justice held that the exemption for 'material in the course of completion' did not apply to opinions or advice issued by one administrative department to another other than during the course of a permit procedure, ruling that, whilst the permit procedure may not be finished, the opinion or advice is final and therefore access to it may not be refused.[16]

Article 7 of the Directive provides for active dissemination of environmental information by public authorities; it transposes Article 5 of the Aarhus Convention into EU law. Article 5 of the Aarhus Convention is particularly general and vague and leaves a large margin of discretion to Contracting Parties. Directive 2003/4 did not go significantly beyond the provisions of the Convention. It asked Member States, though, to publish a national report on the state of the environment at least every four years (Article 7(3) of the Directive), which the majority of the EU Member States does not appear to do.

Overall, it can be fairly stated that the provisions of the Convention on access to environmental information were correctly taken up by Directive 2003/4.

There are a number of other EU regulations and directives which deal with the question of access to information, such as the Regulations on chemical substances and products,[17] on pesticides[18] and on genetically modified food and feed,[19] on

[15] Case C-266/09 *Stichting Natuur en Milieu* [2010] ECR I-13119, judgment of 16 December 2010.

[16] Case C-321/96 *Mecklenburg* [1999] ECR 1999, p I-3809.

[17] Regulation 1907/2006 concerning the registration, evaluation, authorisation and restriction of chemicals (REACH) [2006] OJ L396/1, Article 118.

[18] Regulation 1107/2009 concerning the placing of plant protection products on the market [2009] OJ L309/1, Article 63.

[19] Regulation 1829/2003 on genetically modified food and feed [2003] OJ L268/1, Article 29s: Article 30(6) provides that the competent authorities shall ensure 'appropriate confidentiality'; such a formula is not in compliance with the restricted provision of the Aarhus Convention.

biocidal products[20] and the Directive on the deliberate release into the environment of genetically modified organisms.[21] This legislation[22] was enacted with a very active participation of vested interest groups. The relationship between their provisions and the Aarhus Convention has not been analysed by the Court of Justice. In particular, the question of what kind of information the producer of a substance or a product may keep confidential, when he applies for a permit, will need to be clarified. At present, there is a tendency of keeping essential information which is relevant for the permit procedure confidential. As the Aarhus Convention only allows such information to be kept confidential 'where such confidentiality is protected by law in order to protect a legitimate economic interest' (Art 4(4)(d)), the balance between producer's interests and the right of citizens to know will have to be struck on a case-by-case basis. As the Aarhus Convention prevails over secondary EU law (see above), the fact that an EU regulation or directive declares a specific information confidential, is not in itself sufficient to refuse access to it.

In several pieces of EU legislation, a provision was inserted stating that 'disclosure [of the following information] shall normally be deemed to undermine the commercial interests' of the applicant for an authorisation.[23] This reversal of the burden of proof is not compatible with the approach taken by Art 4(4) of the Convention in relation to exemptions from disclosure. The long lists of information that normally follow a provision of this nature need to be examined carefully to see whether the restriction claimed is 'legitimate' within the meaning of Art 4(4)(d) of the Convention.

Access to Environmental Information Held by the EU

The existence of Directive 90/313 on access to environmental information contributed to the insertion, into the Final Act on the Treaty of European Union (TEU) of 1992, of Declaration No 17, which invited the EU institutions to take measures in order to increase transparency and public access to information.[24] Subsequently, the Council and the Commission adopted legal instruments on

[20] Regulation 528/2012 concerning the placing on the market of biocidal products [2012] OJ L167/1, Article 63.

[21] Directive 2001/18 on the deliberate release into the environment of genetically modified organisms [2001] OJ L106/1, Article 25.

[22] This product-related legislation is mentioned here for the sake of a coherent presentation, though the authorisation to market the substance or product is sometimes given by EU authorities (REACH, genetically modified food and feed, active substances for pesticides and biocides), sometimes by national authorities (GMO releases, pesticides).

[23] Regulation 1907/2006 (n 17), Art 118(2); Regulation 1107/2009 (n 18), Art 63(2); Regulation 1829/2003 (n 19), Art 29s; Regulation 528/2012 (n 20), Art 66(2).

[24] Maastricht Treaty on European Union [1992] OJ C191, Declaration No 17: 'The Conference considers that transparency of the decision-making process strengthens the democratic nature of the institutions and the public confidence in the administration...'

access to documents which avoided, though, giving rights to individual persons.[25] The Amsterdam Treaty on European Union then inserted an Article 255 into the EC Treaty which largely corresponds to the present Article 15 TFEU. It gave a right of access to documents to persons living within the EC and to EU citizens, but limited this right to the Commission, the Council and the European Parliament.

Implementation provisions concerning Article 255 were laid down in Regulation 1049/2001.[26] In order to take account of the existence of the Aarhus Convention, an Article 2(6) was inserted into that Regulation which reads: 'This Regulation shall be without prejudice to rights of public access to documents held by the institutions which might follow from instruments of international law or acts of the institutions implementing it'; a recognition that the provisions of the Aarhus Convention prevailed over the provisions of Regulation 1049/2001.

Regulation 1049/2001 dealt with access to documents in general. In order to deal specifically with environmental information and to implement the Aarhus Convention with regard to the EU institutions and bodies, Regulation 1367/2006 was adopted.[27] It contained a chapter on access to environmental information which declared that Regulation 1049/2001 should apply to requests for access to environmental information (Article 3). In this way, all the exceptions provided for in Regulation 1049/2001 were meant to apply in cases where access to environmental information was requested. Regulation 1367/2006 only took over the provisions of the Aarhus Convention which stated that an overriding public interest should be presumed to exist, when information on emissions into the environment was asked for; furthermore, the exceptions of Article 4 of Regulation 1049/2001 had to be interpreted narrowly, taking into account the public interest in disclosure.

This legislative construction had as a consequence that EU institutions, and in particular the EU Commission, treated requests for access to information, as if the Aarhus Convention—and also Article 2(6) of Regulation 1049/2006—did not exist. Unfortunately, this practice was also followed, occasionally, by the General Court which went so far as to apply an exception which was contained in Article 4 of Regulation 1049/2001, but not in the Aarhus Convention, to a case where it accepted that access to information was refused.[28]

[25] Code of Conduct concerning public access to Council and Commission documents [1993] OJ L340/1; Decision 93/731 on public access to Council documents [1993] OJ L340/43; Commission Decision 94/90 on public access to Commission documents [1994] OJ L46/58.

[26] Regulation 1049/2001 regarding public access to European Parliament, Council and Commission documents [2001] OJ L145/43.

[27] Regulation 1367/2006 on the application of the provisions of the Aarhus Convention on access to information, public participation in decision-making and access to justice in environmental matters to Community institutions and bodies [2006] OJ L264/13.

[28] Case T-362/08 *IFAW v Commission*, judgment of 13 January 2011, with comment from L Krämer, (2011) *Journal for European and Environmental Planning Law*, p 225. On appeal the judgment was quashed, however, on other procedural grounds.

Regulation 1049/2001, and thus EU law, is not in compliance with the Aarhus Convention in particular concerning the conditions under which a request for access may be refused. The following discrepancies exist:

a) Regulation 1049/2001 provides that requests for access shall be refused, where they undermine the protection of 'defence and military matters'. The Aarhus Convention only refers to 'national defence'. 'Military matters' may include the administration of a military airport, the pollution of soil or waters by military activities, etc. There is no reason to refuse access to information for all military matters.
b) Regulation 1049/2001 provides that access to information shall be refused, where it undermines the 'financial, monetary or economic policy of the Community or a Member State'. Such an exception does not exist in the Aarhus Convention. EU law is thus insofar not in compliance with the Convention.
c) Regulation 1049/2001 provides that requests for access to information shall be refused, where disclosure would undermine 'commercial interests of a natural or legal person, including intellectual property'. The Aarhus Convention allows requests to be refused, where disclosure would adversely affect the 'confidentiality of commercial and industrial information, where such confidentiality is protected by law in order to protect a legitimate economic interest'. The exception by Regulation 1049/2001 is thus much larger: under the Aarhus Convention, there must first be specific legislation to protect the commercial information. And second—much more important—the legislative provision is not sufficient in itself: it must also be meant to protect a 'legitimate' interest (see Art 4(4)(d) of the Convention). In this way, the Aarhus Convention wanted to exclude 'protectionist' provisions which just had in mind the interests of the economic operators, but did not consider the public interest in disclosing information. The EU exception is thus not compatible with the Aarhus Convention.
d) Regulation 1049/2001 provides that information shall not be disclosed which undermines the confidentiality of 'court proceedings and legal advice'. The Aarhus Convention provides an exception for 'the course of justice'. With regard to court proceedings, the Court of Justice held that disclosure of the submissions made by the parties to the EU Courts could be withheld, as disclosure would disturb the smooth course of Justice.[29] However, normally submissions had to be disclosed after the end of the court procedure in question, as then the disclosure of pleadings could not any more 'undermine' the course of justice.
e) An exception for 'legal advice' does not exist under the Aarhus Convention. The Court of Justice ruled that in legislative processes, the legal advice given

[29] Cases C-514/07P, C-528/07P and 532/07P to 517/07 *API*, judgment of 21 September 2010.

by the Council's Legal Service had to be disclosed[30] and could only under very exceptional circumstances be withheld.[31]

f) Regulation 1049/2001 provides for an exception, where disclosure could undermine 'the purpose of inspections, investigations and audits' (Article 4(2)). The Aarhus Convention allows an exception where the disclosure would adversely affect 'the ability of a public authority to conduct an enquiry of a criminal or disciplinary nature' (Article 4(4)(c)). Regulation 1049/2001 is thus much broader than the Convention. Moreover, the Commission tries to subsume under this exception all the documents established under Article 258 TFEU, an understanding which is neither compatible with the Aarhus Convention nor even with Regulation 1049/2001.[32] In *ClientEarth v Commission*, the General Court went even so far as to subsume all studies which the Commission made on the conformity of national environmental law with EU law, to be part of the procedure under Article 258 TFEU and thus capable of not being disclosed by the Commission.[33] The Court of Justice has not yet finally decided on this question.

As regards the collective and active dissemination of environmental information, Article 4 of Regulation 1367/2006 correctly transposes the general requirements of the Aarhus Convention into EU law. Article 4(4) of the Regulation requires that a report on the EU state of the environment is published at regular intervals 'not exceeding four years'. The European Environment Agency which is charged to produce this report, publishes it every *five* years, relying on Article 2(vi) of Regulation 1210/90,[34] ignoring that Regulation 1210/90 was, in this regard, substituted by Regulation 1367/2006.

Generally, the EU institutions and bodies have a tendency to interpret the exceptions of Regulation 1049/2001 broadly and to disregard largely the public interest in disclosure. Where a refusal of disclosure appears difficult, they try to delay answers to requests as long as possible, frequently also in the hope that the applicant loses interest in the issue. Access to environmental information will thus often have to be sought against the reserved practice of the EU institutions. The EU institutions are far from applying Article 1(1) TEU that decisions should be taken as openly as possible according to its letter and to its spirit.[35]

[30] See Recital 6 to Regulation 1049/2006: 'Wider access should be granted to documents in cases where the institutions are acting in their legislative capacity, including under delegated powers'.

[31] Cases C-39/05P and C-52/05P *Sweden and Turco v Council*, judgment of 1 September 2008.

[32] An enquiry, investigation or audit has the objective to obtain factual information, if necessary even without or against the will of the investigated person. Under Article 258 TFEU, however, no information can be extracted from Member States against their will. See further L Krämer, 'Access to Letters of Formal Notice and Reasoned Opinions in Environmental Law Matters' (2003) *European Environmental Law Review* 197.

[33] Case T-111/11 *Client Earth v Commission*, judgment of 13 September 2013. The judgment was appealed (case C-612/13P).

[34] Regulation 1210/90 [1990] OJ L120/1.

[35] The EU Treaties use the terms 'open' and 'transparent' not less than five times, apart from Article 1(1) TEU also in Articles 9(3) and 11(2) TEU and in Articles 15(1) and 298 TFEU.

Participation in Decision-Making

Member State Level

With regard to *projects*, the EU adopted Directive 2003/35/EC[36] to give effect to the Aarhus Convention by amending the EIA Directive (now Directive 2011/92/EU)[37] and the Industrial Emissions Directive (now Directive 2010/75/EU).[38] Overall, the two Directives correctly transpose the provisions of Article 6 of the Aarhus Convention into EU law. The following observations are nonetheless necessary:

a) Directive 2011/92 and Directive 2010/75 provide for a specific, intergovernmental procedure for assessing the effects of a project which may have transboundary effects.[39] At least some Member States refer, for transboundary projects, *exclusively* to this intergovernmental procedure. However, the Aarhus Convention set out no specific procedure for transboundary projects. And it prohibits, in Article 3(9), any discrimination as to citizenship, nationality or domicile. This means that the individual right of participation in decision-making may not be substituted by an intergovernmental procedure. It may therefore be necessary in a case with significant transboundary effects both to undertake the intergovernmental procedure and to consult the public who will be affected by those transboundary effects.
b) The Aarhus Convention provides that the public concerned shall be informed, among others, of 'an outline of the main alternatives studied by the applicant' (Article 6(6(e)). This formula is repeated by Articles 5(3)(d) and 6(2)(e) of the Espoo Convention on environmental impact assessment in a transboundary context, to which the EU adhered.[40] This Convention provides in Annex II(b) that the public should obtain 'a description, where appropriate, of reasonable alternatives (for example, locational or technological) to the proposed activity, and also the no action alternative'. This should have been incorporated into Directive 2011/92 and Directive 2010/75, but was not. The present formula does not oblige the applicant to study alternatives to his project proposal. However, a new Environmental Impact Assessment Directive (Directive 2014/52/EU) was passed in April 2014 and once it comes into force it will amend Directive 2011/92 so as (inter alia) to require the applicant to provide a 'description of the reasonable alternatives (for example

36 Directive 2003/35 providing for public participation in respect of the drawing up of certain plans and programmes relating to the environment [2003] OJ L156/17.
37 Directive 2011/92 (n 3), Article 6. It should be noted that the Aarhus Convention does not require to ensure public participation in the process of environment impact assessments.
38 Directive 2010/75 (n 4), Article 24 and Annex IV.
39 Directive 2011/92 (n 3), Article 7; Directive 2010/75 (n 4), Article 26.
40 Decision of 15 October 1996. That Decision was not published.

in terms of project design, technology, location, size and scale) studied by the developer'.[41] This new requirement comes into force on 16 May 2017.

c) Directive 2011/92 and Directive 2010/75 do not clarify that the public has a right of obtaining access to all studies made and opinions delivered during the permitting or impact assessment process, as provided for in Article 6(6) of the Aarhus Convention. Administrations frequently refuse access to such documents with the argument that the final decision on the permit or impact assessment has not yet been taken. The Court of Justice clarified, though, that such studies and opinion are themselves 'final' documents and must therefore be disclosed, even before the final permitting or impact assessment decision is taken.[42]

With regard to *plans and programmes*, Directive 2003/35 provides, in one single Article, for basic rules, leaving the details for ensuring the participation to the EU Member States; therefore, the enforcement of this Directive is particularly important.

The field of application of Directive 2003/35 is extremely narrow and does not comply with the provisions of the Aarhus Convention: Article 7 of the Convention covers all 'plans and programmes related to the environment'. Directive 2003/35 only refers to management plans for waste, batteries, packaging and packaging waste, nitrates in water and air quality assessment and management and even lists the different EU directives which provided for the elaboration of such plans.[43] However, there are numerous other plans and programmes which relate to the environment. Such plans are either foreseen by EU legislation—in the sectors of water, air, waste, noise, nature conservation, renewable energies, climate change, fisheries, agriculture, etc—or in national legislation—such as town and country planning, energy, transport, regional policy, etc. The absence of participation provisions for all these different plans is a very considerable deficiency of EU legislation.

This omission is not repaired by the adoption of the Strategic Environmental Assessment Directive 2001/42/EC,[44] for three main reasons: first, this Directive only covers those plans or programmes which form the basis for projects that require, under Directive 2011/92, an environmental impact assessment. However, there are numerous other plans and programmes—including those of an economic or financial nature—which stand on their own and do not form the basis of later projects. These plans and programmes are not made subject of a decision on public participation.

Secondly, Directive 2001/42 only applies to plans and programmes which are 'required by legislative, regulatory or administrative provisions' and which 'set the

[41] See Annexes IV, para 2 of Directive 2011/92, as amend by Directive 2014/52 (2014) OJ L 124/1.

[42] *Mecklenburg* (n 16).

[43] See Directive 2003/35 (n 36), Annex I.

[44] Directive 2001/42 on the environment assessment of the effects of certain plans and programmes on the environment [2001] OJ L197/30.

framework for development consent' (see Articles 2(a) and 3(2)(a) respectively). Article 7 of the Convention does not have those provisos. At the time of writing, a communication to the Aarhus Convention Compliance Committee is pending, alleging that as a result of these restrictions to Directive 2001/42's scope, the EU has not properly implemented Article 7 of the Convention.[45]

Thirdly, participation in the decision-making of a plan or programme itself is not the same as participation in the decision-making of an environmental impact assessment. It is clear that a national, regional or local authority is not bound, in its decision on a plan or programme, by the negative result of the environmental impact assessment. Arguments which the public may have, might be irrelevant for the impact assessment procedure, but might be very relevant for the decision on the plan or programme.

As mentioned, Directive 2003/35 excludes numerous plans and programmes of its application, because it only applies to those plans listed in Annex I. Directive 2001/42 excludes plans and programmes on small areas (Article 3(3) and financial and budget plans (Article 3(8)). For both exclusions, no justification can be found in the Aarhus Convention.

Neither Directive 2003/35 nor Directive 2001/42 took over the wording of Article 6(4) of the Aarhus Convention, according to which the public participation shall take place '*when all options are open and effective public participation can take place*'. Both Directives mention instead that the participation shall be '*effective*'. It is submitted, however, that this is not necessarily the same thing.

Directive 2001/42 provides for an intergovernmental participation procedure where a plan or programme may have effects on another Member State. The Directive does not state that in such a case, the citizens of that other Member State have a direct right of their own to participate in the decision-making procedure established by the Directive, so that Article 7 would have to be applied cumulatively with Article 6 on the participation rights of citizens. Otherwise, citizens of that neighbouring Member State would be discriminated because of their nationality.[46]

Projects, Plans and Programmes—EU Level

Regulation 1367/2006[47] seeks to transpose the requirements of the Aarhus Convention regarding public participation in decision-making by EU institutions and bodies.

The Regulation does not deal with participation in EU projects. Indeed, the EU does not issue permits for the realisation of projects which are listed in Annex I, though it does authorise the placing on the market of substances and products, such as pesticides, chemicals or genetically modified food. However, Article 6 of

[45] ACCC/C/2014/101 (European Union).
[46] See above in relation to transboundary public participation in relation to projects.
[47] Regulation 1367/2006 (n 27).

the Aarhus Convention does not oblige Contracting Parties to provide for participation with regard to such decisions.

With regard to plans and programmes, Regulation 1367/2006 provides for participation in plans and programmes related to the environment that are elaborated by EU institutions or bodies. Plans or programmes are only those, the elaboration of which is required by EU law and which contribute to the achievement of one of the objectives of EU environmental policy. The restriction to plans or programmes which are required, is not compatible with the Aarhus Convention.

Regulation 1367/2006 excludes financial and budgetary plans or programmes and emergency plans for civil protection. None of these exclusions is found in the Aarhus Convention.

The general provisions from the Aarhus Convention, that participation shall take place when all options are open and shall be effective, are taken over by the Regulation. The minimum time for the public to give comments is fixed at eight weeks (Article 9).

The Regulation does not address the problem of languages. In order to be able to participate effectively, the public must be able to obtain the relevant documents in its own language. This proves difficult with 23 official EU languages. In practice, the Commission organises public consultation in one (English), in very rare situations in three languages (English, French, German). This practice is not compatible with the requirement of an effective participation.

In general, the Commission proceeds to *consultation* on draft plans or programmes which it prepares, but does not organise citizens' *participation*. There is no serious attempt to enter into a dialogue with civil society, on how environment-related plans or programmes should be structured, organised, monitored and implemented. The consultation procedure which follows two communications of the Commission of 2002,[48] is unilateral and does not try to exchange opinions.

An example of this EU approach to participation is the Aarhus Convention's amendment regarding genetically modified organisms (GMOs). The new Article 6 bis of the Convention, together with Annex I bis, provides that the Contracting Parties of the Convention should adopt provisions for effective public participation in decisions on the deliberate release into the environment of GMOs. The EU adhered to this amendment,[49] but declared that its existing legislation already complied with the amendment so that no amendment was necessary.[50] However, the existing provisions just provide that citizens may comment, within 30 days, on the European Food Safety Authority's opinion whether a GMO release should be authorised or not.[51] The participation provisions with regard to GMOs are thus not in compliance with the Aarhus Convention.

[48] Commission, Towards a reinforced culture of consultation and dialogue—Proposal for general principles and minimm standards for consultation of interested parties by the Commission, COM (2002) 277 and General principles and minimum standards for consultation of interested parties by the Commission, COM (2002) 704.

[49] Decision 2006/957 [2006] OJ L386/46.

[50] ibid Recital 4.

[51] Regulation 1829/2003 (n 19), Article 6/7; the same provision is found in Directive 2001/18 (n 21), Article 24.

There are, dispersed in different EU legislative instruments, numerous plans or programmes which relate to the environment, but which do not provide for any public participation. They cannot all be discussed here. Examples are: the working plan which the Commission shall elaborate according to Article 16 of the Directive on energy saving from products;[52] the annual working plan which the Commission shall adopt according to Article 8 of the Regulation on European standardisation;[53] or the participation in the elaboration of the EU environmental action programmes[54] or the financial instrument LIFE to support environmental activities.[55] A very important recent plan is the Commission's plan for a 'Europe 2020' strategy.[56] This strategy gives priority to issues on growth and jobs; it considerably affects environmental issues, as environmental issues are reduced, in that strategy, on climate change and energy issues—which means in practice that all other environmental concerns shall be of secondary or even less importance for the Commission. Any participation of the public did not take place, before the Commission adopted its strategy.

Plans or programmes which the Commission prepares are accompanied by an impact assessment of the possible effects of the plan or programme on economic, social and environmental aspects. This impact assessment is made public, however, only together with the adopted proposal for a plan or programme itself. This practice contradicts Article 9(3)(b) of Regulation 1367/2006 which provides that the public shall be informed of 'the environmental impact or assessment relevant to the plan or programme under preparation, where available'. As the Commission's impact assessment is made, before the Commission adopts its proposal, the reservation 'where available' is irrelevant: the assessment is always available. The Commission practice is thus not in compliance with Regulation 1367/2006.

Access to Justice

National Level

In questions, where access to environmental information was refused, in full or in part, Directive 2003/4 provides that such access shall be available in all EU Member States.

[52] Directive 2009/125 establishing a framework for the setting of eco-design requirements for energy related products [2009] OJ L285/10.

[53] Regulation 1025/2012 on European standardisation [2012] OJ L316/12.

[54] Commission, 'Proposal on the 7th EU Environmental Action Programme' COM (2012) 710;

[55] Regulation 1293/2013 on the establishment of a programme for the environment and climate action (LIFE) and repealing Regulation 614/2007, (2013) OJ 347/185.

[56] Commission, Europe 2020—a strategy for smart, sustainable and inclusive growth, COM (2010) 2020.

As regards access to justice for lack of participation in decision-making, Directives 2011/92 (environmental impact assessment) and Directive 2010/75 (permitting of industrial activities) both provide that natural or legal persons may challenge 'the substantive or procedural legality of decisions, acts or omissions subject to public participation'.[57] These provisions stem from Directive 2003/35[58] and comply with the provisions of the Aarhus Convention. There is no analogous provision in relation to plans and programmes,[59] although it is likely that the general principle of effectiveness of EU law requires a similar result where the provisions of Directive 2003/35 or Directive 2001/42 in relation to plans and programmes have not been complied with.

In 2003, the Commission published a proposal for a directive on general access to justice in environmental matters to provide for co-ordinated transposition of the requirements of Article 9 of the Convention.[60] However, the Council did not discuss the proposal in detail, as several Member States were of the opinion that the EU lacked competence to legislate on matters concerning access to justice.

In 2011, the EU Court of Justice held that Article 9(3) of the Convention could not directly be invoked by private persons before courts (in other words, it did not have direct effect), but nonetheless held that a national court was:[61]

> ... in order to ensure effective judicial protection in the fields covered by EU environmental law, to interpret its national law in a way which, to the fullest extent possible, is consistent with the objectives laid down in Article 9(3) of the Aarhus Convention.

It is not clear what exactly is meant by this formula that the national court should interpret its national law 'to the fullest extent possible' in line with Article 9(3) of the Aarhus Convention. Several studies on the practice of access to justice in environmental matters in the 28 Member States revealed rather large discrepancies. In view of this, the European Commission sought to kick-start the debate on a new access to justice Directive in March 2012, through its Communication 'Improving the delivery of benefits from EU environment measures: building confidence through better knowledge and responsiveness'.[62] In March 2013, the European Parliament expressed regret that work on the Directive had previously stalled.[63] Further work led to a public consultation from June to September

[57] Directive 2011/92 (n 3), Article 11. Directive 2010/75 (n 4), Article 25; however, this Article 25 mentions 'subject to Article 24' instead of talking of public participation. Article 24 deals with the right of access to information and the right of public participation.

[58] Directive 2003/35 (n 36).

[59] The Aarhus Convention does not address this question either; Article 9(2) only refers to Article 6 of the Convention which deals with projects (activities), whereas the participation in plans and programmes is mentioned in Article 7 of the Convention.

[60] Commission, Proposal for a directive on access to justice in environmental matters COM (2003) 624; see also the support of the European Parliament to the proposal [2004] OJ C103E/626.

[61] Case C-240/09 *Lesoochranárske zoskupenie* [2011] ECR I-1255.

[62] COM (2012) 95, 7 March 2012.

[63] European Parliament, 'Improving the delivery of benefits from EU environmental measures', Document P7_TA(2013)0077 at para 29.

2013, which sought the views of the general public and all stakeholders to assess whether legislative action at EU level would add value in ensuring effective and non-discriminatory access to justice in environmental matters across the EU Member States and to identify those issues where targeted legislative action would be needed.[64] In the face of strong opposition from some Member States, however, in particular the United Kingdom, the Commission withdrew its proposal for an access to justice Directive in 2014.

Access to justice by persons and organisations in environmental matters is also partly regulated in the Directive on environmental liability.[65] According to Article 12 of that Directive, a natural or legal person may draw the attention of public authorities of environmental damage having occurred or being imminent and request them to take action. Provided this information shows 'in a plausible manner that environmental damage exist', the authorities shall have to decide whether they initiate restoration measures. Against that decision, access to the national court is possible, in order to have the procedural and substantial legality of the decision, act or failure to act checked (Article 13).

With the ratification of the Aarhus Convention, the Convention became part of EU law. Under Article 17 TEU, the Commission 'shall ensure the application of the treaties, and of measures adopted by the institutions pursuant to them'. It was mentioned above that the EU, by adhering to the Aarhus Convention, committed itself to ensuring that all the provisions of the Convention, including Article 9(3), would be applied throughout the territory of the EU. At present, this is far from being the case. It would thus be the obligation of the EU Commission to take legal action or other efficient and effective measures against those Member States which did not take the necessary legislative measures to make Article 9(3) fully operational in their countries. This omission is an omission of the EU to comply with its obligations under the Aarhus Convention.

Access to the EU Courts

Regulation 1367/2006 provides for an internal review procedure: an environmental organisation which meets certain criteria laid down in Article 11 of the Regulation, is entitled to make a request for internal review to the EU institution or body that adopted an administrative act (Article 11). The request shall state the grounds for the review—which are no further specified in the Regulation—and be introduced within six weeks. A written reply shall be given within 12 weeks—exceptionally within 18 weeks—which state the reasons of the EU institution or body. Against this internal review decision, the NGO may institute proceedings before the Court of Justice 'in accordance with the relevant provisions of the Treaty' (Article 12).

[64] http://ec.europa.eu/environment/consultations/access_justice_en.htm.

[65] Directive 2004/35 on environmental liability with regard to the prevention and remedying of environmental damage [2004] OJ L143/56.

This procedure does not fully implement Article 9(3) and (4) of the Aarhus Convention, since it is limited to environmental NGOs rather than the public generally. Moreover, the Convention does not either restrict access to the courts to administrative acts.[66] The procedure in Regulation 1367/2006 also does not contain the express safeguards in Article 9(4) of the Convention that such proceedings shall provide for 'injunctive relief' and be 'fair', 'equitable' and not 'prohibitively expensive'. There is also no requirement that the person or body conducting the review under Article 11 is independent of the original decision-maker. Fairness would require that another, neutral institution or body than the one whose decision is attacked, decides on the internal review.

Access to the EU courts is not automatically granted to those environmental organisations which are entitled to introduce a request for internal review. The Commission had made such a proposal,[67] but the European Parliament and the Council had rejected it and instead provided in Article 12 of Regulation 1367/2006 that access is only granted in accordance with the provisions of Article 263(4) TFEU.

Access to the EU courts is therefore only possible, where the individual person or the environmental organisation is either addressed by a decision of an EU institution, or where it is 'directly and individually concerned' by it; since the end of 2009, there is a third possibility: access to the Courts is possible by a natural or legal person against 'a regulatory act which is of direct concern and does not entail implementing measures' (Article 263(4) TFEU).[68]

The jurisprudence of the EU Court of Justice was particularly restrictive with regard to the criterion of 'direct and individual concern'. Based on a judgment of 1963,[69] the Court's approach has been that the applicant had to be characterised by specific features which made him different from all other persons being in a similar position. Even when an applicant claimed that there was a risk to life or health, his application was not admissible, if other persons were in the same situation; the Court did not discuss whether such an interpretation was compatible with the human rights of the applicant.[70]

[66] The General Court, in cases T-338/08 *Stichting Natuur en Milieu v Commission*, judgment of 14 June 2012, and T-396/09 *Vereniging Milieudefensie v Commission*, judgment of 14 June 2012, held that the internal review procedure under Regulation 1367/2006 was also open against regulatory acts. (These judgments were quashed on appeal, See cases C-405/12P *Commission v Stichting Natuur en Milieu*, judgment of 13 January 2013; C-401/12P *Council and Commission v Milieu-Defensie*, judgment of 13 January 2015.

[67] Commission, Proposal for a Regulation of the European Parliament and of the Council on the application of the provisions of the Aarhus Convention on Access to Information, Public Participation in Decision-making and Access to Justice in Environmental Matters to EC institutions and bodies, COM (2003) 622.

[68] This new provision appears not to apply to EU secondary legislation and therefore challenges to such legislation will still have to be brought on the basis that the applicant has 'direct and individual concern'. See Case C-583/11/P *Inuit Tapiriit Kanatami v Parliament and Council*, judgment of 3 October 2013.

[69] Case 25/62 *Plaumann v Commission* [1963] ECR 199.

[70] See Case C-321/95P *Greenpeace ao v Commission* [1998] ECR I-1651 (CJEU); Case T-219/95R *Danielsson ao v Commission* [1995] ECR II-3051 (General Court).

The result of this jurisprudence was that since 1963, not one single application by a non-governmental organisation or a private person in environmental matters was held admissible. It remains to be seen, whether the Court will change its interpretation of Article 263(4) TFEU in the light of the EU Charter on Fundamental Rights[71] or the European Convention on Human Rights and Fundamental Freedoms, to which the EU is bound to adhere in the future.

Significantly, in response to a communication brought by ClientEarth, the Aarhus Convention Compliance Committee held in 2011 that the restrictive access to the EU Courts according to the jurisprudence of the Court of Justice, is not compatible with the Aarhus Convention.[72] It remains to be seen if the Court of Justice modifies its principles relating to standing to bring challenges under Article 263 TFEU in the light of this ruling.

Concluding Remarks

The EU has correctly and completely transposed the provisions of the Aarhus Convention on access to environmental information in relation to information held by Member States' authorities. In contrast, the application of those provisions to the EU institutions and bodies is deficient. A considerable number of provisions of EU Regulation 1049/2001 are not in compliance with the Convention.

Public participation in decision-making is likewise relatively well regulated for decisions on projects. However, EU legislation only requires that *some* national plans and programmes related to the environment are subject to a participation procedure. At EU level, several plans and programmes adopted by the EU institutions and bodies and related to the environment do not foresee any public participation. What is worse, the EU institutions consider 'consultation' to be equivalent to 'participation' which is not under the Aarhus Convention. Also, the EU ignores that there are 23 official languages and that, in order to make participation effective, citizens have to be informed in their own language *so* that they can also make their comments in their own language. It therefore does not appear that there has been complete implementation by the EU of Article 7 of the Convention.

On access to justice, there is still no comprehensive EU legislation regulating access to the national courts in environmental matters. And access to the EU courts on environmental matters—other than regarding access to information—is, until now, in practice impossible, so that EU law is not in compliance with the Aarhus Convention.

It can only be hoped that the Aarhus Convention Compliance Committee and the EU Court of Justice soon come out with rulings that highlight and, insofar as possible, deal with the lacunas in the EU's implementation of the Convention.

[71] European Charter for Fundamental Freedoms [2000] OJ C364/1.
[72] ACCC/C/2008/32 (European Community).

The Substantive Rights

6

Access to and Collection of Environmental Information

DAVID BLUNDELL[1]

Introduction

The 'first pillar' environmental information provisions of the Aarhus Convention establish a freedom of information regime relating to environmental information which is powerful and detailed. They are significant not only for the substantive rights they create but also for the pivotal role they have played in the development of European Union ('EU') legislation on access to environmental information. They were highly influential in the enactment of Directive 2003/4/EC,[2] following the more limited success of Directive 90/313/EEC. Directive 2003/4/EC has been implemented in domestic law by the Environmental Information Regulations 2004 (the '2004 Regulations').[3] The influence of the Aarhus Convention is thus deep and fundamental in both EU and domestic law.

Background: Influence of and on EU Law

EU action in this field began much earlier. The European Community ('EC') Action Programme on the Environment of 1987 had called for devising 'ways of improving public access to information held by environmental authorities'.[4] This was followed by a Resolution of 19 October 1987 on the continuation and implementation of an EC policy and action programme on the environment,[5] which declared the importance of concentrating Community action on certain priority

[1] Barrister, Landmark Chambers, London.
[2] Directive 2003/4 on public access to environmental information and repealing Council Directive 90/313/EEC [2003] OJ L41/26.
[3] SI 1992/3240.
[4] [1987] OJ C70/3.
[5] [1987] OJ C289/3.

areas, including better access to information on the environment. Similarly, the European Parliament had stressed in its Opinion on the fourth action programme by the EC on the environment[6] that 'access to information for all must be made possible by a specific Community programme'.

The result was the enactment of Council Directive 90/313/EEC of 7 June 1990 on the freedom of access to information on the environment. The objective of the Directive was to 'ensure freedom of access to, and dissemination of, information on the environment held by public authorities and to set out the basic terms and conditions on which such information should be made available': Article 1.

Member States were required to implement the Directive by 31 December 1992 at the latest. There was provision in Article 8 for Member States to report to the Commission four years after the implementation date on 'the experience gained in the light of which the Commission shall make a report to the European Parliament and the Council together with any proposal for revision which it may consider appropriate'.

The Directive was not a wholehearted success. The Commission wrote to the (then) 15 Member States reminding them of their four-year reporting obligations on 25 July 1996. It provided them with a questionnaire listing the matters which, at a minimum, the national reports were expected to cover. The reminder did not have the desired effect, as by 31 December 1996 only one report had been sent to the Commission.[7] A reminder was sent to the Member States concerned at the beginning of 1997, urging them to send the reports as soon as possible. This was to no effect. The Commission subsequently launched multiple infraction proceedings in the course of 1997 against the recalcitrant Member States. Perhaps unsurprisingly, this had the desired effect. However, in the Commission's opinion the reports 'varied in the amount of useful detail provided'.[8]

The Commission then noted the recent signing of the Aarhus Convention, including by the EC.[9] In a passage which provides an interesting insight into the development of the Convention, as well as into the importance of the involvement of non-governmental organisations (NGOs) in the process, the Commission stated that:[10]

> Although the first draft of the provisions in the Convention relating to access to environmental information were largely inspired by the Directive, subsequent negotiations highlighted the weaknesses or shortcomings of the latter in the light of experience

[6] [1987] OJ C156/138.

[7] Commission Report on the experience gained in the application of Directive 90/313/EEC: COM (2000) 400 of 29 June 2000, p 3.

[8] Ibid, p 4. The Commission concluded that 'Most of the reports contained no, or only very limited, statistical data. Some included a significant amount of data relevant to the national experience but from which no firm conclusions can be drawn at the Community level.'

[9] The EC signed the Convention on 25 June 1998, as did the United Kingdom ('UK'). The Convention was approved on behalf of the EC by Council Decision 2005/370.

[10] See Report (n 7) pp 8–9.

gained in its application. NGOs concerned with the environment participated actively and constructively in the negotiations on an equal footing with national delegations. The Commission considers that the final text of the Convention represents a clear advance on the provisions of the Directive.

In light of the weaknesses that had been identified in Directive 90/313/EEC, the Commission proposed a replacement Directive which would align EC law with the position under the Convention. In view of the Commission's previous endorsement of the Convention and the EC's expression of satisfaction with its terms, it was no surprise that it proved highly influential in the drafting of the replacement Directive envisaged by the Commission in 2000. Directive 2003/4/EC (the 'Environmental Information Directive') was the result and the new Directive is heavily based on the Convention. In its declaration at the time of approving the Convention on 17 February 2005, the EC stated that it 'has already adopted several legal instruments, binding on its Member States, implementing provisions of this Convention' and went on expressly to refer to Directive 2003/4/EC. Further, the fifth recital to the 2003 Directive provides that:

> Provisions of Community law must be consistent with [the Aarhus] Convention with a view to its conclusion by the European Community.

In addition, and reflecting the fact that the EC was itself a party to the Convention, the Convention also led to a Regulation dealing with the application of the Convention to the EU itself: Regulation 1367/2006.[11] The 2006 Regulation applies the earlier Regulation 1049/2001[12] regarding public access to European Parliament, Council and Commission documents to applications for environmental information held by the EU institutions and does so by reference to the Aarhus Convention.

The Environmental Information Provisions of the Aarhus Convention

The key provisions of the Aarhus Convention on environmental information are Articles 4 and 5. Article 4 sets out the general right of the public to gain access to existing information on request, also known as 'passive' access to information; Article 5 sets out the duties of States Parties to collect and disseminate information on their own initiative, also known as 'active' access to information.[13]

[11] Regulation (EC) 1367/2006 on the application of the provisions of the Aarhus Convention on Access to Information, Public Participation in Decision-making and Access to Justice in Environmental Matters to Community institutions and bodies [2006] OJ L264/13.

[12] Regulation (EC) 1049/2001 regarding public access to European Parliament, Council and Commission documents [2001] OJ L145/43.

[13] See p 75 of *The Aarhus Convention: An Implementation Guide*, 2nd edn (UNECE, 2014).

Article 4: Access to Information

Article 4 provides, so far as is relevant, as follows:

> 1. Each Party shall ensure that, subject to the following paragraphs of this article, public authorities, in response to a request for environmental information, make such information available to the public, within the framework of national legislation, including, where requested and subject to subparagraph (b) below, copies of the actual documentation containing or comprising such information:
> (a) Without an interest having to be stated;
> (b) In the form requested unless:
> (i) It is reasonable for the public authority to make it available in another form, in which case reasons shall be given for making it available in that form; or
> (ii) The information is already publicly available in another form.
> 2. The environmental information referred to in paragraph 1 above shall be made available as soon as possible and at the latest within one month after the request has been submitted, unless the volume and the complexity of the information justify an extension of this period up to two months after the request. The applicant shall be informed of any extension and of the reasons justifying it.

Thus Article 4(1) includes the primary right of access to environmental information. Its principal characteristics are as follows:

(1) It is dependent on a request being made. This is to be contrasted with the distinct right of dissemination under Article 5, discussed below.
(2) The right to information is not subject to having to demonstrate any 'interest' in it or in anything concerning it.[14] Motive is therefore irrelevant (subject, possibly, to the exemption of manifestly unreasonable requests under Article 4(3)(b), again discussed below).
(3) Where requested, the authority shall supply copies of the 'actual documentation containing or comprising the information'. In such circumstances, summaries or excerpts would not be acceptable.
(4) The information is to be provided in the form requested. The Implementation Guide gives the non-exhaustive examples of paper, electronic media, videotape or recording.[15] That requirement is subject to the proviso in Article 4(1)(b), which allows an authority to provide it in a different form where it is reasonable to do so or not to provide it in the form requested if it is already publicly available in another form.
(5) The time limit for the provision of the information is 'as soon as possible and at the latest within one month after the request has been submitted', unless the volume and complexity of the information justify an extension up to a maximum total period of two months. Where an extension is

[14] In its first published decision, the Compliance Committee found a breach of this principle by Kazakhstan: ACCC/C/2004/1: see paragraph 25.
[15] Implementation Guide (n 13) p 80.

claimed, the applicant must be informed of the fact together with the reasons for it.

It is notable that the Convention does not specify the form of the request. Thus, any request meeting the requirements of Article 4, whether oral or written, will be caught by Article 4(1). Similarly, Article 4(1) does not require the requesting party to refer to the Convention, the implementing national legislation or even the fact that the request is for environmental information. However, as noted by the Implementation Guide, such references are good practice[16] since they facilitate the work of the implementing parties and avoid delays. In communication ACCC/C/2007/21 (European Community), the Compliance Committee noted that, where a public authority does not recognise a request as an environmental information request, it may not be aware of the potential legal obligations, thus causing problems with compliance.[17]

Further, the requirement to honour the form in which the information is requested means that, subject to the limited exceptions in Article 4(1)(b), an applicant for information would be able to request sight of the original documentation itself.

The Compliance Committee takes the obligation to provide the information in the form requested seriously. In communication ACCC/C/2008/24 (Spain), the Compliance Committee found Spain to be in breach of this requirement where, in responding to a request for information in electronic format or CD-ROM, it provided it instead in paper form. This consisted of a document of more than 600 pages at a cost of €1,200—a CD-ROM would have cost only €13. The requesting individual could not afford the cost of the full document and so took only 34 pages, as well as dropping a request for additional plans for which a further charge would have been levied. The Committee found that Spain's approach significantly limited public access to environmental information.

As to the exceptions in Article 4(1)(b), the public authority may provide the requested information in another form if it is reasonable to do so or if it is already publicly available in another form. The Implementation Guide suggests that 'publicly available' means 'easily accessible to the member of the public requesting the information' and that 'another form' means that 'the available information is the functional equivalent of the form requested, not a summary, and that the information should be available in its entirety'.[18]

As regards timing, the time limits in Article 4 are maxima: the parties are to make the requested information available 'as soon as possible'. The Convention does not specify how time is to be calculated, or from when time runs, for the

[16] Ibid, p 80.
[17] See paragraphs 34 and 35.
[18] Implementation Guide (n 13) p 81.

purposes of the outer one- and two-month time limits. It is thus for the administrative law of the individual States Parties to calculate such matters.[19]

Compliance with the time limits in the Convention is important for ensuring that applicants are able to use the information to engage with related administrative decision-making processes. In ACCC/C/2008/24 (Spain), Spain failed to provide the requested information until four months after the request was made. The request related to pending land use determinations. In the time it took for Spain to respond, a modification was made to the relevant land use plan. Spain escaped censure on that aspect of the complaint only because the Convention was not in force at the relevant time. But the Committee held it to be in breach in the same case where it later took seven months to respond to a request. The Committee emphasised that at the end of the extended two-month period, the only option for the public authority was to provide the information or to rely on one of the exceptions in Article 4(3) or (4). Although extensions could be granted, the total time for all extensions could not exceed two months after the submission of the original request: paragraph 74.

Exemptions

Article 4(3) and (4) provide for a series of exemptions from the duty of disclosure. Both are expressed in terms of discretionary powers of refusal—'A request for environmental information *may* be refused' (emphasis added). But their operation is different. The exemptions in Article 4(3) are not subject to any additional criterion for their engagement, beyond the particular requirements of each category. The Article 4(4) exemptions, on the other hand, are all expressed to apply only where disclosure would 'adversely affect' the particular protected category of information.[20]

Article 4(3)

The Article 4(3) exemption is engaged in three situations, namely where:

(1) The public authority does not hold the requested environmental information (subparagraph (a));
(2) The request is manifestly unreasonable or formulated in too general a manner (subparagraph (b)); and
(3) The request concerns 'material in the course of completion' or internal communications of public authorities where such an exemption is provided for

[19] This is also the view of the Implementation Guide: see p 82.

[20] In Case C-71/10 *Office of Communications v Information Commissioner* [2012] Env LR 7, the CJEU ruled, on a reference from the UK Supreme Court ([2010] 10 UKSC 3, [2010] Env LR 20) that the exceptions under Directive 2003/4 could be applied cumulatively so that where an exception considered individually did not justify non-disclosure, a combination of exceptions could do so.

in national law or customary practice 'taking into account the public interest served by disclosure' (subparagraph (c)).

The first category is reasonably straightforward, requiring simply that a public authority demonstrate that it does not have in its possession the environmental information which is sought. That will be a question of fact in each case. Article 4(3)(a) specifies only that the authority does not 'hold' the information; it does not specify that it must be held in a particular form. It will, therefore, be important for an authority subject to such a request to ensure that all media in which it holds environmental information are checked to ensure that they do not contain the requested material.

In addition, the fact that a public authority does not hold information which has been requested of it is not the end of its obligations as far as Article 4 is concerned. Article 4(5) provides that, in those circumstances, the authority shall 'as promptly as possible' inform the applicant of the public authority to which it 'believes' it is possible to apply for the information requested or transfer the request to that authority and inform the applicant accordingly. The trigger for this informative obligation is a belief on the part of the first public authority that it knows of another authority which holds the information. That is a low threshold, which is notably not qualified by having to be reasonable (although such a qualification may well be implied). Where it has such a belief, it will have to tell the individual as promptly as possible. Promptness in these circumstances is likely to be measured having regard to all the circumstances. Unlike the primary obligation in paragraph (1), no particular outer time limit is specified. However, in light of the decision in ACCC/C/2008/24 (Spain) emphasising that a State Party must rely on one of the exemptions within the extended two-month period or release the material, the responding party would certainly have to provide information about the other public authority within that time. Indeed, given that the obligation is to provide that information 'as promptly as possible' it is likely that a more rapid response will be required in many cases.

Finally, public authorities have a choice between informing the applicant of the identity of the second authority and passing on the request to that authority itself, before informing the applicant. However, the Implementation Guide advises that 'the most timely and effective method' is to require public authorities to transfer requests directly. In its communication on ACCC/C/2009/37 (Belarus), the Compliance Committee considered the operation of the 'onward referral' mechanism in Article 4(5). It identified two conditions to be met in order for reliance on the 'onward referral' mechanism to be justified. First, the request must be referred to another 'public authority': paragraph 66. In principle, it was acceptable for some functions relating to the maintenance and distribution of environmental information to be delegated to private entities. But, for the purposes of access to information, they should be treated as falling within the definition of a public authority: paragraph 67. Secondly, onward referral must not compromise compliance with the requirements of Article 5: paragraph 68.

The second category of exemption under Article 4(3) provides protection against vexatious requests—described in Article 4(3)(b) as 'manifestly unreasonable'—or ones which are formulated too generally. In terms of the 'manifestly unreasonable' test, there is no need for a request to be, for example, repetitious. The notion of unreasonableness is a broad one. Domestic lawyers will need to beware of falling into the trap of conflating the test with that of *Wednesbury* unreasonableness in public law.[21] There is no suggestion in the text of Article 4 or elsewhere that the term should be given anything other than its ordinary, broad meaning; compare the approach of the domestic courts to the use of the term 'unreasonable' in planning policy relating to costs applications.[22] The exemption covers a potentially very wide range of flawed requests. The Implementation Guide suggests that where States Parties decide to provide for this exemption, they will need to define '"manifestly unreasonable" so as to assist public authorities in determining when a request is so unreasonable that it may be refused ... and to protect the public's interest that the test will not be applied arbitrarily'.[23] The Guide also suggests that volume and complexity will not suffice under this head because they are already listed as reasons for extending the time limit for a reply from one to two months under Article 4(2).[24] As for requests which are 'too general', this provides protection to public authorities by enabling them to demand a degree of specificity in the requests that are made. Again, there is no definition of 'too general' in the Convention and the Implementation Guide advises states to provide guidance on the issue.[25]

As for the third category of exemption under Article 4(3), it has two limbs. First, it covers material 'in the course of completion'. On its face, this would appear to cover draft documentation, whether reports, policies or other materials, which was not yet finalised. Understood in that sense, it has an analogue in the common law exemption from the duty to publish drafts of a policy which is still in the course of evolution.[26] However, the Implementation Guide takes a different approach, suggesting that 'the mere status of something as a draft alone does not automatically bring it under the exception'.[27] Rather, it would cover 'individual documents that are actively being worked on by the public

[21] *Associated Provincial Picture Houses Ltd v Wednesbury Corporation* [1948] KB 223.

[22] *Manchester City Council v. Secretary of State for the Environment* [1988] JPL 774.

[23] Implementation Guide (n 13) p 84.

[24] This approach to volume and complexity was confirmed in the Compliance Committee's findings in submission ACCC/S/2004/1 (Romania v Ukraine) and communication ACCC/C/2004/3 (Ukraine): paragraph 33 of the Committee's Findings and Recommendations. There were other practical options open to the State Party in such circumstances, such as providing the information in electronic form, indicating where the information could be viewed and facilitating such viewing or indicating the charge to be applied.

[25] Implementation Guide (n 13) p 84.

[26] *R (Lumba) v Secretary of State for the Home Department* [2011] UKSC 12, [2012] 1 AC 245, per Lord Dyson at 268H [38].

[27] Implementation Guide (n 13) p 85.

authority'. The commentary in the Guide is of some importance on this issue and bears citation:

> Once those documents are no longer in the 'course of completion' they may be released, even if they are still unfinished and even if the decision to which they pertain has not yet been resolved. 'In the course of completion' suggests that the document will have more work done on it within some reasonable time frame. Other articles of the Convention also give some guidance as to how Parties might interpret 'in the course of completion'. Articles 6, 7 and 8 concerning public participation require certain draft documents to be accessible for public review. Thus, drafts of documents such as permits, EIAs, policies, programmes, plans and executive regulations that are open for comment under the Convention would not be 'materials in the course of completion' under this exception.

The need to interpret the individual exceptions within the context of the Convention as a whole supports this analysis, given the terms of Articles 6, 7 and 8 to which the Guidance refers. But it demonstrates that there may well be a difference here with the requirements of domestic common law as analysed in *Lumba*.[28] Whereas draft policies in other areas of public law may be exempt from disclosure, that is unlikely to be the case for policies relating to environmental matters which engage the Convention.

The decision in ACCC/C/2010/53 (United Kingdom) is an interesting example of the application of this exception. It concerned a request for access to raw environmental data on air pollution which had been collected from a monitoring station but not yet subjected to data correction. The Committee held that the raw data fell within the definition of environmental information in the Convention and fell to be disclosed. Any concerns about the data in its raw form could be met by disclosure with the express caveat that the data were not yet processed according to the agreed and regulated process for processing raw environmental data.

The second limb of the third category of exemption under Article 4(3) is an apparently broader category of exemption covering 'internal communications of public authorities'. The Implementation Guide makes the point that if the material has been disclosed to a third party, it could no longer be considered 'internal'.

These two limbs of the exception in Article 4(3) are both subject to two important qualifications: the exemption must itself be provided for in national law or customary practice, and there is a public interest test for disclosure in any event. The qualification that such an exemption must be provided for in national law or customary practice is important and, in effect, means that the Convention does not introduce any new exemption on this ground where none exists in the law or practice of a signatory state. The Convention does not explain what is meant by 'customary practice' but the Implementation Guide advises that 'this may differ according to the administrative law of an implementing party'.[29] The public interest qualification also provides an important brake on public

[28] *Lumba* (n 26).
[29] Implementation Guide (n 13) p 84.

authorities automatically resorting to this exemption to prevent release of internal communications. They will need to be able to demonstrate that the public interest would not be served by disclosure.

Article 4(4)

The exemptions in Article 4(4) cover the following areas:

(1) The confidentiality of public authority proceedings, where such confidentiality is provided for under national law (subparagraph 4(4)(a));
(2) International relations, national defence or public security (subparagraph 4(4)(b));
(3) The course of justice, the ability of a person to receive a fair trial or the ability of a public authority to conduct an enquiry of a criminal or disciplinary nature (subparagraph 4(4)(c));
(4) The confidentiality of commercial and industrial information, where such confidentiality is protected by law in order to protect a legitimate economic interest—but subject to the principle that information on emissions which is relevant for the protection of the environment shall be disclosed (subparagraph 4(4)(d));
(5) Intellectual property rights (subparagraph 4(4)(e));
(6) The confidentiality of personal data and/or files relating to a natural person where that person has not consented to the disclosure of the information to the public, where such confidentiality is provided for in national law (subparagraph 4(4)(f));
(7) The interests of a third party which has supplied the information requested without that party being under or capable of being put under a legal obligation to do so, and where that party does not consent to the release of the material (subparagraph 4(4)(g)); or
(8) The environment to which the information relates, such as the breeding sites of rare species (subparagraph 4(4)(h)).

All of the categories in Article 4(4) are subject to a test of adverse impact: that is, the exemptions are only triggered where the disclosure of the information would 'adversely affect' the protected interest in question. Of some interest is the fact that there is no direct equivalent of legal professional privilege. However, it is possible that the scope of the exemption in Article 4(4)(c) would be capable of covering material which would be subject to legal professional privilege in domestic law. Although there is no guidance on the standard of proof to be applied to the adverse effect requirement, the Implementation Guide points out that the use of the word 'would' before 'adversely affect' requires a greater degree of certainty that the request will have an adverse effect than in other Convention provisions (for example, Article 6(1)(b)).[30]

[30] Ibid, p 86.

In addition, the exemptions are all subject to the following rejoinder at the end of Article 4(4):

> The aforementioned grounds for refusal shall be interpreted in a restrictive way, taking into account the public interest served by disclosure and taking into account whether the information requested relates to emissions into the environment.

Thus there are three relevant considerations for a public authority seeking to apply one of the Article 4(4) exemptions: first, they must be interpreted restrictively; secondly, the public interest in disclosure must be taken into account; and, thirdly, it is relevant (presumably in favour of disclosure, although this is not explicitly stated) whether the information relates to environmental emissions. Each of those three factors narrows the scope for application of an Article 4(4) exemption. In its findings in ACCC/C/2007/21 (European Community), the Compliance Committee commented on the requirements for a strict interpretation and the operation of the public interest in response to an attempt to rely on the exception in Article 4(4)(d). At paragraph 30(c), it held that:

> The Committee wishes to point out that this exemption may not be read as meaning that public authorities are only required to release environmental information where no harm to the interests concerned is identified. Such a broad interpretation of the exemption would not be in compliance with article 4, paragraph 4, of the Convention which requires interpreting exemptions in a restrictive way, taking into account the public interest served by disclosure. Thus, in situations where there is a significant public interest in disclosure of certain environmental information and a relatively small amount of harm to the interests involved, the Convention would require disclosure.[31]

The individual categories of exception are dealt with in more detail below.

Proceedings of Public Authorities

There is no guidance on the scope of the term 'proceedings' in the Convention. However, it is most likely to apply to the internal processes of such authorities, rather than their interactions with the outside world through their statutory powers.[32] Otherwise, the exception would cover an excessively broad range of material. The exception has to be provided for under national law.

International Relations, National Defence or Public Security

This exception covers well-established areas of high policy. There is no definition of the terms in the Convention. The Implementation Guide suggests that the terms will fall to be interpreted by reference to their 'generally accepted meaning' in international law.[33]

[31] See also the discussion in the Implementation Guide (n 13) at p 91 on the interaction between the Convention and the public interest tests in the EU's Transparency Regulation (Regulation 1049/2001) and Aarhus Regulation (Regulation 1367/2006).

[32] This is also the view expressed in the Implementation Guide (n 13) p 86.

[33] Ibid, p 86.

Course of Justice, Fair Trial Rights, Public Authority Criminal or Disciplinary Enquiries

This wide exception covers three aspects of what could broadly be described as the administration of justice: the course of justice, the ability of a person to receive a fair trial or the ability of a public authority to conduct an enquiry of a criminal or disciplinary nature. The course of justice will relate to proceedings which are on-going, rather than historic litigation.[34] The reference to the right to a fair trial, whilst not developed further in the Convention, would be likely to be interpreted in light of the guarantees under domestic law. In the United Kingdom, that would cover both common law principles of natural justice and the rights enshrined in Article 6 of the European Convention on Human Rights (the 'ECHR'), by virtue of the Human Rights Act 1998. The reference to local authority enquiries of a criminal and disciplinary nature raises questions of classification of proceedings and penalties under domestic law.[35]

Confidentiality of Commercial and Industrial Information

This category of exception protects the confidentiality of commercial and industrial information, whether held by private or public bodies. Its breadth of application is narrowed in three important respects. First, the confidentiality must be protected by law. Thus there must be an identifiable legal basis in national law on which to base a claim to the exception. The exception does not provide a new free-standing basis for non-disclosure but rather preserves any such protection recognised in law. Secondly, non-disclosure must be required to protect a 'legitimate economic interest'. There is no further guidance in the Convention as to what might constitute a 'legitimate' interest (or, for that matter, what constitutes an 'economic' interest). The legitimacy of any claimed economic interest is likely to be a source of future litigation and disagreement. The Implementation Guide gives the interesting example of enterprises operating monopolies, such as certain State-run enterprises, being unable to claim the exception because they have no competitors: disclosure of information could not cause an adverse effect, because there is no other party who could take advantage of the information.[36] Thirdly, the exception does not cover information on emissions which is relevant to the environment. Such information must still be disclosed. This final 'exception to the exception' implies that there is information on emissions which is not relevant to the environment and

[34] See Ibid, p 87.

[35] The classification of such matters in relation to the guarantees under Article 6 ECHR has been subject to much litigation in the European Court of Human Rights: see, for example, *Engel v Netherlands* (1976) 1 EHRR 647, paragraph 81.

[36] Implementation Guide (n 13) p 88. This is an increasingly rare situation in the United Kingdom, but still common in some other Convention States. Although there is a logic to the Guide's analysis, the scope of 'adverse effect' is not defined by the Convention and it is possible that a State-run enterprise could still be adversely affected by disclosure for other reasons.

which could still be disclosed. In practice, it is difficult to conceive of what such information might cover. As to the meaning of 'emissions' for this exception, the Implementation Guide refers to the definition in Article 3(4) of Directive 2010/75/EU,[37] the Industrial Emissions Directive, which covers 'direct or indirect release of substances, vibrations, heat or noise from individual or diffuse sources in the installation into air, water or land'.[38]

Intellectual Property Rights

Although the absence of any express restriction on the scope of the intellectual property rights to which this exception applies suggests that such matters will be determined by national law, the Compliance Committee has found breaches of Article 4 where domestic law applies such rights too broadly. In ACCC/C/2005/15 (Romania), the Compliance Committee considered a complaint that Romanian domestic law recognised the intellectual property in an environmental impact assessment ('EIA') report of its author. Publication was prohibited without the author's express consent. The Committee held that since EIA studies were prepared for the public file in an administrative procedure, their authors should not be able to prevent disclosure on the grounds of intellectual property rights: paragraph 28. The application of intellectual property laws to such studies in some countries 'by no means' justified a general prohibition on disclosure: paragraph 29. The Committee continued, at paragraph 30:

> Therefore, the Committee doubts very much that this exemption could ever be applicable in practice in connection with EIA documentation. Even if it could be, the grounds for refusal are to be interpreted in a restrictive way, taking into account the public interest served by disclosure. Decisions on exempting parts of the information from disclosure should themselves be clear and transparent as to the reasoning for non-disclosure. Furthermore, disclosure of EIA studies in their entirety should be considered as the rule, with the possibility for exempting parts of them being an exception to the rule. A general exemption of EIA studies from disclosure is therefore not in compliance with article 4, paragraph 1, in conjunction with article 4, paragraph 4, and article 6, paragraph 6, in conjunction with article 4, paragraph 4, of the Convention.[39]

Confidential Personal Data

Article 4(4)(f) provides an exception where disclosure would adversely affect the confidentiality of personal data and/or files relating to a natural person, where

[37] Directive 2010/75/EU on industrial emissions (integrated pollution prevention and control) (recast) [2010] OJ L334/17.

[38] Implementation Guide (n 13) p 88.

[39] In its decision on submission ACCC/S/2004/01 (Romania) and complaint ACCC/C/2004/03 (Ukraine), the Committee considered a complaint about a refusal of access to EIA reports on the grounds that they were the property of the developer. It held, at paragraph 31, that 'The issue of ownership is not of relevance in this matter, as information is used in decision-making by a public authority and should be provided to it for that purpose by the developer.'

that person has not consented to the disclosure of the information to the public and where such confidentiality is provided for by national law. The exception can be waived by an individual, but the terms of the exception suggest that a person could consent to limited disclosure of the data to particular bodies or other individuals without waiving his right to rely on it against the public at large. As with some of the other exceptions, there is a need for the confidentiality in the data and/or files to be recognised by national law.

Third Party Interests

The purpose of this exception is to 'encourage the free flow of information from private persons to the government'.[40] It is engaged where a person voluntarily provided the information requested without being legally obliged to do so. Furthermore, the person must have refused consent to its disclosure to the public.

The Environment to which the Information Relates

This exception operates as a safeguard for the environment and applies where the disclosure of the requested information would adversely affect the environment to which the information relates. The exception includes a single example: the breeding sites of rare species. The purpose of the exception is to protect the environment from exploitation through the provision of information.

The possibility of redaction and partial disclosure of documents is expressly covered by Article 4(6). Public authorities are required to ensure that, where information exempt under Article 4(3)(c) or (4) is capable of being 'separated out without prejudice to the confidentiality of the information exempted', they make available the remainder of the environmental information which has been requested. It will be necessary in each such case to evaluate whether the disclosure of non-exempt information would be likely to cause prejudice to the maintenance of the exemption in relation to the remaining information. Relevant considerations in that regard are likely to be whether the non-exempt information would indirectly identify the exempt information or reveal its nature or harm the underlying interest protected by the particular exemption.

Article 4(7) provides details of the means of refusal. Where the authority refuses a request, the refusal must be in writing but only if the request was in writing or the applicant so requests. The refusal must include reasons and give information on the Article 9 review procedure. Mirroring the requirement to provide information as soon as possible and at the latest within one month in Article 4(2) (unless the complexity of the request justifies an extension up to a total of two months), Article 4(7) provides for a refusal to take place in the same timeframe. Again, as with Article 2(2), the applicant is to be informed of any extension and the reasons for it.[41]

40 Implementation Guide (n 13) p 89.

41 For an example of a finding of non-compliance with Article 4(7), see ACCC/C/2008/30 (Moldova).

Article 4(8) allows States Parties to the Convention to permit their public authorities to charge for the provision of information, such charges not exceeding 'a reasonable amount'. Where authorities intend to make such charges, they are required to make available to applicants a schedule of charges, indicating the circumstances in which they may be levied or waived and when the supply of information will be conditional on advance payment of a charge.

The requirement that any charge shall not exceed a 'reasonable' amount is an important one. In ACCC/C/2008/24 (Spain), the Spanish authorities were censured for having imposed a charge of around €2 per sheet (scheduled charges ranged from €2.05 and €2.15 per sheet). Plans cost a further €10 each to copy. The case concerned a planning application; the cost of copying non-planning materials in the authority concerned was much lower and the cost in the region concerned (Murcia) was only €0.03 per sheet. The Committee had regard to the case-law of the CJEU and the UK Information Tribunal in deciding whether the charges were reasonable.[42] Unsurprisingly, at paragraphs 77–79, it concluded that they were not. It was striking in that case that, as noted above, the applicant had reduced the scope of its request following the imposition of such high charges. Thus it could genuinely be said that the charges had had a negative impact on access to justice.

Article 5

Article 5 is entitled 'Collection and Dissemination of Environmental Information' and sets out the 'active' environmental information requirement. It is a highly prescriptive provision which includes measures to ensure that public authority information systems are effective in providing publicly accessible information, including the progressive provision of information on 'electronic databases which are easily accessible to the public through public telecommunications networks': Article 5(3). It also includes provision for each State Party to publish and disseminate a national report on the state of the environment at regular intervals not exceeding three or four years. The Article 5 provisions are without prejudice to the exemptions in Article 4(3) and (4).

[42] The Committee considered Case C-217/97 *Commission v Germany* [1999] ECR I-5087, concerning Directive 90/313 in fn 8 to paragraph 77 of its communication. The Committee relied on paragraph 47 of the *Germany* case where the CJEU had held that 'any interpretation of what constitutes "a reasonable cost" for the purpose of [Directive 90/313] which may have the result that persons are dissuaded from seeking to obtain information or which may restrict their right of access to information must be rejected. [...] consequently, the term "reasonable" for the purposes of Article 5 of the Directive must be understood as meaning that it does not authorise the Member States to pass on to those seeking information the entire amount of the costs, in particular indirect ones, actually incurred for the State budget in conducting an information search.' In fn 9 to paragraph 77, the Committee noted the decision of the UK Information Tribunal in *David Markinson v Information Commissioner* (EA/2005/0014, 14 March 2006), where the Tribunal had held: 'the Council should adopt as a guide price the sum of 10p per A4 sheet, as identified in the good practice guidance on access to and charging for planning information published by the Office of the Deputy Prime Minister and as recommended by the DCA ... The Council should be free to exceed that guide price figure only if it can demonstrate that there is a good reason for it to do so.'

The primary obligation in relation to the collection and dissemination of environmental information in Article 5 is Article 5(1) which provides that:

> Each party shall ensure that:
>
> (a) Public authorities possess and update environmental information which is relevant to their functions;
> (b) Mandatory systems are established so that there is an adequate flow of information to public authorities about proposed and existing activities which may significantly affect the environment;
> (c) In the event of any imminent threat to human health or the environment, whether caused by human activities or due to natural causes, all information which could enable the public to take measures to prevent or mitigate harm arising from the threat and is held by a public authority is disseminated immediately and without delay to members of the public who may be affected.

'Environmental information' is defined in Article 2(3). However, the scope of the Article 5(1)(a) obligation is limited only to that environmental information which is 'relevant' to the functions of public authorities. Thus, to take the example provided by the Implementation Guide, a water authority would be expected to possess and update information concerning water resources but not necessarily air emissions data.[43] The requirement to 'possess' such information will necessarily mean that the authority 'holds' it for the purposes of Article 4.

The means of possessing and updating such information is not expressly covered by the Convention. The Implementation Guide suggests that signatory states should establish systems to ensure a regular flow of information from operators, monitoring systems, researchers and others to the responsible public authorities.[44] There is an obvious overlap with the requirements of Article 5(1)(b) which requires mandatory systems to be established to ensure an 'adequate flow' of information to public authorities about 'proposed and existing activities which may significantly affect the environment'. However, the requirement of Article 5(1)(a) is, on its face, a broader one: the information which authorities must possess and update is environmental information relevant to their functions; Article 5(1)(b) refers to a narrower category of information because of the two qualifications that relate to 'proposed and existing' activities and that those activities 'may significantly affect the environment'. Nonetheless, compliance with the obligation in Article 5(1)(b) is likely to go a long way to ensuring compliance with Article 5(1)(a).

The 'mandatory systems' envisaged by Article 5(1)(b) could include mandatory monitoring and research programmes, or mandatory systems of self-monitoring and record keeping on emissions.[45] Where monitoring responsibilities are delegated to specialised agencies, there may be a question as to whether those bodies are 'public authorities' for the purposes of Article 2(2)(b) or (c).[46]

[43] Implementation Guide (n 13) p 97.
[44] In ACCC/C/2012/68 (EU and UK), the Committee noted, at paragraph 88, the use of a '*carbon calculator*' at a wind farm as a means of collecting data.
[45] Implementation Guide (n 13) p 97.
[46] The Implementation Guide suggests that they will be public authorities insofar as they meet the requirements of the definition thereof in Article 2.

In the UK, such systems are commonly imposed by way of conditions attached to planning permissions and environmental permits. Such mechanisms are expressly recognised by the Implementation Guide.[47] In particular, the Compliance Committee has held that, at a minimum Article 5(1) covers EIA studies in their entirety, including specific methodologies of assessment and modelling techniques used in their preparation.[48]

The concept of 'significantly affect' in Article 5(1)(b) is not further defined in the Convention. In the absence of any qualification that the effect must be adverse, it is clear that either a negative or a positive effect would suffice for the purposes of Article 5(1)(b). As a guide to the concept of 'significance', the Implementation Guide refers to both the Espoo Convention and the EIA Directive.[49]

Article 5(1)(c) requires the public to be informed in the event of environmental emergencies. The trigger for such an information exercise is the existence of an 'imminent threat' to human health or the environment.[50] Thus, actual harm is not required. Information enabling the public to take measures to prevent or mitigate harm must be disseminated 'immediately and without delay'. It must be made available to the members of the public who may be affected.

Article 5(2) relates to the manner in which environmental information is made available to the public. It must be transparent and effectively accessible. 'Effectively accessible' is described in the Implementation Guide as meaning that:[51]

> [T]he established information systems should go beyond simply making the information available to the public. Records, databases and documents may be considered effectively accessible when, for example, the public can easily search within them for specific

[47] Ibid, p 98.

[48] ACCC/C/2005/15 (Romania) at paragraph 27.

[49] The reference to the Espoo Convention is to the United Nations Economic Commission for Europe ('UNECE') Convention on Environmental Impact Assessment in a Transboundary Context; the reference to the EIA Directive is to Directive 2011/92/EU [2012] OJ L26/1, amended by Directive 2014/52/EU [2014] OJ L124/1. Article 6, paragraph 1 of Appendix III to the Espoo Convention identifies the criteria of size, location and effects as indicators of whether an activity is likely to have a significant adverse transboundary impact. Annex III to the EIA Directive identifies characteristics of the project, location of the project and characteristics of the potential impact for determining whether a proposed activity should be subject to EIA.

[50] The requirement to provide information in circumstances involving a risk to human health or the environment has been recognised in other international regimes. In international law, the UNECE Industrial Accidents Convention includes provisions on access to information, public participation and access to justice. Article 9(1), (2) and (3) contain similar protection to Article 5(1)(c) of the Aarhus Convention. In Guerra v Italy (1998) 26 EHRR 357, the European Court of Human Rights found that, by failing to provide timely information on the risk of accidents at a fertilizer factory, Italy breached the applicant's rights under Article 8 of the European Convention on Human Rights. However, it held that the freedom to receive information in Article 10(2) did not include a positive obligation on the state to collect and disseminate information of its own motion. At the EU level, a series of directives have covered major accident hazards of certain industrial activities: see, for example, the series of directives stemming from the Seveso accident of 1976, most recently Directive 2012/18/EU on the control of major-accident hazards involving dangerous substances, amending and subsequently repealing Council Directive 96/82/EC [2012] OJ L197/1.

[51] Implementation Guide (n 13) p 101. At p 100, the Guide states that 'within the framework of national legislation' means both that the obligations and mechanisms in Article 5(2) must have been transposed into their national laws and also that the States Parties have some flexibility over implementation.

pieces of information, or when the public has easy access through convenient office hours, locations, equipment such as copy machines, etc.

The various subparagraphs of Article 5(2) set out the different ways in which States Parties must ensure that information is transparent and effectively accessible. Subparagraph (a) includes a requirement for 'meta-information'—information about information. The public must be provided with 'sufficient information' about the type and scope of information that is held, the basic terms and conditions under which it is made available and accessible and the process by which it can be obtained. The means of doing so contemplated by the Implementation Guide are information publications, announcements in government publications, announcements on government websites, television or radio public service announcements or as part of environmental information catalogues.[52]

Subparagraph (b) requires the establishment and maintenance of practical arrangements. The examples set out in this provision are publicly accessible lists, registers of files (subparagraph (a)(i)), requiring officials to support the public in seeking access to information under the Convention (subparagraph (a)(ii)) and the identification of points of contact (subparagraph (a)(iii)). By subparagraph (c), the States Parties must provide access to the environmental information in the lists, registers or files in subparagraph (b)(i) free of charge. This is in contrast to Article 4(8), whereby public authorities are allowed to make a reasonable charge for supplying information. There is thus a distinction in terms of the costs regime between supplying environmental information and providing access to it.

Article 5(3) requires that States Parties shall progressively make environmental information available in electronic databases which are 'easily available to the public through public telecommunications networks'. The Convention thus recognises the increasing importance of electronic databases and the internet in ensuring ready access to information. Article 5(3) suggests certain types of specified information that should be available in this way without imposing an absolute obligation to do so: reports on the state of the environment as referred to in Article 5(4); texts of legislation on or relating to the environment; as appropriate, policies, plans and programmes on or relating to the environment, and environmental agreements; and other information, to the extent that the availability of such information in this form would facilitate the application of national law implementing the Convention. Importantly, the obligation only exists to the extent that such information is already available in electronic form. The Convention does not, therefore, require States Parties to put environmental information held in other forms into an electronic form. The Implementation Guide suggests that the purpose of this final provision is 'to avoid imposing on public authorities an obligation to scan or type in handwritten or oral

[52] Implementation Guide (n 13) p 102.

submissions from the public as well as older documents that might not exist in electronic form'.[53]

Article 5(4) requires the publication and dissemination at regular intervals of a national report on the state of the environment. The wording of Article 5(4) is particularly unusual as regards timing: the reports must be produced 'at regular intervals not exceeding three or four years'. If publication at four-yearly intervals is sufficient to meet the requirements of Article 5(4) it is not clear what the reference to three years really adds (apart, perhaps, from suggesting that the publication should be more regular if possible). Provided they are already available in electronic form, Article 5(3) will require that they progressively be made available in electronic databases easily accessible to the public through public telecommunications networks.

Article 5(5) includes a specific dissemination requirement to the public at large. Three categories of document are listed but the use of the words '*inter alia*' makes clear that they are not exhaustive: legislation and policy documents such as documents on strategic policies, programmes and action plans relating to the environment, and progress reports on their implementation, prepared at various levels of government (subparagraph (a)); international treaties, conventions and agreements on environmental issues (subparagraph (b)); and other significant international documents on environmental issues as appropriate (subparagraph (c)). The obligation is similar to that in Article 5(1)(c) relating to imminent threats to human health or the environment, but is broader in so far as it exists vis-à-vis the public at large and concerns a wider category of information. Subparagraph (a) needs to be seen in the context also of the requirements of Articles 7 and 8, which concern public participation in plans, programmes, policies, law-making and rule-making. The Implementation Guide suggests that the use of the term 'relating to the environment' arguably includes a broader range of information 'such as policies on transport, energy, agriculture or mining as these relate to the environment through their impacts or otherwise'.[54]

Whereas Article 5(1) concerns the establishment of systems to ensure the flow of environmental information from those carrying out activities which impact on the environment to public authorities, Article 5(6) obliges 'operators whose activities have a significant impact on the environment' to inform the public directly of the environmental impact of their activities and products. There is no definition of 'operators'. The Implementation Guide suggests that it 'can be a

[53] Implementation Guide (n 13) p 107. The Guide also stresses, at p 106, that 'It is important that the electronic versions do not replace other forms of the same information, as computers and public telecommunications networks are not readily accessible to all members of the public in every country. The wholesale replacement of traditional forms of information storage might not satisfy the requirement that information should be truly accessible to the public, at least in the short term.'

[54] Implementation Guide (n 13) p 109. At EU level, there is the EU Eco-Management and Audit Scheme ('EMAS') governed by Regulation (EC) 1221/2009 on the voluntary participation by organisations in a Community eco-management and audit scheme (EMAS) [2009] OJ L342/1. Details of the Scheme are set out in the Implementation Guide at p 111.

private enterprise or governmental body that conducts activities with a significant impact on the environment'.[55] Such information must be provided regularly. The Convention recognises that some countries already have voluntary systems for the provision of this type of information to the public, with the references to 'eco-labelling' and 'eco-auditing'. The Implementation Guide defines these practices as follows:[56]

> Eco-labelling is a system that includes information about the environmental impacts of the process for manufacturing a product and the contents of the product directly on the label…
>
> Eco-auditing is a system that reports on environmentally relevant information about the inputs, processes and outputs of a manufacturing activity.

Article 5(7) requires States Parties to publish information that helps the public understand the functioning and background of governmental decision-making on the environment. It covers:

1) Facts and analyses of facts which are considered relevant and important in framing major environmental policy proposals (subparagraph (a));
2) Available explanatory material on dealing with the public in matters falling within the scope of the Convention (subparagraph (b)); and
3) Information on the performance of public functions or the provision of public services relating to the environment by government at all levels (subparagraph (c)).

The word 'facts' in subparagraph (a) could include 'factual information like water and air quality data, natural resource use statistics etc', while 'analyses of facts' could cover 'cost-benefit analyses, EIAs and other analytical information used in framing proposals and decisions'.[57]

Article 5(8) deals with product information and requires the States Parties to develop mechanisms with a view to ensuring that sufficient such information is made available to the public in a manner which enables consumers to make informed environmental choices. One means of doing so is eco-labelling, as mentioned in Article 5(6).[58]

Article 5(9) requires the establishment of pollution inventories or registers. Such records are often referred to as a 'pollutant release and transfer register' ('PRTR'). The records must be on a 'structured, computerized and publicly accessible database', compiled through standardised reporting. The records may include inputs, releases and transfers of a specified range of substances and products, including water, energy and resource use, from a specified range of activities to environmental media and to on-site and off-site treatment and

[55] Ibid, p110.
[56] Ibid, p 110.
[57] Ibid, p 112.
[58] The Implementation Guide also refers to establishing codes of conduct and the IS 14021 standard on self-declared environmental claims.

disposal sites. The obligation in Article 5(9) is subject to the requirement in Article 10(2)(i), whereby States Parties undertook to review their experiences in implementing the provision at their first meeting. They were required to consider what steps were necessary to develop further the Article 5(9) system, taking account of international processes and developments, including 'the elaboration of an appropriate instrument concerning pollution release and transfer registers or inventories which could be annexed to this Convention'. This resulted in the adoption of the Protocol on PRTRs at the Fifth EfE Ministerial Conference in Kiev, in May 2003, at an extraordinary session of the Meeting of the Parties. It came into force on 8 October 2009.

Finally, Article 5(10) makes clear that the obligations in Article 5 are without prejudice to the right of Parties to refuse to disclose certain environmental information in accordance with Article 4(3) and (4). However, as the Implementation Guide makes clear, there may be certain circumstances, particularly concerning imminent threats to human health and the environment, where the public interest in dissemination under Article 5(1)(c) will override any grounds for refusing disclosure under Article 4.[59]

[59] Ibid, p 117.

7

Public Participation in Environmental Decision-Making, Plan-Making and Executive Regulations—Articles 6, 7 and 8 of the Aarhus Convention

SIMON RICKETTS[1] AND JULIET MUNN[2]

Introduction

Articles 6, 7 and 8 of the Aarhus Convention ('the Convention') form the Second Pillar of the Convention and set minimum standards that Parties (ie Member States) must apply in ensuring that there is adequate public participation in environmental decision-making. Article 6 applies to consenting procedures for specified types of projects. Article 7 applies to plans, programmes and policies which relate to the environment. Article 8 applies to executive regulations and legally binding instruments.

A large number of complaints received by the Aarhus Convention Compliance Committee ('ACCC') arise from alleged breaches of Articles 6 and/or 7. The public participation principles embodied in these two articles overlap in some respects with common law principles in relation to lawful consultation.[3] They also overlap with EU requirements in relation to Environmental Impact Assessment ('EIA') and Strategic Environmental Assessment ('SEA') which are part of the EU's implementation of its own obligations under the Convention.

[1] Partner, King Wood & Mallesons LLP, London.
[2] Associate, King Wood & Mallesons LLP, London.

[3] The common law principles require that: (a) consultation is undertaken while proposals are still at their formative stage; (b) adequate information is provided to allow consultees to properly respond; (c) adequate time is allowed for consultees to properly respond; and (d) conscientious consideration is given to the responses to the consultation. See *R v North and East Devon Health Authority ex parte Coughlan* [2001] QB 213. In *The Bard Campaign and David Bliss v Secretary of State for Communities and Local Government* [2009] EWHC 308(Admin) Walker J observed, with apparent approval, that the claimants had not suggested that these principles were inconsistent with Articles 6–7 of the Aarhus Convention.

Article 6 sets out a series of requirements which must be met when the Article is engaged. The requirements of paragraphs 3, 4 and 8 of Article 6 also apply to Article 7. This chapter first sets out the types of decision which must meet the requirements of Article 6 or 7 respectively and then takes in turn each of the respective public participation requirements. Finally, we address Article 8, which is so far the lesser known sibling of Articles 6 and 7.

Is Article 6 or Article 7 Engaged?

Article 6 applies to decisions on 'specific activities' whilst Article 7 applies to plans, programmes and policies, in both instances relating to the environment.

The ACCC has expressed the view that it is the legal function and effect of a decision which will establish whether the decision falls within Article 6 or Article 7, rather than its label in domestic legislation.[4] For example, what was described as a detailed plan for the establishment of a landfill site under Lithuanian law was treated by the ACCC as a decision under Article 6 rather than Article 7[5] as a result of its practical effect.

Specific Activities (Article 6)

Article 6 of the Convention is implemented in the EU through Directive 2011/92/EU *on the assessment of the effects of certain public and private projects on the environment* (the 'EIA Directive')[6] and Directive 2008/1/EC *on integrated pollution prevention and control* (the 'IPPC Directive').[7] In England and Wales these Directives are implemented into national legislation through a variety of Regulations which reflect the public participation requirements set out in the Directives.

The 'specific activities' to which Article 6 refers are listed in Annex I of the Convention.[8] A full list of these activities is set out at Appendix 1. There is an overlap between the activities listed in Annex I of the Convention and those in Annex I of the EIA Directive, although the two are not identical (with Annex I of the Convention being wider, with more specific thresholds, than Annex 1 of the EIA Directive). For example, both pieces of legislation list thermal power stations as activities, yet the Directive requires the heat output to be 300 megawatts or more whereas the Convention only requires a minimum output of 50 megawatts.

[4] ACCC/C/2005/12 (Albania).
[5] ACCC/2006/16 (Lithuania).
[6] [2012] OJ L26/1.
[7] [2008] OJ L24/8.
[8] See Appendix 1 of this book.

Section 20 of Annex I of the Aarhus Convention states that the definition of Specific Activities will include:

> Any activity not covered by paragraphs 1–19 above where public participation is provided for under an environmental impact assessment procedure in accordance with national legislation.

Therefore, even if an activity is not covered by Annex I of the Convention, if EIA would be required under national legislation, then the relevant decision-making procedure must be compliant with Article 6.

The ambit of Article 6 is also widened by Article 6(1)(b), which states that each Party:

> shall in accordance, with its national law, also apply the provisions of this article to decisions on proposed activities not listed in Annex I which may have a significant effect on the environment. To this end, Parties shall determine whether such a proposed activity is subject to these provisions.

Whether a project will be caught by this provision will therefore depend on (i) its likely environmental impact and (ii) on whether the project is subject to public participation under national legislation. The ACCC has interpreted the second limb of this test to require an explicit reference to Article 6 in domestic legislation or that the provisions of Article 6 'be reflected in one way or another in the domestic legalisation in respect of activities not listed in Annex I of the Convention'[9] in respect of activities not covered in Annex I. In ACCC/C/2008/35 (Georgia) the ACCC held that the fact that Georgian legislation contained general provisions on public participation was not sufficient to engage Article 6(1)(b) in respect of a specific decision to grant long-term forest licences.

Article 6(1)(c) states that activities relating to national defence can be excluded on a case by case basis, if the need for compliance would have an adverse effect on the purpose of the activity.

Plan or Programme (Article 7)

The Convention does not define either 'plan' or 'programme'. However these terms are also set out in Directive 2001/42/EC *on the assessment of the effects of certain plans and programmes on the environment* ('the SEA Directive')[10] which is implemented in England and Wales through the Environmental Assessment of Plans and Programmes Regulations 2004 ('the SEA Regulations').[11] The ACCC has drawn upon the SEA Directive, and guidance on its interpretation, when defining 'plans' under Article 7.[12]

[9] ACCC/C.2008/95 (Georgia).
[10] [2001] OJ L197/30.
[11] SI 2004/1633.
[12] ACCC/C/2005/12 (Albania).

The purpose of the SEA Directive, as described in Article 1, is to:

> provide for a high level of protection of the environment and to contribute to the integration of environmental considerations into the preparation and adoption of plans and programmes with a view to promoting sustainable development, by ensuring that, in accordance with this Directive, an environmental assessment is carried out of certain plans and programmes which are likely to have significant effects on the environment.

'Plans and programmes' are defined in Article 2(a) of the SEA Directive (transposed in England and Wales by Reg 2(1) of the SEA Regulations) as follows:

> 'plans and programmes' shall mean plans and programmes, including those co-financed by the European Community, as well as any modifications to them:
>
> which are subject to preparation and/or adoption by an authority at national, regional or local level or which are prepared by an authority for adoption, through a legislative procedure by Parliament or Government, andwhich are required by legislative, regulatory or administrative provisions.

The European Commission SEA Guidance: Implementation of Directive 2001/42 on the Assessment of the effects of certain plans and programmes on the environment ('the Commission SEA Guidance') states at paragraphs 3.3 to 3.4 that, in identifying whether a proposal constitutes a plan or programme for the purposes of the SEA Directive, a broad approach should be used in the light of the wide scope of the SEA Directive and that 'that the terms should be taken to cover any formal statement which goes beyond aspirations and sets out an intended course of future action'. At paragraph 3.5, the Commission SEA Guidance advises that the concept of a 'plan' could include a document 'which sets out how the authority proposes to carry out or implement a scheme or policy', which could include 'laying down rules or guidance as to the kind of development which might be appropriate or permissible in particular areas'. Paragraph 3.6 advises that 'programmes' are usually thought of as 'a plan covering a set of projects in a given area, such as a scheme for regeneration of an urban area, comprising a number of separate construction projects'.

The definition of 'plan or programme' has been considered in the European and UK Courts. In particular, the Court of Justice of the European Union (the 'CJEU') discussed the meaning of the second limb of Article 2(a) SEA Directive in *Inter-Environnement Bruxelles ASBL v Région de Bruxelles-Capitale*[13] and specifically as to whether

> the word 'required' in Article 2(a) of that directive be understood as excluding from the definition of 'plans and programmes' plans which are provided for by legislative provisions but the adoption of which is not compulsory...?

The CJEU held that decisions which are regulated by law but whose adoption is not compulsory in all circumstances, may meet the definition of the 'plan or programme' under the SEA Directive.

[13] Case C-567/10 *Inter-Environnement Bruxelles ASBL v Région de Bruxelles-Capitale* [2012] 2 CMLR 30.

It is important to note however that Article 3 of the SEA Directive states that 'an environmental assessment [...] shall be carried out for plans and programmes [...] which are likely to have significant environmental effects'. This is narrower than the wording of Article 7 which states that public participation must be sought during the preparation of 'plans and programmes relating to the environment'. Therefore, although the SEA Directive may be of use in identifying a 'plan or programme', its ambit is not as far reaching as that of Article 7 of the Convention.

The ACCC identified this inconsistency in ACCC/C/2006/16 (Lithuania), where it determined, in the context of a waste plan, that in Lithuanian legislation public participation requirements only applied to those plans or programmes which would be subject to SEA. There was no evidence that these requirements extended to other plans and programmes relating to the environment.

The UK Supreme Court considered the definition of 'plan or programme' and the interaction between the SEA Directive and the Convention in the *HS2* case.[14] This case considered the question of whether the UK Government's decision to promote a high speed train line from London to the north of the UK, announced in a 2013 Command Paper entitled 'High Speed Rail: Investing in Britain's Future—Decisions and Next Steps' (the 'DNS') should have been preceded by SEA.

The claimant argued that the DNS was a 'plan or programme' under the SEA Directive as it was 'required' by the 'administrative provisions' within a March 2010 Command Paper. The issue of whether the DNS was a 'plan or programme' was considered at every stage of the proceedings. However, the Supreme Court held that, as a result of finding that the Command Paper did not 'set the framework for future development consent', the issue of whether the DNS was 'required' by the Command Paper did not require a reference to the CJEU.

The Supreme Court in *HS2* was constituted of an enlarged panel of seven Justices.[15] The claimants argued that any plan or programme for the purpose of the Convention must also be a plan or programme for the purposes of the SEA Directive. In this submission they relied on the fact that the Public Participation Directive (Directive 2003/35/EC),[16] which amended European environment legislation to render it compliant with the Convention, did not amend the SEA Directive. This was because it was considered that the SEA Directive was compliant with the public participation requirements of the Convention and therefore did not require amendment.[17]

[14] *R (HS2 Action Alliance Ltd & Others) v Secretary of State for Transport* [2014] 1 WLR 324.

[15] The Supreme Court Rules state that more than five justices should sit on a panel if: the Court is being asked to depart, or may depart, from a previous decision; the case is of high constitutional importance; the case is of great public importance; where there is a conflict between decisions in the House of Lords, Judicial Committee of the Privy Council and/or the Supreme Court has to be reconciled; or a case raising an important point in relation to the European Convention on Human Rights.

[16] [2003] OJ L156/17.

[17] See recital (10) and Article 2(5) Public Participation Directive.

In the Court of Appeal, Lord Justice Sullivan, in his dissenting judgment, stated:

> I am troubled by the conclusion of the Master of the Rolls and Lord Justice Richards that because the DNS does not in their view set the framework for future development consent it is difficult to see how Article 7 of Aarhus can have been intended to apply to it. We know that the Government did, in fact, engage in a comprehensive consultation exercise prior to the adoption of the DNS (see paragraphs 84–109 above). In my judgment, a conclusion that even if there had been no consultation prior to the adoption of the DNS there would have been no breach of Article 7 of Aarhus would not be in accordance with the purposive interpretation of EU environmental legislation that has been consistently adopted by the CJEU.

The Supreme Court, however, disagreed. Lord Carnwath stated:

> [52] To my mind there is a more fundamental objection to Mr Elvin's (Council for the Claimant) argument. There is no reason to assume that article 7 and the SEA Directive are intended to cover exactly the same ground. The differences in wording are clear and must be assumed to be deliberate. Indeed the UNECE guidance on the Convention (The Aarhus Convention: An Implementation Guide 2nd Ed 2013 pp 118–119) accepts that its reference to plans and programmes relating to the environment is broader than the equivalent definition in the SEA Directive. The SEA Directive must be interpreted and applied in its own terms. If this falls short of full compliance with the Aarhus Convention, it does not invalidate the directive so far as it goes. It simply means that a possible breach of the Convention may have to be considered as a separate and additional issue. In the present case the point is academic because no such breach is alleged.

This reasoning follows that given by Attorney General Kokott in her opinion in *Inter-Environnment Bruxelles*:

> [22.] At the hearing, Inter-Environment Bruxelles and Others also relied on the public participation provided for in Article 7 of the Aarhus Convention and Article 2 of Directive 2003/35/EC. Under that Convention, the public is to be given the opportunity to participate in all plans and programmes relating to the environment, but an environmental report is not expressly required. If it were the case that the SEA Directive transposed that international law obligation in its entirety in respect of the European Union, there would be good reason to apply it above and beyond the wording of the SEA Directive, that is to say to all plans and programmes relating to the environment.
>
> [23.] However, the SEA Directive does not contain any indication that it is designed to transpose Article 7 of the Aarhus Convention. Rather, recital 10 in the preamble to Directive 2003/35 shows that, in this regard, the Convention is to be transposed only in relation to plans and programmes under European Union law—more specifically by Directive 2003/35 in relation to certain measures but, in future, by specific rules laid down in the relevant legislative act. Article 2(5) of Directive 2003/35 simply makes it clear that an environmental assessment in accordance with the SEA Directive is sufficient from the point of view of public participation.
>
> [24.] The objectives of Article 7 of the Aarhus Convention do not therefore justify an interpretation of the SEA Directive that is contrary to the recognisable intention of the legislature.

It seems clear therefore that the SEA Directive, by restricting the 'plans and programmes' that it applies to those 'required by legislative, regulatory or administrative provisions' and to those which 'are likely to have significant environmental effects' does not comply with the requirements of the Convention. It remains to be seen how the European Commission will deal with this issue. At the time of writing, the unsuccessful appellants in the *HS2* case have a communication pending before the ACCC in which they allege that, based upon the Supreme Court's approach in that case, the narrower scope of the SEA Directive compared to Article 7 of the Convention means that the EU is in breach of its duty to implement Article 7.[18]

ACCC Decision-Making

The ACCC considered the factual issue of whether a decision falls within Article 6 or Article 7 in the case of ACCC/C/2005/12 (Albania) which concerned a complaint about a series of decisions in relation to a proposed industrial park which was to include oil and gas pipelines, installations for the storage of petroleum, three thermal nuclear power plants and a refinery. The ACCC chose to focus on two decisions, namely Decision 8, which approved the site of the proposed industrial park, and Decision 20 which approved the construction of the proposed thermal electric power station ('TES').

Decision 20 related to activities that are listed in Annex I and designated the site where the specific activities were to take place. It was also clear that subsequent decisions would be needed further to Decision 20 in order to carry out the construction and operation of the TES. Accordingly the ACCC held that on balance, as this decision concerned the carrying on of a specific Annex I activity in a particular place, it was more akin to an Article 6 decision. Decision 8 however was considered to be equivalent to a 'zoning' decision that is, it determined, with a certain degree of formality, that particular activities may be carried out in a defined area, and, was accordingly determined to fall within Article 7.

Examples of decisions that have been held to fall within Article 6 of the Convention include:

(a) a decision to proceed, subject to the necessary permits with the construction of a 110 kv overhead transmissions line in Kazakhstan;[19]
(b) a detailed plan, equivalent to a principal planning permission, setting out the proposed location and the basic parameters of a landfill in Lithuania;[20] and
(c) resolutions taken for the purpose of implementing a project for the construction and management of a plant for the incineration of household waste and associated sorting-methanisation centre in France.[21]

[18] ACCC/C/2014/101 (European Union).
[19] ACCC/C/2004/2 (Kazakhstan).
[20] ACCC/2006/16 (Lithuania).
[21] ACCC/C/2007/22 (France).

Multiple Decisions

In situations where multiple decisions are required to be taken in respect of a project, for example the multiple permit requirements needed for the construction of a power station, the ACCC has held that it does not consider that Article 6 requirements will necessarily apply to each of these decisions. Rather, where one particular permitting decision covers the significant environmental effects of the project, it may be sufficient for public participation to be restricted to this decision. However, if significant environmental effects are dealt with through a variety of permits and decisions, the public participation requirements under Article 6 must be discharged at every stage.[22] See also the discussion below on tiered decision-making.

The Requirements of Article 6

Information to be Provided in an 'Adequate, Timely and Effective Manner'

Article 6(2) of the Convention provides:

> The public concerned should be informed, either by public notice or individually as appropriate, early in the environmental decision-making procedure, and in an adequate, timely and effective manner, inter-alia of:
> (a) The proposed activity and the application on which a decision will be taken;
> (b) The nature of possible decisions or the draft decision;
> (c) The public authority responsible for making the decision;
> (d) The envisaged procedure, including, as and when this information can be provided:
>   (i) The commencement of the procedure;
>   (ii) The opportunities for the public to participate;
>   (iii) The time and venue of any envisaged public hearing;
>   (iv) An indication of the public authority from which relevant information can be obtained and where the relevant information has been deposited for examination by the public;
>   (v) An indication of the relevant public authority or any other official body to which comments or questions can be submitted and of the time schedule for transmittal of comments or questions; and
>   (vi) An indication of what environmental information relevant to the proposed activity is available; and
> (e) The fact that the activity is subject to a national or transboundary environmental impact assessment procedure.

[22] ACCC/C/2006/17 (European Community).

'Public Concerned'

First, the definition of '*public concerned*' includes all those people affected by the particular decision, namely:

> the public affected or likely to be affected by, or having an interest in, the environmental decision-making; for the purposes of this definition, non-governmental organisations promoting environmental protection and meeting the requirements under national law shall be deemed to have an interest (Article 2(5)).

This definition is replicated in the EIA Directive. For example, in ACCC/2004/2 (Kazakhstan) the ACCC held that the residents living along the route of the proposed power line were plainly 'public concerned' and therefore should have received notice of hearings held in respect of the power line.

'Public Notice'

'Public notice' may take a number of forms. Notices in newspapers, on the internet and on television have all been held to meet the definition. However, journalistic articles, either in newspapers or on television, commenting on a particular project or on the relevant decision-making process, will not constitute public notice.[23]

'Early in the Environmental Decision-Making Procedure'

This requirement is discussed in detail in the context of Article 6(4) below.

'Adequate'

In order for a public notice to be 'adequate' it must properly describe the nature of the proposed decision to allow the public to comprehend the information which they are required to assess. Inaccurate notifications, or those that do not provide sufficient information for the public to determine the decisions that are to be made, will not be held to be adequate. For example, in ACCC/C/2006/16 (Lithuania) the public were informed that they could participate in the decision-making procedure in respect of 'development possibilities of waste management in the Vilnius region' rather than that they were being invited to comment on a major landfill site proposed for their neighbourhood. This notice was held not to be adequate.

'Effective'

The ACCC has described 'effective' public consultation as meaning that 'public authorities should seek to provide a means of informing the public which ensures

[23] ACCC/C/2009/37 (Belarus).

that all those who potentially could be concerned have a reasonable chance to learn about proposed activities and their possibilities to participate'.[24] Whether a notice was effective is a factual question. For example, in ACCC/2006/16 (Lithuania) the ACCC held that a notice published in a weekly official journal with a readership of only 500 was ineffective, whereas if the notice had been published in a daily popular newspaper this would have sufficed. In ACCC/C/2009/43 (Armenia) a notice was published in the national newspapers, on the internet and publicised through local TV networks. As the public concerned comprised a small rural community, the ACCC held that there would have been little access to national press or the internet, but the use of local television was sufficient to render the notice effective.

Further, effective public participation does not require a particular number of inquiries or hearings to be heard; rather it is essential that adequate information be provided in relation to them and that they be held in an open and transparent manner. In ACCC/C/2007/22 (France) the ACCC held that, contrary to allegations made, the French Government was not in breach for publishing notice of the public inquiries in two local newspapers and only holding inquiries in three locations, rather than holding them in a number of more varied locations, in respect of a waste disposal plant. As these inquiries were open to all and had been appropriately publicised, these were deemed by the ACCC to have provided adequate and effective forums for public participation.

The ACCC has considered a complaint brought against the European Community by Lithuania in which the complainant accused the European Community of failing correctly to implement Article 6(2) of the Convention through the EIA Directive and IPPC Directive. The ACCC found in favour of the European Community, holding that although neither Directive directly repeats the requirement that information should be provided to the public in an '*adequate, timely and effective manner*', equivalent requirements are contained within the Directives.[25]

Reasonable Time Frames

Article 6(3) of the Convention states that:

> The public participation procedures shall include reasonable time frames for the different phases, allowing sufficient time for informing the public in accordance with paragraph 2 above and for the public to participate effectively during the environmental decision making.

This requirement was considered in detail by the ACCC in Lithuania[26] where it was held that

> the requirement to have 'reasonable time frames' implies that the public should have sufficient time to get acquainted with the documentation and to submit comments taking

[24] ACCC/2006/16 (Lithuania), ACCC/C/2007/22 (France).
[25] ACCC/C/2006/17 (European Community).
[26] ACCC/2006/16 (Lithuania).

into account, inter-alia, the nature, complexity and size of a proposed activity. A time frame which may be reasonable for a small simple project with only local impact may well not be reasonable in case of a major complex project.

Further, the reasonableness requirement applies to both the time frame provided for inspecting documents and that for making comments.

What could be considered a 'reasonable time frame' will be fact specific and will turn on the nature of the proposed development and the volume of documentation. By way of example, the ACCC has previously held that:

(a) 10 working days to review documents in relation to a major landfill was insufficient;[27]
(b) 20 days for consideration of the documents relating to a refinery proposal was not compliant with Article 6(3). This was particularly the case as the information was only available during these 20 days on two computers from which no copies could be made;[28]
(c) one week for the examination of documents in respect of a mining project was not a reasonable time-frame;[29] and
(d) six weeks to allow the public to inspect documents and prepare for a public inquiry in respect of a waste incinerator was sufficient.[30]

The ACCC has also said that a flexible approach to setting deadlines for public participation, in order to allow such deadlines to reflect the size or complexity of the proposed development, is not in itself inconsistent with the requirements of Article 6(3). However, only a minimum period for public participation may be fixed by a Party. Any setting of a maximum timeframe would be likely to be a breach of the Convention[31] as the timeframe chosen may not be appropriate for all decisions.

Public Concerned

For public participation to be effective it is essential that the definition of 'public concerned' is correctly interpreted. The ACCC considered this requirement in a complaint made in respect of the Czech Republic's EIA legislation. In Czech legislation at the EIA stage of any project the relevant legislation provides for public participation. However participation in subsequent decisions, such as permitting decisions, is limited to those who are 'parties' to any proceedings which relate to properties or land use. This excludes the majority of the public, including tenants, from the subsequent decision—making processes. The ACCC found that, as environmental decision—making requirements will extend to the decisions following the EIA process, effective public participation is required at

27 Ibid.
28 ACCC/C/2009/36 (Spain).
29 ACCC/C/2009/43 (Armenia).
30 ACCC/C/2007/22 (France).
31 ACCC/C/2009/37 (Belarus).

each of these subsequent stages, and therefore these restrictions were in breach of the Convention.[32]

Public Participation Should take Place when all Options are Open

Article 6(4) of the Convention states that:

> Each Party shall provide for early public participation, when all options are open and effective public participation can take place.

Article 6(4) needs to be seen in the context of tiered decision-making. That is that 'at each stage of decision-making certain options are discussed and selected with the participation of the public and each consecutive stage of decision-making addresses only the issues within the options already selected at the preceding stage.'[33]

Therefore where, as is often the case, a proposed development will be the subject of sequential decisions (for example in the case of a power plant this might include separate permits for the siting, construction and operation of the plant) there is some flexibility as to when public participation is required. However, the key is that where options have been closed as a result of a previous decision without public participation, participation in relation to a subsequent decision will not rectify this deficiency. This is true even if a full EIA will be carried out at a later stage in relation to the entirety of the development.[34]

Where there has been no public participation at an early stage of a decision-making process, and therefore the scope of any subsequent decision has already been narrowed, it will not be sufficient that there is the technical possibility that options could be re-introduced at a later stage. There must instead be a realistic and practical possibility that this may occur. For example in ACCC/C/2007/22 (France) the ACCC rejected the argument that there had been a breach of Article 6(4) in respect of an application put before the Prefect who, it was claimed by the communicant, could not examine particular aspects of the application. The ACCC held that, as about 50 applications before the Prefect are refused each year in France, the Prefect was neither formally nor informally prevented from refusing the application on procedural or substantive grounds.

Whether all options remain open when public participation takes place will therefore be a matter of fact. For example, that public participation may be sought on the technical aspects of a project after the construction of a project has been completed, or after the permit for construction has been granted, will not automatically lead to a breach of Article 6(4) as long as it is realistic that technological and operational options are still in consideration. However, if political,

32 ACCC/C/2010/50 (Czech Republic).

33 ACCC/2006/16 (Lithuania), ACCC/C/2006/17 (European Community), ACCC/C/2009/38 (United Kingdom).

34 ACCC/C/2009/43 (Armenia).

commercial or design constraints would effectively foreclose the availability of any technical or operational choices, it is unlikely to be considered that these options remain open at the time of the public participation.[35] For example, in ACCC/C/2005/12 (Albania) public participation on the environmental impact of a proposed thermal power station could not be considered to have been carried out when all the options were open. The public had been precluded from having an input on the location of the installation as that decision had been taken previously without adequate public participation.

Applicants to Enter into Discussions with Public Concerned and Provide Requisite Information

Article 6(5) of the Convention states that:

> Each Party should, where appropriate, encourage prospective applicants to identify the public concerned, to enter into discussions and to provide information regarding the objectives of their application before applying for a permit.

It is clear that this Article requires a project promoter to take a proactive approach to public participation in respect of its proposed application. However, the ACCC has held that it is not sufficient for a Party to rely solely on the applicant to ensure compliance with Article 6 as it is implicit throughout the Article that certain information must be provided by, and comments should be returned to, the public authority.[36] This does not mean that the public authority cannot delegate its public participation functions to various bodies, or even individuals, but the ACCC considers that promoters and their consultants will not have the requisite level of independence to comply with the requirements of the Convention. Nevertheless, it will still be appropriate for promoters to be engaged in the public participation process but this must be supplementary to, rather than instead of, the mandatory public authority engagement process.[37]

Examination of Information

Article 6(6) of the Convention states that:

> Each Party shall require the competent public authorities to give the public concerned access for examination, upon request where so required under national law, free of charge and as soon as it becomes available, to all information relevant to the decision-making referred to in this article that is available at the time of the public participation procedure, without prejudice to the right of Parties to refuse to disclose certain

[35] ACCC/C/2008/26 (Austria), ACCC/2006/16 (Lithuania).

[36] ACCC/C/2006/16 (Lithuania).

[37] ACCC/C/2009/37 (Belarus).

information in accordance with article 4, paragraphs 3 and 4. The relevant information shall include at least, and without prejudice to the provisions of article 4:

(a) A description of the site and the physical and technical characteristics of the proposed activity, including an estimate of the expected residues and emissions;
(b) A description of the significant effects of the proposed activity on the environment;
(c) A description of the measures envisaged to prevent and/or reduce the effects, including emissions;
(d) A non-technical summary of the above;
(e) An outline of the main alternatives studied by the applicant; and
(f) In accordance with national legislation, the main reports and advice issued to the public authority at the time when the public concerned shall be informed in accordance with paragraph 2 above.

Article 4 of the Convention, referred to above, sets out requirements for access to environmental information. Article 6(6) differs from Article 4 in that it only requires the provision of the information set out in the Article during the public participation procedure. At any other time the public has to rely on the provisions of Article 4.

The information which is required to be made available under Article 6(4) is not limited to the provision of an environmental statement; it is designed to ensure that the public concerned are well informed about the proposed development, and therefore that any public participation is effective. The ACC has held that the information provided should relate to all of the potential significant effects and should not be limited in any way.[38]

Information requested by the public may be refused in certain circumstances on the basis of intellectual property rights but this exception will be very limited and is unlikely to apply to any EIA information.[39]

The ACCC has held that although Article 6(4) precludes a charge being imposed for the examination of environmental information, this does not prevent a charge being made for the copying of documents.[40]

Opportunity to Submit Comments During the Public Participation Process

Article 6(7) of the Convention states that:

> Procedures for public participation shall allow the public to submit, in writing, or as appropriate, at a public hearing or inquiry with the applicant, any comments, information, analyses or opinions that it considers relevant to the proposed activity.

[38] ACCC/C/2004/2 (Kazakhstan).
[39] ACCC/C/2005/15 (Romania).
[40] ACCC/2008/24 (Spain).

For there to be adequate public participation under Article 6 it is imperative that the public be provided with the means to comment on the proposals which they are being consulted on. The ACCC has held that in situations where this is not possible a Party will be in breach of Article 6. For example in ACCC/2006/16 (Lithuania) the ACCC held that provisions in Lithuanian law which only allowed the public to submit 'motivated proposals' which contain reasoned arguments were in breach of the Convention, whilst in ACCC/C/2009/37 (Belarus) the fact that the public could only comment during the hearing process and that there were no facilities to allow comments to be made directly to the public authority was also inconsistent with the Convention.

Comments must also not be limited to the consideration of environmental impacts of the proposed development. Rather, for the requirements of Article 6(7) to be met, the public must be entitled to submit comments on any aspect of the development that it considers relevant.[41]

Public Comments Must be Taken into Account when Making Decision

Article 6(8) of the Convention states that:

> Each Party shall ensure that in the decision due account is taken of the outcome of the public participation.

In ACCC/2008/24 (Spain) the ACCC held that in its view the requirement under Article 6(8) was quite clear that

> the obligation to take due account in the decision of the outcome of the public participation cannot be considered as a requirement to accept all comments, reservations or opinions submitted. However, while it is impossible to accept in substance all the comments submitted, which may often be conflicting, the relevant authority must still seriously consider all the comments received.

It is also imperative that the decision contains a description of the manner in which comments received from the public were taken into account. This was made clear in ACCC/C/2012/68 (United Kingdom) where the ACCC noted that 'the obligation to take account of the outcome of public participation should be interpreted as the obligation that the written reasoned decision includes a discussion on how the public participation was taken into account'.

It is not sufficient for such comments simply to be disregarded or ignored in the making of the decision. For example, it was held in ACCC/C/2004/3 (Ukraine), that a decision taken one week after the publication of the relevant environmental statement could not have taken into account the comments received in response to the statement.

[41] ACCC/C/2010/50 (Czech Republic).

Informing the Public of Any Decision

Article 6(9) of the Convention states that:

> Each Party shall ensure that, when the decision has been taken by the public authority, the public is promptly informed of the decision in accordance with the appropriate procedures. Each Party shall make accessible to the public the text of the decision along with the reasons and considerations on which the decision is based.

This requirement does not place an obligation on the public authority to publish the decision that is made but, rather, to make the public aware of the decision and to make the decision and the reasons behind the decision accessible to the public. The public authority therefore has to apply its discretion as to how to publicise both its decision and reasons and how to make them accessible. However, in order to be able to comply with this requirement it will first be essential that the public authority actually keep a record of the decision and its reasoning. The ACCC has found that under Belarusian law the lack of a requirement to prepare a statement of reasons in respect of decisions and the lack of any requirement for public authorities to keep any record of such conclusions was a breach of Article 6(9).[42]

The ACCC has determined, in respect of timing, that informing the public of a decision 15 days after it was made may be compliant with Article 6(9) depending on the particular circumstances in each case but that any such time period must be 'reasonable' particularly in light of the access to justice considerations set out at Article 9 of the Convention.[43]

Public Participation Must be Repeated where Operating Conditions are Updated

Article 6(10) of the Convention states that:

> Each party shall ensure that, when a public authority reconsiders or updates the operating conditions for an activity referred to in paragraph 1, the provisions of paragraph 2 to 9 of this article are applied mutatis mutandis, and where appropriate.

This provision requires that public participation in accordance with Article 6 must be repeated where a decision that would be subject to Article 6 is revised, renewed or updated. This includes situations where decisions which were made before the Convention entered into force, but which would have been subject to Article 6, are renewed.[44] The ACCC has stated that, although there is some discretion in Article 6(10) as to when it would be appropriate to submit such decisions to public participation, for the Party does not have absolute discretion to determine whether or not it is appropriate. It must exercise its discretion in the light

[42] ACCC/C (Belarus).
[43] ACCC/2006/16 (Lithuania).
[44] ACCC/C/2009/43 (Armenia).

of the objectives of the Convention and in particular of Article 6.[45] It is also not a defence to a breach of Article 10 that the updated decision would contain stricter environmental conditions than the original decision.[46]

Genetically Modified Organisms

Article 6(11) of the Convention states that:

> Each Party shall, within the framework of its national law, apply, to the extent feasible and appropriate, provisions of this article to decisions on whether to permit the deliberate release of genetically modified organisms into the environment.

This Article does not appear to have been considered by the ACCC as yet.

The Requirements of Article 7

Article 7 of the Convention provides:

> Each Party shall make appropriate practical and/or other provisions for the public to participate during the preparation of plans and programmes relating to the environment, within a transparent and fair framework, having provided the necessary information to the public. Within this framework, article 6, paragraphs 3, 4 and 8, shall be applied. The public which may participate shall be identified by the relevant public authority, taking into account the objectives of this Convention. To the extent appropriate, each Party shall endeavour to provide opportunities for public participation in the preparation of policies relating to the environment.

The requirements that must be met when considering a decision that would fall within Article 7 will be identically applied to those which fall under the relevant paragraphs of Article 6, discussed above. The case law on such requirements will be applicable under either article.

The UK was recently found to be in a breach of Article 7.[47] This concerned the June 2010 adoption of the UK's National Renewable Energy Action Plan ('NREAP') which Member States were required to publish under the Renewable Energy Directive (Directive 2009/28/EC).[48] The complainant alleged that the adoption of the NREAP was in breach of Article 7 as:

> The plan was approved in a 'fast track' manner in spite of unresolved environmental issues, thus precluding open and effective public participation early, when all options were open. [... and]

[45] ACCC/C/209/41 (Slovakia).

[46] Ibid.

[47] ACCC/C/2012/68 (United Kingdom).

[48] Directive 2009/28/EC of the European Parliament and of the Council of 23 April 2009 on the promotion of the use of energy from renewable sources and amending and subsequently repealing Directives 2001/77/EC and 2003/30/EC [2009] OJ L140/16.

> [the] Authorities failed to take due account of the outcome of public participation, as evidenced by the one-page only document of comments, that ignored a significant number of informed submissions critical of the authorities' assessment of renewable potential.

The ACCC found that NREAPs are plans or programmes under Article 7 and that, as a result of the failure of the UK Government properly to consult on the adoption of the NREAP, it was in breach. The ACCC went on to state that the fact that the UK's Renewable Energy Strategy, which informed the NREAP, was subject to public participation did not rectify this breach given their different legal status and functions in the EU and UK legal frameworks respectively.

A further communication against the UK alleging a breach of Article 7 in respect of alleged failings in the public consultation leading to the DNS Command Paper that was the subject of the *HS2* litigation referred to above. It is alleged that the failure to provide environmental information on the reasonable alternatives to the proposals set out in the consultation paper leading to the DNS meant that the consultation was not effective. The ACCC has declared the communication admissible and it is likely to be determined in late 2015/early 2016.[49]

The Scope and Requirements of Article 8

Article 8 of the Convention states that:

> Each Party shall strive to promote effective public participation at an appropriate stage, and while options are still open, during the preparation by public authorities of executive regulations and other generally applicable legally binding rules that may have a significant effect on the environment.
>
> To this end, the following steps should be taken:
>
> (a) Time-frames sufficient for effective participation should be fixed;
> (b) Draft rules should be published or otherwise made publicly available; and
> (c) The public should be given the opportunity to comment, directly or through representative consultative bodies.
>
> The result of the public participation shall be taken into account as far as possible.

There has so far been no consideration of Article 8 by the ACCC or on the distinction between those decisions which should be considered under Article 7 and those that should be considered under Article 8. One possible example of an instrument in the UK context which is within the scope of Article 8 is a safeguarding direction issued under s 74 of the Town and Country Planning Act 1990 and Article 25 of the Town and Country Planning (Development Management Procedure) Order 2010 to protect land required for potential development from other development

[49] ACCC/C/2014/100 (United Kingdom).

which may conflict with it. In *R (HS2 Action Alliance) v Secretary of State for Transport*,[50] the Court of Appeal held that the safeguarding directions for HS2 were not a 'plan or programme that set the framework for development consent' within the meaning of the SEA Directive. If on that analysis the directions are also not a 'plan or programme relating to the environment' within the meaning of Article 7 of the Convention, then it may be that they constitute 'executive regulations' or 'generally applicable legally binding rules' within the scope of Article 8 insofar as by preventing all development other than that which they are intended to facilitate they may have significant environmental effects.

[50] *R (HS2 Action Alliance) v Secretary of State for Transport* [2014] EWCA Civ 1578.

8

Access to Justice: Review Procedures and Costs

JAMES MAURICI QC[1]

Introduction

Article 9 contains the 'third pillar' of the Aarhus Convention on access to justice. The purpose of which is

> to provide procedures and remedies to members of the public so they can have the rights enshrined in the Convention on access to environmental information and environmental decision-making, as well as national laws relating to the environment, enforced by law.[2]

It has been the area in which in the UK the Aarhus Convention has had its greatest impact, most notably, as regards costs.

Indeed the first mention of the Aarhus Convention in an English case came in the context of costs and Article 9: see *R (Burkett) v Hammersmith, Fulham LBC (Costs)*.[3] The matter has continued to trouble the Courts since, see for example the recent judgments by the Supreme Court in *R (Edwards) v Environment Agency*[4] and the European Court of Justice ('CJEU') in *Commission v UK*.[5]

Scope

The scope of Article 9 is not straightforward.

The Aarhus Convention Implementation Guide ('the Guide') says that '[t]he provisions on access to justice essentially apply to all matters of environmental

[1] Barrister, Landmark Chambers, London.
[2] See the 'Aarhus Implementation Guide' (2nd edn, 2013) ('the Guide') p 193.
[3] *R (Burkett) v Hammersmith, Fulham LBC (Costs)* [2005] CP Rep 11per Carnwath LJ (as he then was).
[4] *R (Edwards) v Environment Agency* [2014] 1 WLR 55.
[5] Case C-530/11 *Commission v UK* [2014] QB 98885/.

law' but the position is more complicated because different requirements apply in respect of different categories of case.[6]

There are three broad categories of case within the scope of Art 9:

(i) Challenges to decisions on requests for environmental information (Art 9(1));
(ii) Challenges to decisions, acts, or omissions concerning the permitting of activities covered by Art 6 of the Convention (Art 9(2));
(iii) Challenges to other acts or omissions 'by private persons and public authorities which contravene provisions of its national law relating to the environment' (Art 9(3)).[7]

Before discussing scope further it is worth exploring the different protections provided for in respect of these categories:

(i) In Art 9(1) cases there must be an independent and impartial body established by law which is available to any person who has requested information and which can review the decision made on that request;
(ii) In Art 9(2) cases there must be:
   a. a review procedure must be made available to '"members of the public concerned" (a) Having a sufficient interest or, alternatively, (b) Maintaining impairment of a right, where the administrative procedural law of a Party requires this as a precondition';
   b. before an independent and impartial body established by law;[8]
   c. to challenge 'the substantive and procedural legality' of the decision etc in issue;
(iii) In Art 9(3) cases the requirement is that 'where they meet the criteria, if any, laid down in its national law, members of the public have access to

[6] See the Guide (n 2) p 193.

[7] Directive 2003/35/EC of the European Parliament and of the Council providing for public participation in respect of the drawing up of certain plans and programmes relating to the environment amending with regard to public participation and access to justice Council Directives 85/337/EEC and 96/61/EC [2003] OJ L156/17 ('the PP Directive') transposed into Directive 85/337/EEC [1985] OJ L175/40 ('the EIA Directive') and Directive 96/61/EC [1996] OJ L257/26 ('the IPPC Directive') via Articles 10a and 15a (respectively), Article 9(2) and (4) of the Aarhus Convention but not Article 9(3) or (5): see Case C-240/09 *Lesoochranarske Zoskupenie VLK v Ministerstvo Zivotneho Prostredia Slovenskej Republiky* [2012] QB 606.

[8] See the discussion in the Guide (n 2) at pp 195–96 as to whether Ombudsmen are within the scope of Art 9. In ACCC/45 and 60 the ACCC held that planning appeals in England and Wales to the Secretary of State are not governed by Art 9—these are part of the Art 6 decision-making process:
'84. The Committee notes that the right of an applicant to appeal to the Secretary of State for Communities and Local Government or to the Secretary of State's Planning Inspectors are not procedures under article 9, paragraph 2, of the Convention. They are instead procedures by way of which an applicant whose planning decision has been refused may appeal that decision before an executive body, not constituting a court of law or independent and impartial body established by law. This is so even though in the course of such an appeal members of the public concerned may be heard. If the procedure results in a retaking of the decision at stake, then, depending on the proposed activity under consideration, it engages article 6 of the Convention. Similarly, the latter would be the case if the Secretary of State calls in an application for its own determination.'

administrative or judicial procedures to challenge' the acts or omissions in issue.[9]

Under Art 9(4) in relation to all three categories of case (that is those under Art 9(1), (2) and (3)) there must be 'adequate and effective remedies, including injunctive relief as appropriate, and be fair, equitable, timely and not prohibitively expensive'.[10]

Art 9(1) applies to any appeal or other proceedings challenging a decision on a request for environmental information. Its scope is thus relatively straightforward.[11]

Art 9(2) is said to apply to 'any decision, act or omission[12] subject to the provisions of article 6 and, where so provided for under national law and without prejudice to paragraph 3 below, of other relevant provisions of this Convention'.

Article 6(1)(a) of the Convention applies to 'decisions on whether to permit proposed activities listed in annex I'. Annex I lists a number of major project types and is broadly modelled on Annex I to the Environmental Impact Assessment Directive ('the EIAD').[13]

Article 6(1)(b) provides that it also applies 'in accordance with its national law' to 'decisions on proposed activities not listed in annex I which may have a significant effect on the environment'.[14] This would it seems include other projects

[9] The Guide (n 2) pp 208–09 suggests that while Art 9(3) is silent on requiring review on substantive and procedural legality, that is what is required under Art 9(3). No textual support for this can be found in the Convention though.

[10] There is a useful table showing the different requirements for the three types of case in the Guide (n 2) p 197–98.

[11] See the Guide (n 2) p 199.

[12] The Guide suggests a wide approach should be taken to 'decision, act or omission' under Art 9(2): 'the public concerned within the meaning of this paragraph can obtain review of any "decision, act or omission". For instance, a governmental decision or act that limits the participants at a public hearing, or the holding of a public hearing very late in the process, may be subject to review. Review may also be available if the administration fails to take an action or make a decision required by the Convention, for example by failing to notify certain members of the public concerned or to take due account of the outcome of their participation. Examples of other issues of legality that may be challenged under this provision might include EIA screening decisions, permit conditions that fail to meet applicable technical standards or failures to consider nature conservation or environmental quality standards in permit procedures'.

On EIA screening decisions see ACCC/C/45 and 60 at para 83 and also ACCC/C/2010/50 (Czech Republic) at para 82. And see also ACCC/C/2006/17 (European Community) holding that the absence of any review procedure of a permit until after construction had started constituted non-compliance with the Convention.

[13] See the PP Directive) amending the Environmental Assessment Directive (then the EIA Directive) and Directive 96/61/EC concerning integrated pollution prevention and control (later codified into Directive 2008/1/EC ('the IPPC Directive') so as to transpose the Aarhus Convention. The EIA Directive and its amendments have now been codified into Directive 2011/92/EU, see Articles 1(2) and 11 for the Aarhus provisions on access to justice. The IPPC Directive has now been replaced byDirective 2010/75/EU on industrial emissions (integrated pollution prevention and control) (recast) [2010] OJ L334/17 ('the Industrial Emissions Directive'): see Article 25 for the Aarhus access to justice provision.

[14] And it adds 'To this end, Parties shall determine whether such a proposed activity is subject to these provisions...'

determined under national law giving effect to the EIAD to be 'likely to have a significant effect on the environment'.[15]

It is noteworthy Art 9(2) also refers to any decision, act or omission subject to 'other relevant provisions of this Convention', ie other than Art 6 but only 'where so provided for under national law'. The Guide explains,[16] that the effect of this is that 'Parties are free to extend the review procedures prescribed in article 9, paragraph 2, to cover other provisions in the Convention' and gives Arts 3, 5 7 and 8 as examples. The application of Art 9(2) to cases outside Art 6 is thus voluntary and this means it can be critical in establishing whether Art 9(2) applies to determine whether the decision, act or omission under challenge is governed by Art 6 or is within the scope of some other Article, eg Arts 7 or 8: see eg ACCC/C/2004/8 at para 35; ACCC/C/2008/26 at para 58[17] and ACCC/2005/11 at paras 31 and 32. Where what is under challenge does not fall within the scope of Art 9(2) but nonetheless concerns other provisions of the Convention it is likely instead to fall within the scope of Art 9(3) (see below).

Article 9(3) provides that without prejudice to Art 9(1) and (2)

> each Party shall ensure that, where they meet the criteria, if any, laid down in its national law, members of the public have access to administrative or judicial procedures to challenge acts and omissions by private persons and public authorities which contravene provisions of its national law relating to the environment (emphasis added).

Article 9(3) applies to challenges to 'acts and omissions' but not (like Art 9(2)) 'decisions'[18] of both private persons and public authorities[19] 'which contravene provisions of its national law relating to the environment'.[20] In ACCC/2005/11 the ACCC said at para 26:

[15] See in England: the Town and Country Planning (Environmental Impact Assessment) Regulations 2011, SI 2011/1824; it would thus include Annex II projects where they were screened and found to be likely to have significant effects on the environment. And see also ACCC/C/2010/50 (Czech Republic) at para 82 recognising the EIA screening process as also serving as the relevant determination under Art 6(1)(b).

[16] The Guide (n 2) p 202.

[17] 'Given that no permitting decisions within the purview of article 6 of the Convention are at stake, the Committee concludes that article 9, paragraph 2, and consequently paragraph 4 of the Convention, does not apply in the present case, with respect to the proposed introduction of a 7.5 tonnage restriction for lorries on route B 320.' And see also ACCC/C/2008/27 (United Kingdom) at para 43.

[18] It is understood that it was argued (but not decided) in one case that the new Civil Procedure Rule (CPR) Aarhus costs rules were inapplicable on the grounds that (i) Art 9(3) was concerned only with acts and omissions by public authorities, not decisions and (ii) (relevant in that case) that the claim did not engage national law relating to the environment: see in a preliminary (unreported) hearing in *R (Save Britain's Heritage and the Victorian Society) v Sheffield City Council* [2013] EWHC 2456 (Admin). This line of argument was not accepted in *Venn v SSCLG* [2014] EWCA Civ 1539 at para 13.

[19] Art 9(2) as it is concerned with permitting decisions is thus likely only ever to concern proceedings against public authorities; as it is they who are able to grant such consents.

[20] See ACCC/C/2005/11 (Belgium) at para 28 'Article 9, paragraph 3, is applicable to all acts and omissions by private persons and public authorities contravening national law relating to the environment. For all these acts and omissions, each Party must ensure that members of the public "where they meet the criteria, if any, laid down in its national law" have access to administrative or judicial procedures to challenge the acts and omissions concerned. Contrary to paragraph 2 of article 9, however, paragraph 3 does not refer to "members of the public concerned", but to "members of the public"'.

> The Convention obliges the Parties to ensure access to justice for three generic categories of acts and omissions by public authorities. Leaving aside decisions concerning access to information, the distinction is made between, on the one hand, acts and omissions related to permits for specific activities by a public authority for which public participation is required under article 6 (article 9, paragraph 2) and, on the other hand, all other acts and omissions by private persons and public authorities which contravene national law relating to the environment (article 9, paragraph 3). It is apparent that the rationales of paragraph 2 and paragraph 3 of article 9 of the Convention are not identical.[21]

Where a decision is within the scope of either Art 9(2) or (3) the protections in Art 9(4) (that there be 'adequate and effective remedies, including injunctive relief as appropriate, and be fair, equitable, timely and not prohibitively expensive') apply;[22] the more detailed provisions on standing and for review on the basis of 'substantive and procedural legality' in Art 9(2) though would it seems be inapplicable to a case governed solely by Art 9(3).[23]

Focusing on Art 9(3), its scope turns on the scope of environmental law;[24] a subject that has much exercised academics in this field but has (as yet) rarely troubled practitioners. The following points should be noted:

(i) In ACCC/C/2006/18 the ACCC held that 'national law relating to the environment' covered EU law within the EU Member States (see para 27).
(ii) It seems clear that nuisance actions, even between private parties, is also covered: see ACCC/C/2008/33 at paras 44–45.[25]

[21] In that communication it was also said by the ACCC that Art 9(3) was 'intended to provide members of the public with access to adequate remedies against acts and omissions which contravene environmental laws, and with the means to have existing environmental laws enforced and made effective'; and see also para 34 on the different scope of Arts 9(2) and (4) 'To the extent that a town planning permit should not be considered a permit for a specific activity as provided for in article 6 of the Convention, the decision is still an act by a public authority. As such it may contravene provisions of national law relating to the environment. Thus, Belgium is obliged to ensure that in these cases members of the public have access to administrative or judicial procedures to challenge the acts concerned, as set out in article 9, paragraph 3'.

[22] See eg ACCC/C/2004/6 (Kazakhstan) at para 31.

[23] See ACCC/C/2005/11 (Belgium) at para 29 'When determining how to categorize a decision under the Convention, its label in the domestic law of a Party is not decisive. Rather, whether the decision should be challengeable under article 9, paragraph 2 or 3, is determined by the legal functions and effects of a decision, i.e. on whether it amounts to a permit to actually carry out the activity'.

[24] See ACCC/C/C2008/33 (United Kingdom), 'Article 9, paragraph 3, of the Convention, as opposed to article 9, paragraph 2, of the Convention, does not explicitly refer to either substantive or procedural legality. Instead it refers to "acts or omissions [...] which contravene its national law relating to the environment". Clearly, the issue to be considered in such a review procedure is whether the act or omission in question contravened any provision—be it substantive or procedural—in national law relating to the environment.'

[25] 'Private nuisance is a tort (civil wrong) under the United Kingdom's common law system. A private nuisance is defined as an act or omission generally connected with the use or occupation of land which causes damage to another person in connection with that other's use of land or interference with the enjoyment of land or of some right connected with the land. The Committee finds that in the context of the present case, the law of private nuisance is part of the law relating to the environment of the Party concerned, and therefore within the scope of article 9, paragraph 3, of the Convention.' And see also the communications in ACCC/C85 and 86. In these cases, the ACCC is considering two communications alleging that the United Kingdom was in breach of Article 9 of the Convention on the ground that private

(iii) In ACCC/C/2006/18 the ACCC confirmed that Art 9(3) extended to challenges to acts and omissions concerning wildlife (see para 24).

(iv) The Guide says:

> First, as regards 'contravening national law relating to the environment', it does not have to be established prima facie, i.e., before the review, that there has been a violation. Rather, there must have been an allegation by the member of the public that there has been an act or omission violating national law relating to the environment (see ACCC/C/2006/18 (Denmark) discussed above). Second, national laws relating to the environment are neither limited to the information or public participation rights guaranteed by the Convention, nor to legislation where the environment is mentioned in the title or heading. Rather, the decisive issue is if the provision in question somehow relates to the environment. Thus, also acts and omissions that may contravene provisions on, among other things, city planning, environmental taxes, control of chemicals or wastes, exploitation of natural resources and pollution from ships are covered by paragraph 3, regardless of whether the provisions in question are found in planning laws, taxation laws or maritime laws. This was illustrated in the Compliance Committee's findings on communication ACCC/C/2005/11 (Belgium), where the Committee assessed Belgian planning laws under article 9, paragraph 3, and in its findings on Bulgarian planning law in communication ACCC/C/2011/58.425

(v) In *Venn v Secretary of State for Communities and Local Government*,[26] Lang J held that not every planning decision will engage environmental matters falling within the Convention but that the challenge in that case on the ground that the inspector failed to apply policies on protecting gardens from development did raise environmental matters within the meaning of the Convention. The Court of Appeal in *Venn v Secretary of State for Communities and Local Government* (n 18) upheld the view of Lang J that the scope of environmental law for the purposes of Article 9 of the Convention needed to be read in the light of the wide definition of 'environmental information' in Article 2(3) and that this included administrative matters likely to affect 'the state of land' such that it was 'arguably broad enough to catch most, if not all, planning matters' (see paragraph 11). The Secretary of State argued (see paragraph 14) that the policies in issue

law nuisance proceedings are 'prohibitively expensive' for claimants seeking to challenge environmentally deleterious acts. The first communication, ACCC/C/85/2013 (United Kingdom), brought by the Environmental Law Foundation, alleged that s 46 of the Legal Aid Sentencing and Punishment of Offenders Act results in non-compliance because it means that a successful claimant cannot recover the premium for 'after the event' costs insurance from the defendant. The communicant's case was that this means that the expense of insuring against a potentially large costs liability is prohibitive. The second communication, ACCC/C/86/2013 (United Kingdom), brought by Alyson Austin, alleged that her intended nuisance claim against Miller Argent (South Wales) Ltd, who undertake coal extraction activities in the vicinity of her home, would be 'prohibitively expensive' because of the potential costs liability she would face if the claim were to fail. Her application for a protective costs order failed before the High Court but an appeal was pending before the Court of Appeal at the time of the hearing before the ACCC. See also *Austin v Miller Argent (South Wales) Ltd* [2015] 1 WLR 62 and *Coventry v Lawrence* [2014] 3 WLR 555.

[26] *Venn v Secretary of State for Communities and Local Government* [2014] JPL 447.

in the claim were 'not a provision of national law, and the complaint was not that it had been contravened, but that there had been a failure to take it into account as a material consideration in accordance with section 70(2) of the 1990 Act. Insofar as the Claimant was alleging a contravention of national law, it was a contravention of section 70(2), which could not be characterised as a law relating to the environment. It was submitted that a distinction should be drawn between section 70(2) and other enactments which were 'specifically environmental laws', such as sections 80 and 82 of the Environmental Protection Act 1990, section 55(2) of the Clean Air Act 1993, and section 2(4) of the Noise Act 1996'. The Court of Appeal rejected this 'ingenious' argument saying:

> 15 … The UK has a sophisticated Town and Country Planning system, and Parliament has chosen to implement much of the UK's environmental protection through that system. One obvious example is the Environmental Impact Assessment process, which is tied to the grant of planning permission. Another example is the requirement that local development plan documents must include policies that are designed to ensure that development in each local plan area contributes to the mitigation of, and adaptation to, climate change: see section 19(1A) of the Planning and Compulsory Purchase Act 2004 ("the 2004 Act").
>
> 16 As a consequence, it is a characteristic of the UK's approach to environmental protection that much (if not most) of the detail is contained, not in statutory regulations, but in policies, both national policies adopted by the Government (the NPPF), and local policies adopted by local planning authorities in their development plan documents. When preparing their local development plan documents local planning authorities must have regard to national policies; including the NPPF: see section 19(2)(a) of the 2004 Act. Decision makers are then required by section 70(2) to have regard to such policies; and if the policies are contained in the development plan they must be followed unless material considerations indicate otherwise: see section 38(6) of the 2004 Act (paragraph 22 of the judgment).
>
> 17 Given that this is the way in which the UK has chosen to implement a great deal of environmental protection "within the framework of its national legislation", it would deprive Article 9(3) of much of its effect if a distinction was drawn between the policies, both national and local, which do relate to the environment, and the law which does not directly relate to the environment, but which requires those policies which do relate to the environment to be prepared, and then to be taken into account, and in certain cases to be followed unless material considerations indicate otherwise. It would not be consistent with the underlying purpose of Aarhus to adopt an interpretation of Article 9(3) which would, at least in the UK, deprive it of much of its effect: see paragraphs 49 and 50 of the Brown Bear case (paragraph 12 above). In the Aarhus context the UK's combination of statute and policy, with the former requiring that the latter be prepared, taken into account and in some instances followed, is properly characterised as "national law relating to the environment".
>
> 18 For these reasons, I endorse the Judge's conclusion that the Claimant's section 288 application falls within Article 9(3) of Aarhus.

The increased focus on the scope of the Convention in English law comes from the fixed costs rules (in CPR 45.43) for 'Aarhus Convention claims', that is a judicial review 'of a decision, act or omission all or part of which is subject to the provisions of the UNECE convention on Access to Information, Public Participation in Decision-Making and Access to Justice in Environmental Matters'.[27] However, the very wide way this new rule is phrased may mean that precise debates about the scope of Art 9 itself are beside the point. On the face of these CPR rules, it would appear from their wording that a local authority would be entitled to the protection of the fixed costs regime in a judicial review of central government. That would arguably be to take an approach wider that the ACCC has. The ACCC in communication ACCC/C/2012/68 opined that:

> 80. The present complaint was submitted as a 'communication', on behalf of the Avich and Kilchrenan Community Council, a body with statutory duties within the Party concerned (UK). In this respect, the Committee considers whether the complaint at issue qualifies as a communication under paragraphs 18 of the annex to decision I/7.
>
> 81. In order to define the nature of the complaint, the Committee examines the role of community councils in Scotland. Although community councils have statutory duties in terms of licensing and planning, they have no regulatory decision-making functions and are essentially voluntary bodies established within a statutory framework. They mainly act to further the interests of the community and take action in the interest of the community as appears to be expedient and practicable, including representing the view of the community regarding planning applications. In addition, community councils rely on grants from local authorities and voluntary donations. Community Council members furthermore operate on a voluntary basis and do not receive payment for the services.
>
> 82. The Committee was also informed by the Party concerned (UK) that the representations from the Avich and Kilchrenan Community Council with regard to the projects at stake were recorded under the same section as representations from members of the public and non-governmental organizations.
>
> 83. Based on the above, in particular the role of the council to represent the interests of the community in planning matters and the fact council members provide their services on a voluntary basis, the Committee decides to consider the present complaint as a communication under paragraph 18 of the annex to decision I/7.

It would appear from this that a public authority that was not essentially a voluntary body providing services on a voluntary basis and which instead exercised 'regulatory decision-making functions' would not be regarded as a member of the public able to bring a communication.

This decision is consistent with *R (Halebank Parish Council) v Halton Borough Council* (unreported, 30 April 2012) where HHJ Raynor QC held, in considering a protective costs order (PCO) application, that the claimant, a parish council, fell within the definition of the 'public' for the purposes of the Aarhus Convention.

[27] See CPR 45.41–45.44 and the Practice Direction (PD) Part 45 at paras 5.1–5.2, the text of which is at Appendix 10 of this book.

It is also relevant to note the background as to why these provisions of the CPR were introduced. The 'Cost Protection for Litigants in Environmental Judicial Review Claims' was published in response to the consultation carried out by Government on 28 August 2012. The focus was on individual members of the public and non-governmental organisations (NGOs); it was not anticipated that public authorities would seek to use the provisions to litigate against each other. Moreover, the distinction between the 'public' on whom rights are conferred and 'public authorities' on whom obligations are imposed lies at the heart of the Aarhus Convention: see for example the seventh, eighth and ninth recitals and the definitions section in Art 2. The definition of 'public' in Art 2(4) of the Convention is 'one or more natural or legal persons, and in accordance with national legislation or practice, their associations, organizations or groups'. The definition is designed to capture actors other than public authorities. A specific reference to public authorities also being covered by this term would surely have been included if that were intended, given the reference to 'associations, organizations or groups' and the mention that is made of 'individual citizens, non-governmental organizations and the private sector' in relation to the protection of the environment in the thirteenth recital. Moreover, 'public authority' is separately defined in Art 2 and includes 'Government at national, regional and other level'. The fundamental distinction between the public and 'public authorities' is also emphasised by the Guide. Thus the Guide notes in its introduction that 'The Aarhus Convention grants the public rights and imposes on Parties and public authorities obligations regarding access to information and public participation…' and that

> Whilst most multilateral environmental agreements cover obligations that Parties have to each other, the Aarhus Convention covers obligations that Parties have to the public. It goes further than any other environmental convention in imposing clear obligations on Parties and public authorities towards the public…

Further, in commenting on the definitions in Art 2 of the Convention ('Party', 'public authority', 'the public', 'the public concerned', etc), the Guide notes that 'The Convention primarily sets out obligations for Parties (contracting Parties to the Convention) and public authorities (government bodies and persons or bodies performing government functions at national, regional or other levels)…'[28] See also the Advocate-General's opinion in *Commission v UK* where she refuted any suggestion that the financial circumstances of public authorities, and the costs risks they faced, had any relevance in Aarhus Convention terms.[29] If that view is correct then it would further undermine any suggestion that local authorities are entitled to Aarhus costs protection.

However, in a lengthily reasoned costs order dated 16 October 2014 following the unsuccessful judicial review claim by the London Borough of Hillingdon

[28] The Guide (n 2) p 5.
[29] *Commission v UK* (n 5) paras 77–80.

('LBH') alleging that the safeguarding directions issued to protect land required for the HS2 railway were adopted in breach of the Strategic Environmental Assessment Directive 2001/42/EC,[30] Lindblom J held that the LBH was entitled to an Aarhus Convention costs cap under CPR r 45.41–45.44 and CPR PD 5.1–5.2.[31] His reasoning was, firstly, that the Aarhus costs cap regime in the CPR 'relates to claims of a particular nature rather than to any particular type or category of claimant', and that

> local authorities and other public bodies are not included. Nor is there any qualification in terms of the claimant's means, or its ability to fund the proceedings, or the likelihood of its being able to meet from its own resources any order for costs which might be made in favour of another party.

He held that because the CPR rules were 'entirely unambiguous' on this point, resort to the Aarhus Convention to achieve a strained interpretation of them was not permissible. Nonetheless, he went on to reject the Secretary of State's submission that 'the concept of access to justice for members of the public under article 9 of the Aarhus Convention must necessarily exclude a local authority bringing a claim in the interests of those living in its area'. He held that neither the Convention, nor the Compliance Committee's decision in ACCC/C/2012/68, nor the Guide

> preclude the possibility of [Article 9's scope extending to] one public authority acting in the public interest when it seeks judicial review of a decision made by another authority, even though its own administrative acts may themselves be subject to scrutiny by the court in proceedings brought by an individual claimant.[32]

Finally, Art 9 also it seems restricts the use of judicial review ouster clauses in respect of matters within its scope: see ACCC/C/2004/8[33] and see also the discussion of the availability of judicial review in respect of UK legislative acts granting development consent in ACCC/C/ C/2011/61.[34]

[30] Directive 2001/42/EC of the European Parliament and of the Council of 27 June 2001 on the assessment of the effects of certain plans and programmes on the environment [2001] OJ L197/30.

[31] For the determination of the substantive issues in the case, see *R (HS2 Action Alliance Ltd) v Secretary of State for Transport* [2014] EWHC 2759 (Admin) and on appeal [2014] EWCA Civ 1578.

[32] An appeal by the Secretary of State against Lindblom J's order was dismissed very shortly before this book went to print: see *R (HS2 Action Alliance Ltd) v Secretary of State for Transport* [2015] EWCA Civ 203. The Court of Appeal agreed with Lindblom J. on the interpretation of the CPR rules and declined to rule on the definitions under Article 2 of the Convention given that it was unnecessary to do so in the light of the position under the CPR being unambiguous.

[33] At para 38.

[34] '60. Article 9, paragraph 2, of the Convention requires Parties to ensure access to procedures for review of decisions, acts and omissions subject to article 6. This provision addresses standing, as well as the scope of review, that should comprise the substantive and procedural legality of the act. To comply with the Convention, the Party concerned must ensure that within its domestic legal system all criteria required under article 9, paragraph 2, of the Convention, also those extending beyond EU law and the 1998 Human Rights Act, are met in regard to hybrid bills processes.

61. The Committee examines in particular the scope of the review procedures after the adoption of the Crossrail Act (or any act adopted further to a hybrid bill procedure authorizing a specific activity). In the case of the Crossrail Act no such challenge was brought before a court of law. Thus, the Committee is not in position to determine whether the legal remedies available under the law of the Party concerned would have enabled members of the public concerned to challenge the Crossrail Act as required under article 9, paragraph 2, of the Convention.'

The Issue of Standing

Under Art 9(1) the position is straightforward; 'any person' who has requested information must be entitled to access the review procedures.[35]

Article 9(2) requires that Parties ensure '"that members of the public concerned" (a) Having a sufficient interest or, alternatively, (b) Maintaining impairment of a right, where the administrative procedural law of a Party requires this as a precondition, have access to a review procedure'. It is also said that '[w]hat constitutes a sufficient interest and impairment of a right shall be determined in accordance with the requirements of national law and consistently with the objective of giving the public concerned wide access to justice within the scope of this Convention'.

Article 9(2) provides in addition that

> the interest of any non-governmental organization meeting the requirements referred to in article 2, paragraph 5, shall be deemed sufficient for the purpose of subparagraph (a) above. Such organizations shall also be deemed to have rights capable of being impaired for the purpose of subparagraph (b) above.

Article 2(5) provides:

> 'The public concerned' means the public affected or likely to be affected by, or having an interest in, the environmental decision-making; for the purposes of this definition, non-governmental organizations promoting environmental protection and meeting any requirements under national law shall be deemed to have an interest.

Article 9(2) thus gives special protection, in terms of standing to 'non-governmental organizations promoting environmental protection'.

Under Art 9(3) the Convention says rather less, seemingly allowing the Parties to set their own criteria for standing: 'each Party shall ensure that, where they meet the criteria, if any, laid down in its national law, members of the public have access to administrative or judicial procedures'.

A number of ACCC decisions and cases decided in Luxembourg have dealt with standing issues under the Aarhus Convention. The standing rules in judicial review in England & Wales are very liberal; far more so than those in many other European countries. This has meant that in terms of domestic case-law on standing there is rather less in the way of learning.

A number of the ACCC decisions and CJEU cases have concerned the privileged position of environmental NGOs under Art 9.

The first of these cases to consider is the CJEU's decision in *Bund für Umwelt und Naturschutz Deutschland, Landesverband Nordrhein—Westfalen eV v Bezirksregierung Arnsberg*.[36] In that case Trianel—the intervener in the main

[35] See the Guide (n 2) pp 199–200.

[36] Case C-115/09 *Bund für Umwelt und Naturschutz Deutschland, Landesverband Nordrhein—Westfalen eV v Bezirksregierung Arnsberg* [2011] 3 CMLR 15.

proceedings—intended to construct and operate a coal-fired power station in Lünen. The power station was within eight kilometers of five areas designated as special areas of conservation within the meaning of the Habitats Directive.[37] Friends of the Earth initiated proceedings for the annulment of consents granted for the power station relying on alleged infringements of the provisions transposing into German law the Habitats Directive and, in particular, Article 6 thereof. The case thus fell within the scope of Art 9(2) of the Aarhus Convention. A reference was made to the CJEU. One of the issues raised was described thus by the CJEU:

> 35 … the referring court asks essentially whether Article 10a of Directive 85/337[38] precludes legislation which does not permit non-governmental organisations promoting environmental protection, as referred to in Article 1(2) of [the EIA Directive] to rely before the courts, in an action contesting a decision authorising projects likely to have 'significant effects on the environment' for the purposes of Article 1(1) of Directive [the EIA Directive], on the infringement of a rule which protects only the interests of the general public and not the interests of individuals. The referring court also asks the Court whether Article 10a of [the EIA Directive] precludes such legislation in general or only in so far as it does not permit an organisation of that nature to rely before the courts on particular provisions of environment law, whether of Community or purely national origin.
>
> 36 It emerges from the order for reference that the question is justified by the fact that the applicable national legislation makes the admissibility of an action such as that brought by the applicant in the main proceedings conditional upon the applicant showing that the administrative decision contested impairs an individual right which, under national law, can be categorised as an individual public-law right.

The CJEU held that:

> 45 … although the national legislature is entitled to confine to individual public-law rights the rights whose infringement may be relied on by an individual in legal proceedings contesting one of the decisions, acts or omissions referred to in Article 10a of [the EIA Directive], such a limitation cannot be applied as such to environmental protection organisations without disregarding the objectives of the last sentence of the third paragraph of Article 10a of [the EIA Directive].
>
> 46 If, as is clear from that provision, those organisations must be able to rely on the same rights as individuals, it would be contrary to the objective of giving the public concerned wide access to justice and at odds with the principle of effectiveness if such organisations were not also allowed to rely on the impairment of rules of EU environment law solely on the ground that those rules protect the public interest. As the dispute in the main proceedings shows, that very largely deprives those organisations of the possibility of verifying compliance with the rules of that branch of law, which, for the most part,

[37] Council Directive 92/43/EEC of 21 May 1992 on the conservation of natural habitats and of wild fauna and flora [1992] OJ L206/7.

[38] Implementing inter alia Art 9(2) of the Aarhus Convention.

address the public interest and not merely the protection of the interests of individuals as such.

47 It follows first that the concept of 'impairment of a right' cannot depend on conditions which only other physical or legal persons can fulfil, such as the condition of being a more or less close neighbour of an installation or of suffering in one way or another the effects of the installation's operation.

48 It follows more generally that the last sentence of the third paragraph of Article 10a of [the EIA Directive] must be read as meaning that the 'rights capable of being impaired' which the environmental protection organisations are supposed to enjoy must necessarily include the rules of national law implementing EU environment law and the rules of EU environment law having direct effect ...

59 ... non-governmental organisations promoting environmental protection, as referred to in Article 1(2) of that directive, can derive from the last sentence of the third paragraph of Article 10a of [the EIA Directive] a right to rely before the courts, in an action contesting a decision authorising projects 'likely to have significant effects on the environment' for the purposes of Article 1(1) of [the EIA Directive], on the infringement of the rules of national law flowing from Article 6 of the Habitats Directive, even where, on the ground that the rules relied on protect only the interests of the general public and not the interests of individuals, national procedural law does not permit this.

The second case is *Djurgarden-Lilla Vartans Miljoskyddsforening v Stockholms Kommun genom dess Marknamnd*.[39] The Municipality of Stockholm concluded a contract with a private company to construct a tunnel through the hills in Northern Djurgården to house electricity cable. The Environmental Chamber of the District Court of Stockholm (miljödomstolen vid Stockholms tingsrätt) granted development consent to carry out the works. The Djurgården environmental association (Djurgården-Lilla Värtans Miljöskyddsförening) sought to appeal against that decision, but the action was held to be inadmissible, on the basis that it did not fulfil the condition set down in the relevant national law, which required an environmental association to have 2,000 members to be entitled to appeal. The case again raised standing issues under Art 9(2).[40] The Djurgården environmental association appealed and a reference was made to the CJEU, asking inter alia, (i) whether Art 10a of the EIA Directive implied that members of the public concerned were to have access to a review procedure to challenge a granting of development consent even where they had had an opportunity to participate in the decision-making procedure; and (ii) whether Member States were permitted, under the Directive, to allow small local environmental associations to participate in the decision-making procedure but to have no right

[39] Case C-263/08 *Djurgarden-Lilla Vartans Miljoskyddsforening v Stockholms Kommun genom dess Marknamnd* [2009] ECR I-9967.

[40] Sweden lodged a reservation to Art 9(2) of the Aarhus Convention restricting the ability of environmental organisations 'to subject decisions by local administrative authorities to review by a court of law ...'. The reservation concludes by stating: 'The Government intends that Sweden will very shortly comply with Article 9(2) in its entirety.'

of access to a review procedure to challenge the decision subsequently taken. The CJEU held that

> members of the public concerned, within the meaning of art.1(2) and 10a of Directive 85/337, must be able to have access to a review procedure to challenge the decision by which a body attached to a court of law of a Member State has given a ruling on a request for development consent, regardless of the role they might have played in the examination of that request by taking part in the procedure before that body and by expressing their views (para 39).

The CJEU also held that the EIA Directive 'precludes a provision of national law which reserves the right to bring an appeal against a decision on projects which fall within the scope of that directive solely to environmental protection associations which have at least 2,000 members' (para 52). The CJEU said:

> 44 As regards non-governmental organisations which promote environmental protection, art.1(2) of Directive 85/337, read in conjunction with art.10a thereof, requires that those organisations 'meeting any requirements under national law' are to be regarded either as having 'sufficient interest' or as having a right which is capable of being impaired by projects falling within the scope of that directive.
>
> 45 While it is true that art.10a of Directive 85/337 , by its reference to art.1(2) thereof, leaves to national legislatures the task of determining the conditions which may be required in order for a non-governmental organisation which promotes environmental protection to have a right of appeal under the conditions set out above, the national rules thus established must, first, ensure 'wide access to justice' and, secondly, render effective the provisions of Directive 85/337 on judicial remedies. Accordingly, those national rules must not be liable to nullify Community provisions which provide that parties who have a sufficient interest to challenge a project and those whose rights it impairs, which include environmental protection associations, are to be entitled to bring actions before the competent courts.
>
> 46 From that point of view, a national law may require that such an association, which intends to challenge a project covered by Directive 85/337 through legal proceedings, has as its object the protection of nature and the environment.
>
> 47 Furthermore, it is conceivable that the condition that an environmental protection association must have a minimum number of members may be relevant in order to ensure that it does in fact exist and that it is active. However, the number of members required cannot be fixed by national law at such a level that it runs counter to the objectives of Directive 85/337 and in particular the objective of facilitating judicial review of projects which fall within its scope.
>
> 48 In that connection, it must be stated that, although Directive 85/337 provides that members of the public concerned who have a sufficient interest in challenging projects or have rights which may be impaired by projects are to have the right to challenge the decision which authorises it, that directive in no way permits access to review procedures to be limited on the ground that the persons concerned have already been able to express their views in the participatory phase of the decision-making procedure established by art.6(4) thereof.

49 Thus, the fact relied on by the Kingdom of Sweden, that the national rules offer extensive opportunities to participate at an early stage in the procedure in drawing up the decision relating to a project is no justification for the fact that judicial remedies against the decision adopted at the end of that procedure are available only under very restrictive conditions.

50 Furthermore, Directive 85/337 does not exclusively concern projects on a regional or national scale, but also projects more limited in size which locally based associations are better placed to deal with. As the Advocate General notes, in point 78 of her Opinion, the rule of the Swedish legislation at issue is such as to deprive local associations of any judicial remedy.

51 The Swedish Government, which acknowledges that at present only two associations have at least 2, 000 members and thereby satisfy the condition laid down in para.13 of Ch.16 of the Environment Act, has in fact submitted that local associations could contact one of those two associations and ask them to bring an appeal. However, that possibility in itself is not capable of satisfying the requirements of Directive 85/337 as, first, the associations entitled to bring an appeal might not have the same interest in projects of limited size and, secondly, they would be likely to receive numerous requests of that kind which would have to be dealt with selectively on the basis of criteria which would not be subject to review. Finally, such a system would give rise, by its very nature, to a filtering of appeals directly contrary to the spirit of the directive which, as stated in para. 33 of this judgment, is intended to implement the Aarhus Convention.

Third, in ACCC/2005/11 the ACCC was concerned with Belgium where the courts apply general standing rules to environmental NGOs thus requiring them to show a direct, personal and legitimate interest. The ACCC was unable to determine whether the case fell under Art 9(2) or 9(3), and thus examined the position under both (see para 34). Under Art 9(2) the ACCC was clear that there would be non-compliance). Turning to Art 9(3), the ACCC said:

34. To the extent that a town planning permit should not be considered a permit for a specific activity as provided for in article 6 of the Convention, the decision is still an act by a public authority. As such it may contravene provisions of national law relating to the environment. Thus, Belgium is obliged to ensure that in these cases members of the public have access to administrative or judicial procedures to challenge the acts concerned, as set out in article 9, paragraph 3. This provision is intended to provide members of the public with access to adequate remedies against acts and omissions which contravene environmental laws, and with the means to have existing environmental laws enforced and made effective. When assessing the Belgian criteria for access to justice for environ mental organizations in the light of article 9, paragraph 3, the provision should be read in conjunction with articles 1 to 3 of the Convention, and in the light of the purpose reflected in the preamble, that 'effective judicial mechanisms should be accessible to the public, including organizations, so that its legitimate interests are protected and the law is enforced.'

35. While referring to 'the criteria, if any, laid down in national law', the Convention neither defines these criteria nor sets out the criteria to be avoided. Rather, the

Convention is intended to allow a great deal of flexibility in defining which environmental organizations have access to justice. On the one hand, the Parties are not obliged to establish a system of popular action ('actio popularis') in their national laws with the effect that anyone can challenge any decision, act or omission relating to the environment. On other the hand, the Parties may not take the clause 'where they meet the criteria, if any, laid down in its national law' as an excuse for introducing or maintaining so strict criteria that they effectively bar all or almost all environmental organizations from challenging act or omissions that contravene national law relating to the environment.

36. Accordingly, the phrase 'the criteria, if any, laid down in national law' indicates a self restraint on the parties not to set too strict criteria. Access to such procedures should thus be the presumption, not the exception. One way for the Parties to avoid a popular action ('action popularis') in these cases, is to employ some sort of criteria (e.g. of being affected or of having an interest) to be met by members of the public in order to be able to challenge a decision.

However, this presupposes that such criteria do not bar effective remedies for members of the public …

38. Up to the point of entry into force of the Convention for Belgium, the general criteria for standing of environmental organizations before the Council of State have not differed from those of natural persons. According to this practice, to be able to challenge a town planning permit or a plan before the Council of State, an environmental organization must thus claim a direct, personal and legitimate interest. It must also prove that, when acting in accordance with its statutory goals, the goals do not coincide with the protection of a general interest or a personal interest of its members. Hence, federations of environmental organizations have generally not been able to meet this criterion, since their interest is not seen as distinct from the interests of its members. Moreover, according to this practice, two criteria must be fulfilled in order to appreciate the general character of the organization's statutory goal, a social and a geographical criterion. The case is not admissible if the objective of the organization is so broadly defined that it is not distinct from a general interest. As to the geographical criterion, an act cannot be challenged by an organization if the act refers to a well-defined territory and the activities of organization are not territorially limited or cover a large geographical area, unless the organization also has a specifically defined social objective. Furthermore, an organization whose objective expands to a large territory may only challenge an administrative act if the act affects the entire or a great part of the territory envisaged by the organization's statutes.

39. The Convention does not explicitly refer to federations of environmental organizations. If, in the jurisdiction of a Party, standing is not granted to such federations, it is possible that, to the extent that member organizations of the federation are able to effectively challenge the act or omission in question, this may suffice for complying with article 9, paragraph 3. If, on the other hand, due to the criteria of a direct and subjective interest for the person, no member of the public may be in a position to challenge such acts or omissions, this is too strict to provide for access to justice in accordance with the Convention. This is also the case if, for the same reasons, no environmental organization is able to meet the criteria set by the Council of State.

40. The Convention does not prevent a Party from applying general criteria of the sort found in Belgian legislation. However, even though the wordings of the relevant Belgian laws do not as such imply a lack of compliance, the jurisprudence of the Belgian courts, as reflected in the cases submitted by the Communicant, implies a too restrictive access to justice for environmental organizations. In its response, the Party concerned contends that the Communicant 'presents an unbalanced image by its "strategic use" of jurisprudence,' and that 'the difficulties that the BBL experiences by the Communicant to bring an action in court are not representative for environmental NGOs in general'. In the view of the Committee, however, the cases referred to show that the criteria applied by the Council of State so far seem to effectively bar most, if not all, environmental organizations from challenging town planning permits and area plans that they consider to contravene national law relating to the environment, as under article 9, paragraph 3. Accordingly, in these cases, too, the jurisprudence of the Council of State appears too strict. Thus, if maintained by the Council of State, Belgium would fail to provide for access to justice as set out in article 9, paragraph 3, of the Convention. By failing to provide for effective remedies with respect to town planning permits and decisions on area plans, Belgium would then also fail to comply with article 9, paragraph 4.[41]

[41] See also ACCC/2006/18:

'21. As far as access to justice is concerned, Danish courts maintain the general criteria that, to have standing, the person concerned, whether a physical or legal person, must have a concrete, significant and individual interest in the case. Danish court practice on access to courts for non-governmental organizations in matters relating to nature protection is scarce and not that well established, and generally rather restrictive towards non-governmental organizations. Yet, some relevant jurisprudence has developed since the entry into force of the Convention for Denmark. In particular, the jurisprudence of the Western High Court (Vestre Landsret), as reflected in its decision of 2001 *(Danmarks Sportfiskerforbund and Lemvig og Omegns Sportfiskerforening vs. Miljø- & Energiministeriet, Skov- og Naturstyrelsen and Naturklagenævnet [Danish Angler Society and Lemvig and Omegn's Angler Society vs. Ministry of the Environment and Energy, Forest and Nature Agency, and Nature Protection Board of Appeal]*, U.2001.1594V) indicates that at least some nation-wide as well as local non-governmental organizations concerned with the protection of wildlife can bring cases to court for an injunction. In this case, the organizations challenged decisions to allow the introduction of beavers into certain areas. While the case differs from that of challenging the culling of birds, it shows that such organizations can be considered to have a sufficiently concrete, significant and individual interest to go to court.

...

29. As the Committee has pointed out in its findings and recommendations with regard to communication ACCC/C/2005/11 (Belgium) (ECE/MP.PP/C.1/2006/4/Add.2, paras. 29-37), while article 9, paragraph 3, refers to 'the criteria, if any, laid down in national law', the Convention neither defines these criteria nor sets out the criteria to be avoided. Rather, the Convention is intended to allow a great deal of flexibility in defining which members of the public have access to justice. On the one hand, the Parties are not obliged to establish a system of popular action ('actio popularis') in their national laws with the effect that anyone can challenge any decision, act or omission relating to the environment. On other the hand, the Parties may not take the clause 'where they meet the criteria, if any, laid down in its national law' as an excuse for introducing or maintaining so strict criteria that they effectively bar all or almost all environmental organizations or other members of the public from challenging act or omissions that contravene national law relating to the environment. This interpretation of article 9, paragraph 3, is clearly supported by the Meeting of the Parties, which in paragraph 16 of decision II/2 (promoting effective access to justice) invites those Parties which choose to apply criteria in the exercise of their discretion under article 9, paragraph 3, 'to take fully into account the objective of the Convention to guarantee access to justice'.

The CJEU has further considered the standing requirements under the Aarhus Convention in two other cases.

First, *Commission of the European Communities v Ireland*,[42] which focussed on Art 9(2). In that case and where the Commission argued that the criterion of 'substantial interest' required for seeking judicial review in Irish domestic public law was stricter than that of 'sufficient interest' in the Aarhus Convention and transposed in the PP Directive.

The CJEU stated:

> ... Member States must ensure that, in accordance with the relevant national legal system, members of the public concerned having a sufficient interest, or alternatively, maintaining the impairment of a right, where the administrative procedural law of a Member State requires this as a precondition, have access to a review procedure under the conditions specified in those provisions, and must determine what constitutes a sufficient interest and impairment of a right consistently with the objective of giving the public concerned wide access to justice.[43]

The CJEU noted that Ireland had adopted provisions under which the right of access to justice in this area 'depends directly' on the applicants' interest.[44] The Court added

> ... there is no need to ascertain whether the criterion of substantial interest as applied and interpreted by the Irish courts corresponds to the sufficient interest referred to in Directive 2003/35 [which inserted article 10a into Directive 85/337] as that would lead to calling into question the quality of the transposition having regard, in particular, to the competence of the Member States recognised by that directive to determine what constitutes a sufficient interest consistently with the objective which that directive pursues (at para 84).

30. When evaluating whether a Party complies with article 9, paragraph 3, the Committee pays attention to the general picture, i.e. to what extent national law effectively has such blocking consequences for members of the public in general, including environmental organizations, or if there are remedies available for them to actually challenge the act or omission in question. In this evaluation article 9, paragraph 3, should be read in conjunction with articles 1 to 3 of the Convention, and in the light of the purpose reflected in the preamble, that 'effective judicial mechanisms should be accessible to the public, including organizations, so that its legitimate interests are protected and the law is enforced.

...

42. While the Committee is not convinced that the Party concerned fails to comply with the Convention, it notes the limited case law with regard to standing for non-governmental organisations in these situations. As far as standing for such organisations is concerned, it therefore stresses the importance of applying the approach reflected in the decision by the Western High Court in 2001, referred to in paragraph 21, mutatis mutandis, as a minimum standard of access to justice in cases relating to the protection of wildlife.'

[42] Case C-427/07 *Commission of the European Communities v Ireland* [2009] ECR I-6277; [2010] Env LR 8.

[43] ibid para 82.

[44] ibid para 83.

Under Irish law, the applicant was required to prove a peculiar and personal interest of significant weight which is affected by or connected with the development in question (*Harding v Cork County Council*).[45] When considering that test, Kokott AG stated:

> 66. Under Directive 2003/35 , that is to say under the first sentence of the third paragraph of art.10a of the EIA Directive and the first sentence of the third paragraph of art.15a of Directive 96/61, the Member States are to determine what constitutes a sufficient interest and impairment of a right. This is admittedly to be done consistently with the objective of giving the public concerned wide access to justice. However, an even more restrictive access rule is also possible, namely the requirement to maintain the impairment of a right. The directive thus leaves it to the Member States to define 'sufficient interest', without laying down any mandatory minimum standard.
>
> ...
>
> 69. However, in order to determine what constitutes sufficient interest to bring an action, a balance must necessarily be struck. Effective enforcement of the law militates in favour of wide access to the courts. On the other hand, it is possible that many court actions are unnecessary because the law has not been infringed. Unnecessary actions not only burden the courts, but also in some cases adversely affect projects, whose implementation can be delayed. Factors such as an increasing amount of legislation or a growing litigiousness of citizens, but also a change in environmental conditions, can affect the outcome of that balancing exercise. Accordingly, it cannot be automatically inferred from more generous access to the courts that was previously available that a more restrictive approach would be incompatible with the objective of wide access.

The Court found Irish law to be compatible with the PP Directive on the issue of standing though there were findings against Ireland on other grounds including costs.[46]

Second, in *Lesoochranárske Zoskupenie VLK*,[47] a Grand Chamber of the CJEU concluded, in relation to Article 9(3) of the Aarhus Convention and

[45] *Harding v Cork County Council* [2008] IECS 27.

[46] On costs it is submitted that the Advocate-General in *Commission v UK* (n 5) has misunderstood the effect of Case C-456/08 *Commission v Ireland* [2010] ECR I-859. That case stands as authority only for the proposition that a discretion not to award costs at the end of a set of proceedings is by itself not sufficient to amount to transposition. It does not stand as authority, as the Advocate-General in Case C-530/11 seems to suggest at §39, for the proposition that any element of judicial discretion in rules on costs is contrary to EU law. That view is also inconsistent with the acceptance by Advocate-General Kokott and the CJEU in *Edwards* itself (see (n 4) and below) that a system of PCOs can in principle be relied upon in order to transpose the Directive: see especially paras 16 and 38 of the CJEU's judgment in *Edwards*. See also *Road Sense v Scottish Ministers* [2011] CSOH 10 at paras 14–17. In *R (Garner) v Elmbridge Borough Council* [2011] 1 Costs LR 48, Sullivan LJ recorded the submission made in that case, in a similar vein, namely that it 'is not sufficient to rely on an exercise of judicial discretion after the event (see Case C-427/07 *Commission v Ireland* (n 40) paras 92 to 94). 'A PCO must be made in order to avoid the chilling effect of an open ended exposure to liability for the respondent and the two interested parties' costs ...' (see para 21). Moreover at para 39, Garner Sullivan LJ said '[t]he fact that such an award [of costs] might not be made as an exercise of judicial discretion was insufficiently certain for the purposes of Article 10a (see *Commission v Ireland*)'.

[47] C-240/09 *Lesoochranárske Zoskupenie VLK* [2011] 2 CMLR 43.

questions of standing, that while Article 9(3) did not have direct effect, it was for the national court 'to interpret its national law in a way which, to the fullest extent possible, is consistent with the objectives laid down in Article 9(3) of the Aarhus Convention'. In that case a Slovakian association which had the objective of protection of the environment, applied to the Slovakian Ministry of the Environment to be a party to administrative proceedings relating to the grant of derogations to the system of protection for species such as the brown bear, access to protected countryside areas, or the use of chemical substances in such areas. This was rejected and this was challenged in the Courts. In those proceedings the Court made a reference to the CJEU as to the effect of Art 9(3) of the Aarhus Convention.

The CJEU held that it had jurisdiction to interpret Art 9(3) of the Convention. In this regard it noted that the PP Directive does not cover fully the implementation of the obligations resulting from Art 9(3) of the Aarhus Convention and that, consequently, its Member States are responsible for the performance of these obligations. However, it found, it cannot be inferred that the dispute in the main proceedings does not fall within the scope of EU law because a specific issue which has not yet been subject to EU legislation may fall within the scope of EU law if it relates to a field covered in large measure by it. The CJEU held:

> 45. It must be held that the provisions of Article 9(3) of the Aarhus Convention do not contain any clear and precise obligation capable of directly regulating the legal position of individuals. Since only members of the public who meet the criteria, if any, laid down by national law are entitled to exercise the rights provided for in Article 9(3), that provision is subject, in its implementation or effects, to the adoption of a subsequent measure.
>
> 46. However, it must be observed that those provisions, although drafted in broad terms, are intended to ensure effective environmental protection.
>
> 47. In the absence of EU rules governing the matter, it is for the domestic legal system of each Member State to lay down the detailed procedural rules governing actions for safeguarding rights which individuals derive from EU law, in this case the Habitats Directive, since the Member States are responsible for ensuring that those rights are effectively protected in each case (see, in particular, Case C-268/06 *Impact* [2008] ECR I2483, paragraphs 44 and 45).
>
> 48. On that basis, as is apparent from well-established case-law, the detailed procedural rules governing actions for safeguarding an individual's rights under EU law must be no less favourable than those governing similar domestic actions (principle of equivalence) and must not make it in practice impossible or excessively difficult to exercise rights conferred by EU law (principle of effectiveness) (Impact, paragraph 46 and the case-law cited).
>
> 49. Therefore, if the effective protection of EU environmental law is not to be undermined, it is inconceivable that Article 9(3) of the Aarhus Convention be interpreted in such a way as to make it in practice impossible or excessively difficult to exercise rights conferred by EU law.

50. It follows that, in so far as concerns a species protected by EU law, and in particular the Habitats Directive, it is for the national court, in order to ensure effective judicial protection in the fields covered by EU environmental law, to interpret its national law in a way which, to the fullest extent possible, is consistent with the objectives laid down in Article 9(3) of the Aarhus Convention.

51. Therefore, it is for the referring court to interpret, to the fullest extent possible, the procedural rules relating to the conditions to be met in order to bring administrative or judicial proceedings in accordance with the objectives of Article 9(3) of the Aarhus Convention and the objective of effective judicial protection of the rights conferred by EU law, so as to enable an environmental protection organisation, such as the zoskupenie, to challenge before a court a decision taken following administrative proceedings liable to be contrary to EU environmental law (see, to that effect, Case C-432/05 *Unibet* [2007] ECR I2271, paragraph 44, and Impact, paragraph 54).

52. In those circumstances, the answer to the first and second questions referred is that Article 9(3) of the Aarhus Convention does not have direct effect in EU law. It is, however, for the referring court to interpret, to the fullest extent possible, the procedural rules relating to the conditions to be met in order to bring administrative or judicial proceedings in accordance with the objectives of Article 9(3) of that convention and the objective of effective judicial protection of the rights conferred by EU law, in order to enable an environmental protection organisation, such as the zoskupenie, to challenge before a court a decision taken following administrative proceedings liable to be contrary to EU environmental law.

While the CJEU has thus been astute to ensure that the Member States do not apply an overly restrictive approach to the standing, especially of NGOs, it has not addressed though its own failings in this regard and which were the subject of a ACCC decision (ACCC/C/2008/32 (European Community)). Article 263(4) TFEU sets out the test for standing for non-privileged applicants in an action for annulment. It provides that a natural or legal person will have standing in one of three scenarios: (i) if the act is addressed to the applicant; (ii) if the act is of direct and individual concern to the applicant; or (iii) if the challenge is to a regulatory act that is of direct concern to the claimant and does not entail implementing measures. As is well-known, these tests are interpreted very restrictively: see eg *Plaumann*;[48] and see also *P Inuit Tapiriit Kanatami and Others v European Parliament and Council*.[49]

In ACCC/C/2008/3, ClientEarth complained that the 'individual concern' requirement was incompatible with the EU's obligations under Article 9 of the Aarhus Convention. The Compliance Committee issued its findings in April 2011. It reviewed the European jurisprudence on standing and 'individual concerned', but did not make a finding of non-compliance because the previous cases

[48] *Plaumann* [1964] CMLR 29.

[49] Case C-583/11 *P Inuit Tapiriit Kanatami and Others v European Parliament and Council* [2014] QB 648.

pre-dated the entry into force of the Convention. Nevertheless, the Committee did state (findings dated 24 August 2011):

> the Committee is also convinced that if the examined jurisprudence of the EU Courts on access to justice were to continue, unless fully compensated by adequate administrative review procedures, the Party concerned would fail to comply with article 9, paragraph 3 of the Convention ([88]).
>
> a new direction of the jurisprudence of the EU courts should be established in order to ensure compliance with the Convention ([97]).

As mentioned above standing requirements in England & Wales are very liberal. There are two cases where standing has directly been addressed in the context of the Aarhus Convention.

First, in *Ashton v Secretary of State for Communities and Local Government and Coin Street Community Builders Ltd*,[50] the appellant was a local resident whose property was affected by the development. He was a member of the Waterloo Community Development Group ('WCDG'). He did not make any representations to the local authority or at the public inquiry. He stated that he had asked WCDG to make representations on his behalf. The Court of Appeal rejected his s 288 challenge on the merits but went on to consider whether he would in any event have been a 'person aggrieved'. Pill LJ in his judgment considered Article 10a of the EIA Directive, the Stockholm case and *Commission v Ireland*. He concluded:

> 53 The following principles may be extracted from the authorities and applied when considering whether a person is aggrieved within the meaning of s.288 of the 1990 Act:
>
> 1. Wide access to the courts is required under s.288 (art.10a, *N'Jie*).[51]
> 2. Normally, participation in the planning process which led to the decision sought to be challenged is required. What is sufficient participation will depend on the opportunities available and the steps taken (*Eco-Energy*,[52] *Lardner*).[53]
> 3. There may be situations in which failure to participate is not a bar (*Cumming*,[54] cited in *Lardner*).
> 4. A further factor to be considered is the nature and weight of the person's substantive interest and the extent to which it is prejudiced (*N'Jie* and *Lardner*). The sufficiency of the interest must be considered (art.10a).
> 5. This factor is to be assessed objectively. There is a difference between feeling aggrieved and being aggrieved (*Lardner*).
> 6. What might otherwise be a sufficient interest may not be sufficient if acquired for the purpose of establishing a status under s.288 (*Morbaine*).[55]

[50] *Ashton v Secretary of State for Communities and Local Government and Coin Street Community Builders Ltd* [2011] 1 P & CR 5.

[51] *Attorney General of the Gambia v N'Jie* [1961] AC 617.

[52] *Eco-Energy (GB) Ltd v First Secretary of State* [2004] EWCA Civ 1566; [2005] 2 P & CR 5.

[53] *Lardner v Renfrewshire Council* 1997 SCLR 454; 1997 SC 104.

[54] *Cumming v Secretary of State for Scotland* 1992 SC 463; 1993 SLT 228.

[55] *Morbaine Ltd v First Secretary of State & Ors* [2004] EWHC 1708 (Admin); [2005] JPL 377.

7. The participation factor and the interest factor may be interrelated in that it may not be possible to assess the extent of the person's interest if he has not participated in the planning procedures (*Lardner*).
8. While recognising the need for wide access to the courts, weight may be given, when assessing the prior participation required, and the interests relied on, to the public interest in the implementation of projects and the delay involved in judicial proceedings (A.G. Kokott in *Ireland*).[56]

54 I do not consider that the appellant had standing under s.288 to bring the present claim. His participation in the planning process was insufficient in the circumstances to acquire standing. He was not an objector to the proposal in any formal sense and did not make representations, either oral or written, at the properly constituted Public Inquiry. Mere attendance at parts of the hearing and membership of WCDG, which has not brought proceedings in this court, were insufficient. I agree with the judge's conclusion set out at [32] above.

55 Moreover, the absence of representations before or at the Inquiry about the loss of amenity at his property, either personally or by WCDG, deprived CSCB and the local planning authority of the opportunity to test the extent of the alleged loss and to call evidence in response. That being so, the Inspector, the fact-finding tribunal, was not in a position to assess the extent of the loss and whether it amounts to a sufficient interest. This Court cannot make good that deficiency.

56 I make no finding as to whether the appellant would also fail under the interest limb of the test, though it appears to me likely that he would do so. A major project, approved following proper public consultation and a Public Inquiry, should not readily be challengeable on this or other grounds on the basis of a grievance about amenity such as the appellant's appears to be. What is a sufficient interest will always be a question of fact and degree. That reinforces the need to place the facts relied on before the decision maker during the planning process.

That case while not discussed expressly in *Walton v Scottish Ministers*,[57] *Ashton* would now have to be considered in the light of the wide approach taken by the Supreme Court in that case to the 'person aggrieved test'. And see also *JB Trustees Ltd v Secretary of State for Communities and Local Government*.[58]

Second, in *Coedbach Action Team Ltd v Secretary of State for Energy and Climate Change*,[59] there was a standing issue. Coedbach applied for a PCO in respect of its application for judicial review of a consent for a biomass fuelled power station granted by the Secretary of State. Coedbach was a limited company formed by local residents as a response to a proposal to build two biomass power stations in Wales which Coedbach was opposing. There were ongoing appeals in respect of those

[56] *Commission v Ireland* (n 40).
[57] *Walton v Scottish Ministers* [2012] UKSC 44; [2013] PTSR 5.
[58] *JB Trustees Ltd v Secretary of State for Communities and Local Government* [2013] EWHC 3555 (Admin).
[59] *Coedbach Action Team Ltd v Secretary of State for Energy and Climate Change* [2010] EWHC 2312 (Admin); [2011] 1 Costs LR 70. This was upheld on appeal: [2010] EWCA Civ 1494.

proposals. Meanwhile the Secretary of State granted consent under the Electricity Act 1989 for a biomass power station in England and directed that planning permission be deemed to be granted under the Town and Country Planning Act 1990 s 90(2). Coedbach did not object to the applications for consent and played no part in the process until it issued an application for permission to apply for judicial review of that decision out of a concern that the decision might influence the decisions in respect of the Welsh proposals. The issue of standing arose in the context of the PCO application, and Coedbach's attempt to rely on the Aarhus Convention:

> 29 I accept the submissions made on behalf of the defendant and Interested Party that the claimant is not a member of the public concerned and it is not a person having a sufficient interest. The claimant is a limited company whose aims and objects are made clear, unequivocally, in its Memorandum of Association. Its aim is to protect a particular local environment. The claimant played no part in the decision-making process leading to the grant of the consents to the Interested Party. But for the coincidence that the planning appeals with which the claimant is concerned were in progress at a time when the defendant's decision was made it is clear, in my judgment, that the claimant would have shown no interest in challenging the lawfulness of the defendant's decision. The claimant readily accepts that its sole purpose in challenging the defendant's decision is to prevent it becoming material to the decisions to be made in the planning appeals in which the claimant is an objector.
>
> 30 During the course of the hearing there was some debate as to the status and/or relevance of the defendant's decision in the planning appeals. I accept the submission of Mr Maurici that the defendant's decision can be no more than a material consideration. It cannot be said, as was suggested by Mr Kimblin, that part of the reasoning of the defendant in support of his decision constitutes an expression of the defendant's policy which would be binding upon an Inspector appointed by the Welsh Ministers to conduct the planning appeals in which the claimant appears as an objector. Even if the defendant's decision is treated as a material consideration by the Inspector considering the appeals I infer that it will be but one of a host of factors which will be considered. Mr Kimblin did not suggest before me that the acceptance of the defendant's decision as a material consideration would be, in effect, determinative of the planning appeals.
>
> 31 In any event it must be borne in mind when assessing whether the claimant has a sufficient interest for the purposes of the Directive that if the defendant's decision is treated as a material consideration and if the appeals are allowed the claimant has the ability to challenge those decisions under s 288 Town and Country Planning Act 1990.
>
> 32 Mr Maurici prays in aid the claimant's ability to challenge any successful appeals under s 288 as a free standing reason why the defendant's decision in these proceedings should not be the subject of judicial review. He may be right. In my judgment, however, the existence of this 'alternative remedy' is also relevant, at least in the context of a case such as the present, in assessing whether the claimant is a member of the public concerned having a sufficient interest for the purposes of the Directive. I do not accept that this alternative remedy is illusory. It is illusory only if the claimant so conducts its affairs that it has no funds to mount a challenge under s 288. That

is a matter of choice for the claimant. In my judgment the existence of the right to challenge any decisions in the appellate process which are adverse to the claimant's objectives is a factor which militates against the conclusion that the claimant is a member of the public concerned having a sufficient interest when challenging the defendant's decision.

33 I have reached the clear conclusion that the claimant is not a member of the public concerned for the purposes of the Directive. That being so the Directive is not material to my decision upon whether or not to grant a protective costs order.

34 I should make two further points in this context for completeness. Mr Kimblin acknowledges that the claimant can bring itself within the Directive only if it establishes that it has a sufficient interest. It cannot, for example, assert that it is maintaining the impairment of a right; further, Mr Kimblin does not suggest that the claimant brings itself within the Directive because it is a nongovernmental organisation falling within the provisions of Article 1(2).[60]

'Substantive and Procedural Legality'

In ACCC/C/2008/33 the ACCC expressed concern as to the adequacy of judicial review on standard public law grounds in the UK but 'based on the information before it in the context of the current communication, the Committee does not go so far as to find the Party concerned to be in non-compliance with Article 9, paragraphs 2 or 3, of the Convention'. The Committee said:

123. Article 9, paragraph 2, of the Convention addresses both substantive and procedural legality. Hence, the Party concerned has to ensure that members of the public have access to a review procedure before a court of law and/or another independent body established by law which can review both the substantive and procedural legality of decisions, acts and omissions in appropriate cases.

124. Article 9, paragraph 3, of the Convention, as opposed to article 9, paragraph 2, of the Convention, does not explicitly refer to either substantive or procedural legality. Instead it refers to 'acts or omissions [...] which contravene its national law relating to the environment'. Clearly, the issue to be considered in such a review procedure is whether the act or omission in question contravened any provision—be it substantive or procedural—in national law relating to the environment.

125. The Committee finds that the Party concerned allows for members of the public to challenge certain aspects of the substantive legality of decisions, acts or omissions subject to article 9, paragraphs 2 and 3, of the Convention, including, inter alia, for material

[60] On standing see also now the views of the Supreme Court in *Walton v Scottish Ministers* [2013] PTSRSI and also more recently, *Zurich Assurance Ltd v Winchester City Council* [2014] EWHC 758 (Admin) and *JB Trustees Ltd v Secretary of State for Communities and Local Government* [2014] JPL 656.

error of fact; error of law; regard to irrelevant considerations and failure to have regard to relevant considerations; jurisdictional error; and on the grounds of Wednesbury unreasonableness (see paras. 87–89 above). The Committee, however, is not convinced that the Party concerned, despite the above-mentioned challengeable aspects, meets the standards for review required by the Convention as regards substantive legality. In this context, the Committee notes for example the criticisms by the House of Lords, and the European Court of Human Rights, of the very high threshold for review imposed by the Wednesbury test.

126. The Committee considers that the application of a 'proportionality principle' by the courts in England and Wales could provide an adequate standard of review in cases within the scope of the Aarhus Convention. A proportionality test requires a public authority to provide evidence that the act or decision pursued justifies the limitation of the right at stake, is connected to the aim(s) which that act or decision seeks to achieve and that the means used to limit the right at stake are no more than necessary to attain the aim(s) of the act or decision at stake. While a proportionality principle in cases within the scope of the Aarhus Convention may go a long way towards providing for a review of substantive and procedural legality, the Party concerned must make sure that such a principle does not generally or prima facie exclude any issue of substantive legality from a review.

127. Given its findings in paragraphs 125 and 126 above, the Committee expresses concern regarding the availability of appropriate judicial or administrative procedures, as required by article 9, paragraphs 2 and 3, of the Convention, in which the substantive legality of decisions, acts or omissions within the scope of the Convention can be subjected to review under the law of England and Wales. However, based on the information before it in the context of the current communication, the Committee does not go so far as to find the Party concerned to be in non-compliance with article 9, paragraphs 2 or 3, of the Convention.

The English Courts have rejected this concern, most recently by the Divisional Court in *R (Evans) v Attorney General*:[61]

130 I do not think the provisions of article 9 of the Aarhus Convention really tell against that conclusion. On the contrary, article 9(1) in general terms, so far as concerns requests under article 4 (access to environmental information), requires 'access to a review procedure' by an independent and impartial body established by law. That generality of approach is reflected in article 6(2) of the Directive itself.

131 It is true that article 9(2) of the Aarhus Convention requires access to such a body 'to challenge the substantive and procedural legality of any decision': albeit that is dealing specifically with requests under article 6 (public participation in decisions on specific activities) and such language is not in fact deployed in article 9(1) of the Aarhus Convention. It is also true that the Implementation Guide to the Aarhus Convention 2nd ed (2013), p 199 asserts that the entitlement to challenge the 'substantive and procedural legality' is 'implicit' in article 9(1) also; and the 2011 recommendations of the

[61] *R (Evans) v Attorney General* [2013] EWHC 1960 (Admin); [2013] 3 WLR 1631.

Implementation Committee had indicated concern as to whether a judicial review procedure, of the model adopted under the law of England and Wales, meet the standards of review said to be required by the Aarhus Convention with regard to substantive legality. But the point was tentatively put by the Implementation Committee: and there was, at all events, no finding that the United Kingdom was in non-compliance with article 9 of the Aarhus Convention : see para 127. Moreover, while the Implementation Guide itself may properly be taken into account, it is not binding: any more than are the views of the Implementation Committee.

132 Mr Swift cited *R (Evans) v Secretary of State for Communities and Local Government* [2013] EWCA Civ 114, a case on the Town and Country Planning (Environmental Impact Assessment) (England and Wales) Regulations 1999 (SI 1999/293). Among other things, in that case, article 9 of the Aarhus Convention fell to be considered, including the suggested need for assessment by a court of the substantive and procedural legality of an environmental decision, at para 33. It was observed by Beatson LJ, at para 37 of his judgment (with which Sir Stanley Burnton and Patten LJ agreed), that the expressed concerns of the Aarhus Convention Compliance Committee did not bind the English courts and in any event did not 'identify the variations in the intensity of *Wednesbury* review that reflect the nature of the interests affected'.

133 As may be gathered from what I have previously said, I attach considerable importance to the principle reaffirmed by Beatson LJ in this last sentence. Judicial review is a procedure consistent with the requirements of article 9(4) of the Aarhus Convention. It is a flexible procedure, enabling an appropriate intensity of review where such intensity of review is called for: see also the analogous reasoning of the Court of Appeal in *T-Mobile (UK) Ltd v Office of Communications* [2009] 1 WLR 1565—a competition case dealing with Parliament and Council Directive 2002/21/EC. In the present kind of case, close scrutiny by the court is called for: and such close scrutiny of the reasons given for the accountable person's opinion must require—and has here required—a close scrutiny by the court of the initial *1668 decision to withhold. Indeed, if there were substantive or procedural illegality or irregularity in the original decision such a review by the court, under section 53, should reveal it. In my view, that amply complies with the requirements of article 6(2) of Directive 2003/4.

However, in the Court of Appeal in that case ([2014] 2 WLR 1334) it was said:

Nature of the review required by article 6(2)

68 We heard a good deal of argument on the question whether article 6(2) requires a full reconsideration of the merits by the court de novo or whether some form of judicial review is sufficient. I have reached a decision on the third issue without addressing this question. In deference to the submissions of counsel, however, it is right that I should say something about it. Miss Rose relies on the statement of Sullivan LJ in the *Department for the Environment case* [2012] PTSR 1299 (see para 42 above) and submits that article 6(2) requires the court to consider de novo for itself the propriety of releasing the information …

69 Mr Swift says that we should prefer the approach of Beatson LJ in *R (Evans) v Secretary of State for Communities and Local Government* [2013] JPL 1027. This case involved a different Directive (the 'Environmental Impact Assessment Directive':

> Council Directive 85/337/EEC as subsequently amended) which concerned environmental impact assessments and which contained provisions derived from the Aarhus Convention. Beatson LJ (with whom the other members of the court agreed) decided that orthodox Wednesbury review is compatible with the requirements of the 'access to justice' provisions in the Directive. But since (i) the case involves a different Directive and (ii) the statement of Sullivan LJ is binding on us, I shall not lengthen this judgment by elaborating on the differences between the two Directives to which Miss Rose drew our attention.
>
> ...
>
> 73 If I had considered that it was necessary to decide what kind of review is required by article 6(2) , I would have been inclined to hold that it was not acte clair and to make a reference to the Court of Justice. It seems to me that it is not clear that in relation to article 6(2) the approach of Sullivan LJ in the *Department for the Environment case* [2012] PTSR 1299 is to be preferred to that of Beatson LJ in the *Evans* case [2013] JPL 1027. The policy imperatives of the Aarhus Convention and the Directive are clear enough in broad terms. The difficult question is whether a Wednesbury review is sufficiently flexible to meet the requirements of article 6(2).

The matter is now going to the Supreme Court.

Costs

The final findings of the ACCC in ACCC/C/2008/33 as regards costs in the UK are at paras 129–136:

> 129. The Committee considers that the 'costs follow the event rule', contained in rule 44.3(2) of the Civil Procedure Rules, is not inherently objectionable under the Convention, although the compatibility of this rule with the Convention depends on the outcome in each specific case and the existence of a clear rule that prevents prohibitively expensive procedures. In this context, the Committee considers whether the effects of 'costs follow the event rule' can be softened by legal aid, CFAs and PCOs as well as by the considerable discretionary powers that the courts have in interpreting and applying the relevant law. At this stage, however, at least four potential problems emerge with regard to the legal system of E&W. First, the 'general public importance', 'no private interest' and 'in exceptional circumstances' criteria applied when considering the granting of PCOs. Second, the limiting effects of (i) the costs for a claimant if a PCO is applied for and not granted and (ii) PCOs that cap the costs of both parties. Third, the potential effect of cross-undertakings in damages on the costs incurred by a claimant. Fourth, the fact that in determining the allocation of costs in a given case, the public interest nature of the environmental claims under consideration is not in and of itself given sufficient consideration.
>
> 130. While the courts in E&W have applied a flexible approach to *Corner House* criteria when considering the granting of PCOs, including the 'general public importance', 'no private interest' and 'exceptional circumstances' criteria, they have also indicated

that, given the ruling in *Corner House*, there are limits to this flexible approach. The Committee notes the numerous calls by judges suggesting that the Civil Procedure Rules Committee take legislative action in respect of PCOs, also in view of the Convention (see paragraph 102 above). These calls have to date not resulted in amendment of the Civil Procedure Rules so as to ensure that all cases within the scope of article 9 of the Aarhus Convention are accorded the standards set by the Convention. The Convention, amongst other things, requires its Parties to 'provide adequate and effective remedies' which shall be 'fair, equitable [...] and not prohibitively expensive'. The Committee endorses the calls by the judiciary and suggests that the Party concerned amend the Civil Procedure Rules in the light of the standards set by the Convention.

131. Within such considerations the Committee finds that the Party concerned should also consider the cost that may be incurred by a claimant in those cases where a PCO is applied for but not granted, as suggested in Appendix 3 to the Sullivan Report. The Committee endorses this recommendation.

132. The Committee also notes the limiting effect of reciprocal cost caps ...

134. Moreover, in accordance with its findings in ACCC/C/2008/23 (UK) and ACCC/C/2008/27 (UK), the Committee considers that in legal proceedings within the scope of article 9 of the Convention, the public interest nature of the environmental claims under consideration does not seem to be given sufficient consideration in the apportioning of costs by the courts.

135. The Committee concludes that despite the various measures available to address prohibitive costs, taken together they do not ensure that the costs remain at a level which meets the requirements under the Convention. At this stage, the Committee considers that the considerable discretion of the courts of E&W in deciding the costs, without any clear legally binding direction from the legislature or judiciary to ensure costs are not prohibitively expensive, leads to considerable uncertainty regarding the costs to be faced where claimants are legitimately pursuing environmental concerns that involve the public interest. The Committee also notes the Court of Appeal's judgment in *Morgan v. Hinton Organics*, which held that the principles of the Convention are 'at most' a factor which it 'may' (not must) take into account, 'along with a number of other factors, such as fairness to the defendant'. The Committee in this respect notes that 'fairness' in article 9, paragraph 4, refers to what is fair for the claimant, not the defendant.

136. In the light of the above, the Committee concludes that the Party concerned has not adequately implemented its obligation in article 9, paragraph 4, to ensure that the procedures subject to article 9 are not prohibitively expensive. In addition, the Committee finds that the system as a whole is not such as 'to remove or reduce financial [...] barriers to access to justice', as article 9, paragraph 5, of the Convention requires a Party to the Convention to consider.

In the Cultra Residents' Association case (ACCC/C/2008/27) in relation to the expansion of Belfast City Airport, the Aarhus Compliance Committee found that an order for the claimant to pay £39,454 following the dismissal of its claim for judicial review was prohibitively expensive. By contrast in the Morgan case (ACCC/2008/23), the Committee held that an adverse costs order of £5,130 was not prohibitively expensive. There is a further decision against the UK involving costs at the permission stage: see ACCC/C/2012/77.[62]

Following the decision of the ACCC in ACCC/C/2008/33 in England and Wales new fixed costs rules (in CPR 45.43) for 'Aarhus Convention claims' were introduced, these provide for fixed costs in respect of a judicial review[63] 'of a decision, act or omission all or part of which is subject to the provisions of the UNECE convention on Access to Information, Public Participation in Decision-Making and Access to Justice in Environmental Matters': see CPR 45.41–45.44 and the PD 45 at paras 5.1–5.2. Two limits are set: on the costs recoverable by a defendant from a claimant (£5,000 where the claimant is an individual and £10,000 in any other circumstances) and; on the costs recoverable by a claimant from a defendant (£35,000). No provision is made in the rules to vary these terms; if a claimant wants some other order as to costs s/he can still apply for a PCO, eg limiting a claimant's liability below £5000.[64] The amendments do not apply to a claim commenced before 1 April 2013. CPR 45.44 provides that if a claimant states it is an Aarhus Convention claim in the claim form then it is unless the defendant challenges that in Acknowledgement of Service and the Court determines it is not such a case. If the Court decides it is not, the rules provide that it will usually award no costs in relation to determination of that issue, if it decides it is such a case then the Defendant will normally be ordered to pay indemnity costs.

> These rules apply only at first instance. On appeals the relevant rule is CPR 52.9A.
>
> Orders to limit the recoverable costs of an appeal
>
> 52.9A.—(1) In any proceedings in which costs recovery is normally limited or excluded at first instance, an appeal court may make an order that the recoverable costs of an appeal will be limited to the extent which the court specifies.
>
> (2) In making such an order the court will have regard to—
> (a) the means of both parties;
> (b) all the circumstances of the case; and
> (c) the need to facilitate access to justice.
>
> (3) If the appeal raises an issue of principle or practice upon which substantial sums may turn, it may not be appropriate to make an order under paragraph (1).
>
> (4) An application for such an order must be made as soon as practicable and will be determined without a hearing unless the court orders otherwise.[65]

There had been some suggestion that in environmental appeals governed by these rules the PCO granted below or the fixed costs rules imposed in Aarhus

[62] www.unece.org/env/pp/pubcom.html.

[63] The Court of Appeal in *Venn* confirmed that the CPR did not apply to non-judicial review claims, eg, a claim under s 288 of the Town and Country Planning Act 1990. It also held that because this was a deliberate exclusion the ability to obtain PCO's in cases not governed by the EIA or IE Directives was limited to satisfying the *Corner House* criteria.

[64] See *R (Botley Parish Action Group) v Eastleigh Borough Council* [2014] EWHC 3488 (Admin) on the application of these rules where there are multiple claimants.

[65] See on this rule, *The Manchester College v Hazel* [2013] EWCA Civ 281.

Convention claims should also apply to the appeal costs, eg that there be no further exposure to costs for appealing. That view is not supported by the decision of the Supreme Court in *R (Edwards) v Environment Agency*,[66] where Lord Carnwath said:

> 23 A number of significant points can be extracted from the *Edwards* judgment [of the CJEU]... The same criteria are to be applied on appeal as at first instance.
>
> 24 I do not understand the last point as intended to imply that the same order must be made at each stage of the proceedings, or that there should be a single global figure covering all potential stages, but rather that the same principles should be applied to the assessment at each stage, taking account of costs previously incurred. In her 2013 opinion in *Commission of the European Union v United Kingdom* (Case C-530/11), the Advocate General said of the court's reasoning on this point:
>
> 'that finding cannot be interpreted as meaning that in assessing the permissible cost burden in appeal proceedings the costs already incurred in courts below may be ignored. Instead, each court must ensure that the costs at all levels of jurisdiction taken together are not prohibitive or excessive' (para 23).
>
> 25 However, as she had recognised in her earlier opinion (2012 opinion in *R (Edwards) v Environment Agency (No 2)* (Case C-260/11) [2013] 1 WLR 2914, paras 58–61), while 'prohibitive costs must be prevented at all levels of jurisdiction', the considerations may differ at each level. Thus, on the one hand, as she notes, the decision of the House of Lords as the final court was potentially of special significance, because it alone had a duty to make a reference to the European court in case of doubt as to EU law. On the other hand, it is possible that after the decision by the lower court, public interest in the further continuation of the proceedings would be reduced. Accordingly, she said, it was compatible with Aarhus tests 'to re-examine at each level of jurisdiction the extent to which prohibitive costs must be prevented'.

In this regard it is relevant to consider ACCC/C/2008/24; a communication to the Aarhus Compliance Committee. In that case, concerning Spain, the Aarhus Compliance Committee took note of 'the evidence demonstrating that in practice if a natural or legal person loses in the court of first instance against a public authority, appeals the decision and loses again, the related costs are being imposed on the appellant; it stressed that if this trend reflected a general practice of courts of appeal in Spain regarding costs, this would also constitute non-compliance with article 9, paragraph 4': see the findings of the first addendum to the report of the Compliance Committee of its 26th meeting.[67] That finding, had it been allowed to stand, would have supported the Appellant's case as now advanced before this Court. However, the Meeting of the Parties declined to endorse this as a finding (see para 27 of the Report on the fourth session of the Meeting of the Parties) and accordingly it has no status.

[66] *R (Edwards) v Environment Agency* (n 4).

[67] At para 110 and para 117.

In Scotland see the Act of Sederunt (Rules of the Court of Session Amendment) (Protective Expenses Orders in Environmental Appeals and Judicial Reviews) 2013, whichapplies to appeals as well as first instance judicial review cases, but not to all Aarhus cases only those within scope of EIA Directive and the IPPC Directive (now the IE Directive); caps of £5000 and £30000. Northern Ireland has introduced rules similar to England.

The main issue which has occupied the domestic Courts in recent times in relation to costs and Aarhus is the question whether the cost of litigation is or is not 'prohibitively expensive' to be decided on an 'objective' basis by reference (for example) to the ability of an 'ordinary' member of the public to meet the potential liability for costs, or should it be decided on a 'subjective' basis by reference to the means of the particular claimant, or upon some combination of the two bases?[68]

In *R (Garner) v Elmbridge Borough Council*,[69] the Court of Appeal said that

> [w]hether or not the proper approach to the 'not prohibitively expensive requirement under Article 10a' should be a wholly objective one, I am satisfied that a purely *subjective* approach, as was applied by Nicol J, is not consistent with the objectives underlying the directive.[70]

The issue was referred by the Supreme Court in *R (Edwards) v Environment Agency* [2011] 1 WLR 79.[71] Lord Hope noted

> that the test which the court must apply to ensure that the proceedings are not prohibitively expensive remains in a state of uncertainty. The balance seems to lie in favour of the objective approach, but this has yet to be finally determined.

The CJEU in *R (Edwards) v Environment Agency (No 2)*[72] held that:

> 40 That assessment cannot, therefore, be carried out solely on the basis of the financial situation of the person concerned but must also be based on an objective analysis of the amount of the costs, particularly since, as has been stated in para 32 of the present judgment, members of the public and associations are naturally required to play an active role in defending the environment. To that extent, the cost of proceedings must not appear, in certain cases, to be objectively unreasonable. Thus, the cost of proceedings must neither exceed the financial resources of the person concerned nor appear, in any event, to be objectively unreasonable.

[68] This was a matter touched on in the first Sullivan Report *Ensuring Access to Environmental Justice in England and Wales—Report of the Working Group on Access to Environmental Justice* back in May 2008 (see below) but has only in the last year or so come to prominence. The Sullivan Report said 'we consider ... costs, whether actual or risked, would be "prohibitively expensive" if they would reasonably prevent an "ordinary" member of the public from embarking on the challenge falling within the terms of Aarhus ...' (see pp 12 and 34). A footnote on p 12 of the Report also said in respect of the phrase 'an "ordinary" member of the public' that this refers to the 'elusive concept of a member of a public who is neither very rich nor very poor, and would not be entitled to legal aid ...'.

[69] *R (Garner) v Elmbridge Borough Council* (n 44).

[70] ibid para 46.

[71] *R (Edwards) v Environment Agency* (n 4).

[72] Case C-260/11 *R (Edwards) v Environment Agency (No 2)* [2013] 1 WLR 2914.

41 As regards the analysis of the financial situation of the person concerned, the assessment which must be carried out by the national court cannot be based exclusively on the estimated financial resources of an 'average' applicant, since such information may have little connection with the situation of the person concerned.

42 The court may also take into account the situation of the parties concerned, whether the claimant has a reasonable prospect of success, the importance of what is at stake for the claimant and for the protection of the environment, the complexity of the relevant law and procedure and the potentially frivolous nature of the claim at its various stages: see, by analogy, *DEB Deutsche Energiehandels-und Beratungsgesellschaft mbH v Bundesrepublik Deutschland* (Case C-279/09) [2010] ECR I-13849 , para 61.

43 It must also be stated that the fact, put forward by the Supreme Court of the United Kingdom, that the claimant has not been deterred, in practice, from asserting his or her claim is not in itself sufficient to establish that the proceedings are not, as far as that claimant is concerned, prohibitively expensive for the purpose (as set out above) of Directives 85/337 and 96/61.

44 Lastly, as regards the question whether the assessment as to whether or not the costs are prohibitively expensive ought to differ according to whether the national court is deciding on costs at the conclusion of first instance proceedings, an appeal or a second appeal, an issue which was also raised by the referring court, no such distinction is envisaged in Directives 85/337 and 96/61 , nor, moreover, would such an interpretation be likely to comply fully with the objective of the European Union legislature, which is to ensure wide access to justice and to contribute to the improvement of environmental protection.

45 The requirement that judicial proceedings should not be prohibitively expensive cannot, therefore, be assessed differently by a national court depending on whether it is adjudicating at the conclusion of first instance proceedings, an appeal or a second appeal.

46 It must therefore be held that, where the national court is required to determine, in the context referred to in para 41 of the present judgment, whether judicial proceedings on environmental matters are prohibitively expensive for a claimant, it cannot act solely on the basis of that claimant's financial situation but must also carry out an objective analysis of the amount of the costs. It may also take into account the situation of the parties concerned, whether the claimant has a reasonable prospect of success, the importance of what is at stake for the claimant and for the protection of the environment, the complexity of the relevant law and procedure, the potentially frivolous nature of the claim at its various stages, and the existence of a national legal aid scheme or a costs protection regime.

47 By contrast, the fact that a claimant has not been deterred, in practice, from asserting his claim is not of itself sufficient to establish that the proceedings are not prohibitively expensive for him.

48 Lastly, that assessment cannot be conducted according to different criteria depending on whether it is carried out at the conclusion of first instance proceedings, an appeal or a second appeal.

Lord Carnwath in *Edwards*[73] said:

> 3 A number of significant points can be extracted from the Edwards judgment. (i) First, the test is not purely subjective. The cost of proceedings must not exceed the financial resources of the person concerned nor 'appear to be objectively unreasonable', at least 'in certain cases'. (The meaning of the latter qualification is not immediately obvious, but it may be better expressed in the German version 'in Einzelfällen', meaning simply 'in individual cases'.) The justification is related to the objective of the relevant European legislation (referred to in para 32 of the judgment), which is to ensure that the public 'plays an active role' in protecting and improving the quality of the environment. (ii) The court did not give definitive guidance as to how to assess what is 'objectively unreasonable'. In particular it did not in terms adopt Sullivan LJ's suggested alternative of an 'objective' assessment based on the ability of an 'ordinary' member of the public to meet the potential liability for costs. While the court did not apparently reject that as a possible factor in the overall assessment, 'exclusive' reliance on the resources of an 'average applicant' was not appropriate, because it might have 'little connection with the situation of the person concerned'. (iii) The court could also take into account what might be called the 'merits' *66 of the case: that is, in the words of the court, 'whether the claimant has a reasonable prospect of success, the importance of what is at stake for the claimant and for the protection of the environment, the complexity of the relevant law and procedure, the potentially frivolous nature of the claim at its various stages' (para 42). (iv) That the claimant has not in fact been deterred for carrying on the proceedings is not 'in itself' determinative. (v) The same criteria are to be applied on appeal as at first instance.[74]

The CJEU in *Commission v UK*[75] largely followed the analysis in *Edwards*.[76] It found that the UK was, as at 22 May 2010, in breach of its obligations imposed by the PP Directive transposing (in part) Article 9 of the Aarhus Convention, to ensure that costs in environmental proceedings are not 'prohibitively expensive'. The Commission argued judicial decision-making was inherently incapable of being relied upon to implement EU law. On that the CJEU said at para 36, 'it cannot be considered that every judicial practice is uncertain and inherently incapable of meeting those requirements'. The CJEU found though that judicial practice in respect of PCOs was, as at 22 May 2010, not sufficiently certain but did not go on to consider what would be considered to be sufficiently certain in this regard; what it did recognise though was that in principle, judicial practice was capable of effecting implementation in this context. The Commission's case that reciprocal caps breached the requirements of the Aarhus Convention, and which the Advocate-General appeared to express some agreement with, was rejected on the basis of lack of evidence.

[73] *R (Edwards) v Environment Agency* [2014] 1 WLR 55.
[74] See also *Eaton v Natural England & another* [2013] EWCA Civ 628.
[75] *Commission v UK* (n 5).
[76] *R (Edwards) v Environment Agency* (n 72).

The focus of the case-law has largely been on public law proceedings; although nuisance was the subject of the judgment of Carnwath LJ as he then was in *Morgan v Hinton Organics (Wessex) Ltd*.[77] There are some forthcoming ACCC cases which will consider the UK nuisance costs rules, see further above and also the decisions in *Austin v Miller Argent* and *Coventry v Lawrence*.[78]

Interim Relief

Article 9(4) requires that there be, for the purposes of cases under Art 9(1)–(3), 'adequate and effective remedies, including injunctive relief'.

In *Commission v UK*[79] the Advocate-General has advised the Court to rule that the general requirement for cross-undertakings for injunctions (save in Scotland) means that the UK is non-compliant with the Aarhus-inspired provisions of the PP Directive. She held that such an undertaking fell within the scope of the protection for 'prohibitive expense'.[80] She acknowledged that in practical terms in many cases legal proceedings themselves stopped projects proceeding.[81] She rejected an argument that the Court might exercise its discretion not to seek a cross-undertaking was sufficient for these purposes.[82] She said:

> 91. Of greater significance is the United Kingdom's argument that the obligation to pay damages is compatible with the principle of effectiveness, that is to say, it does not render excessively difficult or impossible in practice the exercise of rights conferred by European Union law.
>
> 92. That argument is based on the valid premise that, subject to compliance with the principles of equivalence and effectiveness, the Member States have discretion in implementing Article 10a of the EIA Directive and Article 15a of the IPPC Directive. (53) Moreover, that discretion is also not called into question by the principle of effective legal protection—to which the principle of effectiveness is related—set out in the first paragraph of Article 47 of the Charter of Fundamental Rights. (54)
>
> 93. For that reason, the possibility cannot be excluded that, in principle, the Member States may provide for an obligation to pay damages in connection with interim relief measures which pertains also to the exercise of rights conferred by European Union law. This applies in particular in proceedings between private parties as a measure of that kind necessarily interferes with the rights of the opposing party.

[77] *Morgan v Hinton Organics (Wessex) Ltd* [2009] EWCA Civ 107; [2009] CP Rep 26 and ACCC/C/2008/23 (United Kingdom).
[78] See n 25.
[79] *Commission v UK* (n 5).
[80] ibid paras 84–87.
[81] ibid paras 88–89.
[82] ibid para 89.

> …
>
> 98. In the proceedings covered by Article 10a of the EIA Directive and Article 15a of the IPPC Directive, additional weight is attached to those considerations as the public interest in the enforcement of environmental law is given special recognition there. Consequently, applicants in those proceedings deserve protection against excessive or prohibitive costs which goes further than the protection afforded by the principle of effectiveness and the right to effective legal protection.
>
> …
>
> 101. None the less, the possibility of taking action against the misuse of interim relief is not precluded. However, the need to prevent or punish misuse does not require the grant of interim relief to be conditional on an undertaking to pay damages. Instead, in cases of that kind, it would suffice to refuse the interim relief or, where the misuse is discovered only subsequently, to grant damages on the normal basis.
>
> 102. Consequently, the United Kingdom has failed to fulfil its obligations under Articles 3(7) and 4(4) of Directive 2003/35 by reason of the fact that the courts in England and Wales, as well as Gibraltar, and in Northern Ireland may make necessary measures granting interim relief in proceedings covered by those provisions conditional on an undertaking to pay damages.

The CJEU held that the requirement that proceedings should not be prohibitively expensive applied also to the costs resulting from measures which the national court might impose as a condition for the grant of interim measures in the context of disputes falling within the Aarhus Convention. It said that the conditions under which the national court granted such interim relief were, in principle, a matter for national law alone, provided that the principles of equivalence and effectiveness were observed. It said that cross-undertakings, was not necessarily precluded; but that, since it was incumbent on the court to make sure that the resulting financial risk for the claimant was also included when it assessed whether the proceedings were prohibitively expensive, the system of cross-undertakings operating in England and Wales in respect of the grant of interim relief constituted an additional element of uncertainty and imprecision so far as concerned compliance with the requirement that proceedings should not be prohibitively expensive; and that, accordingly, by failing to transpose the inserted articles correctly, the United Kingdom had failed to fulfil its obligations under the relevant Directives.

In any event there is now a Practice Direction on interim relief in Aarhus cases, see PD25A: 5.1A. This pre-dates the opinion and judgment in *Commission v UK* but was not considered as it is outside the *ratione temporis* of that case. It requires the Court to consider cross-undertaking if making an interim injunction order; but that is subject to para 5.1B. If interim relief is sought in an Aarhus Convention claim and the Court is satisfied that an injunction is needed to prevent significant environmental damage and to preserve the factual basis of the proceedings, the Court in considering whether to require a cross-undertaking must have particular regard to need to ensure that it does not make the claim prohibitively expensive. It will also give directions to ensure the case is heard promptly.

Fair, Equitable and Timely

In ACCC/C/2008/27 the ACCC made clear that what this requires is fairness for a claimant not a defendant; or presumably an affected interested party. It said:

> The Committee in this respect also stresses that 'fairness' in article 9, paragraph 4, refers to what is fair for the claimant, not the defendant, a public body. The Committee, moreover, finds that fairness in cases of judicial review where a member of the public is pursuing environmental concerns that involve the public interest and loses the case, the fact that the public interest is at stake should be accounted for in allocating costs. The Committee accordingly finds that the manner in which the costs were allocated in this case was unfair within the meaning of article 9, paragraph 4, of the Convention and thus, amounted to non-compliance.

In *Commission v UK* the Advocate-General in the context of costs made similar comments:

> 77. Moreover, that objective of the Aarhus Convention serves to refute the argument of the United Kingdom in relation to the limited resources of the relevant authorities. It is admittedly the case that funds spent by the authorities on legal proceedings cannot be used to fulfil their primary tasks. However, the Convention accepts this. That is also appropriate since the judicial enforcement of environmental law or the risk of a legal challenge forces the authorities to exercise particular care in applying the law in this area.[83]

Examples of matters found not to be fair and equitable include:

a. A court not notifying a party of a hearing or communicating its decision: see ACCC/C/2004/6;
b. The costs order in ACCC/C/2008/23 (see above);
c. A legal aid rule excluding small NGOs from legal aid: ACCC/C/2009/36.

In terms of the 'timely' requirement, this involves:

a. First, Courts making decisions in an expeditious way: see ACCC/C/2008/24.
b. Second, a requirement for fair, equitable and timely rules on delay in bringing legal challenges.

The decision of the Aarhus Compliance Committee in ACCC/C/2008/33 said this on the delay rules:

> 138. The Committee finds that the three month requirement specified in CPR rule 54.5 (1) is not as such problematic under the Convention, also in comparison with the time limits applicable in other Parties to the Convention. However, the Committee considers that the courts in England and Wales have considerable discretion in reducing the time limits by interpreting the requirement under the same provision that an application for a judicial review be filed 'promptly' (see paras. 113–116). This may result in a

[83] *Commission v UK* (n 5).

claim for judicial review not being lodged promptly even if brought within the three-month period. The Committee also considers that the courts in England and Wales, in exercising their judicial discretion, apply various moments at which a time may start to run, depending on the circumstances of the case (see para. 117). The justification for discretion regarding time limits for judicial review, the Party concerned submits, is constituted by the public interest considerations which generally are at stake in such cases. While the Committee accepts that a balance needs to be assured between the interests at stake, it also considers that this approach entails significant uncertainty for the claimant. The Committee finds that in the interest of fairness and legal certainty it is necessary to (i) set a clear minimum time limit within which a claim should be brought, and (ii) time limits should start to run from the date on which a claimant knew, or ought to have known of the act, or omission, at stake.

> 139. As was pointed out with regard to the costs of procedures (see para. 134 above), the Party concerned cannot rely on judicial discretion of the courts to ensure that the rules for timing of judicial review applications meet the requirements of article 9, paragraph 4. On the contrary, reliance on such discretion has resulted in inadequate implementation of article 9, paragraph 4. The Committee finds that by failing to establish clear time limits within which claims may be brought and to set a clear and consistent point at which time starts to run, i.e., the date on which a claimant knew, or ought to have known of the act, or omission, at stake, the Party concerned has failed to comply with the requirement in article 9, paragraph 4, that procedures subject to article 9 be fair and equitable.

DEFRA's response to the Aarhus Compliance Committee said:

> Recommendation to review the rules regarding the timeframe for the bringing of applications for judicial review identified in paragraph 139 of the findings in case ACCC/C/2008/33 to ensure that the legislative measures involved are fair and equitable and amount to a clear and transparent framework.
>
> The UK notes the Committee's findings that by failing to establish clear time limits within which claims may be brought in England and Wales and to set a clear and consistent point at which time starts to run, the UK fails to comply with the requirement of Article 9(4) of the Convention. As indicated to the committee in our comments on the draft compliance committee findings, we are considering the issue of time limits for judicial review proceedings with a view to ensuring that we get the balance right between enabling environmental claims to be made and avoiding unnecessary delay. The Ministry of Justice has consulted with the Administrative Court judiciary on the issue of whether the term 'promptly' should be retained or whether the time limit should simply specify a maximum period and whether it would be appropriate to set the clock running when the applicant becomes aware or should have become aware of the decision to be challenged, and are now considering whether further public consultation would be appropriate.

The compatibility of the promptness rule in judicial review with EU law has also been considered in the EU context: see *R (Berky) v Newport CC*.[84] In *Berky*

[84] *R (Berky) v Newport CC* [2012] EWCA Civ 378.

the Court of Appeal considered the impact of the CJEU's decision in *Uniplex (UK) Ltd v NHS Business Services Authority*,[85] which was a public procurement case in which a promptness rule identical to that in judicial review was said to be incompatible with EU law. The application of *Uniplex* to EU cases outside procurement was considered in *Berky*. The Court of Appeal was of the view that such an issue itself required a reference to the CJEU if it was to be the determinative issue (see para 37 and 77 of the judgment per Carnwath LJ and Sir Richard Buxton).

CPR 54.5(5) and (6) now provide bespoke rules for decisions under the planning acts (as defined in s 336 of the Town and Country Planning Act 1990, see CPR 54.5(A1)): there is a six week time limit, and no promptness requirement. This is though not applicable to environmental cases not governed by these Acts where the promptness requirement may remain an issue requiring a reference.

In *R (Hollins) v Cornwall CC*,[86] the Court (Richards LJ, on a permission to appeal application) said:

> There is nothing in the EIA directive or the Aarhus convention to prevent the court applying the judicial review time limits. The importance of timely challenges in public law matters generally is well recognised. The authorities stress that timeliness is of particular importance in planning matters, which indeed is why the three month time limit as previously existed has recently been reduced to a six week time limit in such cases. I acknowledge of course that the court's discretion to extend time is an important and even essential safeguard, but it needs to be used sparingly and not in such a way as to risk undermining the general rule.

[85] Case C-406/08 *Uniplex (UK) Ltd v NHS Business Services Authority* [2010] 2 CMLR 47.

[86] *R (Hollins) v Cornwall CC* [2013] EWCA Civ 1691. See also *R (Lymington River Association) v SSCLG* [2014] EWCA Civ 1190.

9

The Aarhus Convention and NGOs

CAROL DAY[1]

NGOs and the Negotiation of the Convention

The growth of the UK conservation movement was driven by the formation of NGOs[2] such as the National Trust in 1895, the Royal Society for the Protection of Birds ('RSPB') in 1889 and the Society for the Promotion of Nature Reserves (later the Royal Society of Wildlife Trusts) in 1912. Environmental NGOs currently enjoy their highest ever membership. The National Trust and the RSPB each have in excess of one million members (contrast the Conservative Party with a membership of around 134,000).[3] Existing alongside the larger NGOs are a plethora of specialist NGOs concerned about pretty much every order of biodiversity—be they bats, butterflies or cetaceans. Finally, there are, at any time, groupings of local people formed to oppose particular proposals (such as the HS2 Action Alliance or the Frack Free Balcombe Residents' Association). While these may start as informal groupings of aggrieved local residents, they can rapidly become media savvy, socially networked experts in planning, policy and law.

All of these organisations rely on environmental legislation emanating from all levels (from the regional, through to the national, European and international) to pursue their objectives. However, there is perhaps one international agreement that has played a greater role in enabling NGOs and groups to exercise their democratic rights to protect the environment than any other—the Aarhus Convention.

After the fall of the Berlin wall in 1989 and the breakup of the Soviet Union in 1991, the Aarhus Convention became a key part of the democratisation of Central

[1] Carol Day was in-house Solicitor for WWF-UK between 2000 and 2013, during which time she lead its work on the Aarhus Convention. She was also the Coordinator of the Coalition for Access to Justice for the Environment (CAJE, comprising seven NGOs) between 2004 and 2013. She is now a part-time Legal Consultant for the Royal Society for the Protection of Birds (RSPB) and runs the Environmental Planning and Litigation Service (EPLS) for law firm Leigh Day.

[2] A Non-Governmental Organisation (NGO) is neither a part of a government nor a conventional 'for-profit' business.

[3] www.bbc.co.uk/news/uk-politics-24143443.

Europe, Eastern Europe, the Caucasus region and Central Asia.[4] In October 1995, the Economic Commission for Europe hosted an 'Environment for Europe' conference in Bulgaria during which a number of Ministerial Declarations were made.[5] On the basis of these documents, a special session of the ECE Committee on Environmental Policy met in 1996 and decided to establish an *ad hoc* Working Group with the mandate to prepare a draft convention on access to environmental information and public participation in environmental decision-making.[6] The basis for the Convention was Principle 10 of the 1992 Rio Declaration,[7] which requires individuals to have appropriate access to information held by public bodies concerning the environment, the opportunity to participate in decision-making processes and effective access to judicial and administrative proceedings, including redress and remedy.

The mandate recorded that negotiations should proceed without delay so that the Convention could be finalised by the Committee before an 'Environment for Europe' Conference hosted in Denmark in 1998. The Committee specifically invited NGOs, particularly those involved in the 'Environment for Europe' process, to participate and at the first meeting of the Working Party the Director of the ECE Environment and Human Settlements Division welcomed the presence of the many NGOs and expressed hope that this would strengthen the Convention.

The Working Group met 10 times between June 1996 and March 1998,[8] with senior UK civil servants attending on every occasion. NGOs were invited to form an NGO Coalition and take seats at the negotiating table. To an extent apparently unprecedented in the negotiation of Multilateral Environmental Agreements ('MEAs'), the NGO 'observers' were given their own 'flag' of identification at the table and the right to request the floor and offer the views of civil society at each stage of the negotiating process. They were able to lobby governmental delegates in the corridors and coffee shops and they offered specific language for the Convention, some of which was accepted by the delegates from participating countries.[9] Other NGOs that were consistently represented throughout the

[4] Svitlana Kravchenko, *Strengthening Implementation of MEAs: The Innovative Aarhus Compliance Mechanism* (2005) Paper given to the 7th UNECE Conference available at http://unece.org/conference/7/vol1/Kravchenko.pdf.

[5] Ministerial Declarations accessible via www.unece.org/env/efe/historyofefe/history.en2011_3.html.

[6] See Document ECE/CEP/18 (Annex I) available at www.unece.org/fileadmin/DAM//env/documents/1996/cep/ece.cep.18.e.pdf.

[7] Principle 10 of the Rio Declaration states: 'Environmental issues are best handled with the participation of all concerned citizens at the relevant level. At the national level, each individual shall have access to information concerning the environment that is held by public authorities, including information on hazardous materials and activities in their communities, and the opportunity to participate in decision-making processes. States shall facilitate and encourage public awareness and participation by making information widely available. Effective access to justice and administrative proceedings, including redress and remedy, shall be provided. See www.unep.org/Documents.Multilingual/Default.asp?documentid=78&articleid=1163.

[8] Reports of the meetings can be found in the Archives of the UNECE website at www.unece.org/env/pp/adwg.html.

[9] Kravchenko (n 4).

process including the International Council for Environmental Law ('ICEL'), the Regional Environmental Centre for Central and Eastern Europe ('REC') and the World Conservation Union ('IUCN').

Negotiations around the wording of the draft Convention are recorded on the UNECE website,[10] although in general no distinction is made between the observations made by country delegations or the NGOs. However, there are occasions in which it is apparent that, while the NGO Coalition was only able to participate in certain discussions as an observer (it was generally excluded from EU-coordinating discussions)[11] and lost several battles,[12] it substantially influenced the text of the Convention.[13]

Although provisions on access to justice were included from the outset[14] it was not until the fifth session of the Working Group that, under the leadership of the Belgian delegation, the provisions were developed more fully and the end of the Working Group sessions that it became a true 'pillar' of the Convention and fully reflected in the title. At this point, there was general agreement that there should be a requirement for legal review mechanisms in respect of access to information and public participation requirements[15] provided for by national legislation to be both '*timely*' and '*fair, open, transparent, equitable and not prohibitively expensive*'. With regard to access to justice in environmental matters more generally delegations expressed a mixed approach, some opposed to any provisions on the basis that this would be inconsistent with the agreed scope of the Convention. However, it was recognised that the Convention could include an explicit right for NGOs and/or other individuals meeting certain criteria to challenge unlawful acts or omissions by private persons or public authorities that contravened specific provisions of national environmental law.[16]

Both the UK delegation and the NGO Coalition introduced proposals for a compliance mechanism in the sixth session of the Working Group. However, it is noted in the ninth session that the NGOs '*deplored the minimalist nature of the new text adopted in respect of non-compliance*'[17] on the basis that, *inter alia*,

[10] *Supra*, n 8. See the list of weblinks at Appendix 14 to this book.

[11] See the reports of the eighth and ninth sessions, in which the NGO Coalition expressed dismay at the lack of transparency of the positions of Member States of the EU during discussions on Article 3 (eighth report page 3, para 15 and ninth report page 2, para 7) (*supra*, n 8).

[12] See, for example, the report of the sixth session in which the NGO Coalition expressed unease at the blanket exclusion of bodies acting in a legislative capacity from the scope of the Convention (*supra*, n 8).

[13] See, in particular, negotiations around the definition of environmental information at the third session, support for a proposal by the Belgian, Danish and Italian delegations to include a provision on the right to a healthy environment and express reference to 'future generations' in the sixth and eighth sessions, the development of provisions on access to justice in the eighth session, opposition to the weakening of public participation provisions in the ninth session and the mandatory nature of the compliance mechanism in the tenth session (*supra*, n 8).

[14] Included originally as Article 6 of the Convention.

[15] As covered by the then Article 5 of the Convention.

[16] See report of the fifth session, page 11, available at www.unece.org/env/pp/adwg.html.

[17] At this stage appearing as Article 14.

contracting Parties at their first meeting shall simply *consider* the establishment of a compliance mechanism. The NGOs did not consider this wording reflected the support expressed in the Working Group for a Belgian proposal introduced in the previous session essentially requiring the Conference of the Parties to establish a subsidiary body for implementation that could consider communications from members of the public and make recommendations to the Party concerned.

At the final Working Group session, the NGO Coalition delivered a long and powerful statement regarding the near-finalised text of the Convention, criticising the final text in relation to Genetically Modified Organisms (GMOs) as 'indefensible'. It also expressed a desire for NGOs to enjoy the same level of participation in Meetings of the Parties[18] (a proposal supported by Austria, Denmark and the Netherlands) and expressed regret that, in light of the fact the Convention linked international human rights law and environmental law, the Convention included provisions on compliance that fell short of minimal international human rights standards established over more than 20 years previously. In particular, it deplored the dilution of earlier proposals on the compliance mechanism and the resulting text, which were described by the UK as the weakest compliance provision of any international environmental law instrument. Finally, the Coalition (supported by Ukraine, Albania, Poland and Norway) presented a revised proposal on hazardous and radioactive waste movements. It described the proposal as giving governments such an extremely wide discretion on implementation that, as an NGO delegation, it debased itself by putting it forward. However, it considered it necessary to at least establish the principle that such movements must be subject to public participation.[19]

The Working Group adopted its final report in March 1998 and the Convention was duly signed by 35 countries at Aarhus, Denmark, on 25 June 1998. NGOs lobbied actively to ensure that the required minimum number of 16 ratifications for the Convention resulted in its entry into force just three years later in October 1991. In the period between signing the Convention in 1998, entry into force in 1991 and the first Meeting of the Parties (MoP) in 2002, a great deal of preparatory work had to take place, including the drafting of proposed Rules of Procedure, preparing proposals for a Bureau of the Convention and Working Group of the Parties to function between Meetings of the Parties, and designing the Compliance Mechanism established by the Convention. As before, NGO representatives were constant participants in all of these processes.[20]

The extent to which NGOs shaped the evolution of the Convention established a platform for civil society to influence its implementation and enforcement. By giving NGOs a clear mandate to participate in the preparation of the instrument, the UNECE created an expectation and a reality in which NGOs could

[18] See Article 19(5) of the Convention.
[19] See report of the tenth session, page s 4–5, available at www.unece.org/env/pp/adwg.html.
[20] Kravchenko (n 4).

continue to be powerful proponents for the Convention. Whilst the final text is (naturally) imperfect from an NGO viewpoint being, as it is, the result of lengthy negotiations between opposing parties, it represents one of the most progressive and pervasive legal instruments available to NGOs today. The 2004 Report of the Panel of Eminent Persons on United Nations—Civil Society Relations (the 'Cardoso Report') identified the Convention's experience in engaging civil society[21] and the Convention has been used to strengthen involvement in other UN negotiations. For example, in the 2009 Copenhagen Climate Change negotiations, as pressure mounted for the talks to produce a meaningful and binding treaty, logistics and site-management broke down at the conference centre and the UN suspended Observer registration, leaving thousands of NGOs literally standing outside in the cold. Delegates sought to rely on the Convention as a basis for greater public participation in the process.[22] Furthermore, the Compliance Committee established under the Convention has transpired to be one of the most accessible and authoritative mechanisms for shaping UK law and policy of its type (see later).

Notwithstanding the above, some meetings (primarily the EU coordination meetings) remain closed to observers. Thus, while NGOs are given the opportunity to be heard in the various fora established under the Convention (albeit often after the Parties have made their interventions), it remains impracticable for civil society to annul the wishes of the contracting Parties when operating *en bloc*. Many NGOs hold the view that closed meetings should be the exception and not the rule and that if a closed session is held it should be communicated in advance along with the justifying exceptional circumstances.[23]

The Importance of the Convention for NGOs

In 1998, the Convention was a new kind of environmental agreement, for the first time explicitly linking human rights and the environment. It was the first instrument to acknowledge that we owe an obligation to future generations and to establish that sustainable development can only be achieved through the involvement of all stakeholders. As discussed above, it was developed (and is now implemented and enforced) with substantial NGO input.

[21] *We the Peoples: Civil Society, the United Nations and Global Governance—Report of the Panel of Eminent Persons on United Nations—Civil Society Relations* United Nations General Assembly 58th Session, 2004, paragraph 85, available at www.unog.ch/80256EDD006B8954/(httpAssets)/09916F545454357BC1256F5C005D4352/$file/A-58-817.pdf.

[22] Winfield J Wilson, 'Legal Foundations for NGO Participation in Climate Treaty Negotiations' (Spring 2010) *Sustainable Development Law & Policy* 54, 69. Available at http://digitalcommons.wcl.american.edu/cgi/viewcontent.cgi?article=1037&context=sdlp.

[23] See, for example, *UNFCCC and the Aarhus Convention: Recommendations How to Improve Public Participation in the Framework of UNFCCC Processes—A Position Paper* (Justice and Environment, 2011). Available at www.justiceandenvironment.org/_files/file/2011%20CC%20PPIF%20position.pdf.

The Convention focuses on the interactions between the public and public authorities in a democratic context. It goes to the heart of the relationship between people and governments, seeking to ensure minimum government standards in relation to accountability, transparency and responsiveness insofar as they relate to environmental protection. It is a particularly useful 'tool' for NGOs in this respect. Firstly, it is pervasive, applying across a broadly defined spectrum of environmental issues,[24] ranging from the state of elements of the environment (air, water, soil, land, landscapes and natural sites), factors (not only energy, noise and radiation but activities or measures including policies, legislation, plans or programmes and cost-benefit and other economic analyses and assumptions used in environmental decision-making) and can extend to the state of human health and safety, conditions of human life, cultural sites and built structures.

Secondly, the Convention is largely concerned with procedural compliance, in that it seeks to ensure minimum standards in the context of information provision, participation in decision-making and the scope and standard of review procedures. In the UK (as with many EU Member States), judicial review ('JR') is the core procedure allowing civil society to challenge the way in which Ministers, Government Departments, local authorities and other public bodies make decisions. The main grounds of review are that the decision-maker has acted outside the scope of its statutory powers or that the decision was made using an unfair procedure. It is theoretically possible to assert that the decision was manifestly unreasonable or irrational (so-called '*Wednesbury* unreasonableness'),[25] but in practice the bar is so high that claimants rarely, if ever, rely on such a ground alone—and are seldom successful in using it.[26] As such, JR is not concerned with the merits of a decision or whether the public body has made the 'right' decision. The only question before the court is whether the public body has acted unlawfully.[27] In particular, it is not the task of the courts to substitute its judgment for that of the decision-maker.

Historically, the limited scope of challenge has rendered JR a somewhat 'blunt' instrument for those seeking to influence the decisions of public bodies. However, the advent of the Convention has prompted some to posit that JR should, to a greater extent in certain environmental matters, concern the merits of the contested decision (see below).

[24] See Article 2(3) Aarhus Convention.

[25] Per Lord Greene MR in *Associated Provincial Picture Houses Ltd v Wednesbury Corporation* [1948] 1 KB 447 at p 230: 'if a decision on a competent matter is so unreasonable that no reasonable authority could ever have come to it, then the courts can interfere ... but to prove a case of that kind would require something overwhelming'.

[26] C Day, *Tackling Barriers to Environmental Justice* (WWF Conference Paper, 2011) p 16, available on the WWF-UK website at: http://assets.wwf.org.uk/downloads/tackling_barriers.pdf.

[27] The court can intervene where there has been an error of fact (although it may be cautious to entertain a fact based challenge), however, case-law makes plain that 'a court of supervisory jurisdiction does not, without more, have the power to substitute its own view of the primary facts for the view reasonably adopted by the body to whom the fact finding power has been entrusted' (*Adan v Newham London Borough Council* [2001] EWCA Civ 1916).

NGOs and the Convention Bodies

Aarhus Convention Compliance Committee

Of all the bodies established under the Convention, the Compliance Committee is proving to be the most influential and pertinent of all from the perspective of civil society.

The Aarhus compliance mechanism was formed pursuant to Decision I/7 of the MoP in 2002[28] and has several innovative features. Firstly, it consists of eight independent experts with recognised competence in the environmental field serving in a personal capacity. This contrasts with other conventions with compliance mechanisms consisting of representatives of governments.[29] The advantages of such a composition are that it provides a more dynamic and flexible structure because members can express their own opinions and do not have an obligation to check with their governments,[30] although it is noted that the Committee's recommendations are ultimately endorsed by the MoP, thus providing contracting Parties with an opportunity to bring diplomatic and political concerns to bear. Secondly, members of the Committee are nominated not only by Parties and Signatories (which is the general rule), but also by NGOs falling within the scope of the Convention.[31] Thirdly, the Committee accepts not only the submissions of Parties and referrals from the Secretariat about non-compliance with the Convention (which is a rule in other conventions)[32] but also communications from the public, including NGOs.[33]

While these safeguards enable the Compliance Committee to operate as an independent and impartial forum, the selection of Committee members and the endorsement of its findings do not escape political pressure. While NGOs are free to nominate candidates to sit on the Committee (and do so at each MoP) there is no vote. If there are too many candidates and the matter cannot be resolved by agreement, delegated representatives (of which NGOs are in the minority) negotiate their interests behind closed doors. Similarly, because the Committee's findings must be endorsed by the MoP in the form of a draft decision, contracting Parties can dispute, or even attempt to veto, the Committee's findings. For example,

[28] See www.unece.org/fileadmin/DAM/env/pp/documents/mop1/ece.mp.pp.2.add.8.e.pdf.

[29] For example, the Espoo Convention on Environmental Impact Assessment in a Trans-boundary Context provides that the Implementation Committee consists of eight Parties to the Convention, each of which appoints a member of the Committee. See www.unece.org/env/eia.

[30] Kravchenko (n 4).

[31] Article 10(5).

[32] See, eg www.unece.org/env/eia.

[33] Article 15 of the Convention provides: '*The Meeting of the Parties shall establish, on a consensus basis, optional arrangements of a non-confrontational, non-judicial and consultative nature for reviewing compliance with the provisions of this Convention. These arrangements shall allow for appropriate public involvement and may include the option of considering communications from members of the public on matters related to this Convention*'. See www.unece.org/env/pp/treaty/text.htm.

during the third MoP in Latvia in 2007, the Ukranian delegation challenged the wording of draft Decision III/6f, but stopped short of making a formal objection to it (instead agreeing to its position being reflected in the final report of the Meeting)[34] in the interests of reaching a consensus. Similarly, at the fifth MoP in Maastricht, the UK delegation requested amendments to draft Decision V/9o concerning Communication ACCC/C/2010/53 (compliance with Article 4(1) of the Convention (access to information and the provision of raw data)).[35]

Notwithstanding the above, the proceedings of the Compliance Committee are remarkably transparent and unfettered by political motivation. According to the Committee's *Modus Operandi*, it was agreed that communications that had, on a preliminary basis, been determined to be admissible should be posted on the UNECE website after they had been forwarded to the Parties concerned[36] to enable the public to monitor the processing of submissions, referrals and communications. In fact, all of the information considered by the Compliance Committee is accessible, unless it falls under the narrow grounds for exemption in Articles 4(3) and (4) of the Convention or if the person submitting it has requested it to be kept confidential on the basis that he or she may be penalised, persecuted or harassed.

The Compliance Committee meetings are open to the public (except for deliberations and decision-making) and a number of NGOs routinely participate as observers, offering their comments on each case. The Committee invites the parties to attend hearings, including the contracting Party (state) concerned (or the Party making a submission) and the member of the public submitting the communication. All those attending can participate in the entire meeting except during closed deliberations involving the adoption of findings and measures and recommendations of the MoP.

While it is not mandatory for Communicants or observers to be represented by a lawyer, some Parties routinely instruct counsel (including the UK), thus increasing the pressure on Communicants to do likewise in order to avoid an inequality of arms.[37] A number of UK NGOs have instructed counsel to act on a *pro bono* basis[38] and fortunately, as yet, legal representation does not appear to be a decisive factor in the Committee's findings.

[34] See the Report of the Third Meeting of the Parties (paragraph 49) at www.unece.org/fileadmin/DAM/env/pp/mop3/ODS/ece_mp_pp_2008_2_e_Report.pdf.

[35] See UK statements available at: www.unece.org/fileadmin/DAM/env/pp/mop5/Statements/frUKC53_05.03.2014.pdf, www.unece.org/fileadmin/DAM/env/pp/mop5/Statements/MOP-5_5b_UK_statement_to_Draft_Decision_V-9o.pdf and www.unece.org/fileadmin/DAM/env/pp/mop5/Statements/MOP5-_5b_-_UK_statement_on_item_5_b_.pdf.

[36] Guidance Document on Aarhus Convention Compliance Committee Compliance Mechanism, 'Modus Operandi', page 8, available at www.unece.org/env/pp/compliance/manualv2.doc.

[37] In Communication C33, the UK was represented by James Eadie QC (First Treasury Counsel) and Angus McCulloch (now QC) at a cost of approximately £18,000 (figure confirmed by Defra in response to a Freedom of Information Act 2000 request).

[38] For example, Stephen Tromans QC represented the Environmental Law Foundation in Communications C85 and 86 and David Wolfe (now QC) acted for CAJE at substantially reduced cost in Communication C33.

The Committee makes recommendations to the MoPs. In addition, the compliance mechanism adopted by the First MoP provides that, with a goal of addressing compliance issues without delay prior to a MoP, the Compliance Committee may, in consultation with the Party concerned, '*provide advice and facilitate assistance to individual Parties regarding the implementation of the Convention*'.[39] Furthermore, with the agreement of the Party concerned, the Committee can (prior to a MoP) take the measures listed in paragraph 37(b), (c) and (d) of the compliance mechanism, namely:

> [M]ake recommendations to the Party concerned; request the Party concerned to submit a strategy, including a time schedule, to the Compliance Committee regarding the achievement of compliance with the Convention and to report on the implementation of this strategy; in cases of communications from the public, make recommendations to the Party concerned on specific measures to address the matter raised by the member of the public.[40]

All Communications and relevant material submitted to the Compliance Committee is available on the UNECE's website,[41] alongside a useful compendium of the Committee's case-law between 2004 and 2011.[42] Whilst the product of a non-confrontational, non-judicial and consultative process,[43] the case-law of the Committee is taken into account by the Court of Justice of the European Union ('CJEU'), which is increasingly requested to adjudicate in Aarhus cases. For example, in the case of *Edwards*, Advocate General Kokott referred to, and in part endorsed, the findings of the Compliance Committee in Communication ACCC/C/2008/33 (United Kingdom) ('Communication C33')[44] concerning Article 9(4) and prohibitive expense in the UK.

The practical ramifications of the Committee's mounting authority are, however, of concern. As of September 2014, there were 98 cases before the Compliance Committee, of which nearly one-third concern UK compliance. While the Committee deals with Communications in a timely and admirably efficient

[39] Decision I/7, Review of Compliance, VI, Consideration By The Compliance Committee, paragraph 36, available at www.unece.org/env/pp/documents/mop1/ece.mp.pp.2.add.8.e.pdf.

[40] *Ibid.*

[41] Thus far, all but one of the Communications before the Compliance Committee have been submitted by the public (see www.unece.org/env/pp/pubcom.html). In 2004, Romania submitted a Communication in respect of Ukraine: www.unece.org/environmental-policy/treaties/public-participation/aarhus-convention/envpptfwg/envppcc/envppsubmissions/ukraine-2004.html. The case-law of the Committee can also be accessed via a database housed in the Access to Justice tab: www.unece.org/environmental-policy/treaties/public-participation/aarhus-convention/envpptfwg/envppatoj/jurisprudenceplatform.html.

[42] A Andrusevych, T Alge, and M Silina (eds), *Case Law of the Aarhus Convention Compliance Committee* (2004–11) available at: www.unece.org/fileadmin/DAM/env/pp/Media/Publications/ACCC_Jurisprudence_Ecoforum_2011.pdf.

[43] Article 15 Aarhus Convention.

[44] Case C-260/11 *R oao David Edwards, Lilian Pallikaropoulos v (i) Environment Agency, (ii) First Secretary of State, (iii) Secretary of State for Environment, Food and Rural Affairs*. See paragraphs 8, 36, 44 and 45 of AG Kokott's Opinion available at: http://curia.europa.eu/juris/document/document.jsf;jsessionid=9ea7d0f130d54361d5d97cc14861b9f5eef901d16cca.e34KaxiLc3eQc40LaxqMbN4OahqMe0?text=&docid=128663&pageIndex=0&doclang=EN&mode=lst&dir=&occ=first&part=1&cid=689817.

manner,[45] the escalating caseload puts an administrative burden on the Secretariat and places considerable time commitments on the Committee members who sit in a personal capacity—travelling to Geneva six times a year for meetings and reading a substantial volume of material in support of each Communication. While Committee members are not precluded from contributing to a discussion concerning their own Party,[46] they must avoid situations that may give rise to a conflict of interest or which may be perceived as giving rise to such a conflict. Thus, in practice, Committee members refrain from preparing draft findings in relation to their own Party. This means that the Committee member doing so is likely to have little or no experience of the legal system or practices under review. It is a testament to the rigour and diligence with which the Committee has approached its task that there have been no criticisms of the factual basis (of which is often a lengthy and detailed examination) upon which findings are made. In coming to its view, the Committee may consider any relevant information submitted to it and it is worth noting that NGOs and civil society generally play an important role in this respect. For example, in Communication C33, concerning the compatibility of the costs regime in UK environmental litigation with Article 9 of the Convention, the Coalition for Access to Justice for the Environment ('CAJE')[47] acted as *amicus curiae* to the Committee and still submits regular information on the evolving UK situation with regard to compliance.

The corollary of the Committee's 'success' is that it is unlikely to be able to function as it is unless its caseload diminishes—which seems unlikely given the increasingly prominence placed on its findings. Thus it may have to move to a more formal footing in future. NGOs and civil society generally also have a role to play in this regard by ensuring that Communications are efficiently presented and well-argued. In this respect, there is a useful Guidance Document on the Compliance Mechanism on the UNECE website.[48]

The Meeting of the Parties

The Meeting of the Parties ('MoP') is the main governing body of the Convention and comprises all Parties to the Convention. Other Signatories and other States as well as intergovernmental and NGOs participate as observers in its meetings. The mandate of the MoP is to keep the implementation of the Convention under review and take the necessary measures required to achieve the purposes of the Convention. The Bureau of the MoP invites an NGO representative to attend meetings as an observer.

[45] OW Pederson, 'Price and Participation: the UK before the Aarhus Convention's Compliance Committee' (2011) *Environmental Law Review*.

[46] MP.PP/C.1/2003/2, para 22.

[47] At the time, the author was the Coordinator of CAJE, which comprises WWF-UK, Friends of the Earth, Greenpeace, The Royal Society for the Protection of Birds, the Campaign for the Protection of Rural England and the Environmental Law Foundation.

[48] See www.unece.org/fileadmin/DAM/env/pp/compliance/CC_GuidanceDocument.pdf.

The Working Group of the Parties

The Working Group of the Parties ('WGP') was established to oversee the implementation of the work programme for the Convention between sessions of the MoP, and as such meets significantly more regularly than the MoP (a minimum of once per year and usually two to three times per year). Large numbers of NGOs routinely attend the MoP and the WGPs (indeed many are in receipt of UNECE funding to enable them to do so) and a coordination 'service' offered by the European Environmental Bureau (EEB) has proven to be an effective way of presenting the views of civil society organisations in a cogent and harmonised manner. NGOs are, however, free (and routinely do) make autonomous interventions to the meetings.

There have also been a number of Task Forces established by the MoPs, which are outlined in chapter one of this book. NGOs routinely attend as observers and are instrumental in ensuring they deliver their aims—not only by lobbying their Parties to attend and participate, but by actively engaging in the activities undertaken by them.

The UK and Costs—A Case Study on NGO Enforcement of the Convention

The power of the Compliance Committee to compel States Parties to implement long-term strategic improvements to the law is perhaps illustrated to best effect in the UK by reference to the issue of legal costs.

In 2005, CAJE[49] submitted a complaint to the European Commission alleging the UK was failing to comply with Article 10a of the EIA Directive,[50] which requires access to the courts to be 'not prohibitively expensive'. Shortly afterwards, CAJE acted as an *amicus curiae* in respect of a Communication submitted to the Compliance Committee regarding the UK's failure to comply with Article 9(4) of the Convention also concerning prohibitive expense.[51] This complaint was largely in response to a perception (shared by CAJE) that the prospects for environmental litigation had been shrinking over a number of years, principally because of the high costs of legal action.[52]

[49] *Supra*, n 47.

[50] Directive 2011/92/EU on the assessment of the effects of certain public and private projects on the environment (codification).

[51] See www.unece.org/env/pp/compliance/Compliancecommittee/33TableUK.html.

[52] For a deeper analysis see RG Lee and R Stech, 'Access to Environmental Justice in England and Wales: Funding Representation for Court Reviews for Administrative Action' in J Steele and WH Van Booms (eds), *Mass Justice, Challenges of Representation and Distribution* (Cheltenham, Edward Elgar, 2011) or OW Pederson, 'Environmental Justice *in* the UK: Uncertainty, Ambiguity and the Law' (2011) 31(2) *Legal Studies* 279.

CAJE's complaint to the European Commission resulted in a letter of formal notice to the UK in October 2007, a Reasoned Opinion in March 2010 and referral to the CJEU in April 2011.[53] Also in 2011, the Compliance Committee found the UK in breach of Articles 9(4), 9(5) and 3(1) of the Convention concerning costs and injunctive relief. The Committee recommended the UK review its system for allocating costs in environmental cases within the scope of the Convention and undertake practical and legislative measures to ensure that such procedures are fair and equitable and not prohibitively expensive and also provide a clear and transparent framework.

Meanwhile, a domestic case concerning the legality of an environmental impact assessment in respect of a cement works in Rugby, Warwickshire (*Edwards*)[54] was making its way to the UK Supreme Court. In this case, the Supreme Court was bound to consider whether legal costs of just under £90,000 incurred by, firstly, David Edwards and latterly, Lilian Pallikaropoulos were 'prohibitively expensive' and thus in breach of the EU Public Participation Directive (PPD) and Article 9(4) of the Convention.[55] The Supreme Court referred a number of questions on the meaning of prohibitive expense to the CJEU—which was already grappling with this issue in the parallel infringement case against the UK arising from the CAJE complaint.[56]

Advocate General Kokott's Opinion in *Edwards* was delivered in October 2012[57] and final judgment in April 2013.[58] The same Advocate General delivered her Opinion in the UK infraction case in September 2013[59] with final judgment in April 2014.[60] Essentially, the CJEU held in both cases that domestic courts cannot look exclusively at the financial means of individual claimants but must also carry out an objective analysis of the amount of the costs. In deciding whether a figure would be 'objectively unreasonable', the court must take a number of other factors into account, including whether the claimant has reasonable prospects of success, the importance of what is at stake for the claimant and for the protection of the

[53] Case C-530/11 *Commission v UK* [2014] QB 988.

[54] *Edwards* (n 44).

[55] Directive 2003/35/EC providing for public participation in respect of the drawing up of certain plans and programmes relating to the environment and amending with regard to public participation and access to justice Council Directives 85/337/EEC and 96/61/EC.

[56] *Ibid.*

[57] *Ibid.* AG Kokott's Opinion dated 18th October 2012 available at: http://curia.europa.eu/juris/document/document.jsf?text=&docid=128663&pageIndex=0&doclang=en&mode=lst&dir=&occ=first&part=1&cid=173998.

[58] *Ibid.* CJEU judgment dated 11th April available at: http://curia.europa.eu/juris/document/document.jsf?text=&docid=136149&pageIndex=0&doclang=en&mode=lst&dir=&occ=first&part=1&cid=174139.

[59] *Edwards* (n 43). AG Kokott's Opinion dated 12th September 2013 available at: http://curia.europa.eu/juris/document/document.jsf?text=&docid=140962&pageIndex=0&doclang=EN&mode=lst&dir=&occ=first&part=1&cid=252337.

[60] *Ibid.* CJEU judgment dated 13th February 2014 available at: http://curia.europa.eu/juris/document/document.jsf?text=&docid=147843&pageIndex=0&doclang=EN&mode=lst&dir=&occ=first&part=1&cid=34589.

environment, the complexity of the relevant law and whether public funding or other costs protection schemes are available.

By the end of 2013, content the CJEU was exhibiting a consistent approach to prohibitive expense, the Supreme Court handed down its judgment in *Edwards.* The Supreme Court essentially confirmed the CJEU approach, but stopped short of providing definitive guidance as to how to assess what is objectively unreasonable. The Court also held that the fact that the claimant has not in fact been deterred for carrying on the proceedings is not itself determinative and that the same criteria are to be applied on appeal as at first instance. However, in applying these factors, the Court made a somewhat surprising order for costs against the claimant, Mrs Lilian Pallikaropoulos, of £25,000.

In response to the findings of the Compliance Committee, and in anticipation of the CJEU proceedings resulting from CAJE's complaint to the Commission, the Civil Procedure Rules ('CPR') were amended in April 2013 in respect of costs and environmental cases. Adverse costs liability for unsuccessful claimants in environmental judicial reviews was capped at £5,000 for individuals and £10,000 for 'all other cases'. However, successful claimants are also subjected to a reciprocal cap of £35,000 inclusive of VAT. With respect to injunctive relief, the court must have regard to the question of prohibitive expense when considering whether a cross-undertaking in damages is required and must make necessary directions to ensure the case is heard at the earliest opportunity.

In making these changes, however, the UK has not, in CAJE's view, gone far enough. In the infraction case, both AG Kokott and the CJEU recognised that the need to ensure the figures of 5k and 10k are both objectively reasonable *and* do not exceed the financial resources of the person concerned. CAJE believes this requires a mechanism for those figures to be reduced (but not increased) when a claimant is patently of limited means (and conversely for the cross-cap of 35k to be increased if a case is particularly complex, for example). Given the need for advance certainty as to the claimant's financial liability,[61] it is arguable that the Aarhus costs regimes in England/Wales and Northern Ireland should be amended to mirror that of Scotland, which already provides for both its 5k cap to be reduced and 30k cross-cap to be increased on cause shown.[62] Secondly, in considering whether the assessment of prohibitive expense can differ depending on whether the national court is adjudicating at the conclusion of first-instance proceedings, an appeal or a second appeal—the CJEU explicitly held that national courts are required to have regard to the costs already incurred by a claimant at earlier levels in the same dispute.

While the CPR amendments represent a significant improvement on the previous position, the 5k adverse costs cap still represents a considerable barrier to many individuals. NGOs and residents groups are finding it more manageable to

[61] *Ibid.* See paragraph 35 of the judgment.

[62] See Scottish Court of Session Rules (Rule 58A.4) available at: www.scotcourts.gov.uk/docs/default-source/rules-and-practice/rules-of-court/court-of-session/chapter58a-1.pdf?sfvrsn=6.

raise 10k and are bringing cases forward, albeit not on the scale purported by the Ministry of Justice.[63] Moreover, a request made under the EIR 2004[64] by Leigh Day in April 2014 confirms the MoJ is making no attempt to collate data on the number of 'Aarhus claims' submitted following the introduction of the new costs rules in April 2013. As such, the UK will be unable to assess with any accuracy whether the new costs rules are improving access to justice. The situation is also made more complex by the fact that a number of reforms to the JR procedure introduced in 2013 and 2014 are undermining improvements to the costs regime. These include a reduction in the time limits for bringing a JR in planning cases from three months to six weeks, the removal of a right to an oral renewal in cases assessed by a judge as 'totally without merit' and the introduction of a new fee for oral renewal of a permission hearing (initially £215 but with proposals to ultimately reflect the 'full costs of the hearing').[65]

However, one thing is clear—these changes would not have been effected but for persistent NGOs and individuals who brought the matter to the attention of the European Commission and the Compliance Committee. The NGOs' efforts were substantially assisted by members of the senior judiciary—most notably Lord Carnwath, Lord Justice Sullivan and Lord Justice Jackson—who lent their considerable expertise and profile to the debate.

Future Areas of Concern

Substantive Legality

Article 9(2) of the Convention requires contracting Parties to ensure that relevant members of the public have access to a review procedure to challenge the procedural and substantive legality of any decision, act or omission subject to Article 6 of the Convention.

The Aarhus wording is imported into Article 10a of the EIA Directive via Article 7 of the EC PPD. Article 9(3) of the Convention does not refer specifically to either substantive or procedural legality, instead referring to '*acts or omissions [...]*

[63] In September 2013, the Government issued a public consultation on further reforms to the procedure for Judicial Review to 'tackle the burden that the growth in unmeritorious judicial reviews has placed on stretched public services'. Despite a failure to provide any empirical evidence, particular attention was drawn to the potential for the 'abuse' of JR (principally by campaigners using JR as a delaying tactic) and the role of JR as a 'brake on economic recovery'. The consultation document is available at: https://consult.justice.gov.uk/digital-communications/judicial-review.

[64] The Environmental Information Regulations 1992 (SI 1992/3240).

[65] Note that at the time of writing, further changes to JR are proposed in Part 4 of the Criminal Justice and Courts Bill including: (i) a presumption that interveners will bear their own costs (and any costs arising to the parties from their intervention); and (ii) a requirement for applicants to provide information on funding at the outset of the judicial review and requiring the courts to have regard to this information in order to consider making costs orders against non-parties to a JR.

which contravene its national law relating to the environment'. As such, the issue to be considered in such a review procedure is whether the act or omission in question contravened any provision—be it procedural or substantive—in national law relating to the environment.

In practice, the main way in which substantive legality can be contested in JR is by applying the *Wednesbury* unreasonableness test where an authority has made a judgment on substantive issues. The courts are acutely aware that it is not their role to substitute their judgment for that of the decision-maker, but in environmental cases, the *Wednesbury* unreasonableness test in practice is very difficult to satisfy. Applications for JR are increasingly procedural (eg was there fair consultation?) or concerned with pure law (did the decision-maker apply the right legal test?)—with the attendant frustrations of 'shoehorning' environmental issues into the traditional JR framework.

Donson and Lee recognised that the primary limitation of judicial review in England and Wales is its focus on procedural, rather than substantive, impropriety.[66] This issue was discussed by the Compliance Committee in Communication C33.[67] The Committee concluded that the UK allows for members of the public to challenge certain aspects of the substantive legality of decisions, acts or omissions subject to Articles 9(2) and (3) including, for example, material errors of fact, errors of law, regard to irrelevant considerations, failure to have regard to relevant considerations, jurisdictional error and *Wednesbury* unreasonableness. However, the Committee was not convinced that the UK, despite these exceptions, meets the standards for review required by the Convention as regards substantive legality. Particular reference was made to criticisms by the House of Lords[68] and the ECtHR,[69] concerning the very high threshold for review imposed by the *Wednesbury* test. While the Committee, on the basis of the information before it in C33, did not go as far as to find the UK in non-compliance with Article 9(2) or (3), it did suggest (perhaps picking up on submissions made by the UK Government during the hearing) that the application of the 'proportionality principle' by the courts in England and Wales could provide a more appropriate standard of review in cases within the scope of the Convention.

Whether the present scope of JR is consistent with Article 9(4) of the Convention has been discussed in a number of recent cases. In *Evans*,[70] the Court of Appeal confirmed that *Wednesbury* unreasonableness is the correct standard of review to apply in cases concerning EIA screening decisions and, similarly (in another case called *Evans*),[71] the Court of Appeal held that JR is a flexible procedure with

[66] F Donson and R Lee, 'Environmental Protection: Public or Private Law' (1996) 1 *Judicial Review* 56.

[67] See www.unece.org/env/pp/compliance/Compliancecommittee/33TableUK.html, paragraphs 121–25.

[68] See, for example, Lord Cooke in *R v Secretary of State for the Home Department, ex parte Daly* [2001] UKHL 26, [2001] 2 AC 532 paragraph 32.

[69] *Smith and Grady v United Kingdom* (1999) 29 EHRR 493, paragraph 138.

[70] *Evans v Secretary of State for Communities and Local Government* [2013] EWCA Civ 115.

[71] *R (on the application of Rob Evans) v (1) Attorney General (2) Information Commissioner* (2013) ([2013] EWHC 1960 (Admin)).

an intensity of review[72] consistent with the requirements of Article 9(4) of the Aarhus Convention.[73]

However, in *Viking*,[74] the Scottish Inner House set out its view of the scope of JR in bleak terms. The case concerns a grant of permission by the Scottish Ministers for the Viking Wind Farm on central Shetland in 2012. The Petitioner (Sustainable Shetland) applied for a JR, seeking reduction of the Scottish Ministers' decision on the grounds, *inter alia*, that they had failed to take into account their duties under the Wild Birds Directive[75] in respect of the Whimbrel. In October 2013, Lady Clark of the Outer House reduced the decision, holding that the Scottish Ministers had failed to comply with their obligations under the Birds Directive. In 2014, the Inner House overturned Lady Clark's Opinion on the basis that her jurisdiction should be confined to an examination as to whether the grant of consent had been a lawful decision as opposed to whether the Scottish Ministers had demonstrated a proper understanding of, and compliance with, the Directive. The Inner House held that the obligation to comply with the Birds Directive is an entirely factual question for the Scottish Ministers to determine and that '*once that conclusion was arrived at, the Wild Birds Directive, and any associated problems of interpretation and application, fell out of the picture as far as this proposal was concerned*'.[76]

This judgment raises a number of concerns. Firstly, as the Scottish Minister's decision letter confirmed a divergence in view as to the potential effect of the wind farm on the UK Whimbrel population (Scottish Natural Heritage (SNH) as statutory advisers (and RSPB) believing the impact to be nationally significant and the Scottish Ministers holding it to be less so), it is arguable that it was appropriate, if not necessary, for Lady Clark to examine whether the Ministers had properly understood or interpreted their duties under the Birds Directive. Secondly, it is puzzling that the Inner House does not refer to the possibility that the Scottish Minister's decision could have been unreasonable in the *Wednesbury* sense. Such a narrow interpretation of the scope of JR is regrettable and, given that this is an EIA development, casts doubt on JR as a mechanism to provide a substantive and procedural review under the Convention.

Cabinet Office Consultation Principles

In 2008, the Government published a Code of Practice on Consultation[77] advocating that consultations should normally last for at least 12 weeks, with

[72] *Ibid*, paragraphs 130–38.

[73] Note this case is currently pending before the Supreme Court.

[74] *Sustainable Shetland v The Scottish Ministers* [2014] CSIH 60—see: www.scotcourts.gov.uk/search-judgments/judgment?id=cdc395a6-8980-69d2-b500-ff0000d74aa7.

[75] Directive 2009/147/EC of the European Parliament and of the Council of 30 November 2009 on the conservation of wild birds.

[76] *Supra*, n 75, paragraph 23 onwards.

[77] See http://webarchive.nationalarchives.gov.uk/+/http://www.bis.gov.uk/policies/bre/consultation-guidance/code-of-practice).

consideration given to longer timescales where appropriate. This document was cited by the UK in its National Implementation Report on the Aarhus Convention in preparation for the Fourth MoP to the Aarhus Convention in Moldova in 2011 in terms of compliance with Articles 3(4), 7 and 8 of the Convention.[78]

In July 2012, the Government substituted the Code of Practice with new 'Consultation Principles',[79] which stated that: '*The amount of time required … might typically vary between two and twelve weeks*' and that '*In some cases there will be no requirement for consultation at all*'. While the principles constitute non-legally binding guidance and may be overridden by existing case-law establishing the legal principles with which public consultation must conform, this signalled a significant change in government policy. For example, implying (as the principles do) that a 12-week consultation period is likely to be the exception rather than the rule may encourage consultation at a later stage in the formulation of policy proposals.

In light of the above, CAJE submitted evidence to the Public Administration Select Committee ('PASC') questioning whether the application of the new Principles to environmental issues would be Aarhus compliant. In practice, consultation periods for new proposals have been radically reduced post Autumn 2012 and NGOs (and coalitions of NGOs in particular) have found it difficult to submit considered responses to a number of proposals for policy reform. Concerns have been raised that the Government may be in breach of the second pillar of the Convention concerning public participation in decision-making.

Future Directions from an NGO Perspective and the Draft EC Proposal on Access to Justice

In the final session of the Working Group in 1998,[80] the EC confirmed that it may be necessary for it to make a declaration on the way in which the Convention applies. On subsequently approving the Convention in 2005, the EU declared that as existing legal instruments did not cover the duties in relation to access to justice arising in Article 9(3) of the Convention, the '*Member States are responsible for the performance of these obligations until the EC adopts provisions of Community law covering the implementation of those obligations*'. In 2003, the Commission presented a proposal for a directive on access to justice in environmental matters, with the aim of establishing minimum requirements on access to administrative and judicial procedures, thus transposing the third pillar of the

[78] Available at: www.unece.org/fileadmin/DAM/env/pp/reporting/NIRs%202011/UK_NIR_2011.pdf.
[79] See www.cabinetoffice.gov.uk/resource-library/consultation-principles-guidance.
[80] *Supra*, n 19.

Aarhus Convention into Community law and the law of the Member States.[81] The European Parliament approved it, but there was such strong opposition in the Council of Ministers that negotiations on the directive have been shelved by each Presidency since Luxembourg in 2005.

In 2011, a growing body of CJEU case-law on access to justice prompted the European Commission to examine the implementation of Articles 9(3) and 9(4) of the Convention in 17 EU Member States.[82] The Chair of the UNECE Access to Justice Task Force drafted a synthesis report drawing together the main conclusions and recommendations of the studies in order to inform a future draft directive. The findings of the synthesis report demonstrated strong support for a revised directive on access to justice to ensure minimum standards across the territory of the EU,[83] particularly with regard to standing, costs and remedies.

However, a number of Member States, including the UK, remain firmly opposed to a draft directive. Indeed, the Government's recent response to the Review of the Balance of Competencies between the UK and the EU on the Environment and Climate Change confirmed that the Prime Minister's Business Taskforce has called on the EU to withdraw proposals on access to justice in environmental matters as it would constitute a '*barrier to business expansion*'.[84] Regrettably, the European Commission has subsequently indicated that it may withdraw a proposal on access to environmental justice[85] included within its proposal for a Seventh Environment Action Programme.[86]

As many now believe a legislative basis for the third pillar of the Convention is urgently needed, the UK's efforts to undermine progress on this issue are deeply disappointing. NGOs will continue to press for an instrument that ensures broad access to justice and early engagement in the decision-making process on the basis that there is an inherent public interest in civil society being able to challenge the legality of the decisions of public and private bodies that affect the environment. However, if past experience is anything to go by, we are in for a long haul. In the interim, NGOs and civil society will continue to rely on the access to justice provisions of this far-sighted and pervasive Convention to assert their participatory rights in the interests of environmental protection.

[81] For more information and for the text of the proposal see http://europa.eu/legislation_summaries/environment/general_provisions/l28141_en.htm.

[82] The author was co-author of the UK study alongside Professor Richard Macrory QC. The reports can be found at: http://ec.europa.eu/environment/aarhus/access_studies.htm.

[83] The synthesis report can be found at: http://ec.europa.eu/environment/aarhus/pdf/2012_access_justice_report.pdf. The author was responsible for presenting the results of the studies in relation to costs to the Task Force on Access to Justice in June 2013. The presentation can be found at: www.unece.org/fileadmin/DAM/env/pp/a.to.j/TF6-2013/2b_Day_Costs.pdf.

[84] See paragraph 2.133 of the Government's response published in February 2014 available at: www.gov.uk/government/uploads/system/uploads/attachment_data/file/284500/environment-climate-change-documents-final-report.pdf.

[85] *Ibid*, paragraph 1.29.

[86] European Commission, 'Living Well, Within the Limits of Our Planet—Proposal for a General Union Environmental Action Programme' (2012). Available at: http://ec.europa.eu/environment/newprg/pdf/7EAP_Proposal/en.pdf.

Review of Parties' Compliance with the Aarhus Convention

10

The Aarhus Convention Compliance Mechanism and Proceedings before its Compliance Committee

VEIT KOESTER*

Introduction

Compliance mechanisms ('CMs') are mechanisms established by parties to international treaties with a view to assisting parties having compliance problems and addressing individual cases of non-compliance. Such mechanisms constitute a relatively new phenomenon in public international law. The first CM was established in 1992 under the 1987 Montreal Protocol to the 1985 Vienna Convention on Substances that Deplete the Ozone Layer. Presently, there are about 20 CMs, almost all of them established under multilateral environmental agreements ('MEAs').

Although the precise nature of individual CMs differ considerably, CMs have a common objective, namely to address non-compliance, ie non fulfillment by contracting parties of their obligations under an international treaty. Principally, non-compliance constitutes a violation of the rule on *pacta sunt servanda*,[1] but the application of the notion of 'non-compliance' instead of the notion of 'breach' indicates the underlying assumption of CMs that parties basically wish to comply with their obligations. Hence, non-compliance is a result of lack of ability or capacity to comply rather than of a deliberate decision to ignore obligations. This

* Chair of the Aarhus Convention Compliance Committee 2003–2011, Chair of the Compliance Committee of the Cartagena Protocol 2004–2009 and Chair of the Compliance Committee of the Protocol on Water and Health to the Convention on the Protection and Use of Transboundary Watercourses and International Lakes, 2010–present. The author wishes to express his gratitude to Aphrodite Smagadi, Environmen tal Affairs Officer at UNECE, Secretary to the Implementation Committee, Espoo Convention Secretariat (former Secretary to the Aarhus Convention Compliance Committee) for having reviewed the draft article and for a number of useful comments. The responsibility for any errors lies, however, solely with the author.

[1] In the words of Article 26 of the 1969 Vienna Convention: 'Every treaty in force is binding upon the parties to it and must be performed by them in good faith.'

is why all CMs, although drafted in various ways, are designed to be of a facilitative and non-confrontational nature.[2]

CMs also share some other features, notably that consideration of non-compliance issues is, in the first instance, normally entrusted to a special, relatively small, body established by the governing body of the treaty—usually named the Conference or the Meeting of the Parties ('COP' or 'MOP')—named an implementation or compliance committee.

One of the existing CMs is the CM of the Aarhus Convention, being the subject of the present paper, focusing on the proceedings before the Compliance Committee.

The Aarhus Convention Compliance Mechanism

The Aarhus Convention Compliance Mechanism is rooted in Article 15 of the Convention on 'Review of Compliance' which reads:

> The Meeting of the Parties shall establish, on a consensus basis, optional arrangements of a non-confrontational, non-judicial and consultative nature for reviewing compliance with the provisions of this Convention. These arrangements shall allow for appropriate public involvement and may include the option of considering communications from members of the public on matters related to this Convention.

Based on this provision the first Aarhus Convention MOP (2002) adopted by consensus 'Decision I/7, Review of Compliance' which establishes the Aarhus Convention Compliance Committee and sets out its structure and functions as well as the procedures for review of compliance.[3] This decision which has only been subjected to a minor amendment, increasing the number of the members of the Committee from eight to nine in the tacit understanding to include three members from each of three regions: Western, Central and Eastern Europe, is the cornerstone of the CM of the Convention.

[2] The academic literature on compliance mechanisms is extensive. More recent literature includes, *inter alia*, J Klabbers, 'Compliance Procedures' in D Bodansky, J Brunnée and E Hey (eds), *The Oxford Handbook of International Environmental Law* (New York, Oxford University Press, 2008) (in paperback) 995–1009, T Treves et alia (eds), *Non-Compliance Procedures and Mechanisms and the Effectiveness of International Environmental Agreements* (The Hague, TMC Asser Press, 2009), G Rose, 'Interlinkages between Multilateral Environmental Agreements: International Compliance Cooperation' in LR Paddock et alia (eds), *Compliance and Enforcement in Environmental Law. Towards More Effective Implementation* (Cheltenham, Edward Elgar Publishing, 2011) 3–32, and A Cardesa-Salzmann, 'Constitutionalising Secondary Rules in Global Environmental Regimes: Non-Compliance Procedures and the Enforcement of Multilateral Environmental Agreements' (2012) 24 *Journal of Environmental Law* 103–32.

[3] Appendix 2 of this book. The decision was amended by MOP Decision II/2 (2005), para 12 to increase the number of the members of the Aarhus Convention Compliance Committee from eight to nine, in order to include three members from the Western, Central and Eastern European regions respectively.

Decision I/7 does not explicitly reiterate the requirements of Article 15 of the Convention on arrangements that the CM be of a non-confrontational and consultative nature. It is clear, however, that in practice the Compliance Committee's procedure under the CM does not involve a confrontation between the initiator of the procedure and the Party concerned ('non-confrontational'), and that it aims at assisting Parties facing compliance problems, thereby meeting these requirements.

The procedure is in practice also 'non-judicial' in the sense that it is not a trial, but the procedure, nevertheless, shares a number of features with trials, especially those related to due process (centered on impartiality, provision of a hearing and a reasoned decision) and procedural safeguards. Furthermore, the outcome of the proceedings before the Compliance Committee, leaving aside a potential politically influenced final decision by MOP, is based on conclusions and findings of a strictly legal character. Hence, the nature of the CM, despite of the wording of Article 15 of the Convention, has been referred to as 'quasi-judicial' and the Compliance Committee as 'an independent and impartial review body of a quasi-judicial nature.'[4]

The Aarhus Convention CM differs from most other CMs in two regards. First, and most importantly the CM may, in addition to submissions by the Parties and referrals by the Secretariat, be triggered by complaints by members of the public (communications) which is highly unusual in respect of environmental treaties.[5] At the time of the adoption of the CM it was the only existing CM allowing for communications, but in the course of the last 10 years a few other similar CMs

[4] C Pitea, 'The Compliance Procedure of the Aarhus Convention: Between Environmental and Human Rights Control Mechanisms' in XVI *The Italian Yearbook of International Law* (Martinus Nijhoff Publishers, Leiden, 2007) 85–116, at 115, and V Koester, 'The Convention on Access to Information, Public Participation in Decision-Making and Access to Justice in Environmental Matters (Aarhus Convention)' in G Ulfstein, T Marauhn and A Zimmermann (eds), *Making Treaties Work, Human Rights, Environment and Arms Control* (Cambridge University Press, Cambridge, 2007) 179–217, at 204. The dilemma, which, however, has not till now materialised, is according to J Klabbers, *International Law* (Cambridge University Press, Cambridge, 2013) 265 that 'the more compliance procedures comes to resemble regular judicial procedures, the less it will operate as originally intended, as a gentle way to persuade parties to comply.'

[5] This is the main reason why the Aarhus Convention CM has attracted a considerable interest from legal scholars. Hence, the literature is vast. Apart from articles referred to in other notes, more recent articles include C Pitea, 'Procedures and Mechanisms for Review of Compliance under the 1998 Aarhus Convention on Access to Information, Public Participation and Access to Justice in Environmental Matters' in Treves et alia (eds), *Non-Compliance Procedures and Mechanisms* (2009) (n 2) 221–49, S Kravchenko, 'Giving the Public a Voice in MEA Compliance Mechanisms' in Paddock et alia (eds), *Compliance and Enforcement* (2011) (n 2) 83–109, A Tanzi and C Pitea, 'The Interplay between EU Law and International Law Procedures in Controlling Compliance with the Aarhus Convention by EU Member States' in M Pallemaerts (ed), *The Aarhus Convention at Ten: Interactions and Tensions between Conventional International Law and EU Environmental Law* (Europa Law Publishing, Groningen, 2011) 369–81, J Jendroska, 'Aarhus Convention Compliance Committee: Origins, Status and Activities' (2011) 8 *Journal for European Environmental and Planning Law* 301–14, A Alf, 'The EU and the Compliance Mechanisms of Multilateral Environmental Agreements: The Case of the Aarhus Convention' in E Morgera (ed), *The External Environmental Policy of the EU* (Cambridge University Press, Cambridge, 2012) 287–303, and J Ebbesson, 'The Aarhus Convention, Access to Justice and Compliance by the UK' (2013) 25 *Environmental Law and Management* 56–60.

have been adopted.[6] In addition to communications from the public, submissions may be made by a Party to the Convention about the compliance either of itself or another Party. The Convention's Secretariat may also refer matters of compliance to the Committee. Communications from the public have proved to be frequently more common, the total to date standing at over 100 compared to *one* Party-to-Party submission and no submissions by one Party about its compliance or referrals by the Secretariat.

Secondly, members of the Compliance Committee, who are elected by the MOP based on nominations by States and NGOs, are, by virtue of a well-established, consistent and firm practice by the MOP, independent in the sense that they do not belong to an executive branch of the Government.[7] All members of the Compliance Committee are lawyers,[8] mostly university professors or privately practicing public interest lawyers, working pro bono.[9] The number of annual meetings and of meeting days have gradually increased to, presently, four to five annual meetings, each of which lasting four to five days.

Powers of the Compliance Committee

Although the immediate task of the Compliance Committee implicitly is to decide whether an alleged instance of non-compliance does indeed amount to non-compliance, its ultimate goal is to further compliance in the future by providing advice, facilitating assistance or making recommendations (either directly or through the MOP) to non-complying Parties. Hence, the CM is a forward-looking mechanism, not a redress mechanism. Accordingly, the Compliance Committee is not empowered to overrule decisions of national courts or administrative authorities, abrogate national laws or intervene directly on a communicant's behalf with the authority about whose act or omission a communicant is complaining about, or to require financial damages to be paid as a result of a Party's non-compliance with its obligations. The Compliance Committee may, however, well conclude that a decision by a domestic court or authority is not in compliance with the

[6] Ie the compliance mechanisms under the 1999 Protocol on Water and Health to the Convention on the Protection and Use of Transboundary Watercourses and International Lakes and the 2003 Protocol on Pollutant Release and Transfer Registers to the 1998 Convention on Access to Information, Public Participation in Decision-Making and Access to Justice in Environmental Matters (Aarhus Convention). Most other CMs may be triggered only by Parties vis-à-vis themselves, by a Party in respect of another Party (submissions) and by the secretariat of a treaty (referral). So far, the Compliance Committee of the Aarhus Convention has in addition to numerous communications only received one party-to-party submission.

[7] The formal requirements, shared with a number of other CMs, being (only) that members act in their personal capacity.

[8] According to para 2 of Decision I/7 Annex the requirement is (only) that the Compliance Committee includes 'persons having legal experience.' In practice, however, all members are and have always, save one member who served for a limited period during the first years of the existence of the CM, been lawyers.

[9] Travel costs (economy class!) and per diems are reimbursed by the Convention's budget through its host organisation, United Nations Commission for Europe (UNECE).

provisions of the Convention, which the Committee has been doing in practice several times.[10]

The Compliance Committee's findings on non-compliance are not legally binding. This, however, may be remedied by an endorsement by the MOP of the decision of the Committee, because such endorsement may constitute a 'subsequent agreement between the parties regarding the interpretation of the treaty or the application of its provisions' which pursuant to Art 31(3)(a) of the 1969 Vienna Convention on the Law of the Treaties must be taken into account for the purposes of the interpretation of a treaty.[11] As of yet the MOP has never set aside findings by the Compliance Committee on non-compliance. Whilst the practice of the MOP is to decide whether or not to endorse the Compliance Committee's findings of non-compliance, its practice in relation to the Compliance Committee's findings of no non-compliance has so far been simply to take note of them.[12] In the rather hypothetical event that the MOP cannot reach consensus owing to disagreement about the interpretation or application of the Convention, the most likely result would be some kind of a political compromise concealing or at least not exposing the disagreement, but, naturally depending on the concrete findings of the Compliance Committee, related circumstances as well as the very nature of the disagreement.

Aside from the ability to make findings of non-compliance with the Convention, the powers of the Compliance Committee are, on the one hand, rather limited in the sense that the provisions of advice and assistance to a non-compliant Party is subject to consultation with that Party and that recommendations directly to the Party concerned require the Party's agreement.[13] The Compliance Committee, however, is entirely free to propose[14] any of the non-compliance response measures listed in the Annex to Decision I/7 by way of recommendations to the MOP.

[10] See for example the Compliance Committee's findings in ACCC/C/2008/33 (United Kingdom of Great Britain and Northern Ireland), adopted on 24 September 2010, on the compatibility with Article 9 of the Convention on the principles set out in English case-law regarding protective costs orders in environmental judicial review litigation.

[11] See generally, G Nolte, 'Reports of the ILC Study Group on Treaties over Time' in G Nolte (ed), *Treaties and Subsequent Practice* (Oxford University Press, Oxford, 2013) 169–386, at 370–77.

[12] See generally, V Koester, 'The Compliance Mechanism of the Aarhus Convention—Outcomes of the Fourth Session of the Meetings of the Parties' (Chisinau, Moldova, 29 June–1 July 2011) and 'A Stock-taking of the Work and Accomplishment of the Compliance Committee' (2011) *Environmental Policy and Law* 196 205.

[13] Decision I/7. Annex, para 36 (a) and (b). In practice, however, Parties almost always accept recommendations when they do not disagree with the findings of the Compliance Committee on non-compliance. The reason, however, that the recommendation in ACCC/2012/68 (European Union and United Kingdom of Great Britain and Northern Ireland), adopted on 24 September 2013, was issued to the MOP (para 108) and not to the UK, was probably due to the recently established practice by the CC of only issuing recommendations directly to the Parties when there is sufficient time to implement the recommendations before the MOP due to consider the decisions. The result of this practice is that recommendations in decisions made by the CC within 1–1½ years before the forthcoming MoP are issued as recommendations to the MoP, ie, in reality representing suggestions to the MoP on what measures the MoP should recommend to the Parties concerned to implement. Hence, the UK ultimately accepted the recommendation.

[14] Decision I/7. Annex, paras 33 and 34 are referring to 'measures' and 'recommendations' which are understood to refer both to measures/recommendations provided for in para 36 and recommendations to the MOP, including recommendations to take one or more of the measures listed in para 37.

By contrast the Compliance Committee has a wide discretion as to how to deal with a communication (a submission or a referral). Thus, the Compliance Committee is not bound to address all issues, points, allegations, objections or arguments reflected in the communication or put forward during its consideration by the communicant or the Party concerned.[15] In the same vein, the Compliance Committee is free to address issues related to the communication which may not emerge directly from the communication. The Compliance Committee has also stated that practice in dealing with communications is that it 'does not exclude when determining issues of non-compliance to take into consideration general rules and principles of international law, including international human rights law.'[16]

Proceedings Before the Compliance Committee

General Remarks

The Compliance Committee has published, as an electronic publication, a guide entitled 'Guidance Document on the Aarhus Convention Compliance Mechanism' ('the Guidance Document')[17] divided into the following six parts: Introduction, Composition, Election and Functions, Modus Operandi, The NGOs and the Compliance Committee, Communications—useful information for the public and the Party concerned, and Annexes.[18] From a procedural point of view the 'Modus Operandi', which describes all the procedural rules of the Compliance Committee, is the most important part. As of yet all such rules have been endorsed by the MOP. Leaving aside a procedural incident which inspired the Committee to adopt detailed guiding principles on the independence and impartiality of Committee Members,[19] major procedural problems have never occurred.

[15] See for example the Compliance Committee's decision in ACCC/C/2010/48 (Austria), adopted on 16 December 2011, 'to focus its considerations on selected issues', because 'some allegations are very broad and general and, with respect to a number of issues the Committee was invited to consult academic writings' (paras 25 and 52).

[16] V Koester, 'The Compliance Committee of the Aarhus Convention—An Overview of Procedures and Jurisprudence' (2007) *Environmental Policy and Law* 83–96, at 87.

[17] Available on the website (n 3). See the weblinks at Appendix 14 to this book.

[18] Annex I—Compliance Committee Operation Procedure (representing a one page summary), Annex II—Checklist for communications, and Annex III—Chair's introduction to formal discussions on the substance of communications and submissions. Annex II was at the Committee's 46th meeting (22–25 September 2014) (doc ECE/MP.PP/C.1/2014/10) replaced by 'Recommended format for communications' which, as of yet, has not been included in the Guidance Document, but is available on the website (n 3).

[19] Guidance Document, 'Conflict of Interest' (see further below).

Since the Guidance Document includes detailed information on all relevant aspects of the proceedings,[20] the overview below is focusing on the main features only and those traits that might be most important or interesting seen from a lawyer's perspective. Furthermore, the Guidance Document is currently under revision which is expected to be completed by the middle of 2015. Some of the potential and most interesting elements resulting from the revision are addressed in 'Main Phases of a Compliance Procedure'below.

It should be noted that aside from the overarching rules of the Annex to Decision I/7, the Compliance Committee is in charge of its own procedure. Accordingly, the Committee has decided to apply, *mutatis mutandis*, the rules of procedure of the MOP.[21] In practice, however, those rules do not play any important role, in particular because procedural decisions are consensus-based. Substantive decision-making is as a matter of principle governed by rules of the Annex to Decision I/7,[22] but hitherto, all substantive decisions have been made by consensus.

The principles set out in the Guidance Document governing proceedings before the Compliance Committee are broadly formulated, ie as guidelines rather than as specific rules, although some of them elaborate upon provisions set out in the Annex to Decision I/7. The overview in 'Main Phases of a Compliance Procedure'below does not distinguish between procedural rules set out in the Annex to Decision I/7 and the principles set out in the Guidance Document. This overview is primarily directed at the procedures related to communications from the public given that these form by far the largest proportion of the Compliance Committee's case-law. However, it is also largely applicable to submissions by one Party about another Party. It should be noted, though, that the procedural steps may vary pending the particularities or specific circumstances in respect of the communications in question. The examples from the case-law of the Compliance Committee are all taken from the period 2011–2014,[23] since earlier examples

[20] The Guidance Document, however, does not (as of yet) include the decision of the Compliance Committee relating to submission to the Committee of disorganised and unstructured information difficult to examine. The decision, reflected in the Report on the 34th meeting of the Compliance Committee (2030 September 2011) (doc ECE.MP.PP.C.1. 2011/8), para 52, inter alia, empowers the chair to decide whether excessive information fulfill the criteria specified by the Committee in the decision. If not, such information would not be processed or considered by the Committee.

[21] Rules of procedure of the MOP are available on the website of the Convention (n 3). Rules 19, 20, 24–27, 29–42, 44, 46, and 48 of those are considered by the Compliance Committee to be the most relevant.

[22] Substantive decision-making is governed by para 35 of Decision I/7 Annex requiring every effort to be made to achieve consensus, but according to the above rules of procedure of the MOP substantive decisions may as a last resort be made by three-quarters of the members being present and voting.

[23] All decisions of the Compliance Committee are accessible on the website of the Committee under the website of the Convention (n 3), and all decisions referred to in the notes below were endorsed by MOP 5 (2014) by its Decisions V/9a-9o comprising the decisions by the MOP relating to 14 findings of the Compliance Committee on non-compliance submitted by the Committee to the MOP.

are set out in the 'Case Law of the Aarhus Convention Compliance Committee 2004-2011'.[24]

The overview does not include handling by the MOP of the decisions of the Compliance Committee,[25] nor does it include monitoring by the Compliance Committee of fulfillment of recommendations of the MOP to a non-compliant Party.[26]

Main Phases of a Compliance Procedure

(i) Triggering Phase

The first phase is obviously a communication, including corroborating information, by a member of the public brought before the Compliance Committee via the Secretariat. The 'Checklist for Communications' included in the Guidance Document has been replaced by 'Recommended Format for Communications' that might be useful also for lawyers.[27]

The Secretariat acknowledges the receipt of the communication, registers the communication, and verifies that all necessary information is provided. The final decision on whether the communication should be forwarded to the Compliance Committee for consideration of preliminary admissibility, however, rests with the Chair and the Vice-chair of the Committee. Provided that the communication in their view is sufficiently well-prepared to be considered by the Committee for a preliminary determination on admissibility at the next meeting of the Committee, the Secretariat informs Committee Members of the communication, and that it will be considered in that respect at the upcoming meeting. Simultaneously the Chair decides which Member of the Committee should serve as 'curator' for the case.[28]

[24] A Andrusevych, T Alge and C Konrad (eds), *Case Law of the Aarhus Convention Compliance Committee 2004-2011*, 2nd edn (RACSE, Lviv, 2011) which is accessible on the internet at www.unece.org/index.php?id=31320. Case law relating to procedural issues is cited under the relevant provisions of the Annex to Decision I/7, Part II, 100–120. An updated version of the publication is expected to be completed, and to be available on the internet, by the middle of 2015.

[25] Theoretically speaking, the MOP may be perceived as a kind of appellate body, but in practice the MOP has not been called upon in that capacity by Parties having been found to be non-compliant by the Compliance Committee. This is evidenced by the fact that all MOP decisions relating to findings of the Committee on non-compliance have been taken by consensus.

[26] On those aspects, see generally Koester, *Stocktaking* (2011) (n 12).

[27] Included at Appendix 3 of this book (an electronic version is available on the website of the Committee). The 'Recommended format' was adopted at the 46th meeting of the Compliance Committee (22–25 September 2014), and will be included in the revised Guidance Document, possibly with some minor amendments. On communications relating to significant events that occurred before the entry into force of the Convention for the Party concerned, see Guidance Document p 33 and eg the decision in ACCC/C/2010/53 (United Kingdom of Great Britain and Northern Ireland), adopted 28 September 2012, in which the Compliance Committee decided not to consider the process leading to the adoption of the Central Edinburgh Traffic Management Scheme, 'because this process was effectively concluded in 2003, before the entry into force of the Convention for the Party concerned' (para 81).

[28] An individual Member who assists the Chair and the Committee with the preparation of the draft decision and more generally to take responsibility for engaging in the details of the communication. The curator also introduces the communication with a view to a determination of its preliminary admissibility.

Based on the outcome of an open dialogue with Parties and stakeholders[29] the Compliance Committee has developed new procedures for processing communications pending determination of preliminary admissibility.[30] The procedures are, however, going to be tested at a couple of meetings of the Committee before their finalisation and inclusion in the revised Guidance Document. The main feature of the new procedures, which most likely is going to be included in those procedures as finally adopted, is that both the communicant and the Party concerned are being informed that the communication will be discussed in open session[31] as to its preliminary admissibility at the next meeting. The communication, together with any attachments, is then posted on the website.[32] At the meeting any representatives of the parties concerned present either in person or via audio-conference may briefly state its view regarding the admissibility. Statements should, according to the new procedures, however, not finally adopted, 'be concise and strictly limited to the issue of admissibility, while leaving aside the substance of the communication'.

The working language of the Compliance Committee is English.[33] This may require translation of communications drafted in one of the two other official languages of the Convention, French or Russian,[34] entailing some delays in respect of the procedures outlined below.

(ii) Initial Handling by the Committee and Determination of Preliminary Admissibility

At the first meeting of the Compliance Committee at which its agenda includes the communication, the Committee will consider whether the communication is preliminary admissible, ie make a preliminary determination on whether the communication is admissible, having regard to requirements for communications set out in the Annex to Decision I/7. In particular

— these requirements provide for a communication to be supported by corroborating information.[35] The refusal of the Compliance Committee to consider in its substantive decision allegations that have not been (sufficiently)

[29] Report on the 45th meeting (29 June–2 July 2014) (doc ECE/MP.PP/C.1/2014/10), para 42.

[30] Available on the website (n 3). See the list of weblinks at Appendix 14 of this book.

[31] Also hitherto the issue of preliminary admissibility was discussed in open session, but the parties concerned were not specifically informed that the communication would be on the agenda of the meeting of the Compliance Committee for such discussion.

[32] The former practice implied that communications were only posted on the website when a determination of preliminary admissibility had been made, but if either of the parties concerned happened to be present at the meeting they would be provided an opportunity to make a statement on the issue of preliminary admissibility. As hitherto observers will be permitted to state their views.

[33] Decision I/7. Annex, para 22.

[34] Guidance Document 35. On translation of corroborating information, see Guidance Document 17. Interpretation is provided at discussions of the substance of the case when the parties concerned are French or Russian speaking.

[35] Decision I/7. Annex, paras 19 and 20.

substantiated is a reflection of this requirement.[36] It is, however, obvious that also objections need to be substantiated, but the Committee is free to consider the evidence presented.

— other requirements to a communication include that it is not 'anonymous', 'an abuse of the right to make communications', 'manifestly unreasonable'[37] or—as supplemented by a decision of the Compliance Committee—not *de minimis*.[38]

In considering admissibility the Compliance Committee also has to take into account the availability of any 'domestic remedies unless the application of the application of the remedy is unreasonably prolonged or obviously does not provide an effective and sufficient means of redress.'[39] This means that exhaustion of domestic remedies is not in every case an absolute requirement for the admissibility of a communication.

Inadmissible communications are not a rare phenomenon. Out of the 60 communications received before MOP 4 (June 2011), 15 were deemed inadmissible, a few of them after a determination on preliminary admissibility had been made. Out of the 40 communications submitted to the Committee between MOP 4 and MOP 5 (June 2014), 10 were found inadmissible.

If the Compliance Committee reaches the preliminary decision that the communication is admissible the Party concerned is formally informed about the communication, its preliminary admissibility, and the corroborating information. The letter to the Party concerned is usually accompanied by specific questions to the Party raised by the Committee. The communicant is also informed, quite often accompanied by questions to clarify the facts and/or allegations of the communication.

The Party concerned has five months to 'submit to the Committee written explanations or statements clarifying the matter and describing any response

[36] See eg the decision in ACCC/C/2010/50 (Czech Republic), adopted on 29 June 2012, para 64, and the decision in ACCC/C/2010/53 (n 27), para 71.

[37] Decision I/7. Annex, para 20 (a), (b) and (d).

[38] See generally Koester, *Stocktaking* (2011) (n 12), including on the approach of the Compliance Committee in respect of communications that might be inadmissible.

[39] Decision I/7. Annex, para 21, to which the fifth session of the MOP (July 2014) referred in Decision V/9 *on general issues of compliance*, para 6 (b) by noting that 'the Committee should ensure that, where domestic remedies have not been utilized and exhausted, it takes account of such remedies'. The decision of the Committee in ACCC/C/2010/59 (Kazakhstan), adopted 28 March 2013, provides not only an example of the application of this provision, but also an example of the freedom of the Committee to decide which aspects of a communication to consider (see in particular para 42 and 'Powers of the Compliance Committee'above). On the last issue, see also eg the decision in ACCC/C/2010/48 (Austria), adopted 16 December 2011, para 52. In ACCC/C/2010/53 (n 27) the Committee decided not to address some allegations relating to access to information and public participation, because the communicant had the possibility to address the issue with the Scottish Information Commissioner and because other domestic remedies were not exhausted (para 71). This decision is in conformity with para 21 of the Annex to Decision I/7 which requires that the issue of domestic remedies is to be taken into account 'at all relevant stages'. In ACCC/C/2012/68 (n 13), para 75, the Committee applied the concept of *lis pendens* by its decision not to consider some allegations with respect to compliance by the EU, because those allegations were currently before the General Court.

it may have made',[40] as well as to respond to specific questions posed by the Committee.[41] The same deadline applies for the communicant.

If the communication is found to be inadmissible the case is closed without further information to the Party concerned. Both inadmissible and preliminary admissible communications are allocated a case number in the meeting report.

(iii) Discussion of the Substance

The general approach of the Compliance Committee is to seek to arrange for a formal discussion[42] of the communication with the parties concerned at the first meeting that takes place more than two weeks after the expiry of the period mentioned above. In practice, however, whether this timescale is possible or feasible does not only depend on the substance of the communication, responses from the parties concerned to questions posed by the Committee, and other circumstances related to the communication, but as well as the Committee's workload. The communicant and the Party concerned are, naturally, given advance notice of the scheduling of the formal discussion, sometimes accompanied by information on specific issues that the Committee wishes to focus on at the discussion.[43]

The formal discussion with the two parties is following a specific pattern outlined in the Modus Operandi. The first issue being addressed is whether the communication is admissible. Normally this, however, simply involves confirming the Compliance Committee's earlier preliminary determination on the admissibility of the communication.[44] The main purpose of the discussion is to clarify the facts and legal issues by means of a constructive dialogue between the Committee and the two parties concerned. The discussion is conducted so as to avoid it becoming confrontational and adversarial.[45] However, participants are entitled to, and often use, legal representation.

The procedure does not provide for an *amicus curiae*-system, but since the procedure is quite flexible, recognising the presence of observers and providing a possibility for them to intervene,[46] the lack of provision on *amici curiae* has not caused any problems.

[40] Decision I/7. Annex, para 23.

[41] The Party concerned may, of course, also use this opportunity to question or disagree with the Compliance Committee's determination on preliminary admissibility, which under the procedure before the introduction of the, not as of yet finally adopted, procedures on the processing of communications pending determination of preliminary admissibility, referred to in 'Main Phases of a Compliance Procedure'above, could remedy the fact that the Party concerned was usually not present when that determination was made.

[42] In practice, a formal discussion corresponds to a hearing, which the Compliance Committee according to Decision I/7. Annex, para 24 may hold.

[43] Travel costs and per diems are being reimbursed by the Convention's budget for eligible State Parties as well as for most communicants.

[44] So much more because this issue has already been discussed with parties concerned under the new, not as of yet finally adopted, procedures referred to in 'Main Phases of a Compliance Procedure' above.

[45] See also Annex III to the Guidance Document.

[46] Observers may equally present comments in writing, before the formal discussion takes place.

(iv) The Committee's Preparation and Adoption of its Decision

After the formal discussion the Compliance Committee will discuss the case in closed session with a view to preparing conclusions and findings, and, if relevant, measures or recommendations ('decision'),[47] sometimes but not always based on a draft decision already prepared by the curator.[48] In the course of such session the Committee may identify further questions to be raised with the Party concerned and/or communicant. Normally, the closed session takes place on the same meeting day as that of the formal discussion so as to allow for a resumed discussion with the parties concerned after the closed session. Further questions may also be identified during the Committee's deliberations after the meeting during which the session of the formal discussion with the parties concerned takes place[49] and, in some cases, the deliberations of the Committee may, pending the circumstances and due to the extensive workload of the Committee, continue at a number of meetings thereafter[50] notwithstanding the possibilities for electronic decision-making.[51]

When the Compliance Committee has agreed on a draft decision it is, following a notice 1–2 days before to the parties concerned in order to allow them to prepare for inquiries from the public and media,[52] being forwarded to the parties concerned who are usually given a delay of one month to provide any comments. The draft decision is also posted on the website of the Committee in order to enable any observers to make comments. As soon as possible after the delay the Committee will proceed formally to adopting the decision, taking into account any comments received.[53]

Decisions of the Compliance Committee are drafted following a specific pattern: The first part, 'I Introduction', presents the basic facts relating to the communication and the Committee's handling of the case. The second part, 'II Summary of facts, evidence and issues', is divided into three subsections, the first of those outlining the legal framework, the second the facts, as presented by the parties involved, and the third substantive issues, namely the specific allegations and how the Party concerned responded. This part usually also includes

[47] The notion of decision is applied in the present paper for practical reasons only to characterise the outcome of the deliberations of the Compliance Committee, because the outcome may vary considerably pending the circumstances. It may include findings on no non-compliance, or findings on non-compliance with recommendations either to the MOP or to the Party concerned, or without recommendations. The notion of decision in the present paper should not be confused with the decision of the MOP, representing deliberations of the MOP on the 'decision' of the Committee.

[48] See n 28.

[49] Over and above the procedure is rather inquisitive, simply because a prerequisite of a decision is a full understanding of the facts and none the least the legal situation at stake.

[50] The average time to reach substantive decisions was in the intersessional period between MOP 2 (2005) and MOP 3 (2008), 389 days from the date of the communication and between MOP 3 (2008) and MOP 4 (2011), 540–570 days. See Koester, *Stocktaking* (2011) (n 12).

[51] Guidance Document 9.

[52] Report of the Compliance Committee on its 45th meeting (29 June–2 July 2014) (doc ECE/MP.PP/C.1/2014/10), para 44.

[53] Decision I/7. Annex para 34.

a section on the exhaustion of domestic remedies, being relevant in particular when the Committee decides to proceed with the consideration of the case, even if domestic remedies are still pending. Part three, 'III Consideration and evaluation by the Committee', is divided into subsections which the Committee considers to be the main issues. When relevant, the Committee will in that part refer to its previous case law.[54] Finally, the fourth part, 'IV Conclusions and recommendations', contains in a first subsection a summary of the main findings and in the second subsection the recommendations of the Committee.

(v) *Finalisation and Communication of the Decision*

The final version of the decision is produced as an official document available in the three UNECE languages and transmitted to the parties concerned, but an advance unedited copy of the decision is being communicated to the parties concerned and being posted on the website, shortly after the meeting during which the Compliance Committee adopted the final text.[55] Until the production of the decision as an official document, editorial and minor substantive changes aiming at correcting errors but without any impact on the conclusion and findings may take place. The final version is being published as a pre-session document, along with the agenda, of the second meeting of the Committee following the finalisation of the decision.[56]

Procedural Safeguards

The Annex to Decision I/7 includes a number of procedural safeguards, most of which have been referred to above, the others including quite detailed rules on conflict of interest and on information gathering as well as rules on confidentiality.[57]

Some key features of the compliance procedure may also be characterised as procedural safeguards, including the openness and transparency of the process, the fact that the draft decision is forwarded to the parties concerned for comments, and that both the draft decision and comments to the draft decision as well as other correspondence with the parties concerned are posted on the website.[58]

[54] See eg the decision in ACCC/C/2011/58 (Bulgaria), adopted 28 September 2012, paras 52 and 53.

[55] Parties are provided a notice 1–2 days before. See n 52 above.

[56] Until 2012, the adopted findings were an addendum to the report of the Committee on the meeting where the findings were adopted. Because of a change in the proceeding of UN documents that set some limitations to the overall length of the UN documents, the practice for the publication of the findings of the Compliance Committee changed: from 2012 onwards, Committee findings are produced as a separate (ie not as an addendum to a report) UN document, bearing their own UN document symbol number, and thus the Committee at the second meeting following the meeting at which it adopted the findings, also has an opportunity to review the editorial changes made and also the translations, before 'confirming' its findings.

[57] Guidance Document, respectively 11–12, 23–26 and 35. Decision I/7. Annex, para 25 includes a few rules on information gathering, and paras 26–31 rather extensive rules on confidentiality.

[58] Meeting reports are obviously equally posted on the website.

In addition, the procedure is flexible and easily adaptable to changing circumstances without foreclosing legal predictability, because substantive procedural rules are not obviously being amended retroactively.

Some Concluding Remarks

The Aarhus Convention CM has been and is being used extensively by the NGO community, and frequently also by individual citizens. No other compliance or implementation committee is handling more cases than the Aarhus Convention Compliance Committee.

It is obvious that the 'success' presents some problems of its own, mainly due to the very construction of the mechanism centered on a committee the members of which having their main occupation elsewhere. The Compliance Committee has, however, been quite innovative to adapt its procedures so as to enable it to handle the steadily increasing number of communications, although decisions in that respect are also governed by other considerations. The introduction of the *de minimis* criterion (see 'Main Phases of a Compliance Procedure' above) is one example, and the decision on excessive disorganised and unstructured information (see 'Proceedings before the Compliance Committee' above) another. A further example is the introduction of summary proceedings in respect of communications reflecting the same legal issues upon which the Committee has already deliberated in previous communications.[59]

Furthermore, the procedures of the Compliance Committee have not caused any major problems. They seem to be appropriate and easily understandable and applicable by those having been engaged in communications. This observation includes also the many lawyers from a variety of countries having represented either communicants or Parties. Arguments over procedure are exceptional.[60]

[59] See Guidance Document 22 and as an example the decision in ACCC/C/2010/45 & ACCC/C/2011/60 (United Kingdom of Great Britain and Northern Ireland), adopted 28 June 2013. When only a part of a communication relates to legal issues already considered by the Compliance Committee, the Committee simply decides not to consider that part of the communication. As an example the Committee decided in ACCC/C/2012/68 (n 13), para 77, not to consider whether the EU had in place a regulatory framework to ensure proper implementation of National Renewable Energy Action Plans 'given that this was considered in its findings on communication ACCC/C/2010/54 concerning compliance by the EU'.

[60] In one case, however, such discussion entailed elaboration by the Compliance Committee of more detailed rules on conflict of interest. See above at n 19, and the discussion as reflected in the Report of the Compliance Committee on its 25th meeting (22–25 September 2009) (doc ECE/MP.PP/C.1/2009/6), paras 6–11 with annexed statements: 1) by the Committee concerning the allegation of a conflict of interest in connection with the communications ACCC/C/2008/23 and ACCC/C/2008/27; 2) by the United Kingdom concerning the issue of conflict of interest with respect to the communications ACCC/C/2008/23 and ACCC/C/2008/27 as well as to ACCC/C/2008/33; and 3) by the communicants in the form of three statements relating to respectively the three communications referred to. The issue of conflict of interest was pursued by the Committee at the following four meetings, see in particular Report of the Compliance Committee on its 26th meeting (15–19

It has to be seen, however, whether the new procedures concerning the processing of communications pending determination of preliminary admissibility that are currently being tested[61] are going to work in an appropriate and feasible manner. In any event, however, the Compliance Committee has to take into account that the fifth session of the MOP in July 2014 noted in one of its decisions

> the need for the Committee to ensure transparency and due process for both communicants and the Parties concerned in respect of communications received from members of the public (including informing the Party concerned, at an early stage, of the receipt of a communication by the Committee).[62]

December 2009) (doc ECE/MP.PP/C.1/2009/8), para 5 and Report of the Compliance Committee on its 29th meeting (21–24 September 2010) (doc ECE/MP.PP/C.1/2010/6), paras 6 and 7 referring to the adoption of the Committee of detailed rules on conflict of interest.

[61] Above at nn 29 and 30.

[62] *Decision V/9 on general issues of compliance*, para 6(a).

Appendix 1—The Aarhus Convention

CONVENTION ON ACCESS TO INFORMATION, PUBLIC PARTICIPATION IN DECISION-MAKING AND ACCESS TO JUSTICE IN ENVIRONMENTAL MATTERS

done at Aarhus, Denmark,
on 25 June 1998

The Parties to this Convention,

Recalling principle 1 of the Stockholm Declaration on the Human Environment,

Recalling also principle 10 of the Rio Declaration on Environment and Development,

Recalling further General Assembly resolutions 37/7 of 28 October 1982 on the World Charter for Nature and 45/94 of 14 December 1990 on the need to ensure a healthy environment for the well-being of individuals,

Recalling the European Charter on Environment and Health adopted at the First European Conference on Environment and Health of the World Health Organization in Frankfurt-am-Main, Germany, on 8 December 1989,

Affirming the need to protect, preserve and improve the state of the environment and to ensure sustainable and environmentally sound development,

Recognizing that adequate protection of the environment is essential to human well-being and the enjoyment of basic human rights, including the right to life itself,

Recognizing also that every person has the right to live in an environment adequate to his or her health and well-being, and the duty, both individually and in association with others, to protect and improve the environment for the benefit of present and future generations,

Considering that, to be able to assert this right and observe this duty, citizens must have access to information, be entitled to participate in decision-making and have access to justice in environmental matters, and acknowledging in this regard that citizens may need assistance in order to exercise their rights,

Recognizing that, in the field of the environment, improved access to information and public participation in decision-making enhance the quality and the implementation of decisions, contribute to public awareness of environmental issues, give the public the opportunity to express its concerns and enable public authorities to take due account of such concerns,

Aiming thereby to further the accountability of and transparency in decision-making and to strengthen public support for decisions on the environment,

Recognizing the desirability of transparency in all branches of government and inviting legislative bodies to implement the principles of this Convention in their proceedings,

Recognizing also that the public needs to be aware of the procedures for participation in environmental decision-making, have free access to them and know how to use them,

Recognizing further the importance of the respective roles that individual citizens, non-governmental organizations and the private sector can play in environmental protection,

Desiring to promote environmental education to further the understanding of the environment and sustainable development and to encourage widespread public awareness of, and participation in, decisions affecting the environment and sustainable development,

Noting, in this context, the importance of making use of the media and of electronic or other, future forms of communication,

Recognizing the importance of fully integrating environmental considerations in governmental decision-making and the consequent need for public authorities to be in possession of accurate, comprehensive and up-to-date environmental information,

Acknowledging that public authorities hold environmental information in the public interest,

Concerned that effective judicial mechanisms should be accessible to the public, including organizations, so that its legitimate interests are protected and the law is enforced,

Noting the importance of adequate product information being provided to consumers to enable them to make informed environmental choices,

Recognizing the concern of the public about the deliberate release of genetically modified organisms into the environment and the need for increased transparency and greater public participation in decision-making in this field,

Convinced that the implementation of this Convention will contribute to strengthening democracy in the region of the United Nations Economic Commission for Europe (ECE),

Conscious of the role played in this respect by ECE and recalling, inter alia, the ECE Guidelines on Access to Environmental Information and Public Participation in Environmental Decision-making endorsed in the Ministerial Declaration adopted at the Third Ministerial Conference "Environment for Europe" in Sofia, Bulgaria, on 25 October 1995,

Bearing in mind the relevant provisions in the Convention on Environmental Impact Assessment in a Transboundary Context, done at Espoo, Finland, on 25 February 1991, and the Convention on the Transboundary Effects of Industrial Accidents and the Convention on the Protection and Use of Transboundary Watercourses and International Lakes, both done at Helsinki on 17 March 1992, and other regional conventions,

Conscious that the adoption of this Convention will have contributed to the further strengthening of the "Environment for Europe" process and to the results of the Fourth Ministerial Conference in Aarhus, Denmark, in June 1998,

Have agreed as follows:

Article 1

OBJECTIVE

In order to contribute to the protection of the right of every person of present and future generations to live in an environment adequate to his or her health and well-being, each Party shall guarantee the rights of access to information, public participation in decision-making, and access to justice in environmental matters in accordance with the provisions of this Convention.

Article 2

DEFINITIONS

For the purposes of this Convention,

1. "Party" means, unless the text otherwise indicates, a Contracting Party to this Convention;

2. "Public authority" means:

(a) Government at national, regional and other level;

(b) Natural or legal persons performing public administrative functions under national law, including specific duties, activities or services in relation to the environment;

(c) Any other natural or legal persons having public responsibilities or functions, or providing public services, in relation to the environment, under the control of a body or person falling within subparagraphs (a) or (b) above;

(d) The institutions of any regional economic integration organization referred to in article 17 which is a Party to this Convention.

This definition does not include bodies or institutions acting in a judicial or legislative capacity;

3. "Environmental information" means any information in written, visual, aural, electronic or any other material form on:

(a) The state of elements of the environment, such as air and atmosphere, water, soil, land, landscape and natural sites, biological diversity and its components, including genetically modified organisms, and the interaction among these elements;

(b) Factors, such as substances, energy, noise and radiation, and activities or measures, including administrative measures, environmental agreements, policies, legislation, plans and programmes, affecting or likely to affect the elements of the environment within the scope of subparagraph (a) above, and cost-benefit and other economic analyses and assumptions used in environmental decision-making;

(c) The state of human health and safety, conditions of human life, cultural sites and built structures, inasmuch as they are or may be affected by the state of the elements of the environment or, through these elements, by the factors, activities or measures referred to in subparagraph (b) above;

4. "The public" means one or more natural or legal persons, and, in accordance with national legislation or practice, their associations, organizations or groups;

5. "The public concerned" means the public affected or likely to be affected by, or having an interest in, the environmental decision-making; for the purposes of this definition, non-governmental organizations promoting environmental protection and meeting any requirements under national law shall be deemed to have an interest.

Article 3

GENERAL PROVISIONS

1. Each Party shall take the necessary legislative, regulatory and other measures, including measures to achieve compatibility between the provisions implementing the information, public participation and access-to-justice provisions in this Convention, as well as proper enforcement measures, to establish and maintain a clear, transparent and consistent framework to implement the provisions of this Convention.

2. Each Party shall endeavour to ensure that officials and authorities assist and provide guidance to the public in seeking access to information, in facilitating participation in decision-making and in seeking access to justice in environmental matters.

3. Each Party shall promote environmental education and environmental awareness among the public, especially on how to obtain access to information, to participate in decision-making and to obtain access to justice in environmental matters.

4. Each Party shall provide for appropriate recognition of and support to associations, organizations or groups promoting environmental protection and ensure that its national legal system is consistent with this obligation.

5. The provisions of this Convention shall not affect the right of a Party to maintain or introduce measures providing for broader access to information, more extensive public participation in decision-making and wider access to justice in environmental matters than required by this Convention.

6. This Convention shall not require any derogation from existing rights of access to information, public participation in decision-making and access to justice in environmental matters.

7. Each Party shall promote the application of the principles of this Convention in international environmental decision-making processes and within the framework of international organizations in matters relating to the environment.

8. Each Party shall ensure that persons exercising their rights in conformity with the provisions of this Convention shall not be penalized, persecuted or harassed in any way for their involvement. This provision shall not affect the powers of national courts to award reasonable costs in judicial proceedings.

9. Within the scope of the relevant provisions of this Convention, the public shall have access to information, have the possibility to participate in decision-making and have access to justice in environmental matters without discrimination as to citizenship, nationality or domicile and, in the case of a legal person, without discrimination as to where it has its registered seat or an effective centre of its activities.

Article 4

ACCESS TO ENVIRONMENTAL INFORMATION

1. Each Party shall ensure that, subject to the following paragraphs of this article, public authorities, in response to a request for environmental information, make such information available to the public, within the framework of national legislation, including, where requested and subject to subparagraph (b) below, copies of the actual documentation containing or comprising such information:

(a) Without an interest having to be stated;

(b) In the form requested unless:

(i) It is reasonable for the public authority to make it available in another form, in which case reasons shall be given for making it available in that form; or

(ii) The information is already publicly available in another form.

2. The environmental information referred to in paragraph 1 above shall be made available as soon as possible and at the latest within one month after the request has been submitted, unless the volume and the complexity of the information justify an extension of this period up to two months after the request. The applicant shall be informed of any extension and of the reasons justifying it.

3. A request for environmental information may be refused if:

(a) The public authority to which the request is addressed does not hold the environmental information requested;

(b) The request is manifestly unreasonable or formulated in too general a manner; or

(c) The request concerns material in the course of completion or concerns internal communications of public authorities where such an exemption is provided for in national law or customary practice, taking into account the public interest served by disclosure.

4. A request for environmental information may be refused if the disclosure would adversely affect:

(a) The confidentiality of the proceedings of public authorities, where such confidentiality is provided for under national law;

(b) International relations, national defence or public security;

(c) The course of justice, the ability of a person to receive a fair trial or the ability of a public authority to conduct an enquiry of a criminal or disciplinary nature;

(d) The confidentiality of commercial and industrial information, where such confidentiality is protected by law in order to protect a legitimate economic interest. Within this framework, information on emissions which is relevant for the protection of the environment shall be disclosed;

(e) Intellectual property rights;

(f) The confidentiality of personal data and/or files relating to a natural person where that person has not consented to the disclosure of the information to the public, where such confidentiality is provided for in national law;

(g) The interests of a third party which has supplied the information requested without that party being under or capable of being put under a legal obligation to do so, and where that party does not consent to the release of the material; or

(h) The environment to which the information relates, such as the breeding sites of rare species.

The aforementioned grounds for refusal shall be interpreted in a restrictive way, taking into account the public interest served by disclosure and taking into account whether the information requested relates to emissions into the environment.

5. Where a public authority does not hold the environmental information requested, this public authority shall, as promptly as possible, inform the applicant of the public authority to which it believes it is possible to apply for the information requested or transfer the request to that authority and inform the applicant accordingly.

6. Each Party shall ensure that, if information exempted from disclosure under paragraphs 3 (c) and 4 above can be separated out without prejudice to the confidentiality of the information exempted, public authorities make available the remainder of the environmental information that has been requested.

7. A refusal of a request shall be in writing if the request was in writing or the applicant so requests. A refusal shall state the reasons for the refusal and give information on access to the review procedure provided for in accordance with article 9. The refusal shall be made as soon as possible and at the latest within one month, unless the complexity of the information justifies an extension of this period up to two months after the request. The applicant shall be informed of any extension and of the reasons justifying it.

8. Each Party may allow its public authorities to make a charge for supplying information, but such charge shall not exceed a reasonable amount. Public authorities intending to make such a charge for supplying information shall make available to applicants a schedule of charges which may be levied, indicating the circumstances in which they may be levied or waived and when the supply of information is conditional on the advance payment of such a charge.

Article 5

COLLECTION AND DISSEMINATION OF ENVIRONMENTAL INFORMATION

1. Each Party shall ensure that:

(a) Public authorities possess and update environmental information which is relevant to their functions;

(b) Mandatory systems are established so that there is an adequate flow of information to public authorities about proposed and existing activities which may significantly affect the environment;

(c) In the event of any imminent threat to human health or the environment, whether caused by human activities or due to natural causes, all information which could enable the public to take measures to prevent or mitigate harm arising from the threat and is held by a public authority is disseminated immediately and without delay to members of the public who may be affected.

2. Each Party shall ensure that, within the framework of national legislation, the way in which public authorities make environmental information available to the public is transparent and that environmental information is effectively accessible, inter alia, by:

(a) Providing sufficient information to the public about the type and scope of environmental information held by the relevant public authorities, the basic terms and conditions under which such information is made available and accessible, and the process by which it can be obtained;

(b) Establishing and maintaining practical arrangements, such as:

(i) Publicly accessible lists, registers or files;

(ii) Requiring officials to support the public in seeking access to information under this Convention; and

(iii) The identification of points of contact; and

(c) Providing access to the environmental information contained in lists, registers or files as referred to in subparagraph (b) (i) above free of charge.

3. Each Party shall ensure that environmental information progressively becomes available in electronic databases which are easily accessible to the public through public telecommunications networks. Information accessible in this form should include:

(a) Reports on the state of the environment, as referred to in paragraph 4 below;

(b) Texts of legislation on or relating to the environment;

(c) As appropriate, policies, plans and programmes on or relating to the environment, and environmental agreements; and

(d) Other information, to the extent that the availability of such information in this form would facilitate the application of national law implementing this Convention,

provided that such information is already available in electronic form.

4. Each Party shall, at regular intervals not exceeding three or four years, publish and disseminate a national report on the state of the environment, including information on the quality of the environment and information on pressures on the environment.

5. Each Party shall take measures within the framework of its legislation for the purpose of disseminating, inter alia:

(a) Legislation and policy documents such as documents on strategies, policies, programmes and action plans relating to the environment, and progress reports on their implementation, prepared at various levels of government;

(b) International treaties, conventions and agreements on environmental issues; and

(c) Other significant international documents on environmental issues, as appropriate.

6. Each Party shall encourage operators whose activities have a significant impact on the environment to inform the public regularly of the environmental impact of their activities and products, where appropriate within the framework of voluntary eco-labelling or eco-auditing schemes or by other means.

7. Each Party shall:

(a) Publish the facts and analyses of facts which it considers relevant and important in framing major environmental policy proposals;

(b) Publish, or otherwise make accessible, available explanatory material on its dealings with the public in matters falling within the scope of this Convention; and

(c) Provide in an appropriate form information on the performance of public functions or the provision of public services relating to the environment by government at all levels.

8. Each Party shall develop mechanisms with a view to ensuring that sufficient product information is made available to the public in a manner which enables consumers to make informed environmental choices.

9. Each Party shall take steps to establish progressively, taking into account international processes where appropriate, a coherent, nationwide system of pollution inventories or registers on a structured, computerized and publicly accessible database compiled through standardized reporting. Such a system may include inputs, releases and transfers of a specified range of substances and products, including water, energy and resource use, from a specified range of activities to environmental media and to on-site and off-site treatment and disposal sites.

10. Nothing in this article may prejudice the right of Parties to refuse to disclose certain environmental information in accordance with article 4, paragraphs 3 and 4.

Article 6

PUBLIC PARTICIPATION IN DECISIONS ON SPECIFIC ACTIVITIES

1. Each Party:

(a) Shall apply the provisions of this article with respect to decisions on whether to permit proposed activities listed in annex I;

(b) Shall, in accordance with its national law, also apply the provisions of this article to decisions on proposed activities not listed in annex I which may have a significant effect on the environment. To this end, Parties shall determine whether such a proposed activity is subject to these provisions; and

(c) May decide, on a case-by-case basis if so provided under national law, not to apply the provisions of this article to proposed activities serving national defence purposes, if that Party deems that such application would have an adverse effect on these purposes.

2. The public concerned shall be informed, either by public notice or individually as appropriate, early in an environmental decision-making procedure, and in an adequate, timely and effective manner, *inter alia*, of:

(a) The proposed activity and the application on which a decision will be taken;

(b) The nature of possible decisions or the draft decision;

(c) The public authority responsible for making the decision;

(d) The envisaged procedure, including, as and when this information can be provided:

(i) The commencement of the procedure;

(ii) The opportunities for the public to participate;

(iii) The time and venue of any envisaged public hearing;

(iv) An indication of the public authority from which relevant information can be obtained and where the relevant information has been deposited for examination by the public;

(v) An indication of the relevant public authority or any other official body to which comments or questions can be submitted and of the time schedule for transmittal of comments or questions; and

(vi) An indication of what environmental information relevant to the proposed activity is available; and

(e) The fact that the activity is subject to a national or transboundary environmental impact assessment procedure.

3. The public participation procedures shall include reasonable time-frames for the different phases, allowing sufficient time for informing the public in accordance with paragraph 2 above and for the public to prepare and participate effectively during the environmental decision-making.

4. Each Party shall provide for early public participation, when all options are open and effective public participation can take place.

5. Each Party should, where appropriate, encourage prospective applicants to identify the public concerned, to enter into discussions, and to provide information regarding the objectives of their application before applying for a permit.

6. Each Party shall require the competent public authorities to give the public concerned access for examination, upon request where so required under national law, free of charge and as soon as it becomes available, to all information relevant to the decision-making referred to in this article that is available at the time of the public participation procedure, without prejudice to the right of Parties to refuse to disclose certain information in accordance with article 4, paragraphs 3 and 4. The relevant information shall include at least, and without prejudice to the provisions of article 4:

(a) A description of the site and the physical and technical characteristics of the proposed activity, including an estimate of the expected residues and emissions;

(b) A description of the significant effects of the proposed activity on the environment;

(c) A description of the measures envisaged to prevent and/or reduce the effects, including emissions;

(d) A non-technical summary of the above;

(e) An outline of the main alternatives studied by the applicant; and

(f) In accordance with national legislation, the main reports and advice issued to the public authority at the time when the public concerned shall be informed in accordance with paragraph 2 above.

7. Procedures for public participation shall allow the public to submit, in writing or, as appropriate, at a public hearing or inquiry with the applicant, any comments, information, analyses or opinions that it considers relevant to the proposed activity.

8. Each Party shall ensure that in the decision due account is taken of the outcome of the public participation.

9. Each Party shall ensure that, when the decision has been taken by the public authority, the public is promptly informed of the decision in accordance with the appropriate procedures. Each Party shall make accessible to the public the text of the decision along with the reasons and considerations on which the decision is based.

10. Each Party shall ensure that, when a public authority reconsiders or updates the operating conditions for an activity referred to in paragraph 1, the provisions of paragraphs 2 to 9 of this article are applied mutatis mutandis, and where appropriate.

11. Each Party shall, within the framework of its national law, apply, to the extent feasible and appropriate, provisions of this article to decisions on whether to permit the deliberate release of genetically modified organisms into the environment.

Article 7

PUBLIC PARTICIPATION CONCERNING PLANS, PROGRAMMES AND POLICIES RELATING TO THE ENVIRONMENT

Each Party shall make appropriate practical and/or other provisions for the public to participate during the preparation of plans and programmes relating to the environment, within a transparent and fair framework, having provided the necessary information to the public. Within this framework, article 6, paragraphs 3, 4 and 8, shall be applied. The public which may participate shall be identified by the relevant public authority, taking into account the objectives of this Convention. To the extent appropriate, each Party shall endeavour to provide opportunities for public participation in the preparation of policies relating to the environment.

Article 8

PUBLIC PARTICIPATION DURING THE PREPARATION OF EXECUTIVE REGULATIONS AND/OR GENERALLY APPLICABLE LEGALLY BINDING NORMATIVE INSTRUMENTS

Each Party shall strive to promote effective public participation at an appropriate stage, and while options are still open, during the preparation by public authorities of executive regulations and other generally applicable legally binding rules that may have a significant effect on the environment. To this end, the following steps should be taken:

(a) Time-frames sufficient for effective participation should be fixed;

(b) Draft rules should be published or otherwise made publicly available; and

(c) The public should be given the opportunity to comment, directly or through representative consultative bodies.

The result of the public participation shall be taken into account as far as possible.

Article 9

ACCESS TO JUSTICE

1. Each Party shall, within the framework of its national legislation, ensure that any person who considers that his or her request for information under article 4 has been ignored, wrongfully refused, whether in part or in full, inadequately answered, or otherwise not dealt with in accordance with the provisions of that article, has access to a review procedure before a court of law or another independent and impartial body established by law.

In the circumstances where a Party provides for such a review by a court of law, it shall ensure that such a person also has access to an expeditious procedure established by law that is free of charge or inexpensive for reconsideration by a public authority or review by an independent and impartial body other than a court of law.

Final decisions under this paragraph 1 shall be binding on the public authority holding the information. Reasons shall be stated in writing, at least where access to information is refused under this paragraph.

2. Each Party shall, within the framework of its national legislation, ensure that members of the public concerned

(a) Having a sufficient interest

or, alternatively,

(b) Maintaining impairment of a right, where the administrative procedural law of a Party requires this as a precondition,

have access to a review procedure before a court of law and/or another independent and impartial body established by law, to challenge the substantive and procedural legality of any decision, act or omission subject to the provisions of article 6 and, where so provided for under national law and without prejudice to paragraph 3 below, of other relevant provisions of this Convention.

What constitutes a sufficient interest and impairment of a right shall be determined in accordance with the requirements of national law and consistently with the objective of giving the public concerned wide access to justice within the scope of this Convention. To this end, the interest of any non-governmental organization meeting the requirements referred to in article 2, paragraph 5, shall be deemed sufficient for the purpose of subparagraph (a) above. Such organizations shall also be deemed to have rights capable of being impaired for the purpose of subparagraph (b) above.

The provisions of this paragraph 2 shall not exclude the possibility of a preliminary review procedure before an administrative authority and shall not affect the requirement of exhaustion of administrative review procedures prior to recourse to judicial review procedures, where such a requirement exists under national law.

3. In addition and without prejudice to the review procedures referred to in paragraphs 1 and 2 above, each Party shall ensure that, where they meet the criteria, if any, laid down in its national law, members of the public have access to administrative or judicial procedures to challenge acts and omissions by private persons and public authorities which contravene provisions of its national law relating to the environment.

4. In addition and without prejudice to paragraph 1 above, the procedures referred to in paragraphs 1, 2 and 3 above shall provide adequate and effective remedies, including injunctive relief as appropriate, and be fair,

equitable, timely and not prohibitively expensive. Decisions under this article shall be given or recorded in writing. Decisions of courts, and whenever possible of other bodies, shall be publicly accessible.

5. In order to further the effectiveness of the provisions of this article, each Party shall ensure that information is provided to the public on access to administrative and judicial review procedures and shall consider the establishment of appropriate assistance mechanisms to remove or reduce financial and other barriers to access to justice.

Article 10

MEETING OF THE PARTIES

1. The first meeting of the Parties shall be convened no later than one year after the date of the entry into force of this Convention. Thereafter, an ordinary meeting of the Parties shall be held at least once every two years, unless otherwise decided by the Parties, or at the written request of any Party, provided that, within six months of the request being communicated to all Parties by the Executive Secretary of the Economic Commission for Europe, the said request is supported by at least one third of the Parties.

2. At their meetings, the Parties shall keep under continuous review the implementation of this Convention on the basis of regular reporting by the Parties, and, with this purpose in mind, shall:

(a) Review the policies for and legal and methodological approaches to access to information, public participation in decision-making and access to justice in environmental matters, with a view to further improving them;

(b) Exchange information regarding experience gained in concluding and implementing bilateral and multilateral agreements or other arrangements having relevance to the purposes of this Convention and to which one or more of the Parties are a party;

(c) Seek, where appropriate, the services of relevant ECE bodies and other competent international bodies and specific committees in all aspects pertinent to the achievement of the purposes of this Convention;

(d) Establish any subsidiary bodies as they deem necessary;

(e) Prepare, where appropriate, protocols to this Convention;

(f) Consider and adopt proposals for amendments to this Convention in accordance with the provisions of article 14;

(g) Consider and undertake any additional action that may be required for the achievement of the purposes of this Convention;

(h) At their first meeting, consider and by consensus adopt rules of procedure for their meetings and the meetings of subsidiary bodies;

(i) At their first meeting, review their experience in implementing the provisions of article 5, paragraph 9, and consider what steps are necessary to develop further the system referred to in that paragraph, taking into account international processes and developments, including the elaboration of an appropriate instrument concerning pollution release and transfer registers or inventories which could be annexed to this Convention.

3. The Meeting of the Parties may, as necessary, consider establishing financial arrangements on a consensus basis.

4. The United Nations, its specialized agencies and the International Atomic Energy Agency, as well as any State or regional economic integration organization entitled under article 17 to sign this Convention but which is not a Party to this Convention, and any intergovernmental organization qualified in the fields to which this Convention relates, shall be entitled to participate as observers in the meetings of the Parties.

5. Any non-governmental organization, qualified in the fields to which this Convention relates, which has informed the Executive Secretary of the Economic Commission for Europe of its wish to be represented at a meeting of the Parties shall be entitled to participate as an observer unless at least one third of the Parties present in the meeting raise objections.

6. For the purposes of paragraphs 4 and 5 above, the rules of procedure referred to in paragraph 2 (h) above shall provide for practical arrangements for the admittance procedure and other relevant terms.

Article 11

RIGHT TO VOTE

1. Except as provided for in paragraph 2 below, each Party to this Convention shall have one vote.

2. Regional economic integration organizations, in matters within their competence, shall exercise their right to vote with a number of votes equal to the number of their member States which are Parties to this Convention. Such organizations shall not exercise their right to vote if their member States exercise theirs, and vice versa.

Article 12

SECRETARIAT

The Executive Secretary of the Economic Commission for Europe shall carry out the following secretariat functions:

(a) The convening and preparing of meetings of the Parties;

(b) The transmission to the Parties of reports and other information received in accordance with the provisions of this Convention; and

(c) Such other functions as may be determined by the Parties.

Article 13

ANNEXES

The annexes to this Convention shall constitute an integral part thereof.

Article 14

AMENDMENTS TO THE CONVENTION

1. Any Party may propose amendments to this Convention.

2. The text of any proposed amendment to this Convention shall be submitted in writing to the Executive Secretary of the Economic Commission for Europe, who shall communicate it to all Parties at least ninety days before the meeting of the Parties at which it is proposed for adoption.

3. The Parties shall make every effort to reach agreement on any proposed amendment to this Convention by consensus. If all efforts at consensus have been exhausted, and no agreement reached, the amendment shall as a last resort be adopted by a three-fourths majority vote of the Parties present and voting at the meeting.

4. Amendments to this Convention adopted in accordance with paragraph 3 above shall be communicated by the Depositary to all Parties for ratification, approval or acceptance. Amendments to this Convention other than those to an annex shall enter into force for Parties having ratified, approved or accepted them on the ninetieth day after the receipt by the Depositary of notification of their ratification, approval or acceptance by at least three fourths of these Parties. Thereafter they shall enter into force for any other Party on the ninetieth day after that Party deposits its instrument of ratification, approval or acceptance of the amendments.

5. Any Party that is unable to approve an amendment to an annex to this Convention shall so notify the Depositary in writing within twelve months from the date of the communication of the adoption. The Depositary shall without delay notify all Parties of any such notification received. A Party may at any time substitute an acceptance for its previous notification and, upon deposit of an instrument of acceptance with the Depositary, the amendments to such an annex shall become effective for that Party.

6. On the expiry of twelve months from the date of its communication by the Depositary as provided for in paragraph 4 above an amendment to an annex shall become effective for those Parties which have not submitted a notification to the Depositary in accordance with the provisions of paragraph 5 above, provided that not more than one third of the Parties have submitted such a notification.

7. For the purposes of this article, "Parties present and voting" means Parties present and casting an affirmative or negative vote.

Article 15

REVIEW OF COMPLIANCE

The Meeting of the Parties shall establish, on a consensus basis, optional arrangements of a non-confrontational, non-judicial and consultative nature for reviewing compliance with the provisions of this Convention. These arrangements shall allow for appropriate public involvement and may include the option of considering communications from members of the public on matters related to this Convention.

Article 16

SETTLEMENT OF DISPUTES

1. If a dispute arises between two or more Parties about the interpretation or application of this Convention, they shall seek a solution by negotiation or by any other means of dispute settlement acceptable to the parties to the dispute.

2. When signing, ratifying, accepting, approving or acceding to this Convention, or at any time thereafter, a Party may declare in writing to the Depositary that, for a dispute not resolved in accordance with paragraph 1 above, it accepts one or both of the following means of dispute settlement as compulsory in relation to any Party accepting the same obligation:

(a) Submission of the dispute to the International Court of Justice;

(b) Arbitration in accordance with the procedure set out in annex II.

3. If the parties to the dispute have accepted both means of dispute settlement referred to in paragraph 2 above, the dispute may be submitted only to the International Court of Justice, unless the parties agree otherwise.

Article 17

SIGNATURE

This Convention shall be open for signature at Aarhus (Denmark) on 25 June 1998, and thereafter at United Nations Headquarters in New York until 21 December 1998, by States members of the Economic Commission for Europe as well as States having consultative status with the Economic Commission for Europe pursuant to paragraphs 8 and 11 of Economic and Social Council resolution 36 (IV) of 28 March 1947, and by regional economic integration organizations constituted by sovereign States members of the Economic Commission for Europe to which their member States have transferred competence over matters governed by this Convention, including the competence to enter into treaties in respect of these matters.

Article 18

DEPOSITARY

The Secretary-General of the United Nations shall act as the Depositary of this Convention.

Article 19

RATIFICATION, ACCEPTANCE, APPROVAL AND ACCESSION

1. This Convention shall be subject to ratification, acceptance or approval by signatory States and regional economic integration organizations.

2. This Convention shall be open for accession as from 22 December 1998 by the States and regional economic integration organizations referred to in article 17.

3. Any other State, not referred to in paragraph 2 above, that is a Member of the United Nations may accede to the Convention upon approval by the Meeting of the Parties.

4. Any organization referred to in article 17 which becomes a Party to this Convention without any of its member States being a Party shall be bound by all the obligations under this Convention. If one or more of such an organization's member States is a Party to this Convention, the organization and its member States shall decide on their respective responsibilities for the performance of their obligations under this Convention. In such cases, the organization and the member States shall not be entitled to exercise rights under this Convention concurrently.

5. In their instruments of ratification, acceptance, approval or accession, the regional economic integration organizations referred to in article 17 shall declare the extent of their competence with respect to the matters governed by this Convention. These organizations shall also inform the Depositary of any substantial modification to the extent of their competence.

Article 20

ENTRY INTO FORCE

1. This Convention shall enter into force on the ninetieth day after the date of deposit of the sixteenth instrument of ratification, acceptance, approval or accession.

2. For the purposes of paragraph 1 above, any instrument deposited by a regional economic integration organization shall not be counted as additional to those deposited by States members of such an organization.

3. For each State or organization referred to in article 17 which ratifies, accepts or approves this Convention or accedes thereto after the deposit of the sixteenth instrument of ratification, acceptance, approval or accession, the Convention shall enter into force on the ninetieth day after the date of deposit by such State or organization of its instrument of ratification, acceptance, approval or accession.

Article 21

WITHDRAWAL

At any time after three years from the date on which this Convention has come into force with respect to a Party, that Party may withdraw from the Convention by giving written notification to the Depositary. Any such withdrawal shall take effect on the ninetieth day after the date of its receipt by the Depositary.

Article 22

AUTHENTIC TEXTS

The original of this Convention, of which the English, French and Russian texts are equally authentic, shall be deposited with the Secretary-General of the United Nations.

IN WITNESS WHEREOF the undersigned, being duly authorized thereto, have signed this Convention.

DONE at Aarhus (Denmark), this twenty-fifth day of June, one thousand nine hundred and ninety-eight.

Annex I

LIST OF ACTIVITIES REFERRED TO IN ARTICLE 6, PARAGRAPH 1 (a)

1. Energy sector:

- Mineral oil and gas refineries;
- Installations for gasification and liquefaction;
- Thermal power stations and other combustion installations with a heat input of 50 megawatts (MW)or more;
- Coke ovens;
- Nuclear power stations and other nuclear reactors including the dismantling or decommissioning of such power stations or reactors 1/ (except research installations for the production and conversion of fissionable and fertile materials whose maximum power does not exceed 1 kW continuous thermal load);
- Installations for the reprocessing of irradiated nuclear fuel;
- Installations designed:

    - For the production or enrichment of nuclear fuel;
    - For the processing of irradiated nuclear fuel or high-level radioactive waste;
    - For the final disposal of irradiated nuclear fuel;
    - Solely for the final disposal of radioactive waste;
    - Solely for the storage (planned for more than 10 years) of irradiated nuclear fuels or radioactive waste in a different site than the production site.

2. Production and processing of metals:

- Metal ore (including sulphide ore) roasting or sintering installations;
- Installations for the production of pig-iron or steel (primary or secondary fusion) including continuous casting, with a capacity exceeding 2.5 tons per hour;
- Installations for the processing of ferrous metals:

    (i) Hot-rolling mills with a capacity exceeding 20 tons of crude steel per hour;
    (ii) Smitheries with hammers the energy of which exceeds 50 kilojoules per hammer, where the calorific power used exceeds 20 MW;
    (iii) Application of protective fused metal coats with an input exceeding 2 tons of crude steel per hour;
- Ferrous metal foundries with a production capacity exceeding 20 tons per day;

- Installations:

    (i) For the production of non-ferrous crude metals from ore, concentrates or secondary raw materials by metallurgical, chemical or electrolytic processes;
    (ii) For the smelting, including the alloying, of non-ferrous metals, including recovered products (refining, foundry casting, etc.), with a melting capacity exceeding 4 tons per day for lead and cadmium or 20 tons per day for all other metals;
- Installations for surface treatment of metals and plastic materials using an electrolytic or chemical process where the volume of the treatment vats exceeds 30 m^3.

3. Mineral industry:

- Installations for the production of cement clinker in rotary kilns with a production capacity exceeding 500 tons per day or lime in rotary kilns with a production capacity exceeding 50 tons per day or in other furnaces with a production capacity exceeding 50 tons per day;
- Installations for the production of asbestos and the manufacture of asbestos-based products;
- Installations for the manufacture of glass including glass fibre with a melting capacity exceeding 20 tons per day;
- Installations for melting mineral substances including the production of mineral fibres with a melting capacity exceeding 20 tons per day;
- Installations for the manufacture of ceramic products by firing, in particular roofing tiles, bricks, refractory bricks, tiles, stoneware or porcelain, with a production capacity exceeding 75 tons per day, and/or with a kiln capacity exceeding 4 m^3 and with a setting density per kiln exceeding 300 kg/m^3.

4. Chemical industry: Production within the meaning of the categories of activities contained in this paragraph means the production on an industrial scale by chemical processing of substances or groups of substances listed in subparagraphs (a) to (g):

(a) Chemical installations for the production of basic organic chemicals, such as:

(i) Simple hydrocarbons (linear or cyclic, saturated or unsaturated, aliphatic or aromatic);
(ii) Oxygen-containing hydrocarbons such as alcohols, aldehydes, ketones, carboxylic acids, esters, acetates, ethers, peroxides, epoxy resins;
(iii) Sulphurous hydrocarbons;
(iv) Nitrogenous hydrocarbons such as amines, amides, nitrous compounds, nitro compounds or nitrate compounds, nitriles, cyanates, isocyanates;

(v) Phosphorus-containing hydrocarbons;
(vi) Halogenic hydrocarbons;
(vii) Organometallic compounds;
(viii) Basic plastic materials (polymers, synthetic fibres and cellulose-based fibres);
(ix) Synthetic rubbers;
(x) Dyes and pigments;
(xi) Surface-active agents and surfactants;

(b) Chemical installations for the production of basic inorganic chemicals, such as:

(i) Gases, such as ammonia, chlorine or hydrogen chloride, fluorine or hydrogen fluoride, carbon oxides, sulphur compounds, nitrogen oxides, hydrogen, sulphur dioxide, carbonyl chloride;
(ii) Acids, such as chromic acid, hydrofluoric acid, phosphoric acid, nitric acid, hydrochloric acid, sulphuric acid, oleum, sulphurous acids;
(iii) Bases, such as ammonium hydroxide, potassium hydroxide, sodium hydroxide;
(iv) Salts, such as ammonium chloride, potassium chlorate, potassium carbonate, sodium carbonate, perborate, silver nitrate;

(v) Non-metals, metal oxides or other inorganic compounds such as calcium carbide, silicon, silicon carbide;

(c) Chemical installations for the production of phosphorous-, nitrogen- or potassium-based fertilizers (simple or compound fertilizers);

(d) Chemical installations for the production of basic plant health products and of biocides;

(e) Installations using a chemical or biological process for the production of basic pharmaceutical products;

(f) Chemical installations for the production of explosives;

(g) Chemical installations in which chemical or biological processing is used for the production of protein feed additives, ferments and other protein substances.

5. Waste management:

- Installations for the incineration, recovery, chemical treatment or landfill of hazardous waste;
- Installations for the incineration of municipal waste with a capacity exceeding 3 tons per hour;
- Installations for the disposal of non-hazardous waste with a capacity exceeding 50 tons per day;
- Landfills receiving more than 10 tons per day or with a total capacity exceeding 25 000 tons, excluding landfills of inert waste.

6. Waste-water treatment plants with a capacity exceeding 150 000 population equivalent.

7. Industrial plants for the:

(a) Production of pulp from timber or similar fibrous materials;

(b) Production of paper and board with a production capacity exceeding 20 tons per day.

8. (a) Construction of lines for long-distance railway traffic and of airports 2/ with a basic runway length of 2 100 m or more;

(b) Construction of motorways and express roads; 3/

(c) Construction of a new road of four or more lanes, or realignment and/or widening of an existing road of two lanes or less so as to provide four or more lanes, where such new road, or realigned and/or widened section of road, would be 10 km or more in a continuous length.

9. (a) Inland waterways and ports for inland-waterway traffic which permit the passage of vessels of over 1 350 tons;

(b) Trading ports, piers for loading and unloading connected to land and outside ports (excluding ferry piers) which can take vessels of over 1 350 tons.

10. Groundwater abstraction or artificial groundwater recharge schemes where the annual volume of water abstracted or recharged is equivalent to or exceeds 10 million cubic metres.

11. (a) Works for the transfer of water resources between river basins where this transfer aims at preventing possible shortages of water and where the amount of water transferred exceeds 100 million cubic metres/year;

(b) In all other cases, works for the transfer of water resources between river basins where the multiannual average flow of the basin of abstraction exceeds 2 000 million cubic metres/year and where the amount of water transferred exceeds 5% of this flow.

In both cases transfers of piped drinking water are excluded.

12. Extraction of petroleum and natural gas for commercial purposes where the amount extracted exceeds 500 tons/day in the case of petroleum and 500 000 cubic metres/day in the case of gas.

13. Dams and other installations designed for the holding back or permanent storage of water, where a new or additional amount of water held back or stored exceeds 10 million cubic metres.

14. Pipelines for the transport of gas, oil or chemicals with a diameter of more than 800 mm and a length of more than 40 km.

15. Installations for the intensive rearing of poultry or pigs with more than:

(a) 40 000 places for poultry;

(b) 2 000 places for production pigs (over 30 kg); or

(c) 750 places for sows.

16. Quarries and opencast mining where the surface of the site exceeds 25 hectares, or peat extraction, where the surface of the site exceeds 150 hectares.

17. Construction of overhead electrical power lines with a voltage of 220 kV or more and a length of more than 15 km.

18. Installations for the storage of petroleum, petrochemical, or chemical products with a capacity of 200 000 tons or more.

19. Other activities:

- Plants for the pretreatment (operations such as washing, bleaching, mercerization) or dyeing of fibres or textiles where the treatment capacity exceeds 10 tons per day;
- Plants for the tanning of hides and skins where the treatment capacity exceeds 12 tons of finished products per day;
- (a) Slaughterhouses with a carcass production capacity greater than 50 tons per day;

  (b) Treatment and processing intended for the production of food products from:

  (i) Animal raw materials (other than milk) with a finished product production capacity greater than 75 tons per day;

  (ii) Vegetable raw materials with a finished product production capacity greater than 300 tons per day (average value on a quarterly basis);

(c) Treatment and processing of milk, the quantity of milk received being greater than 200 tons per day (average value on an annual basis);

- Installations for the disposal or recycling of animal carcasses and animal waste with a treatment capacity exceeding 10 tons per day;
- Installations for the surface treatment of substances, objects or products using organic solvents, in particular for dressing, printing, coating, degreasing, waterproofing, sizing, painting, cleaning or impregnating, with a consumption capacity of more than 150 kg per hour or more than 200 tons per year;
- Installations for the production of carbon (hard-burnt coal) or electrographite by means of incineration or graphitization.

20. Any activity not covered by paragraphs 1-19 above where public participation is provided for under an environmental impact assessment procedure in accordance with national legislation.

21. The provision of article 6, paragraph 1 (a) of this Convention, does not apply to any of the above projects undertaken exclusively or mainly for research, development and testing of new methods or products for less than two years unless they would be likely to cause a significant adverse effect on environment or health.

22. Any change to or extension of activities, where such a change or extension in itself meets the criteria/thresholds set out in this annex, shall be subject to article 6, paragraph 1 (a) of this Convention. Any other change or extension of activities shall be subject to article 6, paragraph 1 (b) of this Convention.

Notes

1/ Nuclear power stations and other nuclear reactors cease to be such an installation when all nuclear fuel and other radioactively contaminated elements have been removed permanently from the installation site.

2/ For the purposes of this Convention, "airport" means an airport which complies with the definition in the 1944 Chicago Convention setting up the International Civil Aviation Organization (Annex 14).

3/ For the purposes of this Convention, "express road" means a road which complies with the definition in the European Agreement on Main International Traffic Arteries of 15 November 1975.

Annex II

ARBITRATION

1. In the event of a dispute being submitted for arbitration pursuant to article 16, paragraph 2, of this Convention, a party or parties shall notify the secretariat of the subject matter of arbitration and indicate, in particular, the articles of this Convention whose interpretation or application is at issue. The secretariat shall forward the information received to all Parties to this Convention.

2. The arbitral tribunal shall consist of three members. Both the claimant party or parties and the other party or parties to the dispute shall appoint an arbitrator, and the two arbitrators so appointed shall designate by common agreement the third arbitrator, who shall be the president of the arbitral tribunal. The latter shall not be a national of one of the parties to the dispute, nor have his or her usual place of residence in the territory of one of these parties, nor be employed by any of them, nor have dealt with the case in any other capacity.

3. If the president of the arbitral tribunal has not been designated within two months of the appointment of the second arbitrator, the Executive Secretary of the Economic Commission for Europe shall, at the request of either party to the dispute, designate the president within a further two-month period.

4. If one of the parties to the dispute does not appoint an arbitrator within two months of the receipt of the request, the other party may so inform the Executive Secretary of the Economic Commission for Europe, who shall designate the president of the arbitral tribunal within a further two-month period. Upon designation, the president of the arbitral tribunal shall request the party which has not appointed an arbitrator to do so within two months. If it fails to do so within that period, the president shall so inform the Executive Secretary of the Economic Commission for Europe, who shall make this appointment within a further two-month period.

5. The arbitral tribunal shall render its decision in accordance with international law and the provisions of this Convention.

6. Any arbitral tribunal constituted under the provisions set out in this annex shall draw up its own rules of procedure.

7. The decisions of the arbitral tribunal, both on procedure and on substance, shall be taken by majority vote of its members.

8. The tribunal may take all appropriate measures to establish the facts.

9. The parties to the dispute shall facilitate the work of the arbitral tribunal and, in particular, using all means at their disposal, shall:

(a) Provide it with all relevant documents, facilities and information;

(b) Enable it, where necessary, to call witnesses or experts and receive their evidence.

10. The parties and the arbitrators shall protect the confidentiality of any information that they receive in confidence during the proceedings of the arbitral tribunal.

11. The arbitral tribunal may, at the request of one of the parties, recommend interim measures of protection.

12. If one of the parties to the dispute does not appear before the arbitral tribunal or fails to defend its case, the other party may request the tribunal to continue the proceedings and to render its final decision. Absence of a party or failure of a party to defend its case shall not constitute a bar to the proceedings.

13. The arbitral tribunal may hear and determine counter-claims arising directly out of the subject matter of the dispute.

14. Unless the arbitral tribunal determines otherwise because of the particular circumstances of the case, the expenses of the tribunal, including the remuneration of its members, shall be borne by the parties to the dispute in equal shares. The tribunal shall keep a record of all its expenses, and shall furnish a final statement thereof to the parties.

15. Any Party to this Convention which has an interest of a legal nature in the subject matter of the dispute, and which may be affected by a decision in the case, may intervene in the proceedings with the consent of the tribunal.

16. The arbitral tribunal shall render its award within five months of the date on which it is established, unless it finds it necessary to extend the time limit for a period which should not exceed five months.

17. The award of the arbitral tribunal shall be accompanied by a statement of reasons. It shall be final and binding upon all parties to the dispute. The award will be transmitted by the arbitral tribunal to the parties to the dispute and to the secretariat. The secretariat will forward the information received to all Parties to this Convention.

18. Any dispute which may arise between the parties concerning the interpretation or execution of the award may be submitted by either party to the arbitral tribunal which made the award or, if the latter cannot be seized thereof, to another tribunal constituted for this purpose in the same manner as the first.

Appendix 2—Decision I/7 of the Meeting of the Parties to the Aarhus Convention

UNITED
NATIONS

E

Economic and Social Council

Distr.
GENERAL

ECE/MP.PP/2/Add.8
2 April 2004

Original: ENGLISH

ECONOMIC COMMISSION FOR EUROPE

Meeting of the Parties to the
Convention on Access to Information,
Public Participation in Decision-making and
Access to Justice in Environmental Matters

REPORT OF THE FIRST MEETING OF THE PARTIES

Addendum

DECISION I/7

REVIEW OF COMPLIANCE

adopted at the first meeting of the Parties
held in Lucca, Italy, on 21-23 October 2002

The Meeting,

Determined to promote and improve compliance with the Convention on Access to Information, Public Participation in Decision-making and Access to Justice in Environmental Matters and recalling its article 15,

Recognizing the necessity for rigorous reporting by the Parties on their compliance with the Convention,

1. Establishes the Compliance Committee for the review of compliance by the Parties with their obligations under the Convention.

2. Decides that the structure and functions of the Compliance Committee and the procedures for the review of compliance shall be those set out in the annex to this decision.

GE.04-30994

Annex

STRUCTURE AND FUNCTIONS OF THE COMPLIANCE COMMITTEE AND PROCEDURES FOR THE REVIEW OF COMPLIANCE

I. STRUCTURE

1. The Committee shall consist of eight members, who shall serve in their personal capacity.

2. The Committee shall be composed of nationals of the Parties and Signatories to the Convention who shall be persons of high moral character and recognized competence in the fields to which the Convention relates, including persons having legal experience.

3. The Committee may not include more than one national of the same State.

4. Candidates meeting the requirements of paragraph 2 shall be nominated by Parties, Signatories and non-governmental organizations falling within the scope of article 10, paragraph 5, of the Convention and promoting environmental protection, for election pursuant to paragraph 7.

5. Unless the Meeting of the Parties, in a particular instance, decides otherwise, the procedure for the nomination of candidates for the Committee shall be the following:

(a) Nominations shall be sent to the secretariat in at least one of the official languages of the Convention not later than 12 weeks before the opening of the meeting of the Parties during which the election is to take place;

(b) Each nomination shall be accompanied by a curriculum vitae (CV) of the candidate not exceeding 600 words and may include supporting material;

(c) The secretariat shall distribute the nominations and the CVs, together with any supporting material, in accordance with rule 10 of the Rules of Procedure.

6. Committee members shall be elected on the basis of nominations in accordance with paragraphs 4 and 5. The Meeting of the Parties shall give due consideration to all nominations.

7. The Meeting of the Parties shall elect the members of the Committee by consensus or, failing consensus, by secret ballot.

8. In the election of the Committee, consideration should be given to the geographical distribution of membership and diversity of experience.

9. The Meeting of the Parties shall, as soon as practicable, elect four members to the Committee to serve until the end of the next ordinary meeting and four members to serve a full term of office. At each ordinary meeting thereafter, the Meeting of the Parties shall elect four members for a full term of office. Outgoing members may be re-elected once for a further full

term of office, unless in a given case the Meeting of the Parties decides otherwise. A full term of office commences at the end of an ordinary meeting of the Parties and runs until the second ordinary meeting of the Parties thereafter. The Committee shall elect its own Chairperson and Vice-Chairperson.

10. If a member of the Committee can no longer perform his or her duties as member of the Committee for any reason, the Bureau of the Meeting of the Parties shall appoint another member fulfilling the criteria in this chapter to serve the remainder of the term, subject to the approval of the Committee.

11. Every member serving on the Committee shall, before taking up his or her duties, make a solemn declaration in a meeting of the Committee that he or she will perform his or her functions impartially and conscientiously.

II. MEETINGS

12. The Committee shall, unless it decides otherwise, meet at least once a year. The secretariat shall arrange for and service the meetings of the Committee.

III. FUNCTIONS OF THE COMMITTEE

13. The Committee shall:

(a) Consider any submission, referral or communication made in accordance with paragraphs 15 to 24 below;

(b) Prepare, at the request of the Meeting of the Parties, a report on compliance with or implementation of the provisions of the Convention; and

(c) Monitor, assess and facilitate the implementation of and compliance with the reporting requirements under article 10, paragraph 2, of the Convention;

and act pursuant to paragraphs 36 and 37.

14. The Committee may examine compliance issues and make recommendations if and as appropriate.

IV. SUBMISSION BY PARTIES

15. A submission may be brought before the Committee by one or more Parties that have reservations about another Party's compliance with its obligations under the Convention. Such a submission shall be addressed in writing to the secretariat and supported by corroborating information. The secretariat shall, within two weeks of receiving a submission, send a copy of it to the Party whose compliance is at issue. Any reply and supporting information shall be submitted to the secretariat and to the Parties involved within three months or such longer period as the circumstances of a particular case may require but in no case later than six months. The secretariat shall transmit the submission and the reply, as well as all corroborating and supporting information, to the Committee, which shall consider the matter as soon as practicable.

16. A submission may be brought before the Committee by a Party that concludes that, despite its best endeavours, it is or will be unable to comply fully with its obligations under the Convention. Such a submission shall be addressed in writing to the secretariat and explain, in particular, the specific circumstances that the Party considers to be the cause of its non-compliance. The secretariat shall transmit the submission to the Committee, which shall consider the matter as soon as practicable.

V. REFERRALS BY THE SECRETARIAT

17. Where the secretariat, in particular upon considering the reports submitted in accordance with the Convention's reporting requirements, becomes aware of possible non-compliance by a Party with its obligations under the Convention, it may request the Party concerned to furnish necessary information about the matter. If there is no response or the matter is not resolved within three months, or such longer period as the circumstances of the matter may require but in no case later than six months, the secretariat shall bring the matter to the attention of the Committee, which shall consider the matter as soon as practicable.

VI. COMMUNICATIONS FROM THE PUBLIC

18. On the expiry of twelve months from either the date of adoption of this decision or from the date of the entry into force of the Convention with respect to a Party, whichever is the later, communications may be brought before the Committee by one or more members of the public concerning that Party's compliance with the Convention, unless that Party has notified the Depositary in writing by the end of the applicable period that it is unable to accept, for a period of not more than four years, the consideration of such communications by the Committee. The Depositary shall without delay notify all Parties of any such notification received. During the four-year period mentioned above, the Party may revoke its notification thereby accepting that, from that date, communications may be brought before the Committee by one or more members of the public concerning that Party's compliance with the Convention.

19. The communications referred to in paragraph 18 shall be addressed to the Committee through the secretariat in writing and may be in electronic form. The communications shall be supported by corroborating information.

20. The Committee shall consider any such communication unless it determines that the communication is:

(a) Anonymous;

(b) An abuse of the right to make such communications;

(c) Manifestly unreasonable;

(d) Incompatible with the provisions of this decision or with the Convention.

21. The Committee should at all relevant stages take into account any available domestic remedy unless the application of the remedy is unreasonably prolonged or obviously does not provide an effective and sufficient means of redress.

22. Subject to the provisions of paragraph 20, the Committee shall as soon as possible bring any communications submitted to it under paragraph 18 to the attention of the Party alleged to be in non-compliance.

23. A Party shall, as soon as possible but not later than five months after any communication is brought to its attention by the Committee, submit to the Committee written explanations or statements clarifying the matter and describing any response that it may have made.

24. The Committee shall, as soon as practicable, further consider communications submitted to it pursuant to this chapter and take into account all relevant written information made available to it, and may hold hearings.

VII. INFORMATION GATHERING

25. To assist the performance of its functions, the Committee may:

(a) Request further information on matters under its consideration;

(b) Undertake, with the consent of any Party concerned, information gathering in the territory of that Party;

(c) Consider any relevant information submitted to it; and

(d) Seek the services of experts and advisers as appropriate.

VIII. CONFIDENTIALITY

26. Save as otherwise provided for in this chapter, no information held by the Committee shall be kept confidential.

27. The Committee and any person involved in its work shall ensure the confidentiality of any information that falls within the scope of the exceptions provided for in article 4, paragraphs 3 (c) and 4, of the Convention and that has been provided in confidence.

28. The Committee and any person involved in its work shall ensure the confidentiality of information that has been provided to it in confidence by a Party when making a submission in respect of its own compliance in accordance with paragraph 16 above.

29. Information submitted to the Committee, including all information relating to the identity of the member of the public submitting the information, shall be kept confidential if submitted by a person who asks that it be kept confidential because of a concern that he or she may be penalized, persecuted or harassed.

30. If necessary to ensure the confidentiality of information in any of the above cases, the Committee shall hold closed meetings.

31. Committee reports shall not contain any information that the Committee must keep confidential under paragraphs 27 to 29 above. Information that the Committee must keep confidential under paragraph 29 shall not be made available to any Party. All other information that the Committee receives in confidence and that is related to any recommendations by the Committee to the Meeting of the Parties shall be made available to any Party upon its request; that Party shall ensure the confidentiality of the information that it has received in confidence.

IX. ENTITLEMENT TO PARTICIPATE

32. A Party in respect of which a submission, referral or communication is made or which makes a submission, as well as the member of the public making a communication, shall be entitled to participate in the discussions of the Committee with respect to that submission, referral or communication.

33. The Party and the member of the public shall not take part in the preparation and adoption of any findings, any measures or any recommendations of the Committee.

34. The Committee shall send a copy of its draft findings, draft measures and any draft recommendations to the Parties concerned and the member of the public who submitted the communication if applicable, and shall take into account any comments made by them in the finalization of those findings, measures and recommendations.

X. COMMITTEE REPORTS TO THE MEETING OF THE PARTIES

35. The Committee shall report on its activities at each ordinary meeting of the Parties and make such recommendations as it considers appropriate. Each report shall be finalized by the Committee not later than twelve weeks in advance of the meeting of the Parties at which it is to be considered. Every effort shall be made to adopt the report by consensus. Where this is not possible, the report shall reflect the views of all the Committee members. Committee reports shall be available to the public.

XI. CONSIDERATION BY THE COMPLIANCE COMMITTEE

36. Pending consideration by the Meeting of the Parties, with a view to addressing compliance issues without delay, the Compliance Committee may:

(a) In consultation with the Party concerned, take the measures listed in paragraph 37 (a);

(b) Subject to agreement with the Party concerned, take the measures listed in paragraph 37 (b), (c) and (d).

XII. CONSIDERATION BY THE MEETING OF THE PARTIES

37. The Meeting of the Parties may, upon consideration of a report and any recommendations of the Committee, decide upon appropriate measures to bring about full compliance with the Convention. The Meeting of the Parties may, depending on the particular question before it and taking into account the cause, degree and frequency of the non-compliance, decide upon one or more of the following measures:

(a) Provide advice and facilitate assistance to individual Parties regarding the implementation of the Convention;

(b) Make recommendations to the Party concerned;

(c) Request the Party concerned to submit a strategy, including a time schedule, to the Compliance Committee regarding the achievement of compliance with the Convention and to report on the implementation of this strategy;

(d) In cases of communications from the public, make recommendations to the Party concerned on specific measures to address the matter raised by the member of the public;

(e) Issue declarations of non-compliance;

(f) Issue cautions;

(g) Suspend, in accordance with the applicable rules of international law concerning the suspension of the operation of a treaty, the special rights and privileges accorded to the Party concerned under the Convention;

(h) Take such other non-confrontational, non-judicial and consultative measures as may be appropriate.

XIII. RELATIONSHIP BETWEEN SETTLEMENT OF DISPUTES AND THE COMPLIANCE PROCEDURE

38. The present compliance procedure shall be without prejudice to article 16 of the Convention on the settlement of disputes.

XIV. ENHANCEMENT OF SYNERGIES

39. In order to enhance synergies between this compliance procedure and compliance procedures under other agreements, the Meeting of the Parties may request the Compliance Committee to communicate as appropriate with the relevant bodies of those agreements and report back to it, including with recommendations as appropriate. The Compliance Committee may also submit a report to the Meeting of the Parties on relevant developments between the sessions of the Meeting of the Parties.

Appendix 3—Format for Communications to the Aarhus Convention Compliance Committee*

I. Information on Correspondent Submitting the Communication

Full name of organization or person(s) submitting the communication:
Permanent address:
Address for correspondence on this matter, if different from permanent address:
Telephone:
E-mail:

If the communication is made by a group of persons, provide the above information for each person and indicate one contact person.

If the communication is submitted by an organization, provide the following information for the contact person authorized to represent the organization in connection with this communication:
Name:
Title/Position:
Telephone:
E-mail:

II. Party Concerned

Name of the Party concerned by the communication:

III. Length of the Communication

The communication should be no more than ten **A4 pages**. If in an exceptionally complex case more than ten pages are required, in no circumstances should the communication be longer than twenty A4 pages.

IV. Facts of the Communication

Detail the facts and circumstances of the alleged non-compliance. Include all matters of relevance to the assessment and consideration of your communication. Explain how you consider that the facts and circumstances described represent a lack of compliance with the provisions the Convention.

* This is the format for communications at the time of publication. Prior to preparing a communication, check the Compliance Committee website, http://www.unece.org/env/pp/pubcom.html, to ensure that you use the latest version.

V. Provisions of the Convention Alleged to be in Non-Compliance

List as precisely as possible the provisions (articles, paragraphs, subparagraphs) of the Convention that you allege the Party concerned has not complied with.

VI. Nature of Alleged Non-Compliance

For each of the above provisions which you allege to be in non-compliance, clearly explain how you consider that the Party concerned has failed to comply with that provision based on the facts of your case. (Provide as attachments to your communication the key supporting documentation that will help to substantiate your allegations).

Also indicate whether the communication concerns a specific case of a person's rights of access to information, public participation or access to justice being violated as a result of the non-compliance of the Party concerned or whether it relates to a general failure by the Party concerned to implement, or to implement correctly, the provisions of the Convention. If you consider that the non-compliance concerns a general failure by the Party concerned, provide as attachments to your communication any key supporting documentation that will help to substantiate that it is a general failure.

VII. Use of Domestic Remedies

Describe which, if any, domestic procedures have been invoked to address the particular matter of non-compliance which is the subject of the communication. Specify which procedures were used, when, which claims were made, what the results were and whether there are any other domestic remedies available.

If no domestic procedures have been invoked or if there are other domestic remedies available, explain why they have not been used. This information will be important for the Compliance Committee's decision on admissibility of the case.

VIII. Use of Other International Procedures

Indicate if any international procedures besides the Aarhus Convention Compliance Committee have been invoked to address the issue of non-compliance which is the subject of the communication. If so, specify which procedures were used, when, which claims were made and what the results were.

IX. Confidentiality

Note that unless you expressly request it, none of the information contained in your communication will be kept confidential. If you are concerned that you may be penalized, harassed or persecuted, you may request that information contained in your communication, including information on your identity, be kept confidential. If you request any information to be kept confidential, clearly indicate which information. It is also helpful for the Committee to know why confidentiality is requested.

X. Supporting Documentation (Copies, Not Originals)

Avoid including extraneous, superfluous or bulky documentation. Attach only documentation essential to your case, including:

- — Relevant national legislation, highlighting the most relevant provisions.
- — Relevant decisions/results of other procedures, highlighting the most relevant sections.
- — Relevant correspondence with the Party concerned's authorities or other documentation substantiating your allegations of non-compliance, highlighting the most relevant sections.

For documents other than key legislation and decisions, there should be no more than **five** attachments (one document per attachment).

For all documentation, highlight those parts which are essential to your case.

Provide all documentation in the original language, together with a legal standard English translation thereof, or if that is not possible, a legal standard translation in either Russian or French.

XI. Signature

Sign and date the communication. If the communication is submitted by an organization, a person authorized to sign on behalf of that organization must sign it.

XII. Sending the Communication

Send the communication by **e-mail and by registered post** to the following address:

Secretary to the Aarhus Convention Compliance Committee

United Nations Economic Commission for Europe
Environment Division
Palais des Nations
CH-1211 Geneva 10, Switzerland
E-mail. aarhus.compliance@unece.org

Clearly Indicate:
"Communication to the Aarhus Convention Compliance Committee"

Appendix 4—Regulation 1049/2001/EC *on public access to Parliament, Council and Commission documents*

31.5.2001 EN Official Journal of the European Communities L 145/43

REGULATION (EC) No 1049/2001 OF THE EUROPEAN PARLIAMENT AND OF THE COUNCIL

of 30 May 2001

regarding public access to European Parliament, Council and Commission documents

THE EUROPEAN PARLIAMENT AND THE COUNCIL OF THE EUROPEAN UNION,

Having regard to the Treaty establishing the European Community, and in particular Article 255(2) thereof,

Having regard to the proposal from the Commission ([1]),

Acting in accordance with the procedure referred to in Article 251 of the Treaty ([2]),

Whereas:

(1) The second subparagraph of Article 1 of the Treaty on European Union enshrines the concept of openness, stating that the Treaty marks a new stage in the process of creating an ever closer union among the peoples of Europe, in which decisions are taken as openly as possible and as closely as possible to the citizen.

(2) Openness enables citizens to participate more closely in the decision-making process and guarantees that the administration enjoys greater legitimacy and is more effective and more accountable to the citizen in a democratic system. Openness contributes to strengthening the principles of democracy and respect for fundamental rights as laid down in Article 6 of the EU Treaty and in the Charter of Fundamental Rights of the European Union.

(3) The conclusions of the European Council meetings held at Birmingham, Edinburgh and Copenhagen stressed the need to introduce greater transparency into the work of the Union institutions. This Regulation consolidates the initiatives that the institutions have already taken with a view to improving the transparency of the decision-making process.

(4) The purpose of this Regulation is to give the fullest possible effect to the right of public access to documents and to lay down the general principles and limits on such access in accordance with Article 255(2) of the EC Treaty.

(5) Since the question of access to documents is not covered by provisions of the Treaty establishing the European Coal and Steel Community and the Treaty establishing the European Atomic Energy Community, the European Parliament, the Council and the Commission should, in accordance with Declaration No 41 attached to the Final Act of the Treaty of Amsterdam, draw guidance from this Regulation as regards documents concerning the activities covered by those two Treaties.

(6) Wider access should be granted to documents in cases where the institutions are acting in their legislative capacity, including under delegated powers, while at the same time preserving the effectiveness of the institutions' decision-making process. Such documents should be made directly accessible to the greatest possible extent.

(7) In accordance with Articles 28(1) and 41(1) of the EU Treaty, the right of access also applies to documents relating to the common foreign and security policy and to police and judicial cooperation in criminal matters. Each institution should respect its security rules.

(8) In order to ensure the full application of this Regulation to all activities of the Union, all agencies established by the institutions should apply the principles laid down in this Regulation.

(9) On account of their highly sensitive content, certain documents should be given special treatment. Arrangements for informing the European Parliament of the content of such documents should be made through interinstitutional agreement.

(10) In order to bring about greater openness in the work of the institutions, access to documents should be granted by the European Parliament, the Council and the Commission not only to documents drawn up by the institutions, but also to documents received by them. In this context, it is recalled that Declaration No 35 attached to the Final Act of the Treaty of Amsterdam provides that a Member State may request the Commission or the Council not to communicate to third parties a document originating from that State without its prior agreement.

(11) In principle, all documents of the institutions should be accessible to the public. However, certain public and private interests should be protected by way of exceptions. The institutions should be entitled to protect their internal consultations and deliberations where necessary to safeguard their ability to carry out their tasks. In assessing the exceptions, the institutions should take account of the principles in Community legislation concerning the protection of personal data, in all areas of Union activities.

(12) All rules concerning access to documents of the institutions should be in conformity with this Regulation.

([1]) OJ C 177 E, 27.6.2000, p. 70.
([2]) Opinion of the European Parliament of 3 May 2001 (not yet published in the Official Journal) and Council Decision of 28 May 2001.

(13) In order to ensure that the right of access is fully respected, a two-stage administrative procedure should apply, with the additional possibility of court proceedings or complaints to the Ombudsman.

(14) Each institution should take the measures necessary to inform the public of the new provisions in force and to train its staff to assist citizens exercising their rights under this Regulation. In order to make it easier for citizens to exercise their rights, each institution should provide access to a register of documents.

(15) Even though it is neither the object nor the effect of this Regulation to amend national legislation on access to documents, it is nevertheless clear that, by virtue of the principle of loyal cooperation which governs relations between the institutions and the Member States, Member States should take care not to hamper the proper application of this Regulation and should respect the security rules of the institutions.

(16) This Regulation is without prejudice to existing rights of access to documents for Member States, judicial authorities or investigative bodies.

(17) In accordance with Article 255(3) of the EC Treaty, each institution lays down specific provisions regarding access to its documents in its rules of procedure. Council Decision 93/731/EC of 20 December 1993 on public access to Council documents [1], Commission Decision 94/90/ECSC, EC, Euratom of 8 February 1994 on public access to Commission documents [2], European Parliament Decision 97/632/EC, ECSC, Euratom of 10 July 1997 on public access to European Parliament documents [3], and the rules on confidentiality of Schengen documents should therefore, if necessary, be modified or be repealed,

HAVE ADOPTED THIS REGULATION:

Article 1

Purpose

The purpose of this Regulation is:

(a) to define the principles, conditions and limits on grounds of public or private interest governing the right of access to European Parliament, Council and Commission (hereinafter referred to as 'the institutions') documents provided for in Article 255 of the EC Treaty in such a way as to ensure the widest possible access to documents,

(b) to establish rules ensuring the easiest possible exercise of this right, and

(c) to promote good administrative practice on access to documents.

Article 2

Beneficiaries and scope

1. Any citizen of the Union, and any natural or legal person residing or having its registered office in a Member State, has a right of access to documents of the institutions, subject to the principles, conditions and limits defined in this Regulation.

2. The institutions may, subject to the same principles, conditions and limits, grant access to documents to any natural or legal person not residing or not having its registered office in a Member State.

3. This Regulation shall apply to all documents held by an institution, that is to say, documents drawn up or received by it and in its possession, in all areas of activity of the European Union.

4. Without prejudice to Articles 4 and 9, documents shall be made accessible to the public either following a written application or directly in electronic form or through a register. In particular, documents drawn up or received in the course of a legislative procedure shall be made directly accessible in accordance with Article 12.

5. Sensitive documents as defined in Article 9(1) shall be subject to special treatment in accordance with that Article.

6. This Regulation shall be without prejudice to rights of public access to documents held by the institutions which might follow from instruments of international law or acts of the institutions implementing them.

Article 3

Definitions

For the purpose of this Regulation:

(a) 'document' shall mean any content whatever its medium (written on paper or stored in electronic form or as a sound, visual or audiovisual recording) concerning a matter relating to the policies, activities and decisions falling within the institution's sphere of responsibility;

(b) 'third party' shall mean any natural or legal person, or any entity outside the institution concerned, including the Member States, other Community or non-Community institutions and bodies and third countries.

---

(1) OJ L 340, 31.12.1993, p. 43. Decision as last amended by Decision 2000/527/EC (OJ L 212, 23.8.2000, p. 9).
(2) OJ L 46, 18.2.1994, p. 58. Decision as amended by Decision 96/567/EC, ECSC, Euratom (OJ L 247, 28.9.1996, p. 45).
(3) OJ L 263, 25.9.1997, p. 27.

Article 4

Exceptions

1. The institutions shall refuse access to a document where disclosure would undermine the protection of:

(a) the public interest as regards:

— public security,

— defence and military matters,

— international relations,

— the financial, monetary or economic policy of the Community or a Member State;

(b) privacy and the integrity of the individual, in particular in accordance with Community legislation regarding the protection of personal data.

2. The institutions shall refuse access to a document where disclosure would undermine the protection of:

— commercial interests of a natural or legal person, including intellectual property,

— court proceedings and legal advice,

— the purpose of inspections, investigations and audits,

unless there is an overriding public interest in disclosure.

3. Access to a document, drawn up by an institution for internal use or received by an institution, which relates to a matter where the decision has not been taken by the institution, shall be refused if disclosure of the document would seriously undermine the institution's decision-making process, unless there is an overriding public interest in disclosure.

Access to a document containing opinions for internal use as part of deliberations and preliminary consultations within the institution concerned shall be refused even after the decision has been taken if disclosure of the document would seriously undermine the institution's decision-making process, unless there is an overriding public interest in disclosure.

4. As regards third-party documents, the institution shall consult the third party with a view to assessing whether an exception in paragraph 1 or 2 is applicable, unless it is clear that the document shall or shall not be disclosed.

5. A Member State may request the institution not to disclose a document originating from that Member State without its prior agreement.

6. If only parts of the requested document are covered by any of the exceptions, the remaining parts of the document shall be released.

7. The exceptions as laid down in paragraphs 1 to 3 shall only apply for the period during which protection is justified on the basis of the content of the document. The exceptions may apply for a maximum period of 30 years. In the case of documents covered by the exceptions relating to privacy or commercial interests and in the case of sensitive documents, the exceptions may, if necessary, continue to apply after this period.

Article 5

Documents in the Member States

Where a Member State receives a request for a document in its possession, originating from an institution, unless it is clear that the document shall or shall not be disclosed, the Member State shall consult with the institution concerned in order to take a decision that does not jeopardise the attainment of the objectives of this Regulation.

The Member State may instead refer the request to the institution.

Article 6

Applications

1. Applications for access to a document shall be made in any written form, including electronic form, in one of the languages referred to in Article 314 of the EC Treaty and in a sufficiently precise manner to enable the institution to identify the document. The applicant is not obliged to state reasons for the application.

2. If an application is not sufficiently precise, the institution shall ask the applicant to clarify the application and shall assist the applicant in doing so, for example, by providing information on the use of the public registers of documents.

3. In the event of an application relating to a very long document or to a very large number of documents, the institution concerned may confer with the applicant informally, with a view to finding a fair solution.

4. The institutions shall provide information and assistance to citizens on how and where applications for access to documents can be made.

Article 7

Processing of initial applications

1. An application for access to a document shall be handled promptly. An acknowledgement of receipt shall be sent to the applicant. Within 15 working days from registration of the application, the institution shall either grant access to the document requested and provide access in accordance with Article 10 within that period or, in a written reply, state the reasons for the total or partial refusal and inform the applicant of his or her right to make a confirmatory application in accordance with paragraph 2 of this Article.

2. In the event of a total or partial refusal, the applicant may, within 15 working days of receiving the institution's reply, make a confirmatory application asking the institution to reconsider its position.

3. In exceptional cases, for example in the event of an application relating to a very long document or to a very large number of documents, the time-limit provided for in paragraph 1 may be extended by 15 working days, provided that the applicant is notified in advance and that detailed reasons are given.

4. Failure by the institution to reply within the prescribed time-limit shall entitle the applicant to make a confirmatory application.

Article 8

Processing of confirmatory applications

1. A confirmatory application shall be handled promptly. Within 15 working days from registration of such an application, the institution shall either grant access to the document requested and provide access in accordance with Article 10 within that period or, in a written reply, state the reasons for the total or partial refusal. In the event of a total or partial refusal, the institution shall inform the applicant of the remedies open to him or her, namely instituting court proceedings against the institution and/or making a complaint to the Ombudsman, under the conditions laid down in Articles 230 and 195 of the EC Treaty, respectively.

2. In exceptional cases, for example in the event of an application relating to a very long document or to a very large number of documents, the time limit provided for in paragraph 1 may be extended by 15 working days, provided that the applicant is notified in advance and that detailed reasons are given.

3. Failure by the institution to reply within the prescribed time limit shall be considered as a negative reply and entitle the applicant to institute court proceedings against the institution and/or make a complaint to the Ombudsman, under the relevant provisions of the EC Treaty.

Article 9

Treatment of sensitive documents

1. Sensitive documents are documents originating from the institutions or the agencies established by them, from Member States, third countries or International Organisations, classified as 'TRÈS SECRET/TOP SECRET', 'SECRET' or 'CONFIDENTIEL' in accordance with the rules of the institution concerned, which protect essential interests of the European Union or of one or more of its Member States in the areas covered by Article 4(1)(a), notably public security, defence and military matters.

2. Applications for access to sensitive documents under the procedures laid down in Articles 7 and 8 shall be handled only by those persons who have a right to acquaint themselves with those documents. These persons shall also, without prejudice to Article 11(2), assess which references to sensitive documents could be made in the public register.

3. Sensitive documents shall be recorded in the register or released only with the consent of the originator.

4. An institution which decides to refuse access to a sensitive document shall give the reasons for its decision in a manner which does not harm the interests protected in Article 4.

5. Member States shall take appropriate measures to ensure that when handling applications for sensitive documents the principles in this Article and Article 4 are respected.

6. The rules of the institutions concerning sensitive documents shall be made public.

7. The Commission and the Council shall inform the European Parliament regarding sensitive documents in accordance with arrangements agreed between the institutions.

Article 10

Access following an application

1. The applicant shall have access to documents either by consulting them on the spot or by receiving a copy, including, where available, an electronic copy, according to the applicant's preference. The cost of producing and sending copies may be charged to the applicant. This charge shall not exceed the real cost of producing and sending the copies. Consultation on the spot, copies of less than 20 A4 pages and direct access in electronic form or through the register shall be free of charge.

2. If a document has already been released by the institution concerned and is easily accessible to the applicant, the institution may fulfil its obligation of granting access to documents by informing the applicant how to obtain the requested document.

3. Documents shall be supplied in an existing version and format (including electronically or in an alternative format such as Braille, large print or tape) with full regard to the applicant's preference.

Article 11

Registers

1. To make citizens' rights under this Regulation effective, each institution shall provide public access to a register of documents. Access to the register should be provided in electronic form. References to documents shall be recorded in the register without delay.

2. For each document the register shall contain a reference number (including, where applicable, the interinstitutional reference), the subject matter and/or a short description of the content of the document and the date on which it was received or drawn up and recorded in the register. References shall be made in a manner which does not undermine protection of the interests in Article 4.

3. The institutions shall immediately take the measures necessary to establish a register which shall be operational by 3 June 2002.

Article 12

Direct access in electronic form or through a register

1. The institutions shall as far as possible make documents directly accessible to the public in electronic form or through a register in accordance with the rules of the institution concerned.

2. In particular, legislative documents, that is to say, documents drawn up or received in the course of procedures for the adoption of acts which are legally binding in or for the Member States, should, subject to Articles 4 and 9, be made directly accessible.

3. Where possible, other documents, notably documents relating to the development of policy or strategy, should be made directly accessible.

4. Where direct access is not given through the register, the register shall as far as possible indicate where the document is located.

Article 13

Publication in the Official Journal

1. In addition to the acts referred to in Article 254(1) and (2) of the EC Treaty and the first paragraph of Article 163 of the Euratom Treaty, the following documents shall, subject to Articles 4 and 9 of this Regulation, be published in the Official Journal:

(a) Commission proposals;

(b) common positions adopted by the Council in accordance with the procedures referred to in Articles 251 and 252 of the EC Treaty and the reasons underlying those common positions, as well as the European Parliament's positions in these procedures;

(c) framework decisions and decisions referred to in Article 34(2) of the EU Treaty;

(d) conventions established by the Council in accordance with Article 34(2) of the EU Treaty;

(e) conventions signed between Member States on the basis of Article 293 of the EC Treaty;

(f) international agreements concluded by the Community or in accordance with Article 24 of the EU Treaty.

2. As far as possible, the following documents shall be published in the Official Journal:

(a) initiatives presented to the Council by a Member State pursuant to Article 67(1) of the EC Treaty or pursuant to Article 34(2) of the EU Treaty;

(b) common positions referred to in Article 34(2) of the EU Treaty;

(c) directives other than those referred to in Article 254(1) and (2) of the EC Treaty, decisions other than those referred to in Article 254(1) of the EC Treaty, recommendations and opinions.

3. Each institution may in its rules of procedure establish which further documents shall be published in the Official Journal.

Article 14

Information

1. Each institution shall take the requisite measures to inform the public of the rights they enjoy under this Regulation.

2. The Member States shall cooperate with the institutions in providing information to the citizens.

Article 15

Administrative practice in the institutions

1. The institutions shall develop good administrative practices in order to facilitate the exercise of the right of access guaranteed by this Regulation.

2. The institutions shall establish an interinstitutional committee to examine best practice, address possible conflicts and discuss future developments on public access to documents.

Article 16

Reproduction of documents

This Regulation shall be without prejudice to any existing rules on copyright which may limit a third party's right to reproduce or exploit released documents.

Article 17

Reports

1. Each institution shall publish annually a report for the preceding year including the number of cases in which the institution refused to grant access to documents, the reasons for such refusals and the number of sensitive documents not recorded in the register.

2. At the latest by 31 January 2004, the Commission shall publish a report on the implementation of the principles of this Regulation and shall make recommendations, including, if appropriate, proposals for the revision of this Regulation and an action programme of measures to be taken by the institutions.

Article 18

Application measures

1. Each institution shall adapt its rules of procedure to the provisions of this Regulation. The adaptations shall take effect from 3 December 2001.

2. Within six months of the entry into force of this Regulation, the Commission shall examine the conformity of Council Regulation (EEC, Euratom) No 354/83 of 1 February 1983 concerning the opening to the public of the historical archives of the European Economic Community and the European Atomic Energy Community [1] with this Regulation in order to ensure the preservation and archiving of documents to the fullest extent possible.

3. Within six months of the entry into force of this Regulation, the Commission shall examine the conformity of the existing rules on access to documents with this Regulation.

Article 19

Entry into force

This Regulation shall enter into force on the third day following that of its publication in the *Official Journal of the European Communities.*

It shall be applicable from 3 December 2001.

This Regulation shall be binding in its entirety and directly applicable in all Member States.

Done at Brussels, 30 May 2001.

For the European Parliament	*For the Council*
The President	*The President*
N. FONTAINE	B. LEJON

(1) OJ L 43, 15.2.1983, p. 1.

Appendix 5—Regulation 1367/2006 *on the application of the Aarhus Convention to Community institutions and bodies*

REGULATION (EC) No 1367/2006 OF THE EUROPEAN PARLIAMENT AND OF THE COUNCIL

of 6 September 2006

on the application of the provisions of the Aarhus Convention on Access to Information, Public Participation in Decision-making and Access to Justice in Environmental Matters to Community institutions and bodies

THE EUROPEAN PARLIAMENT AND THE COUNCIL OF THE EUROPEAN UNION,

Having regard to the Treaty establishing the European Community, and in particular Article 175(1) thereof,

Having regard to the proposal from the Commission,

Having regard to the opinion of the European Economic and Social Committee (1),

After consulting the Committee of the Regions,

Acting in accordance with the procedure laid down in Article 251 of the Treaty, in the light of the joint text approved by the Conciliation Committee on 22 June 2006 (2),

Whereas:

(1) Community legislation in the field of the environment aims to contribute *inter alia* to preserving, protecting and improving the quality of the environment and protecting human health, thereby promoting sustainable development.

(2) The Sixth Community Environment Action Programme (3) stresses the importance of providing adequate environmental information and effective opportunities for public participation in environmental decision-making, thereby increasing accountability and transparency of decision-making and contributing to public awareness and support for the decisions taken. It furthermore encourages, as did its predecessors (4), more effective implementation and application of Community legislation on environmental protection, including the enforcement of Community rules and the taking of action against breaches of Community environmental legislation.

(3) On 25 June 1998 the Community signed the United Nations Economic Commission for Europe (UNECE) Convention on Access to Information, Public Participation in Decision-making and Access to Justice in Environmental Matters (hereinafter the Aarhus Convention). The Community approved the Aarhus Convention on 17 February 2005 (5). Provisions of Community law should be consistent with that Convention.

(4) The Community has already adopted a body of legislation, which is evolving and contributes to the achievement of the objectives of the Aarhus Convention. Provision should be made to apply the requirements of the Convention to Community institutions and bodies.

(5) It is appropriate to deal with the three pillars of the Aarhus Convention, namely access to information, public participation in decision-making and access to justice in environmental matters, in one piece of legislation and to lay down common provisions regarding objectives and definitions. This contributes to rationalising legislation and increasing the transparency of the implementation measures taken with regard to Community institutions and bodies.

(6) As a general principle, the rights guaranteed by the three pillars of the Aarhus Convention are without discrimination as to citizenship, nationality or domicile.

(7) The Aarhus Convention defines public authorities in a broad way, the basic concept being that wherever public authority is exercised, there should be rights for individuals and their organisations. It is therefore necessary that the Community institutions and bodies covered by this Regulation be defined in the same broad and functional way. Under the Aarhus Convention, Community institutions and bodies can be excluded from the scope of application of the Convention when acting in a judicial or legislative capacity. However, for reasons of consistency with Regulation (EC) No 1049/2001 of the European Parliament and of the Council of 30 May 2001 regarding public access to European Parliament, Council and Commission documents (6), the provisions on access to environmental information should apply to Community institutions and bodies acting in a legislative capacity.

(1) OJ C 117, 30.4.2004, p. 52.

(2) Opinion of the European Parliament of 31 March 2004 (OJ C 103 E, 29.4.2004, p. 612), Council Common Position of 18 July 2005 (OJ C 264 E, 25.10.2005, p. 18), and Position of the European Parliament of 18 January 2006 (not yet published in the Official Journal). Legislative resolution of the European Parliament of 4 July 2006 (not yet published in the Official Journal) and Decision of the Council of 18 July 2006.

(3) Decision No 1600/2002/EC of the European Parliament and of the Council of 22 July 2002 laying down the Sixth Community Environment Action Programme (OJ L 242, 10.9.2002, p. 1).

(4) Fourth Community Action Programme for the Environment (OJ C 328, 7.12.1987, p. 1), Fifth Community Action Programme for the Environment (OJ C 138, 17.5.1993, p. 1).

(5) Council Decision 2005/370/EC (OJ L 124, 17.5.2005, p. 1).

(6) OJ L 145, 31.5.2001, p. 43.

(8) The definition of environmental information in this Regulation encompasses information in any form on the state of the environment. This definition, which has been aligned to the definition adopted for Directive 2003/4/EC of the European Parliament and of the Council of 28 January 2003 on public access to environmental information and repealing Council Directive 90/313/EEC ([1]), has the same content as the one laid down in the Aarhus Convention. The definition of 'document' in Regulation (EC) No 1049/2001 encompasses environmental information as defined in this Regulation.

(9) It is appropriate for this Regulation to provide for a definition of plans and programmes taking into account the provisions of the Aarhus Convention, in parallel with the approach followed in relation to the Member States' obligations under existing EC law. 'Plans and programmes relating to the environment' should be defined in relation to their contribution to the achievement, or to their likely significant effect on the achievement, of the objectives and priorities of Community environmental policy. For the ten-year period starting from 22 July 2002, the Sixth Community Environment Action Programme establishes the objectives of Community environmental policy and the actions planned to attain these objectives. At the end of this period, a subsequent environmental action programme should be adopted.

(10) In view of the fact that environmental law is constantly evolving, the definition of environmental law should refer to the objectives of Community policy on the environment as set out in the Treaty.

(11) Administrative acts of individual scope should be open to possible internal review where they have legally binding and external effects. Similarly, omissions should be covered where there is an obligation to adopt an administrative act under environmental law. Given that acts adopted by a Community institution or body acting in a judicial or legislative capacity can be excluded, the same should apply to other inquiry procedures where the Community institution or body acts as an administrative review body under provisions of the Treaty.

(12) The Aarhus Convention calls for public access to environmental information either following a request or by active dissemination by the authorities covered by the Convention. Regulation (EC) No 1049/2001 applies to the European Parliament, the Council and the Commission, as well as to agencies and similar bodies set up by a Community legal act. It lays down rules for these institutions that comply to a great extent with the rules laid down in the Aarhus Convention. It is necessary to extend the application of Regulation (EC) No 1049/2001 to all other Community institutions and bodies.

(13) Where the Aarhus Convention contains provisions that are not, in whole or in part, to be found also in Regulation (EC) No 1049/2001, it is necessary to address those, in particular with regard to the collection and dissemination of environmental information.

(14) For the right of public access to environmental information to be effective, environmental information of good quality is essential. It is therefore appropriate to introduce rules that oblige Community institutions and bodies to ensure such quality.

(15) Where Regulation (EC) No 1049/2001 provides for exceptions, these should apply subject to any more specific provisions in this Regulation concerning requests for environmental information. The grounds for refusal as regards access to environmental information should be interpreted in a restrictive way, taking into account the public interest served by disclosure and whether the information requested relates to emissions in the environment. The term 'commercial interests' covers confidentiality agreements concluded by institutions or bodies acting in a banking capacity.

(16) Pursuant to Decision No 2119/98/EC of the European Parliament and the Council of 24 September 1998 setting up a network for the epidemiological surveillance and control of communicable diseases in the Community ([2]), a network at Community level has already been set up to promote cooperation and coordination between the Member States, with the assistance of the Commission, with a view to improving the prevention and control in the Community of a number of communicable diseases. Decision No 1786/2002/EC of the European Parliament and of the Council ([3]) adopts a programme of Community action in the field of public health that complements national policies. Improving information and knowledge for the development of public health and enhancing the capability to respond rapidly and in a coordinated fashion to threats to health, both of which are elements of this programme, are objectives that are equally fully in line with the requirements of the Aarhus Convention. This Regulation should therefore apply without prejudice to Decision No 2119/98/EC and Decision No 1786/2002/EC.

([1]) OJ L 41, 14.2.2003, p. 26.

([2]) OJ L 268, 3.10.1998, p. 1. Decision as last amended by Regulation (EC) No 1882/2003 (OJ L 284, 31.10.2003, p. 1).

([3]) OJ L 271, 9.10.2002, p. 1. Decision as amended by Decision No 786/2004/EC (OJ L 138, 30.4.2004, p. 7).

(17) The Aarhus Convention requires Parties to make provisions for the public to participate during the preparation of plans and programmes relating to the environment. Such provisions are to include reasonable timeframes for informing the public of the environmental decision-making in question. To be effective, public participation is to take place at an early stage, when all options are open. When laying down provisions on public participation, Community institutions and bodies, should identify the public which may participate. The Aarhus Convention also requires that, to the extent appropriate, Parties shall endeavour to provide opportunities for public participation in the preparation of policies relating to the environment.

(18) Article 9(3) of the Aarhus Convention provides for access to judicial or other review procedures for challenging acts and omissions by private persons and public authorities which contravene provisions of law relating to the environment. Provisions on access to justice should be consistent with the Treaty. It is appropriate in this context that this Regulation address only acts and omissions by public authorities.

(19) To ensure adequate and effective remedies, including those available before the Court of Justice of the European Communities under the relevant provisions of the Treaty, it is appropriate that the Community institution or body which issued the act to be challenged or which, in the case of an alleged administrative omission, omitted to act, be given the opportunity to reconsider its former decision, or, in the case of an omission, to act.

(20) Non-governmental organisations active in the field of environmental protection which meet certain criteria, in particular in order to ensure that they are independent and accountable organisations that have demonstrated that their primary objective is to promote environmental protection, should be entitled to request internal review at Community level of acts adopted or of omissions under environmental law by a Community institution or body, with a view to their reconsideration by the institution or body in question.

(21) Where previous requests for internal review have been unsuccessful, the non-governmental organisation concerned should be able to institute proceedings before the Court of Justice in accordance with the relevant provisions of the Treaty.

(22) This Regulation respects the fundamental rights and observes the principles recognised by Article 6 of the Treaty on the European Union and reflected in the Charter of Fundamental Rights of the European Union, in particular Article 37 thereof,

HAVE ADOPTED THIS REGULATION:

TITLE I

GENERAL PROVISIONS

Article 1

Objective

1. The objective of this Regulation is to contribute to the implementation of the obligations arising under the UNECE Convention on Access to Information, Public Participation in Decision-making and Access to Justice in Environmental Matters, hereinafter referred to as 'the Aarhus Convention', by laying down rules to apply the provisions of the Convention to Community institutions and bodies, in particular by:

(a) guaranteeing the right of public access to environmental information received or produced by Community institutions or bodies and held by them, and by setting out the basic terms and conditions of, and practical arrangements for, the exercise of that right;

(b) ensuring that environmental information is progressively made available and disseminated to the public in order to achieve its widest possible systematic availability and dissemination. To that end, the use, in particular, of computer telecommunication and/or electronic technology, where available, shall be promoted;

(c) providing for public participation concerning plans and programmes relating to the environment;

(d) granting access to justice in environmental matters at Community level under the conditions laid down by this Regulation.

2. In applying the provisions of this Regulation, the Community institutions and bodies shall endeavour to assist and provide guidance to the public with regard to access to information, participation in decision-making and access to justice in environmental matters.

Article 2

Definitions

1. For the purpose of this Regulation:

(a) 'applicant' means any natural or legal person requesting environmental information;

(b) 'the public' means one or more natural or legal persons, and associations, organisations or groups of such persons;

(c) 'Community institution or body' means any public institution, body, office or agency established by, or on the basis of, the Treaty except when acting in a judicial or legislative capacity. However, the provisions under Title II shall apply to Community institutions or bodies acting in a legislative capacity;

(d) 'environmental information' means any information in written, visual, aural, electronic or any other material form on:

(i) the state of the elements of the environment, such as air and atmosphere, water, soil, land, landscape and natural sites including wetlands, coastal and marine areas, biological diversity and its components, including genetically modified organisms, and the interaction among these elements;

(ii) factors, such as substances, energy, noise, radiation or waste, including radioactive waste, emissions, discharges and other releases into the environment, affecting or likely to affect the elements of the environment referred to in point (i);

(iii) measures (including administrative measures), such as policies, legislation, plans, programmes, environmental agreements, and activities affecting or likely to affect the elements and factors referred to in points (i) and (ii) as well as measures or activities designed to protect those elements;

(iv) reports on the implementation of environmental legislation;

(v) cost-benefit and other economic analyses and assumptions used within the framework of the measures and activities referred to in point (iii);

(vi) the state of human health and safety, including the contamination of the food chain, where relevant, conditions of human life, cultural sites and built structures in as much as they are or may be affected by the state of the elements of the environment referred to in point (i) or, through those elements, by any of the matters referred to in points (ii) and (iii);

(e) 'plans and programmes relating to the environment' means plans and programmes,

(i) which are subject to preparation and, as appropriate, adoption by a Community institution or body;

(ii) which are required under legislative, regulatory or administrative provisions; and

(iii) which contribute to, or are likely to have significant effects on, the achievement of the objectives of Community environmental policy, such as laid down in the Sixth Community Environment Action Programme, or in any subsequent general environmental action programme.

General environmental action programmes shall also be considered as plans and programmes relating to the environment.

This definition shall not include financial or budget plans and programmes, namely those laying down how particular projects or activities should be financed or those related to the proposed annual budgets, internal work programmes of a Community institution or body, or emergency plans and programmes designed for the sole purpose of civil protection;

(f) 'environmental law' means Community legislation which, irrespective of its legal basis, contributes to the pursuit of the objectives of Community policy on the environment as set out in the Treaty: preserving, protecting and improving the quality of the environment, protecting human health, the prudent and rational utilisation of natural resources, and promoting measures at international level to deal with regional or worldwide environmental problems;

(g) 'administrative act' means any measure of individual scope under environmental law, taken by a Community institution or body, and having legally binding and external effects;

(h) 'administrative omission' means any failure of a Community institution or body to adopt an administrative act as defined in (g).

2. Administrative acts and administrative omissions shall not include measures taken or omissions by a Community institution or body in its capacity as an administrative review body, such as under:

(a) Articles 81, 82, 86 and 87 of the Treaty (competition rules);

(b) Articles 226 and 228 of the Treaty (infringement proceedings);

(c) Article 195 of the Treaty (Ombudsman proceedings);

(d) Article 280 of the Treaty (OLAF proceedings).

TITLE II

ACCESS TO ENVIRONMENTAL INFORMATION

Article 3

Application of Regulation (EC) No 1049/2001

Regulation (EC) No 1049/2001 shall apply to any request by an applicant for access to environmental information held by Community institutions and bodies without discrimination as to citizenship, nationality or domicile and, in the case of a legal person, without discrimination as to where it has its registered seat or an effective centre of its activities.

For the purposes of this Regulation, the word 'institution' in Regulation (EC) No 1049/2001 shall be read as 'Community institution or body'.

Article 4

Collection and dissemination of environmental information

1. Community institutions and bodies shall organise the environmental information which is relevant to their functions and which is held by them, with a view to its active and systematic dissemination to the public, in particular by means of computer telecommunication and/or electronic technology in accordance with Articles 11(1) and (2), and 12 of Regulation (EC) No 1049/2001. They shall make this environmental information progressively available in electronic databases that are easily accessible to the public through public telecommunication networks. To that end, they shall place the environmental information that they hold on databases and equip these with search aids and other forms of software designed to assist the public in locating the information they require.

The information made available by means of computer telecommunication and/or electronic technology need not include information collected before the entry into force of this Regulation unless it is already available in electronic form. Community institutions and bodies shall as far as possible indicate where information collected before entry into force of this Regulation which is not available in electronic form is located.

Community institutions and bodies shall make all reasonable efforts to maintain environmental information held by them in forms or formats that are readily reproducible and accessible by computer telecommunications or by other electronic means.

2. The environmental information to be made available and disseminated shall be updated as appropriate. In addition to the documents listed in Article 12(2) and (3) and in Article 13(1) and (2) of Regulation (EC) No 1049/2001, the databases or registers shall include the following:

(a) texts of international treaties, conventions or agreements, and of Community legislation on the environment or relating to it, and of policies, plans and programmes relating to the environment;

(b) progress reports on the implementation of the items referred to under (a) where prepared or held in electronic form by Community institutions or bodies;

(c) steps taken in proceedings for infringements of Community law from the stage of the reasoned opinion pursuant to Article 226(1) of the Treaty;

(d) reports on the state of the environment as referred to in paragraph 4;

(e) data or summaries of data derived from the monitoring of activities affecting, or likely to affect, the environment;

(f) authorisations with a significant impact on the environment, and environmental agreements, or a reference to the place where such information can be requested or accessed;

(g) environmental impact studies and risk assessments concerning environmental elements, or a reference to the place where such information can be requested or accessed.

3. In appropriate cases, Community institutions and bodies may satisfy the requirements of paragraphs 1 and 2 by creating links to Internet sites where the information can be found.

4. The Commission shall ensure that, at regular intervals not exceeding four years, a report on the state of the environment, including information on the quality of, and pressures on, the environment is published and disseminated.

Article 5

Quality of the environmental information

1. Community institutions and bodies shall, insofar as is within their power, ensure that any information that is compiled by them, or on their behalf, is up-to-date, accurate and comparable.

2. Community institutions and bodies shall, upon request, inform the applicant of the place where information on the measurement procedures, including methods of analysis, sampling and pre-treatment of samples, used in compiling the information can be found, if it is available. Alternatively, they may refer them to the standardised procedure that was used.

Article 6

Application of exceptions concerning requests for access to environmental information

1. As regards Article 4(2), first and third indents, of Regulation (EC) No 1049/2001, with the exception of investigations, in particular those concerning possible infringements of Community law, an overriding public interest in disclosure shall be deemed to exist where the information requested relates to emissions into the environment. As regards the other exceptions set out in Article 4 of Regulation (EC) No 1049/2001, the grounds for refusal shall be interpreted in a restrictive way, taking into account the public interest served by disclosure and whether the information requested relates to emissions into the environment.

2. In addition to the exceptions set out in Article 4 of Regulation (EC) No 1049/2001, Community institutions and bodies may refuse access to environmental information where disclosure of the information would adversely affect the protection of the environment to which the information relates, such as the breeding sites of rare species.

Article 7

Requests for access to environmental information which is not held by a Community institution or body

Where a Community institution or body receives a request for access to environmental information and where this information is not held by that Community institution or body, it shall, as promptly as possible, but within 15 working days at the latest, inform the applicant of the Community institution or body or the public authority within the meaning of Directive 2003/4/EC to which it believes it is possible to apply for the information requested or transfer the request to the relevant Community institution or body or the public authority and inform the applicant accordingly.

Article 8

Cooperation

In the event of an imminent threat to human health, life or the environment, whether caused by human activities or due to natural causes, Community institutions and bodies shall, upon request of public authorities within the meaning of Directive 2003/4/EC, collaborate with and assist those public authorities in order to enable the latter to disseminate immediately and without delay to the public that might be affected all environmental information which could enable it to take measures to prevent or mitigate harm arising from the threat, to the extent that this information is held by or on behalf of Community institutions and bodies and/or those public authorities.

The first subparagraph shall apply without prejudice to any specific obligation laid down by Community legislation, in particular by Decision No 2119/98/EC and by Decision No 1786/2002/EC.

TITLE III

PUBLIC PARTICIPATION CONCERNING PLANS AND PROGRAMMES RELATING TO THE ENVIRONMENT

Article 9

1. Community institutions and bodies shall provide, through appropriate practical and/or other provisions, early and effective opportunities for the public to participate during the preparation, modification or review of plans or programmes relating to the environment when all options are still open. In particular, where the Commission prepares a proposal for such a plan or programme which is submitted to other Community institutions or bodies for decision, it shall provide for public participation at that preparatory stage.

2. Community institutions and bodies shall identify the public affected or likely to be affected by, or having an interest in, a plan or programme of the type referred to in paragraph 1, taking into account the objectives of this Regulation.

3. Community institutions and bodies shall ensure that the public referred to in paragraph 2 is informed, whether by public notices or other appropriate means, such as electronic media where available, of:

(a) the draft proposal, where available;

(b) the environmental information or assessment relevant to the plan or programme under preparation, where available; and

(c) practical arrangements for participation, including:

(i) the administrative entity from which the relevant information may be obtained,

(ii) the administrative entity to which comments, opinions or questions may be submitted, and

(iii) reasonable time-frames allowing sufficient time for the public to be informed and to prepare and participate effectively in the environmental decision-making process.

4. A time limit of at least eight weeks shall be set for receiving comments. Where meetings or hearings are organised, prior notice of at least four weeks shall be given. Time limits may be shortened in urgent cases or where the public has already had the opportunity to comment on the plan or programme in question.

5. In taking a decision on a plan or programme relating to the environment, Community institutions and bodies shall take due account of the outcome of the public participation. Community institutions and bodies shall inform the public of that plan or programme, including its text, and of the reasons and considerations upon which the decision is based, including information on public participation.

TITLE IV

INTERNAL REVIEW AND ACCESS TO JUSTICE

Article 10

Request for internal review of administrative acts

1. Any non-governmental organisation which meets the criteria set out in Article 11 is entitled to make a request for internal review to the Community institution or body that has adopted an administrative act under environmental law or, in case of an alleged administrative omission, should have adopted such an act.

Such a request must be made in writing and within a time limit not exceeding six weeks after the administrative act was adopted, notified or published, whichever is the latest, or, in the case of an alleged omission, six weeks after the date when the administrative act was required. The request shall state the grounds for the review.

2. The Community institution or body referred to in paragraph 1 shall consider any such request, unless it is clearly unsubstantiated. The Community institution or body shall state its reasons in a written reply as soon as possible, but no later than 12 weeks after receipt of the request.

3. Where the Community institution or body is unable, despite exercising due diligence, to act in accordance with paragraph 2, it shall inform the non-governmental organisation which made the request as soon as possible and at the latest within the period mentioned in that paragraph, of the reasons for its failure to act and when it intends to do so.

In any event, the Community institution or body shall act within 18 weeks from receipt of the request.

Article 11

Criteria for entitlement at Community level

1. A non-governmental organisation shall be entitled to make a request for internal review in accordance with Article 10, provided that:

(a) it is an independent non-profit-making legal person in accordance with a Member State's national law or practice;

(b) it has the primary stated objective of promoting environmental protection in the context of environmental law;

(c) it has existed for more than two years and is actively pursuing the objective referred to under (b);

(d) the subject matter in respect of which the request for internal review is made is covered by its objective and activities.

2. The Commission shall adopt the provisions which are necessary to ensure transparent and consistent application of the criteria mentioned in paragraph 1.

Article 12

Proceedings before the Court of Justice

1. The non-governmental organisation which made the request for internal review pursuant to Article 10 may institute proceedings before the Court of Justice in accordance with the relevant provisions of the Treaty.

2. Where the Community institution or body fails to act in accordance with Article 10(2) or (3) the non-governmental organisation may institute proceedings before the Court of Justice in accordance with the relevant provisions of the Treaty.

TITLE V

FINAL PROVISIONS

Article 13

Application measures

Where necessary, Community institutions and bodies shall adapt their rules of procedure to the provisions of this Regulation. These adaptations shall take effect from 28 June 2007.

Article 14

Entry into force

This Regulation shall enter into force on the third day following that of its publication in the *Official Journal of the European Union*.

It shall apply from 28 June 2007.

This Regulation shall be binding in its entirety and directly applicable in all Member States.

Done at Strasbourg, 6 September 2006.

For the European Parliament
The President
J. BORRELL FONTELLES

For the Council
The President
P. LEHTOMÄKI

Appendix 6—Directive 2003/4 (the Environmental Information Directive)

L 41/26 EN Official Journal of the European Union 14.2.2003

DIRECTIVE 2003/4/EC OF THE EUROPEAN PARLIAMENT AND OF THE COUNCIL

of 28 January 2003

on public access to environmental information and repealing Council Directive 90/313/EEC

THE EUROPEAN PARLIAMENT AND THE COUNCIL OF THE EUROPEAN UNION,

Having regard to the Treaty establishing the European Community, and in particular Article 175(1) thereof,

Having regard to the proposal from the Commission ([1]),

Having regard to the opinion of the European Economic and Social Committee ([2]),

Having regard to the opinion of the Committee of the Regions ([3]),

Acting in accordance with the procedure laid down in Article 251 of the Treaty ([4]) in the light of the joint text approved by the Conciliation Committee on 8 November 2002,

Whereas:

(1) Increased public access to environmental information and the dissemination of such information contribute to a greater awareness of environmental matters, a free exchange of views, more effective participation by the public in environmental decision-making and, eventually, to a better environment.

(2) Council Directive 90/313/EEC of 7 June 1990 on the freedom of access to information on the environment ([5]) initiated a process of change in the manner in which public authorities approach the issue of openness and transparency, establishing measures for the exercise of the right of public access to environmental information which should be developed and continued. This Directive expands the existing access granted under Directive 90/313/EEC.

(3) Article 8 of that Directive requires Member States to report to the Commission on the experience gained, in the light of which the Commission is required to make a report to the European Parliament and to the Council together with any proposal for revision of the Directive which it may consider appropriate.

(4) The report produced under Article 8 of that Directive identifies concrete problems encountered in the practical application of the Directive.

(5) On 25 June 1998 the European Community signed the UN/ECE Convention on Access to Information, Public Participation in Decision-Making and Access to Justice in Environmental Matters ('the Aarhus Convention'). Provisions of Community law must be consistent with that Convention with a view to its conclusion by the European Community.

(6) It is appropriate in the interest of increased transparency to replace Directive 90/313/EEC rather than to amend it, so as to provide interested parties with a single, clear and coherent legislative text.

(7) Disparities between the laws in force in the Member States concerning access to environmental information held by public authorities can create inequality within the Community as regards access to such information or as regards conditions of competition.

(8) It is necessary to ensure that any natural and legal person has a right of access to environmental information held by or for public authorities without his having to state an interest.

(9) It is also necessary that public authorities make available and disseminate environmental information to the general public to the widest extent possible, in particular by using information and communication technologies. The future development of these technologies should be taken into account in the reporting on, and reviewing of, this Directive.

(10) The definition of environmental information should be clarified so as to encompass information in any form on the state of the environment, on factors, measures or activities affecting or likely to affect the environment or designed to protect it, on cost-benefit and economic analyses used within the framework of such measures or activities and also information on the state of human health and safety, including the contamination of the food chain, conditions of human life, cultural sites and built structures in as much as they are, or may be, affected by any of those matters.

(11) To take account of the principle in Article 6 of the Treaty, that environmental protection requirements should be integrated into the definition and implementation of Community policies and activities, the definition of public authorities should be expanded so as to encompass government or other public administration at national, regional or local level whether or not they have specific responsibilities for the environment. The definition should likewise be expanded to include other persons or bodies performing public administrative functions in relation to the environment under national law, as well as other persons or bodies acting under their control and having public responsibilities or functions in relation to the environment.

([1]) OJ C 337 E, 28.11.2000, p. 156 and OJ C 240 E, 28.8.2001, p. 289.
([2]) OJ C 116, 20.4.2001, p. 43.
([3]) OJ C 148, 18.5.2001, p. 9.
([4]) Opinion of the European Parliament of 14 March 2001 (OJ C 343, 5.12.2001, p. 165), Council Common Position of 28 January 2002 (OJ C 113 E, 14.5.2002, p. 1) and Decision of the European Parliament of 30 May 2002 (not yet published in the Official Journal). Decision of the Council of 16 December 2002 and decision the European Parliament of 18 December 2002.
([5]) OJ L 158, 23.6.1990, p. 56.

(12) Environmental information which is physically held by other bodies on behalf of public authorities should also fall within the scope of this Directive.

(13) Environmental information should be made available to applicants as soon as possible and within a reasonable time and having regard to any timescale specified by the applicant.

(14) Public authorities should make environmental information available in the form or format requested by an applicant unless it is already publicly available in another form or format or it is reasonable to make it available in another form or format. In addition, public authorities should be required to make all reasonable efforts to maintain the environmental information held by or for them in forms or formats that are readily reproducible and accessible by electronic means.

(15) Member States should determine the practical arrangements under which such information is effectively made available. These arrangements shall guarantee that the information is effectively and easily accessible and progressively becomes available to the public through public telecommunications networks, including publicly accessible lists of public authorities and registers or lists of environmental information held by or for public authorities.

(16) The right to information means that the disclosure of information should be the general rule and that public authorities should be permitted to refuse a request for environmental information in specific and clearly defined cases. Grounds for refusal should be interpreted in a restrictive way, whereby the public interest served by disclosure should be weighed against the interest served by the refusal. The reasons for a refusal should be provided to the applicant within the time limit laid down in this Directive.

(17) Public authorities should make environmental information available in part where it is possible to separate out any information falling within the scope of the exceptions from the rest of the information requested.

(18) Public authorities should be able to make a charge for supplying environmental information but such a charge should be reasonable. This implies that, as a general rule, charges may not exceed actual costs of producing the material in question. Instances where advance payment will be required should be limited. In particular cases, where public authorities make available environmental information on a commercial basis, and where this is necessary in order to guarantee the continuation of collecting and publishing such information, a market-based charge is considered to be reasonable; an advance payment may be required. A schedule of charges should be published and made available to applicants together with information on the circumstances in which a charge may be levied or waived.

(19) Applicants should be able to seek an administrative or judicial review of the acts or omissions of a public authority in relation to a request.

(20) Public authorities should seek to guarantee that when environmental information is compiled by them or on their behalf, the information is comprehensible, accurate and comparable. As this is an important factor in assessing the quality of the information supplied the method used in compiling the information should also be disclosed upon request.

(21) In order to increase public awareness in environmental matters and to improve environmental protection, public authorities should, as appropriate, make available and disseminate information on the environment which is relevant to their functions, in particular by means of computer telecommunication and/or electronic technology, where available.

(22) This Directive should be evaluated every four years, after its entry into force, in the light of experience and after submission of the relevant reports by the Member States, and be subject to revision on that basis. The Commission should submit an evaluation report to the European Parliament and the Council.

(23) Since the objectives of the proposed Directive cannot be sufficiently achieved by the Member States and can therefore be better achieved at Community level, the Community may adopt measures, in accordance with the principle of subsidiarity as set out in Article 5 of the Treaty. In accordance with the principle of proportionality, as set out in that Article, this Directive does not go beyond what is necessary in order to achieve those objectives.

(24) The provisions of this Directive shall not affect the right of a Member State to maintain or introduce measures providing for broader access to information than required by this Directive,

HAVE ADOPTED THIS DIRECTIVE:

Article 1

Objectives

The objectives of this Directive are:

(a) to guarantee the right of access to environmental information held by or for public authorities and to set out the basic terms and conditions of, and practical arrangements for, its exercise; and

(b) to ensure that, as a matter of course, environmental information is progressively made available and disseminated to the public in order to achieve the widest possible systematic availability and dissemination to the public of environmental information. To this end the use, in particular, of computer telecommunication and/or electronic technology, where available, shall be promoted.

Article 2

Definitions

For the purposes of this Directive:

1. 'Environmental information' shall mean any information in written, visual, aural, electronic or any other material form on:

   (a) the state of the elements of the environment, such as air and atmosphere, water, soil, land, landscape and natural sites including wetlands, coastal and marine areas, biological diversity and its components, including genetically modified organisms, and the interaction among these elements;

   (b) factors, such as substances, energy, noise, radiation or waste, including radioactive waste, emissions, discharges and other releases into the environment, affecting or likely to affect the elements of the environment referred to in (a);

   (c) measures (including administrative measures), such as policies, legislation, plans, programmes, environmental agreements, and activities affecting or likely to affect the elements and factors referred to in (a) and (b) as well as measures or activities designed to protect those elements;

   (d) reports on the implementation of environmental legislation;

   (e) cost-benefit and other economic analyses and assumptions used within the framework of the measures and activities referred to in (c); and

   (f) the state of human health and safety, including the contamination of the food chain, where relevant, conditions of human life, cultural sites and built structures inasmuch as they are or may be affected by the state of the elements of the environment referred to in (a) or, through those elements, by any of the matters referred to in (b) and (c).

2. 'Public authority' shall mean:

   (a) government or other public administration, including public advisory bodies, at national, regional or local level;

   (b) any natural or legal person performing public administrative functions under national law, including specific duties, activities or services in relation to the environment; and

   (c) any natural or legal person having public responsibilities or functions, or providing public services, relating to the environment under the control of a body or person falling within (a) or (b).

   Member States may provide that this definition shall not include bodies or institutions when acting in a judicial or legislative capacity. If their constitutional provisions at the date of adoption of this Directive make no provision for a review procedure within the meaning of Article 6, Member States may exclude those bodies or institutions from that definition.

3. 'Information held by a public authority' shall mean environmental information in its possession which has been produced or received by that authority.

4. 'Information held for a public authority' shall mean environmental information which is physically held by a natural or legal person on behalf of a public authority.

5. 'Applicant' shall mean any natural or legal person requesting environmental information.

6. 'Public' shall mean one or more natural or legal persons, and, in accordance with national legislation or practice, their associations, organisations or groups.

Article 3

Access to environmental information upon request

1. Member States shall ensure that public authorities are required, in accordance with the provisions of this Directive, to make available environmental information held by or for them to any applicant at his request and without his having to state an interest.

2. Subject to Article 4 and having regard to any timescale specified by the applicant, environmental information shall be made available to an applicant:

(a) as soon as possible or, at the latest, within one month after the receipt by the public authority referred to in paragraph 1 of the applicant's request; or

(b) within two months after the receipt of the request by the public authority if the volume and the complexity of the information is such that the one-month period referred to in (a) cannot be complied with. In such cases, the applicant shall be informed as soon as possible, and in any case before the end of that one-month period, of any such extension and of the reasons for it.

3. If a request is formulated in too general a manner, the public authority shall as soon as possible, and at the latest within the timeframe laid down in paragraph 2(a), ask the applicant to specify the request and shall assist the applicant in doing so, e.g. by providing information on the use of the public registers referred to in paragraph 5(c). The public authorities may, where they deem it appropriate, refuse the request under Article 4(1)(c).

4. Where an applicant requests a public authority to make environmental information available in a specific form or format (including in the form of copies), the public authority shall make it so available unless:

(a) it is already publicly available in another form or format, in particular under Article 7, which is easily accessible by applicants; or

(b) it is reasonable for the public authority to make it available in another form or format, in which case reasons shall be given for making it available in that form or format.

For the purposes of this paragraph, public authorities shall make all reasonable efforts to maintain environmental information held by or for them in forms or formats that are readily reproducible and accessible by computer telecommunications or by other electronic means.

The reasons for a refusal to make information available, in full or in part, in the form or format requested shall be provided to the applicant within the time limit referred to in paragraph 2(a).

5. For the purposes of this Article, Member States shall ensure that:

(a) officials are required to support the public in seeking access to information;

(b) lists of public authorities are publicly accessible; and

(c) the practical arrangements are defined for ensuring that the right of access to environmental information can be effectively exercised, such as:

— the designation of information officers;

— the establishment and maintenance of facilities for the examination of the information required,

— registers or lists of the environmental information held by public authorities or information points, with clear indications of where such information can be found.

Member States shall ensure that public authorities inform the public adequately of the rights they enjoy as a result of this Directive and to an appropriate extent provide information, guidance and advice to this end.

Article 4

Exceptions

1. Member States may provide for a request for environmental information to be refused if:

(a) the information requested is not held by or for the public authority to which the request is addressed. In such a case, where that public authority is aware that the information is held by or for another public authority, it shall, as soon as possible, transfer the request to that other authority and inform the applicant accordingly or inform the applicant of the public authority to which it believes it is possible to apply for the information requested;

(b) the request is manifestly unreasonable;

(c) the request is formulated in too general a manner, taking into account Article 3(3);

(d) the request concerns material in the course of completion or unfinished documents or data;

(e) the request concerns internal communications, taking into account the public interest served by disclosure.

Where a request is refused on the basis that it concerns material in the course of completion, the public authority shall state the name of the authority preparing the material and the estimated time needed for completion.

2. Member States may provide for a request for environmental information to be refused if disclosure of the information would adversely affect:

(a) the confidentiality of the proceedings of public authorities, where such confidentiality is provided for by law;

(b) international relations, public security or national defence;

(c) the course of justice, the ability of any person to receive a fair trial or the ability of a public authority to conduct an enquiry of a criminal or disciplinary nature;

(d) the confidentiality of commercial or industrial information where such confidentiality is provided for by national or Community law to protect a legitimate economic interest, including the public interest in maintaining statistical confidentiality and tax secrecy;

(e) intellectual property rights;

(f) the confidentiality of personal data and/or files relating to a natural person where that person has not consented to the disclosure of the information to the public, where such confidentiality is provided for by national or Community law;

(g) the interests or protection of any person who supplied the information requested on a voluntary basis without being under, or capable of being put under, a legal obligation to do so, unless that person has consented to the release of the information concerned;

(h) the protection of the environment to which such information relates, such as the location of rare species.

The grounds for refusal mentioned in paragraphs 1 and 2 shall be interpreted in a restrictive way, taking into account for the particular case the public interest served by disclosure. In every particular case, the public interest served by disclosure shall be weighed against the interest served by the refusal. Member States may not, by virtue of paragraph 2(a), (d), (f), (g) and (h), provide for a request to be refused where the request relates to information on emissions into the environment.

Within this framework, and for the purposes of the application of subparagraph (f), Member States shall ensure that the requirements of Directive 95/46/EC of the European Parliament and of the Council of 24 October 1995 on the protection of individuals with regard to the processing of personal data and on the free movement of such data are complied with ([1]).

3. Where a Member State provides for exceptions, it may draw up a publicly accessible list of criteria on the basis of which the authority concerned may decide how to handle requests.

([1]) OJ L 281, 23.11.1995, p. 31.

4. Environmental information held by or for public authorities which has been requested by an applicant shall be made available in part where it is possible to separate out any information falling within the scope of paragraphs 1(d) and (e) or 2 from the rest of the information requested.

5. A refusal to make available all or part of the information requested shall be notified to the applicant in writing or electronically, if the request was in writing or if the applicant so requests, within the time limits referred to in Article 3(2)(a) or, as the case may be, (b). The notification shall state the reasons for the refusal and include information on the review procedure provided for in accordance with Article 6.

Article 5

Charges

1. Access to any public registers or lists established and maintained as mentioned in Article 3(5) and examination *in situ* of the information requested shall be free of charge.

2. Public authorities may make a charge for supplying any environmental information but such charge shall not exceed a reasonable amount.

3. Where charges are made, public authorities shall publish and make available to applicants a schedule of such charges as well as information on the circumstances in which a charge may be levied or waived.

Article 6

Access to justice

1. Member States shall ensure that any applicant who considers that his request for information has been ignored, wrongfully refused (whether in full or in part), inadequately answered or otherwise not dealt with in accordance with the provisions of Articles 3, 4 or 5, has access to a procedure in which the acts or omissions of the public authority concerned can be reconsidered by that or another public authority or reviewed administratively by an independent and impartial body established by law. Any such procedure shall be expeditious and either free of charge or inexpensive.

2. In addition to the review procedure referred to in paragraph 1, Member States shall ensure that an applicant has access to a review procedure before a court of law or another independent and impartial body established by law, in which the acts or omissions of the public authority concerned can be reviewed and whose decisions may become final. Member States may furthermore provide that third parties incriminated by the disclosure of information may also have access to legal recourse.

3. Final decisions under paragraph 2 shall be binding on the public authority holding the information. Reasons shall be stated in writing, at least where access to information is refused under this Article.

Article 7

Dissemination of environmental information

1. Member States shall take the necessary measures to ensure that public authorities organise the environmental information which is relevant to their functions and which is held by or for them, with a view to its active and systematic dissemination to the public, in particular by means of computer telecommunication and/or electronic technology, where available.

The information made available by means of computer telecommunication and/or electronic technology need not include information collected before the entry into force of this Directive unless it is already available in electronic form.

Member States shall ensure that environmental information progressively becomes available in electronic databases which are easily accessible to the public through public telecommunication networks.

2. The information to be made available and disseminated shall be updated as appropriate and shall include at least:

(a) texts of international treaties, conventions or agreements, and of Community, national, regional or local legislation, on the environment or relating to it;

(b) policies, plans and programmes relating to the environment;

(c) progress reports on the implementation of the items referred to in (a) and (b) when prepared or held in electronic form by public authorities;

(d) the reports on the state of the environment referred to in paragraph 3;

(e) data or summaries of data derived from the monitoring of activities affecting, or likely to affect, the environment;

(f) authorisations with a significant impact on the environment and environmental agreements or a reference to the place where such information can be requested or found in the framework of Article 3;

(g) environmental impact studies and risk assessments concerning the environmental elements referred to in Article 2(1)(a) or a reference to the place where the information can be requested or found in the framework of Article 3.

3. Without prejudice to any specific reporting obligations laid down by Community legislation, Member States shall take the necessary measures to ensure that national, and, where appropriate, regional or local reports on the state of the environment are published at regular intervals not exceeding four years; such reports shall include information on the quality of, and pressures on, the environment.

4. Without prejudice to any specific obligation laid down by Community legislation, Member States shall take the necessary measures to ensure that, in the event of an imminent threat to human health or the environment, whether caused by human activities or due to natural causes, all information held by or for public authorities which could enable the public likely to be affected to take measures to prevent or mitigate harm arising from the threat is disseminated, immediately and without delay.

5. The exceptions in Article 4(1) and (2) may apply in relation to the duties imposed by this Article.

6. Member States may satisfy the requirements of this Article by creating links to Internet sites where the information can be found.

Article 8

Quality of environmental information

1. Member States shall, so far as is within their power, ensure that any information that is compiled by them or on their behalf is up to date, accurate and comparable.

2. Upon request, public authorities shall reply to requests for information pursuant to Article 2(1)b, reporting to the applicant on the place where information, if available, can be found on the measurement procedures, including methods of analysis, sampling, and pre-treatment of samples, used in compiling the information, or referring to a standardised procedure used.

Article 9

Review procedure

1. Not later than 14 February 2009, Member States shall report on the experience gained in the application of this Directive.

They shall communicate the report to the Commission not later than 14 August 2009.

No later than 14 February 2004, the Commission shall forward to the Member States a guidance document setting out clearly the manner in which it wishes the Member States to report.

2. In the light of experience and taking into account developments in computer telecommunication and/or electronic technology, the Commission shall make a report to the European Parliament and to the Council together with any proposal for revision, which it may consider appropriate.

Article 10

Implementation

Member States shall bring into force the laws, regulations and administrative provisions necessary to comply with this Directive by 14 February 2005. They shall forthwith inform the Commission thereof.

When Member States adopt these measures, they shall contain a reference to this Directive or shall be accompanied by such reference on the occasion of their official publication. The methods of making such reference shall be laid down by Member States.

Article 11

Repeal

Directive 90/313/EEC is hereby repealed with effect from 14 February 2005.

References to the repealed Directive shall be construed as referring to this Directive and shall be read in accordance with the correlation table in the Annex.

Article 12

Entry into force

This Directive shall enter into force on the day of its publication in the *Official Journal of the European Union*.

Article 13

Addressees

This Directive is addressed to the Member States.

Done at Brussels, 28 January 2003.

For the European Parliament	*For the Council*
The President	*The President*
P. COX	G. PAPANDREOU

ANNEX

CORRELATION TABLE

Directive 90/313/EEC	This Directive
Article 1	Article 1(a)
	Article 1(b)
Article 2(a)	Article 2(1)
Article 2(b)	Article 2(2)
—	Article 2(3)
—	Article 2(4)
—	Article 2(5)
—	Article 2(6)
Article 3(1)	Article 3(1) and Article 3(5)
Article 3(2)	Article 4(2) and Article 4(4)
Article 3(3)	Article 4(1)(b), (c), (d) and (e)
Article 3(4)	Article 3(2) and Article 4(5)
—	Article 4(1)(a)
—	Article 3(3)
—	Article 3(4)
Article 4	Article 6(1) and Article 6(2)
—	Article 6(3)
Article 5	Article 5(1)
—	Article 5(2)
—	Article 5(3)
Article 6	Article 2(2)(c), Article 3(1)
Article 7	Article 7(1), (2), and (3)
—	Article 7(4)
—	Article 7(5)
—	Article 7(6)
—	Article 8
Article 8	Article 9
Article 9	Article 10
Article 10	Article 13
—	Article 11
—	Article 12

Appendix 7—Directive 2003/35/EC (the Public Participation Directive)

25.6.2003 EN Official Journal of the European Union L 156/17

DIRECTIVE 2003/35/EC OF THE EUROPEAN PARLIAMENT AND OF THE COUNCIL

of 26 May 2003

providing for public participation in respect of the drawing up of certain plans and programmes relating to the environment and amending with regard to public participation and access to justice Council Directives 85/337/EEC and 96/61/EC

THE EUROPEAN PARLIAMENT AND THE COUNCIL OF THE EUROPEAN UNION,

Having regard to the Treaty establishing the European Community, and in particular Article 175 thereof,

Having regard to the proposal from the Commission ([1]),

Having regard to the opinion of the European Economic and Social Committee ([2]),

Having regard to the opinion of the Committee of the Regions ([3]),

Acting in accordance with the procedure laid down in Article 251 of the Treaty ([4]), in the light of the joint text approved by the Conciliation Committee on 15 January 2003,

Whereas:

(1) Community legislation in the field of the environment aims to contribute to preserving, protecting and improving the quality of the environment and protecting human health.

(2) Community environmental legislation includes provisions for public authorities and other bodies to take decisions which may have a significant effect on the environment as well as on personal health and well-being.

(3) Effective public participation in the taking of decisions enables the public to express, and the decision-maker to take account of, opinions and concerns which may be relevant to those decisions, thereby increasing the accountability and transparency of the decision-making process and contributing to public awareness of environmental issues and support for the decisions taken.

(4) Participation, including participation by associations, organisations and groups, in particular non-governmental organisations promoting environmental protection, should accordingly be fostered, including *inter alia* by promoting environmental education of the public.

(5) On 25 June 1998 the Community signed the UN/ECE Convention on Access to Information, Public Participation in Decision-Making and Access to Justice in Environmental Matters (the Århus Convention). Community law should be properly aligned with that Convention with a view to its ratification by the Community.

(6) Among the objectives of the Århus Convention is the desire to guarantee rights of public participation in decision-making in environmental matters in order to contribute to the protection of the right to live in an environment which is adequate for personal health and well-being.

(7) Article 6 of the Århus Convention provides for public participation in decisions on the specific activities listed in Annex I thereto and on activities not so listed which may have a significant effect on the environment.

(8) Article 7 of the Århus Convention provides for public participation concerning plans and programmes relating to the environment.

(9) Article 9(2) and (4) of the Århus Convention provides for access to judicial or other procedures for challenging the substantive or procedural legality of decisions, acts or omissions subject to the public participation provisions of Article 6 of the Convention.

(10) Provision should be made in respect of certain Directives in the environmental area which require Member States to produce plans and programmes relating to the environment but which do not contain sufficient provisions on public participation, so as to ensure public participation consistent with the provisions of the Århus Convention, in particular Article 7 thereof. Other relevant Community legislation already provides for public participation in the preparation of plans and programmes and, for the future, public participation requirements in line with the Århus Convention will be incorporated into the relevant legislation from the outset.

([1]) OJ C 154 E, 29.5.2001, p. 123.
([2]) OJ C 221, 7.8.2001, p. 65.
([3]) OJ C 357, 14.12.2001, p. 58.
([4]) Opinion of the European Parliament of 23 October 2001 (OJ C 112, 9.5.2002, p. 125 (E)), Council Common Position of 25 April 2002 (OJ C 170 E, 16.7.2002, p. 22) and Decision of the European Parliament of 5 September 2002 (not yet published in the Official Journal). Decision of the European Parliament of 30 January 2003 and Decision of the Council of 4 March 2003.

(11) Council Directive 85/337/EEC of 27 June 1985 on the assessment of the effects of certain public and private projects on the environment (¹), and Council Directive 96/61/EC of 24 September 1996 concerning integrated pollution prevention and control (²) should be amended to ensure that they are fully compatible with the provisions of the Århus Convention, in particular Article 6 and Article 9(2) and (4) thereof.

(12) Since the objective of the proposed action, namely to contribute to the implementation of the obligations arising under the Århus Convention, cannot be sufficiently achieved by the Member States and can therefore, by reason of the scale and effects of the action, be better achieved at Community level, the Community may adopt measures in accordance with the principle of subsidiarity as set out in Article 5 of the Treaty. In accordance with the principle of proportionality, as set out in that Article, this Directive does not go beyond what is necessary in order to achieve that objective,

HAVE ADOPTED THIS DIRECTIVE:

Article 1

Objective

The objective of this Directive is to contribute to the implementation of the obligations arising under the Århus Convention, in particular by:

(a) providing for public participation in respect of the drawing up of certain plans and programmes relating to the environment;

(b) improving the public participation and providing for provisions on access to justice within Council Directives 85/337/EEC and 96/61/EC.

Article 2

Public participation concerning plans and programmes

1. For the purposes of this Article, 'the public' shall mean one or more natural or legal persons and, in accordance with national legislation or practice, their associations, organisations or groups.

2. Member States shall ensure that the public is given early and effective opportunities to participate in the preparation and modification or review of the plans or programmes required to be drawn up under the provisions listed in Annex I.

To that end, Member States shall ensure that:

(a) the public is informed, whether by public notices or other appropriate means such as electronic media where available, about any proposals for such plans or programmes or for their modification or review and that relevant information about such proposals is made available to the public including *inter alia* information about the right to participate in decision-making and about the competent authority to which comments or questions may be submitted;

(b) the public is entitled to express comments and opinions when all options are open before decisions on the plans and programmes are made;

(c) in making those decisions, due account shall be taken of the results of the public participation;

(d) having examined the comments and opinions expressed by the public, the competent authority makes reasonable efforts to inform the public about the decisions taken and the reasons and considerations upon which those decisions are based, including information about the public participation process.

3. Member States shall identify the public entitled to participate for the purposes of paragraph 2, including relevant non-governmental organisations meeting any requirements imposed under national law, such as those promoting environmental protection.

The detailed arrangements for public participation under this Article shall be determined by the Member States so as to enable the public to prepare and participate effectively.

Reasonable time-frames shall be provided allowing sufficient time for each of the different stages of public participation required by this Article.

4. This Article shall not apply to plans and programmes designed for the sole purpose of serving national defence or taken in case of civil emergencies.

5. This Article shall not apply to plans and programmes set out in Annex I for which a public participation procedure is carried out under Directive 2001/42/EC of the European Parliament and of the Council of 27 June 2001 on the assessment of the effects of certain plans and programmes on the environment (³) or under Directive 2000/60/EC of the European Parliament and of the Council of 23 October 2000 establishing a framework for Community action in the field of water policy (⁴).

Article 3

Amendment of Directive 85/337/EEC

Directive 85/337/EEC is hereby amended as follows:

1. in Article 1(2), the following definitions shall be added:

(¹) OJ L 175, 5.7.1985, p. 40. Directive as amended by Directive 97/11/EC (OJ L 73, 14.3.1997, p. 5).
(²) OJ L 257, 10.10.1996, p. 26.
(³) OJ L 197, 21.7.2001, p. 30.
(⁴) OJ L 327, 22.12.2000, p. 1. Directive as amended by Decision No 2455/2001/EC (OJ L 331, 15.12.2001, p. 1).

'"the public" means: one or more natural or legal persons and, in accordance with national legislation or practice, their associations, organisations or groups;

"the public concerned" means: the public affected or likely to be affected by, or having an interest in, the environmental decision-making procedures referred to in Article 2(2); for the purposes of this definition, non-governmental organisations promoting environmental protection and meeting any requirements under national law shall be deemed to have an interest;'

2. in Article 1, paragraph 4 shall be replaced by the following:

   '4. Member States may decide, on a case-by-case basis if so provided under national law, not to apply this Directive to projects serving national defence purposes, if they deem that such application would have an adverse effect on these purposes.';

3. in Article 2(3), points (a) and (b) shall be replaced by the following:

   '(a) consider whether another form of assessment would be appropriate;

   (b) make available to the public concerned the information obtained under other forms of assessment referred to in point (a), the information relating to the exemption decision and the reasons for granting it.';

4. in Article 6, paragraphs 2 and 3 shall be replaced by the following paragraphs:

   '2. The public shall be informed, whether by public notices or other appropriate means such as electronic media where available, of the following matters early in the environmental decision-making procedures referred to in Article 2(2) and, at the latest, as soon as information can reasonably be provided:

   (a) the request for development consent;

   (b) the fact that the project is subject to an environmental impact assessment procedure and, where relevant, the fact that Article 7 applies;

   (c) details of the competent authorities responsible for taking the decision, those from which relevant information can be obtained, those to which comments or questions can be submitted, and details of the time schedule for transmitting comments or questions;

   (d) the nature of possible decisions or, where there is one, the draft decision;

   (e) an indication of the availability of the information gathered pursuant to Article 5;

   (f) an indication of the times and places where and means by which the relevant information will be made available;

   (g) details of the arrangements for public participation made pursuant to paragraph 5 of this Article.

   3. Member States shall ensure that, within reasonable time-frames, the following is made available to the public concerned:

   (a) any information gathered pursuant to Article 5;

   (b) in accordance with national legislation, the main reports and advice issued to the competent authority or authorities at the time when the public concerned is informed in accordance with paragraph 2 of this Article;

   (c) in accordance with the provisions of Directive 2003/4/EC of the European Parliament and of the Council of 28 January 2003 on public access to environmental information (*), information other than that referred to in paragraph 2 of this Article which is relevant for the decision in accordance with Article 8 and which only becomes available after the time the public concerned was informed in accordance with paragraph 2 of this Article.

   4. The public concerned shall be given early and effective opportunities to participate in the environmental decision-making procedures referred to in Article 2(2) and shall, for that purpose, be entitled to express comments and opinions when all options are open to the competent authority or authorities before the decision on the request for development consent is taken.

   5. The detailed arrangements for informing the public (for example by bill posting within a certain radius or publication in local newspapers) and for consulting the public concerned (for example by written submissions or by way of a public inquiry) shall be determined by the Member States.

   6. Reasonable time-frames for the different phases shall be provided, allowing sufficient time for informing the public and for the public concerned to prepare and participate effectively in environmental decision-making subject to the provisions of this Article.

   (*) OJ L 41, 14.2.2003, p. 26.'

5. Article 7 shall be amended as follows:

   (a) paragraphs 1 and 2 shall be replaced by the following:

   '1. Where a Member State is aware that a project is likely to have significant effects on the environment in another Member State or where a Member State likely to be significantly affected so requests, the Member State in whose territory the project is intended to be carried out shall send to the affected Member State as soon as possible and no later than when informing its own public, *inter alia*.

(a) a description of the project, together with any available information on its possible transboundary impact;

(b) information on the nature of the decision which may be taken,

and shall give the other Member State a reasonable time in which to indicate whether it wishes to participate in the environmental decision-making procedures referred to in Article 2(2), and may include the information referred to in paragraph 2 of this Article.

2. If a Member State which receives information pursuant to paragraph 1 indicates that it intends to participate in the environmental decision-making procedures referred to in Article 2(2), the Member State in whose territory the project is intended to be carried out shall, if it has not already done so, send to the affected Member State the information required to be given pursuant to Article 6(2) and made available pursuant to Article 6(3)(a) and (b).'

(b) paragraph 5 shall be replaced by the following:

'5. The detailed arrangements for implementing this Article may be determined by the Member States concerned and shall be such as to enable the public concerned in the territory of the affected Member State to participate effectively in the environmental decision-making procedures referred to in Article 2(2) for the project.'

6. Article 9 shall be amended as follows:

(a) Paragraph 1 shall be replaced by the following:

'1. When a decision to grant or refuse development consent has been taken, the competent authority or authorities shall inform the public thereof in accordance with the appropriate procedures and shall make available to the public the following information:

— the content of the decision and any conditions attached thereto,

— having examined the concerns and opinions expressed by the public concerned, the main reasons and considerations on which the decision is based, including information about the public participation process,

— a description, where necessary, of the main measures to avoid, reduce and, if possible, offset the major adverse effects.'

(b) Paragraph 2 shall be replaced by the following:

'2. The competent authority or authorities shall inform any Member State which has been consulted pursuant to Article 7, forwarding to it the information referred to in paragraph 1 of this Article.

The consulted Member States shall ensure that that information is made available in an appropriate manner to the public concerned in their own territory.';

7. the following Article shall be inserted:

'*Article 10a*

Member States shall ensure that, in accordance with the relevant national legal system, members of the public concerned:

(a) having a sufficient interest, or alternatively,

(b) maintaining the impairment of a right, where administrative procedural law of a Member State requires this as a precondition,

have access to a review procedure before a court of law or another independent and impartial body established by law to challenge the substantive or procedural legality of decisions, acts or omissions subject to the public participation provisions of this Directive.

Member States shall determine at what stage the decisions, acts or omissions may be challenged.

What constitutes a sufficient interest and impairment of a right shall be determined by the Member States, consistently with the objective of giving the public concerned wide access to justice. To this end, the interest of any non-governmental organisation meeting the requirements referred to in Article 1(2), shall be deemed sufficient for the purpose of subparagraph (a) of this Article. Such organisations shall also be deemed to have rights capable of being impaired for the purpose of subparagraph (b) of this Article.

The provisions of this Article shall not exclude the possibility of a preliminary review procedure before an administrative authority and shall not affect the requirement of exhaustion of administrative review procedures prior to recourse to judicial review procedures, where such a requirement exists under national law.

Any such procedure shall be fair, equitable, timely and not prohibitively expensive.

In order to further the effectiveness of the provisions of this article, Member States shall ensure that practical information is made available to the public on access to administrative and judicial review procedures.';

8. in Annex I, the following point shall be added:

'22. Any change to or extension of projects listed in this Annex where such a change or extension in itself meets the thresholds, if any, set out in this Annex.';

9. in Annex II, No 13, first indent, the following shall be added at the end:

'(change or extension not included in Annex I)'.

Article 4

Amendment of Directive 96/61/EC

Directive 96/61/EC is hereby amended as follows:

1. Article 2 shall be amended as follows:

   (a) the following sentence shall be added to point 10(b):

   'For the purposes of this definition, any change to or extension of an operation shall be deemed to be substantial if the change or extension in itself meets the thresholds, if any, set out in Annex I.';

   (b) the following points shall be added:

   '13. "the public" shall mean one or more natural or legal persons and, in accordance with national legislation or practice, their associations, organisations or groups;

   14. "the public concerned" shall mean the public affected or likely to be affected by, or having an interest in, the taking of a decision on the issuing or the updating of a permit or of permit conditions; for the purposes of this definition, non-governmental organisations promoting environmental protection and meeting any requirements under national law shall be deemed to have an interest;'

2. in Article 6(1), first subparagraph, the following indent shall be added:

   '— the main alternatives, if any, studied by the applicant in outline.'

3. Article 15 shall be amended as follows:

   (a) paragraph 1 shall be replaced by the following:

   '1. Member States shall ensure that the public concerned are given early and effective opportunities to participate in the procedure for:

   — issuing a permit for new installations,

   — issuing a permit for any substantial change in the operation of an installation,

   — updating of a permit or permit conditions for an installation in accordance with Article 13, paragraph 2, first indent.

   The procedure set out in Annex V shall apply for the purposes of such participation.';

   (b) the following paragraph shall be added:

   '5. When a decision has been taken, the competent authority shall inform the public in accordance with the appropriate procedures and shall make available to the public the following information:

   (a) the content of the decision, including a copy of the permit and of any conditions and any subsequent updates; and

   (b) having examined the concerns and opinions expressed by the public concerned, the reasons and considerations on which the decision is based, including information on the public participation process.';

4. the following Article shall be inserted:

'*Article 15a*

Access to justice

Member States shall ensure that, in accordance with the relevant national legal system, members of the public concerned:

(a) having a sufficient interest, or alternatively,

(b) maintaining the impairment of a right, where administrative procedural law of a Member State requires this as a precondition;

have access to a review procedure before a court of law or another independent and impartial body established by law to challenge the substantive or procedural legality of decisions, acts or omissions subject to the public participation provisions of this Directive.

Member States shall determine at what stage the decisions, acts or omissions may be challenged.

What constitutes a sufficient interest and impairment of a right shall be determined by the Member States, consistently with the objective of giving the public concerned wide access to justice. To this end, the interest of any non-governmental organisation meeting the requirements referred to in Article 2(14) shall be deemed sufficient for the purpose of subparagraph (a) of this Article. Such organisations shall also be deemed to have rights capable of being impaired for the purpose of subparagraph (b) of this Article.

The provisions of this Article shall not exclude the possibility of a preliminary review procedure before an administrative authority and shall not affect the requirement of exhaustion of administrative review procedures prior to recourse to judicial review procedures, where such a requirement exists under national law.

Any such procedure shall be fair, equitable, timely and not prohibitively expensive.

In order to further the effectiveness of the provisions of this Article, Member States shall ensure that practical information is made available to the public on access to administrative and judicial review procedures.';

5. Article 17 shall be amended as follows:
   (a) paragraph 1 shall be replaced by the following:

   '1. Where a Member State is aware that the operation of an installation is likely to have significant negative effects on the environment of another Member State, or where a Member State likely to be significantly affected so requests, the Member State in whose territory the application for a permit pursuant to Article 4 or Article 12(2) was submitted shall forward to the other Member State any information required to be given or made available pursuant to Annex V at the same time as it makes it available to its own nationals. Such information shall serve as a basis for any consultations necessary in the framework of the bilateral relations between the two Member States on a reciprocal and equivalent basis.';

   (b) the following paragraphs shall be added:

   '3. The results of any consultations pursuant to paragraphs 1 and 2 must be taken into consideration when the competent authority reaches a decision on the application.

   4. The competent authority shall inform any Member State, which has been consulted pursuant to paragraph 1, of the decision reached on the application and shall forward to it the information referred to in Article 15(5). That Member State shall take the measures necessary to ensure that that information is made available in an appropriate manner to the public concerned in its own territory.';

6. an Annex V shall be added, as set out in Annex II to this Directive.

Article 5

Reporting and review

By 25 June 2009, the Commission shall send a report on the application and effectiveness of this Directive to the European Parliament and to the Council. With a view to further integrating environmental protection requirements, in accordance with Article 6 of the Treaty, and taking into account the experience acquired in the application of this Directive in the Member States, such a report will be accompanied by proposals for amendment of this Directive, if appropriate. In particular, the Commission will consider the possibility of extending the scope of this Directive to other plans and programmes relating to the environment.

Article 6

Implementation

Member States shall bring into force the laws, regulations and administrative provisions necessary to comply with this Directive by 25 June 2005 at the latest. They shall forthwith inform the Commission thereof.

When Member States adopt these measures, they shall contain a reference to this Directive or shall be accompanied by such a reference on the occasion of their official publication. The methods of making such reference shall be laid down by Member States.

Article 7

Entry into force

This Directive shall enter into force on the day of its publication in the *Official Journal of the European Union.*

Article 8

Addressees

This Directive is addressed to the Member States.

Done at Brussels, 26 May 2003.

For the European Parliament	*For the Council*
The President	*The President*
P. COX	G. DRYS

ANNEX I

PROVISIONS FOR PLANS AND PROGRAMMES REFERRED TO IN ARTICLE 2

(a) Article 7(1) of Council Directive 75/442/EEC of 15 July 1975 on waste ([1]).

(b) Article 6 of Council Directive 91/157/EEC of 18 March 1991 on batteries and accumulators containing certain dangerous substances ([2]).

(c) Article 5(1) of Council Directive 91/676/EEC of 12 December 1991 concerning the protection of waters against pollution caused by nitrates from agricultural sources ([3]).

(d) Article 6(1) of Council Directive 91/689/EEC of 12 December 1991 on hazardous waste ([4]).

(e) Article 14 of Directive 94/62/EC of the European Parliament and of the Council of 20 December 1994 on packaging and packaging waste ([5]).

(f) Article 8(3) of Council Directive 96/62/EC of 27 September 1996 on ambient air quality assessment and management ([6]).

([1]) OJ L 194, 25.7.1975, p. 39. Directive as last amended by Commission Decision 96/350/EC (OJ L 135, 6.6.1996, p. 32).
([2]) OJ L 78, 26.3.1991, p. 38. Directive as last amended by Commission Directive 98/101/EC (OJ L 1, 5.1.1999, p. 1).
([3]) OJ L 375, 31.12.1991, p. 1.
([4]) OJ L 377, 31.12.1991, p. 20. Directive as last amended by Directive 94/31/EC (OJ L 168, 2.7.1994, p. 28).
([5]) OJ L 365, 31.12.1994, p. 10.
([6]) OJ L 296, 21.11.1996, p. 55.

ANNEX II

In Directive 96/61/EC, the following Annex shall be added:

'*ANNEX V*

Public participation in decision-making

1. The public shall be informed (by public notices or other appropriate means such as electronic media where available) of the following matters early in the procedure for the taking of a decision or, at the latest, as soon as the information can reasonably be provided:
   (a) the application for a permit or, as the case may be, the proposal for the updating of a permit or of permit conditions in accordance with Article 15(1), including the description of the elements listed in Article 6(1);
   (b) where applicable, the fact that a decision is subject to a national or transboundary environmental impact assessment or to consultations between Member States in accordance with Article 17;
   (c) details of the competent authorities responsible for taking the decision, those from which relevant information can be obtained, those to which comments or questions can be submitted, and details of the time schedule for transmitting comments or questions;
   (d) the nature of possible decisions or, where there is one, the draft decision;
   (e) where applicable, the details relating to a proposal for the updating of a permit or of permit conditions;
   (f) an indication of the times and places where, or means by which, the relevant information will be made available;
   (g) details of the arrangements for public participation and consultation made pursuant to point 5.
2. Member States shall ensure that, within appropriate time-frames, the following is made available to the public concerned:
   (a) in accordance with national legislation, the main reports and advice issued to the competent authority or authorities at the time when the public concerned were informed in accordance with point 1;
   (b) in accordance with the provisions of Directive 2003/4/EC of the European Parliament and of the Council of 28 January 2003 on public access to environmental information (*), information other than that referred to in point 1 which is relevant for the decision in accordance with Article 8 and which only becomes available after the time the public concerned was informed in accordance with point 1.
3. The public concerned shall be entitled to express comments and opinions to the competent authority before a decision is taken.
4. The results of the consultations held pursuant to this Annex must be taken into due account in the taking of a decision.
5. The detailed arrangements for informing the public (for example by bill posting within a certain radius or publication in local newspapers) and consulting the public concerned (for example by written submissions or by way of a public inquiry) shall be determined by the Member States. Reasonable time-frames for the different phases shall be provided, allowing sufficient time for informing the public and for the public concerned to prepare and participate effectively in environmental decision-making subject to the provisions of this Annex.

(*) OJ L 41, 14.2.2003, p. 26.'

Appendix 8—Directive 2011/92/EU (the Codified Environmental Impact Assessment Directive)

28.1.2012 EN Official Journal of the European Union L 26/1

I

(Legislative acts)

DIRECTIVES

DIRECTIVE 2011/92/EU OF THE EUROPEAN PARLIAMENT AND OF THE COUNCIL

of 13 December 2011

on the assessment of the effects of certain public and private projects on the environment

(codification)

(Text with EEA relevance)

THE EUROPEAN PARLIAMENT AND THE COUNCIL OF THE EUROPEAN UNION,

Having regard to the Treaty on the Functioning of the European Union, and in particular Article 192(1) thereof,

Having regard to the proposal from the European Commission,

After transmission of the draft legislative act to the national parliaments,

Having regard to the opinion of the European Economic and Social Committee [1],

After consulting the Committee of the Regions,

Acting in accordance with the ordinary legislative procedure [2],

Whereas:

(1) Council Directive 85/337/EEC of 27 June 1985 on the assessment of the effects of certain public and private projects on the environment [3] has been substantially amended several times [4]. In the interests of clarity and rationality the said Directive should be codified.

(2) Pursuant to Article 191 of the Treaty on the Functioning of the European Union, Union policy on the environment is based on the precautionary principle and on the principles that preventive action should be taken, that environmental damage should, as a priority, be rectified at source and that the polluter should pay. Effects on the environment should be taken into account at the earliest possible stage in all the technical planning and decision-making processes.

(3) The principles of the assessment of environmental effects should be harmonised, in particular with reference to the projects which should be subject to assessment, the main obligations of the developers and the content of the assessment. The Member States may lay down stricter rules to protect the environment.

(4) In addition, it is necessary to achieve one of the objectives of the Union in the sphere of the protection of the environment and the quality of life.

(5) The environmental legislation of the Union includes provisions enabling public authorities and other bodies to take decisions which may have a significant effect on the environment as well as on personal health and well-being.

(6) General principles for the assessment of environmental effects should be laid down with a view to supplementing and coordinating development consent procedures governing public and private projects likely to have a major effect on the environment.

(7) Development consent for public and private projects which are likely to have significant effects on the environment should be granted only after an assessment of the likely significant environmental effects of those projects has been carried out. That assessment should be conducted on the basis of the appropriate information supplied by the developer, which may be supplemented by the authorities and by the public likely to be concerned by the project in question.

[1] OJ C 248, 25.8.2011, p. 154.
[2] Position of the European Parliament of 13 September 2011 (not yet published in the Official Journal) and decision of the Council of 15 November 2011.
[3] OJ L 175, 5.7.1985, p. 40.
[4] See Annex VI, Part A.

(8) Projects belonging to certain types have significant effects on the environment and those projects should, as a rule, be subject to a systematic assessment.

(9) Projects of other types may not have significant effects on the environment in every case and those projects should be assessed where the Member States consider that they are likely to have significant effects on the environment.

(10) Member States may set thresholds or criteria for the purpose of determining which of such projects should be subject to assessment on the basis of the significance of their environmental effects. Member States should not be required to examine projects below those thresholds or outside those criteria on a case-by-case basis.

(11) When setting such thresholds or criteria or examining projects on a case-by-case basis, for the purpose of determining which projects should be subject to assessment on the basis of their significant environmental effects, Member States should take account of the relevant selection criteria set out in this Directive. In accordance with the subsidiarity principle, the Member States are in the best position to apply those criteria in specific instances.

(12) For projects which are subject to assessment, a certain minimal amount of information should be supplied, concerning the project and its effects.

(13) It is appropriate to lay down a procedure in order to enable the developer to obtain an opinion from the competent authorities on the content and extent of the information to be elaborated and supplied for the assessment. Member States, in the framework of this procedure, may require the developer to provide, inter alia, alternatives for the projects for which it intends to submit an application.

(14) The effects of a project on the environment should be assessed in order to take account of concerns to protect human health, to contribute by means of a better environment to the quality of life, to ensure maintenance of the diversity of species and to maintain the reproductive capacity of the ecosystem as a basic resource for life.

(15) It is desirable to lay down strengthened provisions concerning environmental impact assessment in a transboundary context to take account of developments at international level. The European Community signed the Convention on Environmental Impact Assessment in a Transboundary Context on 25 February 1991, and ratified it on 24 June 1997.

(16) Effective public participation in the taking of decisions enables the public to express, and the decision-maker to take account of, opinions and concerns which may be relevant to those decisions, thereby increasing the accountability and transparency of the decision-making process and contributing to public awareness of environmental issues and support for the decisions taken.

(17) Participation, including participation by associations, organisations and groups, in particular non-governmental organisations promoting environmental protection, should accordingly be fostered, including, inter alia, by promoting environmental education of the public.

(18) The European Community signed the UN/ECE Convention on Access to Information, Public Participation in Decision-Making and Access to Justice in Environmental Matters (the Aarhus Convention) on 25 June 1998 and ratified it on 17 February 2005.

(19) Among the objectives of the Aarhus Convention is the desire to guarantee rights of public participation in decision-making in environmental matters in order to contribute to the protection of the right to live in an environment which is adequate for personal health and well-being.

(20) Article 6 of the Aarhus Convention provides for public participation in decisions on the specific activities listed in Annex I thereto and on activities not so listed which may have a significant effect on the environment.

(21) Article 9(2) and (4) of the Aarhus Convention provides for access to judicial or other procedures for challenging the substantive or procedural legality of decisions, acts or omissions subject to the public participation provisions of Article 6 of that Convention.

(22) However, this Directive should not be applied to projects the details of which are adopted by a specific act of national legislation, since the objectives of this Directive, including that of supplying information, are achieved through the legislative process.

(23) Furthermore, it may be appropriate in exceptional cases to exempt a specific project from the assessment procedures laid down by this Directive, subject to appropriate information being supplied to the Commission and to the public concerned.

(24) Since the objectives of this Directive cannot be sufficiently achieved by the Member States and can therefore, by reason of the scale and effects of the action, be better achieved at Union level, the Union may adopt measures in accordance with the principle of subsidiarity as set out in Article 5 of the Treaty on European Union. In accordance with the principle of proportionality, as set out in that Article, this Directive does not go beyond what is necessary in order to achieve those objectives.

(25) This Directive should be without prejudice to the obligations of the Member States relating to the time limits for transposition into national law of the Directives set out in Annex V, Part B,

HAVE ADOPTED THIS DIRECTIVE:

Article 1

1. This Directive shall apply to the assessment of the environmental effects of those public and private projects which are likely to have significant effects on the environment.

2. For the purposes of this Directive, the following definitions shall apply:

(a) 'project' means:

— the execution of construction works or of other installations or schemes,

— other interventions in the natural surroundings and landscape including those involving the extraction of mineral resources;

(b) 'developer' means the applicant for authorisation for a private project or the public authority which initiates a project;

(c) 'development consent' means the decision of the competent authority or authorities which entitles the developer to proceed with the project;

(d) 'public' means one or more natural or legal persons and, in accordance with national legislation or practice, their associations, organisations or groups;

(e) 'public concerned' means the public affected or likely to be affected by, or having an interest in, the environmental decision-making procedures referred to in Article 2(2). For the purposes of this definition, non-governmental organisations promoting environmental protection and meeting any requirements under national law shall be deemed to have an interest;

(f) 'competent authority or authorities' means that authority or those authorities which the Member States designate as responsible for performing the duties arising from this Directive.

3. Member States may decide, on a case-by-case basis if so provided under national law, not to apply this Directive to projects serving national defence purposes, if they deem that such application would have an adverse effect on those purposes.

4. This Directive shall not apply to projects the details of which are adopted by a specific act of national legislation, since the objectives of this Directive, including that of supplying information, are achieved through the legislative process.

Article 2

1. Member States shall adopt all measures necessary to ensure that, before consent is given, projects likely to have significant effects on the environment by virtue, inter alia, of their nature, size or location are made subject to a requirement for development consent and an assessment with regard to their effects. Those projects are defined in Article 4.

2. The environmental impact assessment may be integrated into the existing procedures for consent to projects in the Member States, or, failing this, into other procedures or into procedures to be established to comply with the aims of this Directive.

3. Member States may provide for a single procedure in order to fulfil the requirements of this Directive and the requirements of Directive 2008/1/EC of the European Parliament and of the Council of 15 January 2008 concerning integrated pollution prevention and control [1].

4. Without prejudice to Article 7, Member States may, in exceptional cases, exempt a specific project in whole or in part from the provisions laid down in this Directive.

In that event, the Member States shall:

(a) consider whether another form of assessment would be appropriate;

(b) make available to the public concerned the information obtained under other forms of assessment referred to in point (a), the information relating to the decision granting exemption and the reasons for granting it;

(c) inform the Commission, prior to granting consent, of the reasons justifying the exemption granted, and provide it with the information made available, where applicable, to their own nationals.

The Commission shall immediately forward the documents received to the other Member States.

The Commission shall report annually to the European Parliament and to the Council on the application of this paragraph.

[1] OJ L 24, 29.1.2008, p. 8.

Article 3

The environmental impact assessment shall identify, describe and assess in an appropriate manner, in the light of each individual case and in accordance with Articles 4 to 12, the direct and indirect effects of a project on the following factors:

(a) human beings, fauna and flora;

(b) soil, water, air, climate and the landscape;

(c) material assets and the cultural heritage;

(d) the interaction between the factors referred to in points (a), (b) and (c).

Article 4

1. Subject to Article 2(4), projects listed in Annex I shall be made subject to an assessment in accordance with Articles 5 to 10.

2. Subject to Article 2(4), for projects listed in Annex II, Member States shall determine whether the project shall be made subject to an assessment in accordance with Articles 5 to 10. Member States shall make that determination through:

(a) a case-by-case examination;

or

(b) thresholds or criteria set by the Member State.

Member States may decide to apply both procedures referred to in points (a) and (b).

3. When a case-by-case examination is carried out or thresholds or criteria are set for the purpose of paragraph 2, the relevant selection criteria set out in Annex III shall be taken into account.

4. Member States shall ensure that the determination made by the competent authorities under paragraph 2 is made available to the public.

Article 5

1. In the case of projects which, pursuant to Article 4, are to be made subject to an environmental impact assessment in accordance with this Article and Articles 6 to 10, Member States shall adopt the necessary measures to ensure that the developer supplies in an appropriate form the information specified in Annex IV inasmuch as:

(a) the Member States consider that the information is relevant to a given stage of the consent procedure and to the specific characteristics of a particular project or type of project and of the environmental features likely to be affected;

(b) the Member States consider that a developer may reasonably be required to compile this information having regard, inter alia, to current knowledge and methods of assessment.

2. Member States shall take the necessary measures to ensure that, if the developer so requests before submitting an application for development consent, the competent authority shall give an opinion on the information to be supplied by the developer in accordance with paragraph 1. The competent authority shall consult the developer and authorities referred to in Article 6(1) before it gives its opinion. The fact that the authority has given an opinion under this paragraph shall not preclude it from subsequently requiring the developer to submit further information.

Member States may require the competent authorities to give such an opinion, irrespective of whether the developer so requests.

3. The information to be provided by the developer in accordance with paragraph 1 shall include at least:

(a) a description of the project comprising information on the site, design and size of the project;

(b) a description of the measures envisaged in order to avoid, reduce and, if possible, remedy significant adverse effects;

(c) the data required to identify and assess the main effects which the project is likely to have on the environment;

(d) an outline of the main alternatives studied by the developer and an indication of the main reasons for his choice, taking into account the environmental effects;

(e) a non-technical summary of the information referred to in points (a) to (d).

4. Member States shall, if necessary, ensure that any authorities holding relevant information, with particular reference to Article 3, make this information available to the developer.

Article 6

1. Member States shall take the measures necessary to ensure that the authorities likely to be concerned by the project by reason of their specific environmental responsibilities are given an opportunity to express their opinion on the information supplied by the developer and on the request for development consent. To that end, Member States shall designate the authorities to be consulted, either in general terms or on a case-by-case basis. The information gathered pursuant to Article 5 shall be forwarded to those authorities. Detailed arrangements for consultation shall be laid down by the Member States.

2. The public shall be informed, whether by public notices or by other appropriate means such as electronic media where available, of the following matters early in the environmental decision-making procedures referred to in Article 2(2) and, at the latest, as soon as information can reasonably be provided:

(a) the request for development consent;

(b) the fact that the project is subject to an environmental impact assessment procedure and, where relevant, the fact that Article 7 applies;

(c) details of the competent authorities responsible for taking the decision, those from which relevant information can be obtained, those to which comments or questions can be submitted, and details of the time schedule for transmitting comments or questions;

(d) the nature of possible decisions or, where there is one, the draft decision;

(e) an indication of the availability of the information gathered pursuant to Article 5;

(f) an indication of the times and places at which, and the means by which, the relevant information will be made available;

(g) details of the arrangements for public participation made pursuant to paragraph 5 of this Article.

3. Member States shall ensure that, within reasonable time-frames, the following is made available to the public concerned:

(a) any information gathered pursuant to Article 5;

(b) in accordance with national legislation, the main reports and advice issued to the competent authority or authorities at the time when the public concerned is informed in accordance with paragraph 2 of this Article;

(c) in accordance with the provisions of Directive 2003/4/EC of the European Parliament and of the Council of 28 January 2003 on public access to environmental information ([1]), information other than that referred to in paragraph 2 of this Article which is relevant for the decision in accordance with Article 8 of this Directive and which only becomes available after the time the public concerned was informed in accordance with paragraph 2 of this Article.

4. The public concerned shall be given early and effective opportunities to participate in the environmental decision-making procedures referred to in Article 2(2) and shall, for that purpose, be entitled to express comments and opinions when all options are open to the competent authority or authorities before the decision on the request for development consent is taken.

5. The detailed arrangements for informing the public (for example by bill posting within a certain radius or publication in local newspapers) and for consulting the public concerned (for example by written submissions or by way of a public inquiry) shall be determined by the Member States.

6. Reasonable time-frames for the different phases shall be provided, allowing sufficient time for informing the public and for the public concerned to prepare and participate effectively in environmental decision-making subject to the provisions of this Article.

Article 7

1. Where a Member State is aware that a project is likely to have significant effects on the environment in another Member State or where a Member State likely to be significantly affected so requests, the Member State in whose territory the project is intended to be carried out shall send to the affected Member State as soon as possible and no later than when informing its own public, inter alia:

(a) a description of the project, together with any available information on its possible transboundary impact;

(b) information on the nature of the decision which may be taken.

The Member State in whose territory the project is intended to be carried out shall give the other Member State a reasonable time in which to indicate whether it wishes to participate in the environmental decision-making procedures referred to in Article 2(2), and may include the information referred to in paragraph 2 of this Article.

2. If a Member State which receives information pursuant to paragraph 1 indicates that it intends to participate in the environmental decision-making procedures referred to in Article 2(2), the Member State in whose territory the project is intended to be carried out shall, if it has not already done so, send to the affected Member State the information required to be given pursuant to Article 6(2) and made available pursuant to points (a) and (b) of Article 6(3).

3. The Member States concerned, each insofar as it is concerned, shall also:

(a) arrange for the information referred to in paragraphs 1 and 2 to be made available, within a reasonable time, to the authorities referred to in Article 6(1) and the public concerned in the territory of the Member State likely to be significantly affected; and

([1]) OJ L 41, 14.2.2003, p. 26.

(b) ensure that the authorities referred to in Article 6(1) and the public concerned are given an opportunity, before development consent for the project is granted, to forward their opinion within a reasonable time on the information supplied to the competent authority in the Member State in whose territory the project is intended to be carried out.

4. The Member States concerned shall enter into consultations regarding, inter alia, the potential transboundary effects of the project and the measures envisaged to reduce or eliminate such effects and shall agree on a reasonable time-frame for the duration of the consultation period.

5. The detailed arrangements for implementing this Article may be determined by the Member States concerned and shall be such as to enable the public concerned in the territory of the affected Member State to participate effectively in the environmental decision-making procedures referred to in Article 2(2) for the project.

Article 8

The results of consultations and the information gathered pursuant to Articles 5, 6 and 7 shall be taken into consideration in the development consent procedure.

Article 9

1. When a decision to grant or refuse development consent has been taken, the competent authority or authorities shall inform the public thereof in accordance with the appropriate procedures and shall make available to the public the following information:

(a) the content of the decision and any conditions attached thereto;

(b) having examined the concerns and opinions expressed by the public concerned, the main reasons and considerations on which the decision is based, including information about the public participation process;

(c) a description, where necessary, of the main measures to avoid, reduce and, if possible, offset the major adverse effects.

2. The competent authority or authorities shall inform any Member State which has been consulted pursuant to Article 7, forwarding to it the information referred to in paragraph 1 of this Article.

The consulted Member States shall ensure that that information is made available in an appropriate manner to the public concerned in their own territory.

Article 10

The provisions of this Directive shall not affect the obligation on the competent authorities to respect the limitations imposed by national laws, regulations and administrative provisions and accepted legal practices with regard to commercial and industrial confidentiality, including intellectual property, and the safeguarding of the public interest.

Where Article 7 applies, the transmission of information to another Member State and the receipt of information by another Member State shall be subject to the limitations in force in the Member State in which the project is proposed.

Article 11

1. Member States shall ensure that, in accordance with the relevant national legal system, members of the public concerned:

(a) having a sufficient interest, or alternatively;

(b) maintaining the impairment of a right, where administrative procedural law of a Member State requires this as a precondition;

have access to a review procedure before a court of law or another independent and impartial body established by law to challenge the substantive or procedural legality of decisions, acts or omissions subject to the public participation provisions of this Directive.

2. Member States shall determine at what stage the decisions, acts or omissions may be challenged.

3. What constitutes a sufficient interest and impairment of a right shall be determined by the Member States, consistently with the objective of giving the public concerned wide access to justice. To that end, the interest of any non-governmental organisation meeting the requirements referred to in Article 1(2) shall be deemed sufficient for the purpose of point (a) of paragraph 1 of this Article. Such organisations shall also be deemed to have rights capable of being impaired for the purpose of point (b) of paragraph 1 of this Article.

4. The provisions of this Article shall not exclude the possibility of a preliminary review procedure before an administrative authority and shall not affect the requirement of exhaustion of administrative review procedures prior to recourse to judicial review procedures, where such a requirement exists under national law.

Any such procedure shall be fair, equitable, timely and not prohibitively expensive.

5. In order to further the effectiveness of the provisions of this Article, Member States shall ensure that practical information is made available to the public on access to administrative and judicial review procedures.

Article 12

1. The Member States and the Commission shall exchange information on the experience gained in applying this Directive.

2. In particular, Member States shall inform the Commission of any criteria and/or thresholds adopted for the selection of the projects in question, in accordance with Article 4(2).

3. On the basis of that exchange of information, the Commission shall if necessary submit additional proposals to the European Parliament and to the Council, with a view to ensuring that this Directive is applied in a sufficiently coordinated manner.

Article 13

Member States shall communicate to the Commission the texts of the provisions of national law which they adopt in the field covered by this Directive.

Article 14

Directive 85/337/EEC, as amended by the Directives listed in Annex V, Part A, is repealed, without prejudice to the obligations of the Member States relating to the time limits for transposition into national law of the Directives set out in Annex V, Part B.

References to the repealed Directive shall be construed as references to this Directive and shall be read in accordance with the correlation table in Annex VI.

Article 15

This Directive shall enter into force on the 20th day following its publication in the *Official Journal of the European Union*.

Article 16

This Directive is addressed to the Member States.

Done at Strasbourg, 13 December 2011.

For the European Parliament	For the Council
The President	*The President*
J. BUZEK	M. SZPUNAR

ANNEX I

PROJECTS REFERRED TO IN ARTICLE 4(1)

1. Crude-oil refineries (excluding undertakings manufacturing only lubricants from crude oil) and installations for the gasification and liquefaction of 500 tonnes or more of coal or bituminous shale per day.

2. (a) Thermal power stations and other combustion installations with a heat output of 300 megawatts or more;

   (b) Nuclear power stations and other nuclear reactors including the dismantling or decommissioning of such power stations or reactors [1] (except research installations for the production and conversion of fissionable and fertile materials, whose maximum power does not exceed 1 kilowatt continuous thermal load).

3. (a) Installations for the reprocessing of irradiated nuclear fuel;

   (b) Installations designed:

      (i) for the production or enrichment of nuclear fuel;

      (ii) for the processing of irradiated nuclear fuel or high-level radioactive waste;

      (iii) for the final disposal of irradiated nuclear fuel;

      (iv) solely for the final disposal of radioactive waste;

      (v) solely for the storage (planned for more than 10 years) of irradiated nuclear fuels or radioactive waste in a different site than the production site.

4. (a) Integrated works for the initial smelting of cast iron and steel;

   (b) Installations for the production of non-ferrous crude metals from ore, concentrates or secondary raw materials by metallurgical, chemical or electrolytic processes.

5. Installations for the extraction of asbestos and for the processing and transformation of asbestos and products containing asbestos: for asbestos-cement products, with an annual production of more than 20 000 tonnes of finished products, for friction material, with an annual production of more than 50 tonnes of finished products, and for other uses of asbestos, utilisation of more than 200 tonnes per year.

6. Integrated chemical installations, i.e. those installations for the manufacture on an industrial scale of substances using chemical conversion processes, in which several units are juxtaposed and are functionally linked to one another and which are:

   (a) for the production of basic organic chemicals;

   (b) for the production of basic inorganic chemicals;

   (c) for the production of phosphorous-, nitrogen- or potassium-based fertilisers (simple or compound fertilisers);

   (d) for the production of basic plant health products and of biocides;

   (e) for the production of basic pharmaceutical products using a chemical or biological process;

   (f) for the production of explosives.

[1] Nuclear power stations and other nuclear reactors cease to be such an installation when all nuclear fuel and other radioactively contaminated elements have been removed permanently from the installation site.

7. (a) Construction of lines for long-distance railway traffic and of airports [1] with a basic runway length of 2 100 m or more;

   (b) Construction of motorways and express roads [2];

   (c) Construction of a new road of four or more lanes, or realignment and/or widening of an existing road of two lanes or less so as to provide four or more lanes, where such new road or realigned and/or widened section of road would be 10 km or more in a continuous length.

8. (a) Inland waterways and ports for inland-waterway traffic which permit the passage of vessels of over 1 350 tonnes;

   (b) Trading ports, piers for loading and unloading connected to land and outside ports (excluding ferry piers) which can take vessels of over 1 350 tonnes.

9. Waste disposal installations for the incineration, chemical treatment as defined in Annex I to Directive 2008/98/EC of the European Parliament and of the Council of 19 November 2008 on waste [3] under heading D9, or landfill of hazardous waste, as defined in point 2 of Article 3 of that Directive.

10. Waste disposal installations for the incineration or chemical treatment as defined in Annex I to Directive 2008/98/EC under heading D9 of non-hazardous waste with a capacity exceeding 100 tonnes per day.

11. Groundwater abstraction or artificial groundwater recharge schemes where the annual volume of water abstracted or recharged is equivalent to or exceeds 10 million cubic metres.

12. (a) Works for the transfer of water resources between river basins where that transfer aims at preventing possible shortages of water and where the amount of water transferred exceeds 100 million cubic metres/year;

    (b) In all other cases, works for the transfer of water resources between river basins where the multi-annual average flow of the basin of abstraction exceeds 2 000 million cubic metres/year and where the amount of water transferred exceeds 5 % of that flow.

    In both cases transfers of piped drinking water are excluded.

13. Waste water treatment plants with a capacity exceeding 150 000 population equivalent as defined in point 6 of Article 2 of Council Directive 91/271/EEC of 21 May 1991 concerning urban waste-water treatment [4].

14. Extraction of petroleum and natural gas for commercial purposes where the amount extracted exceeds 500 tonnes/day in the case of petroleum and 500 000 cubic metres/day in the case of gas.

15. Dams and other installations designed for the holding back or permanent storage of water, where a new or additional amount of water held back or stored exceeds 10 million cubic metres.

16. Pipelines with a diameter of more than 800 mm and a length of more than 40 km:

    (a) for the transport of gas, oil, chemicals;

    (b) for the transport of carbon dioxide (CO_2) streams for the purposes of geological storage, including associated booster stations.

17. Installations for the intensive rearing of poultry or pigs with more than:

    (a) 85 000 places for broilers, 60 000 places for hens;

    (b) 3 000 places for production pigs (over 30 kg); or

    (c) 900 places for sows.

---

(1) For the purposes of this Directive, 'airport' means an airport which complies with the definition in the 1944 Chicago Convention setting up the International Civil Aviation Organisation (Annex 14).

(2) For the purposes of this Directive, 'express road' means a road which complies with the definition in the European Agreement on Main International Traffic Arteries of 15 November 1975.

(3) OJ L 312, 22.11.2008, p. 3.

(4) OJ L 135, 30.5.1991, p. 40.

18. Industrial plants for the production of:

    (a) pulp from timber or similar fibrous materials;

    (b) paper and board with a production capacity exceeding 200 tonnes per day.

19. Quarries and open-cast mining where the surface of the site exceeds 25 hectares, or peat extraction, where the surface of the site exceeds 150 hectares.

20. Construction of overhead electrical power lines with a voltage of 220 kV or more and a length of more than 15 km.

21. Installations for storage of petroleum, petrochemical, or chemical products with a capacity of 200 000 tonnes or more.

22. Storage sites pursuant to Directive 2009/31/EC of the European Parliament and of the Council of 23 April 2009 on the geological storage of carbon dioxide (1).

23. Installations for the capture of CO_2 streams for the purposes of geological storage pursuant to Directive 2009/31/EC from installations covered by this Annex, or where the total yearly capture of CO_2 is 1,5 megatonnes or more.

24. Any change to or extension of projects listed in this Annex where such a change or extension in itself meets the thresholds, if any, set out in this Annex.

---

(1) OJ L 140, 5.6.2009, p. 114.

ANNEX II

PROJECTS REFERRED TO IN ARTICLE 4(2)

1. AGRICULTURE, SILVICULTURE AND AQUACULTURE

(a) Projects for the restructuring of rural land holdings;

(b) Projects for the use of uncultivated land or semi-natural areas for intensive agricultural purposes;

(c) Water management projects for agriculture, including irrigation and land drainage projects;

(d) Initial afforestation and deforestation for the purposes of conversion to another type of land use;

(e) Intensive livestock installations (projects not included in Annex I);

(f) Intensive fish farming;

(g) Reclamation of land from the sea.

2. EXTRACTIVE INDUSTRY

(a) Quarries, open-cast mining and peat extraction (projects not included in Annex I);

(b) Underground mining;

(c) Extraction of minerals by marine or fluvial dredging;

(d) Deep drillings, in particular:

(i) geothermal drilling;

(ii) drilling for the storage of nuclear waste material;

(iii) drilling for water supplies;

with the exception of drillings for investigating the stability of the soil;

(e) Surface industrial installations for the extraction of coal, petroleum, natural gas and ores, as well as bituminous shale.

3. ENERGY INDUSTRY

(a) Industrial installations for the production of electricity, steam and hot water (projects not included in Annex I);

(b) Industrial installations for carrying gas, steam and hot water; transmission of electrical energy by overhead cables (projects not included in Annex I);

(c) Surface storage of natural gas;

(d) Underground storage of combustible gases;

(e) Surface storage of fossil fuels;

(f) Industrial briquetting of coal and lignite;

(g) Installations for the processing and storage of radioactive waste (unless included in Annex I);

(h) Installations for hydroelectric energy production;

(i) Installations for the harnessing of wind power for energy production (wind farms);

(j) Installations for the capture of CO_2 streams for the purposes of geological storage pursuant to Directive 2009/31/EC from installations not covered by Annex I to this Directive.

4. PRODUCTION AND PROCESSING OF METALS

(a) Installations for the production of pig iron or steel (primary or secondary fusion) including continuous casting;

(b) Installations for the processing of ferrous metals:

(i) hot-rolling mills;

(ii) smitheries with hammers;

(iii) application of protective fused metal coats;

(c) Ferrous metal foundries;

(d) Installations for the smelting, including the alloyage, of non-ferrous metals, excluding precious metals, including recovered products (refining, foundry casting, etc.);

(e) Installations for surface treatment of metals and plastic materials using an electrolytic or chemical process;

(f) Manufacture and assembly of motor vehicles and manufacture of motor-vehicle engines;

(g) Shipyards;

(h) Installations for the construction and repair of aircraft;

(i) Manufacture of railway equipment;

(j) Swaging by explosives;

(k) Installations for the roasting and sintering of metallic ores.

5. MINERAL INDUSTRY

(a) Coke ovens (dry coal distillation);

(b) Installations for the manufacture of cement;

(c) Installations for the production of asbestos and the manufacture of asbestos products (projects not included in Annex I);

(d) Installations for the manufacture of glass including glass fibre;

(e) Installations for smelting mineral substances including the production of mineral fibres;

(f) Manufacture of ceramic products by burning, in particular roofing tiles, bricks, refractory bricks, tiles, stoneware or porcelain.

6. CHEMICAL INDUSTRY (PROJECTS NOT INCLUDED IN ANNEX I)

(a) Treatment of intermediate products and production of chemicals;

(b) Production of pesticides and pharmaceutical products, paint and varnishes, elastomers and peroxides;

(c) Storage facilities for petroleum, petrochemical and chemical products.

7. FOOD INDUSTRY

(a) Manufacture of vegetable and animal oils and fats;

(b) Packing and canning of animal and vegetable products;

(c) Manufacture of dairy products;

(d) Brewing and malting;

(e) Confectionery and syrup manufacture;

(f) Installations for the slaughter of animals;

(g) Industrial starch manufacturing installations;

(h) Fish-meal and fish-oil factories;

(i) Sugar factories.

8. TEXTILE, LEATHER, WOOD AND PAPER INDUSTRIES

(a) Industrial plants for the production of paper and board (projects not included in Annex I);

(b) Plants for the pre-treatment (operations such as washing, bleaching, mercerisation) or dyeing of fibres or textiles;

(c) Plants for the tanning of hides and skins;

(d) Cellulose-processing and production installations.

9. RUBBER INDUSTRY

Manufacture and treatment of elastomer-based products.

10. INFRASTRUCTURE PROJECTS

(a) Industrial estate development projects;

(b) Urban development projects, including the construction of shopping centres and car parks;

(c) Construction of railways and intermodal transhipment facilities, and of intermodal terminals (projects not included in Annex I);

(d) Construction of airfields (projects not included in Annex I);

(e) Construction of roads, harbours and port installations, including fishing harbours (projects not included in Annex I);

(f) Inland-waterway construction not included in Annex I, canalisation and flood-relief works;

(g) Dams and other installations designed to hold water or store it on a long-term basis (projects not included in Annex I);

(h) Tramways, elevated and underground railways, suspended lines or similar lines of a particular type, used exclusively or mainly for passenger transport;

(i) Oil and gas pipeline installations and pipelines for the transport of CO_2 streams for the purposes of geological storage (projects not included in Annex I);

(j) Installations of long-distance aqueducts;

(k) Coastal work to combat erosion and maritime works capable of altering the coast through the construction, for example, of dykes, moles, jetties and other sea defence works, excluding the maintenance and reconstruction of such works;

(l) Groundwater abstraction and artificial groundwater recharge schemes not included in Annex I;

(m) Works for the transfer of water resources between river basins not included in Annex I.

11. OTHER PROJECTS

(a) Permanent racing and test tracks for motorised vehicles;

(b) Installations for the disposal of waste (projects not included in Annex I);

(c) Waste-water treatment plants (projects not included in Annex I);

(d) Sludge-deposition sites;

(e) Storage of scrap iron, including scrap vehicles;

(f) Test benches for engines, turbines or reactors;

(g) Installations for the manufacture of artificial mineral fibres;

(h) Installations for the recovery or destruction of explosive substances;

(i) Knackers' yards.

12. TOURISM AND LEISURE

(a) Ski runs, ski lifts and cable cars and associated developments;

(b) Marinas;

(c) Holiday villages and hotel complexes outside urban areas and associated developments;

(d) Permanent campsites and caravan sites;

(e) Theme parks.

13. (a) Any change or extension of projects listed in Annex I or this Annex, already authorised, executed or in the process of being executed, which may have significant adverse effects on the environment (change or extension not included in Annex I);

(b) Projects in Annex I, undertaken exclusively or mainly for the development and testing of new methods or products and not used for more than two years.

ANNEX III

SELECTION CRITERIA REFERRED TO IN ARTICLE 4(3)

1. CHARACTERISTICS OF PROJECTS

The characteristics of projects must be considered having regard, in particular, to:

(a) the size of the project;

(b) the cumulation with other projects;

(c) the use of natural resources;

(d) the production of waste;

(e) pollution and nuisances;

(f) the risk of accidents, having regard in particular to substances or technologies used.

2. LOCATION OF PROJECTS

The environmental sensitivity of geographical areas likely to be affected by projects must be considered, having regard, in particular, to:

(a) the existing land use;

(b) the relative abundance, quality and regenerative capacity of natural resources in the area;

(c) the absorption capacity of the natural environment, paying particular attention to the following areas:

(i) wetlands;

(ii) coastal zones;

(iii) mountain and forest areas;

(iv) nature reserves and parks;

(v) areas classified or protected under Member States' legislation; special protection areas designated by Member States pursuant to Directive 2009/147/EC of the European Parliament and of the Council of 30 November 2009 on the conservation of wild birds (1) and to Council Directive 92/43/EEC of 21 May 1992 on the conservation of natural habitats and of wild fauna and flora (2);

(vi) areas in which the environmental quality standards laid down in Union legislation have already been exceeded;

(vii) densely populated areas;

(viii) landscapes of historical, cultural or archaeological significance.

3. CHARACTERISTICS OF THE POTENTIAL IMPACT

The potential significant effects of projects must be considered in relation to criteria set out in points 1 and 2, and having regard in particular to:

(a) the extent of the impact (geographical area and size of the affected population);

(b) the transfrontier nature of the impact;

(c) the magnitude and complexity of the impact;

(d) the probability of the impact;

(e) the duration, frequency and reversibility of the impact.

---

(1) OJ L 20, 26.1.2010, p. 7.
(2) OJ L 206, 22.7.1992, p. 7.

ANNEX IV

INFORMATION REFERRED TO IN ARTICLE 5(1)

1. A description of the project, including in particular:

   (a) a description of the physical characteristics of the whole project and the land-use requirements during the construction and operational phases;

   (b) a description of the main characteristics of the production processes, for instance, the nature and quantity of the materials used;

   (c) an estimate, by type and quantity, of expected residues and emissions (water, air and soil pollution, noise, vibration, light, heat, radiation, etc.) resulting from the operation of the proposed project.

2. An outline of the main alternatives studied by the developer and an indication of the main reasons for this choice, taking into account the environmental effects.

3. A description of the aspects of the environment likely to be significantly affected by the proposed project, including, in particular, population, fauna, flora, soil, water, air, climatic factors, material assets, including the architectural and archaeological heritage, landscape and the interrelationship between the above factors.

4. A description ([1]) of the likely significant effects of the proposed project on the environment resulting from:

   (a) the existence of the project;

   (b) the use of natural resources;

   (c) the emission of pollutants, the creation of nuisances and the elimination of waste.

5. The description by the developer of the forecasting methods used to assess the effects on the environment referred to in point 4.

6. A description of the measures envisaged to prevent, reduce and where possible offset any significant adverse effects on the environment.

7. A non-technical summary of the information provided under headings 1 to 6.

8. An indication of any difficulties (technical deficiencies or lack of know-how) encountered by the developer in compiling the required information.

([1]) This description should cover the direct effects and any indirect, secondary, cumulative, short, medium and long-term, permanent and temporary, positive and negative effects of the project.

ANNEX V

PART A

Repealed Directive with list of its successive amendments

(referred to in Article 14)

Council Directive 85/337/EEC (OJ L 175, 5.7.1985, p. 40)	
Council Directive 97/11/EC (OJ L 73, 14.3.1997, p. 5)	
Directive 2003/35/EC of the European Parliament and of the Council (OJ L 156, 25.6.2003, p. 17)	Article 3 only
Directive 2009/31/EC of the European Parliament and of the Council (OJ L 140, 5.6.2009, p. 114)	Article 31 only

PART B

List of time limits for transposition into national law

(referred to in Article 14)

Directive	Time limit for transposition
85/337/EEC	3 July 1988
97/11/EC	14 March 1999
2003/35/EC	25 June 2005
2009/31/EC	25 June 2011

ANNEX VI

Correlation table

Directive 85/337/EEC	This Directive
Article 1(1)	Article 1(1)
Article 1(2), first subparagraph	Article 1(2), introductory wording
Article 1(2), second subparagraph, introductory wording	Article 1(2)(a), introductory wording
Article 1(2), second subparagraph, first indent	Article 1(2), point (a), first indent
Article 1(2), second subparagraph, second indent	Article 1(2), point (a), second indent
Article 1(2), third subparagraph	Article 1(2), point (b)
Article 1(2), fourth subparagraph	Article 1(2), point (c)
Article 1(2), fifth subparagraph	Article 1(2), point (d)
Article 1(2), sixth subparagraph	Article 1(2), point (e)
Article 1(3)	Article 1(2), point (f)
Article 1(4)	Article 1(3)
Article 1(5)	Article 1(4)
Article 2(1)	Article 2(1)
Article 2(2)	Article 2(2)
Article 2(2a)	Article 2(3)
Article 2(3)	Article 2(4)
Article 3, introductory wording	Article 3, introductory wording
Article 3, first indent	Article 3, point (a)
Article 3, second indent	Article 3, point (b)
Article 3, third indent	Article 3, point (c)
Article 3, fourth indent	Article 3, point (d)
Article 4	Article 4
Article 5(1)	Article 5(1)
Article 5(2)	Article 5(2)
Article 5(3), introductory wording	Article 5(3), introductory wording
Article 5(3), first indent	Article 5(3), point (a)
Article 5(3), second indent	Article 5(3), point (b)
Article 5(3), third indent	Article 5(3), point (c)
Article 5(3), fourth indent	Article 5(3), point (d)
Article 5(3), fifth indent	Article 5(3), point (e)
Article 5(4)	Article 5(4)
Article 6	Article 6
Article 7(1), introductory wording	Article 7(1), first subparagraph, introductory wording

Directive 85/337/EEC	This Directive
Article 7(1), point (a)	Article 7(1), first subparagraph, point (a)
Article 7(1), point (b)	Article 7(1), first subparagraph, point (b)
Article 7(1), final wording	Article 7(1), second subparagraph
Article 7(2)-7(5)	Article 7(2)-7(5)
Article 8	Article 8
Article 9(1), introductory wording	Article 9, introductory wording
Article 9(1), first indent	Article 9(1), point (a)
Article 9(1), second indent	Article 9(1), point (b)
Article 9(1), third indent	Article 9(1), point (c)
Article 9(2)	Article 9(2)
Article 10	Article 10
Article 10a, first paragraph	Article 11(1)
Article 10a, second paragraph	Article 11(2)
Article 10a, third paragraph	Article 11(3)
Article 10a, fourth and fifth paragraphs	Article 11(4), first and second subparagraphs
Article 10a, sixth paragraph	Article 11(5)
Article 11(1)	Article 12(1)
Article 11(2)	Article 12(2)
Article 11(3)	—
Article 11(4)	Article 12(3)
Article 12(1)	—
Article 12(2)	Article 13
—	Article 14
—	Article 15
Article 14	Article 16
Annex I, point 1	Annex I, point 1
Annex I, point 2, first indent	Annex I, point 2(a)
Annex I, point 2, second indent	Annex I, point 2(b)
Annex I, point 3(a)	Annex I, point 3(a)
Annex I, point 3(b), introductory wording	Annex I, point 3(b), introductory wording
Annex I, point 3(b), first indent	Annex I, point 3(b)(i)
Annex I, point 3(b), second indent	Annex I, point 3(b)(ii)
Annex I, point 3(b), third indent	Annex I, point 3(b)(iii)
Annex I, point 3(b), fourth indent	Annex I, point 3(b)(iv)
Annex I, point 3(b), fifth indent	Annex I, point 3(b)(v)
Annex I, point 4, first indent	Annex I, point 4(a)

Directive 85/337/EEC	This Directive
Annex I, point 4, second indent	Annex I, point 4(b)
Annex I, point 5	Annex I, point 5
Annex I, point 6, introductory wording	Annex I, point 6, introductory wording
Annex I, point 6(i)	Annex I, point 6(a)
Annex I, point 6(ii)	Annex I, point 6(b)
Annex I, point 6(iii)	Annex I, point 6(c)
Annex I, point 6(iv)	Annex I, point 6(d)
Annex I, point 6(v)	Annex I, point 6(e)
Annex I, point 6(vi)	Annex I, point 6(f)
Annex I, points 7-15	Annex I, points 7-15
Annex I, point 16, introductory wording	Annex I, point 16, introductory wording
Annex I, point 16, first indent	Annex I, point 16(a)
Annex I, point 16, second indent	Annex I, point 16(b)
Annex I, points 17-21	Annex I, points 17-21
Annex I, point 22	Annex I, point 24
Annex I, point 23	Annex I, point 22
Annex I, point 24	Annex I, point 23
Annex II, point 1	Annex II, point 1
Annex II, point 2(a), (b) and (c)	Annex II, point 2(a), (b) and (c)
Annex II, point 2(d), introductory wording	Annex II, point 2(d), introductory wording
Annex II, point 2(d), first indent	Annex II, point 2(d)(i)
Annex II, point 2(d), second indent	Annex II, point 2(d)(ii)
Annex II, point 2(d), third indent	Annex II, point 2(d)(iii)
Annex II, point 2(d), final wording	Annex II, point 2(d), final wording
Annex II, point 2(e)	Annex II, point 2(e)
Annex II, points 3-12	Annex II, points 3-12
Annex II, point 13, first indent	Annex II, point 13(a)
Annex II, point 13, second indent	Annex II, point 13(b)
Annex III, point 1, introductory wording	Annex III, point 1, introductory wording
Annex III, point 1, first indent	Annex III, point 1(a)
Annex III, point 1, second indent	Annex III, point 1(b)
Annex III, point 1, third indent	Annex III, point 1(c)
Annex III, point 1, fourth indent	Annex III, point 1(d)
Annex III, point 1, fifth indent	Annex III, point 1(e)
Annex III, point 1, sixth indent	Annex III, point 1(f)
Annex III, point 2, introductory wording	Annex III, point 2, introductory wording

Directive 85/337/EEC	This Directive
Annex III, point 2, first indent	Annex III, point 2(a)
Annex III, point 2, second indent	Annex III, point 2(b)
Annex III, point 2, third indent, introductory wording	Annex III, point 2(c), introductory wording
Annex III, point 2, third indent, point (a)	Annex III, point 2(c)(i)
Annex III, point 2, third indent, point (b)	Annex III, point 2(c)(ii)
Annex III, point 2, third indent, point (c)	Annex III, point 2(c)(iii)
Annex III, point 2, third indent, point (d)	Annex III, point 2(c)(iv)
Annex III, point 2, third indent, point (e)	Annex III, point 2(c)(v)
Annex III, point 2, third indent, point (f)	Annex III, point 2(c)(vi)
Annex III, point 2, third indent, point (g)	Annex III, point 2(c)(vii)
Annex III, point 2, third indent, point (h)	Annex III, point 2(c)(viii)
Annex III, point 3, introductory wording	Annex III, point 3, introductory wording
Annex III, point 3, first indent	Annex III, point 3(a)
Annex III, point 3, second indent	Annex III, point 3(b)
Annex III, point 3, third indent	Annex III, point 3(c)
Annex III, point 3, fourth indent	Annex III, point 3(d)
Annex III, point 3, fifth indent	Annex III, point 3(e)
Annex IV, point 1, introductory wording	Annex IV, point 1, introductory wording
Annex IV, point 1, first indent	Annex IV, point 1(a)
Annex IV, point 1, second indent	Annex IV, point 1(b)
Annex IV, point 1, third indent	Annex IV, point 1(c)
Annex IV, points 2 and 3	Annex IV, points 2 and 3
Annex IV, point 4, introductory wording	Annex IV, point 4, first subparagraph, introductory wording
Annex IV, point 4, first indent	Annex IV, point 4, first subparagraph, point (a)
Annex IV, point 4, second indent	Annex IV, point 4, first subparagraph, point (b)
Annex IV, point 4, third indent	Annex IV, point 4, first subparagraph, point (c)
Annex IV, point 4, final wording	Annex IV, point 5
Annex IV, point 5	Annex IV, point 6
Annex IV, point 6	Annex IV, point 7
Annex IV, point 7	Annex IV, point 8
—	Annex V
—	Annex VI

Appendix 9—Directive 2001/42/EC (the Strategic Environmental Assessment Directive)

DIRECTIVE 2001/42/EC OF THE EUROPEAN PARLIAMENT AND OF THE COUNCIL

of 27 June 2001

on the assessment of the effects of certain plans and programmes on the environment

THE EUROPEAN PARLIAMENT AND THE COUNCIL OF THE EUROPEAN UNION,

Having regard to the Treaty establishing the European Community, and in particular Article 175(1) thereof,

Having regard to the proposal from the Commission ([1]),

Having regard to the opinion of the Economic and Social Committee ([2]),

Having regard to the opinion of the Committee of the Regions ([3]),

Acting in accordance with the procedure laid down in Article 251 of the Treaty ([4]), in the light of the joint text approved by the Conciliation Committee on 21 March 2001,

Whereas:

(1) Article 174 of the Treaty provides that Community policy on the environment is to contribute to, *inter alia*, the preservation, protection and improvement of the quality of the environment, the protection of human health and the prudent and rational utilisation of natural resources and that it is to be based on the precautionary principle. Article 6 of the Treaty provides that environmental protection requirements are to be integrated into the definition of Community policies and activities, in particular with a view to promoting sustainable development.

(2) The Fifth Environment Action Programme: Towards sustainability — A European Community programme of policy and action in relation to the environment and sustainable development ([5]), supplemented by Council Decision No 2179/98/EC ([6]) on its review, affirms the importance of assessing the likely environmental effects of plans and programmes.

(3) The Convention on Biological Diversity requires Parties to integrate as far as possible and as appropriate the conservation and sustainable use of biological diversity into relevant sectoral or cross-sectoral plans and programmes.

(4) Environmental assessment is an important tool for integrating environmental considerations into the preparation and adoption of certain plans and programmes which are likely to have significant effects on the environment in the Member States, because it ensures that such effects of implementing plans and programmes are taken into account during their preparation and before their adoption.

(5) The adoption of environmental assessment procedures at the planning and programming level should benefit undertakings by providing a more consistent framework in which to operate by the inclusion of the relevant environmental information into decision making. The inclusion of a wider set of factors in decision making should contribute to more sustainable and effective solutions.

(6) The different environmental assessment systems operating within Member States should contain a set of common procedural requirements necessary to contribute to a high level of protection of the environment.

(7) The United Nations/Economic Commission for Europe Convention on Environmental Impact Assessment in a Transboundary Context of 25 February 1991, which applies to both Member States and other States, encourages the parties to the Convention to apply its principles to plans and programmes as well; at the second meeting of the Parties to the Convention in Sofia on 26 and 27 February 2001, it was decided to prepare a legally binding protocol on strategic environmental assessment which would supplement the existing provisions on environmental impact assessment in a transboundary context, with a view to its possible adoption on the occasion of the 5th Ministerial Conference 'Environment for Europe' at an extraordinary meeting of the Parties to the Convention, scheduled for May 2003 in Kiev, Ukraine. The systems operating within the Community for environmental assessment of plans and programmes should ensure that there are adequate transboundary consultations where the implementation of a plan or programme being prepared in one Member State is likely to have significant effects on the environment of another Member State. The information on plans and programmes having significant effects on the environment of other States should be forwarded on a reciprocal and equivalent basis within an appropriate legal framework between Member States and these other States.

([1]) OJ C 129, 25.4.1997, p. 14 and OJ C 83, 25.3.1999, p. 13.
([2]) OJ C 287, 22.9.1997, p. 101.
([3]) OJ C 64, 27.2.1998, p. 63 and OJ C 374, 23.12.1999, p. 9.
([4]) Opinion of the European Parliament of 20 October 1998 (OJ C 341, 9.11.1998, p. 18), confirmed on 16 September 1999 (OJ C 54, 25.2.2000, p. 76), Council Common Position of 30 March 2000 (OJ C 137, 16.5.2000, p. 11) and Decision of the European Parliament of 6 September 2000 (OJ C 135, 7.5.2001, p. 155). Decision of the European Parliament of 31 May 2001 and Decision of the Council of 5 June 2001.
([5]) OJ C 138, 17.5.1993, p. 5.
([6]) OJ L 275, 10.10.1998, p. 1.

(8) Action is therefore required at Community level to lay down a minimum environmental assessment framework, which would set out the broad principles of the environmental assessment system and leave the details to the Member States, having regard to the principle of subsidiarity. Action by the Community should not go beyond what is necessary to achieve the objectives set out in the Treaty.

(9) This Directive is of a procedural nature, and its requirements should either be integrated into existing procedures in Member States or incorporated in specifically established procedures. With a view to avoiding duplication of the assessment, Member States should take account, where appropriate, of the fact that assessments will be carried out at different levels of a hierarchy of plans and programmes.

(10) All plans and programmes which are prepared for a number of sectors and which set a framework for future development consent of projects listed in Annexes I and II to Council Directive 85/337/EEC of 27 June 1985 on the assessment of the effects of certain public and private projects on the environment (1), and all plans and programmes which have been determined to require assessment pursuant to Council Directive 92/43/EEC of 21 May 1992 on the conservation of natural habitats and of wild flora and fauna (2), are likely to have significant effects on the environment, and should as a rule be made subject to systematic environmental assessment. When they determine the use of small areas at local level or are minor modifications to the above plans or programmes, they should be assessed only where Member States determine that they are likely to have significant effects on the environment.

(11) Other plans and programmes which set the framework for future development consent of projects may not have significant effects on the environment in all cases and should be assessed only where Member States determine that they are likely to have such effects.

(12) When Member States make such determinations, they should take into account the relevant criteria set out in this Directive.

(13) Some plans or programmes are not subject to this Directive because of their particular characteristics.

(14) Where an assessment is required by this Directive, an environmental report should be prepared containing relevant information as set out in this Directive, identifying, describing and evaluating the likely significant environmental effects of implementing the plan or programme, and reasonable alternatives taking into account the objectives and the geographical scope of the plan or programme; Member States should communicate to the Commission any measures they take concerning the quality of environmental reports.

(15) In order to contribute to more transparent decision making and with the aim of ensuring that the information supplied for the assessment is comprehensive and reliable, it is necessary to provide that authorities with relevant environmental responsibilities and the public are to be consulted during the assessment of plans and programmes, and that appropriate time frames are set, allowing sufficient time for consultations, including the expression of opinion.

(16) Where the implementation of a plan or programme prepared in one Member State is likely to have a significant effect on the environment of other Member States, provision should be made for the Member States concerned to enter into consultations and for the relevant authorities and the public to be informed and enabled to express their opinion.

(17) The environmental report and the opinions expressed by the relevant authorities and the public, as well as the results of any transboundary consultation, should be taken into account during the preparation of the plan or programme and before its adoption or submission to the legislative procedure.

(18) Member States should ensure that, when a plan or programme is adopted, the relevant authorities and the public are informed and relevant information is made available to them.

(19) Where the obligation to carry out assessments of the effects on the environment arises simultaneously from this Directive and other Community legislation, such as Council Directive 79/409/EEC of 2 April 1979 on the conservation of wild birds (3), Directive 92/43/EEC, or Directive 2000/60/EC of the European Parliament and the Council of 23 October 2000 establishing a framework for Community action in the field of water policy (4), in order to avoid duplication of the assessment, Member States may provide for coordinated or joint procedures fulfilling the requirements of the relevant Community legislation.

(20) A first report on the application and effectiveness of this Directive should be carried out by the Commission five years after its entry into force, and at seven-year intervals thereafter. With a view to further integrating environmental protection requirements, and taking into account the experience acquired, the first report should, if appropriate, be accompanied by proposals for amendment of this Directive, in particular as regards the possibility of extending its scope to other areas/sectors and other types of plans and programmes,

(1) OJ L 175, 5.7.1985, p. 40. Directive as amended by Directive 97/11/EC (OJ L 73, 14.3.1997, p. 5).
(2) OJ L 206, 22.7.1992, p. 7. Directive as last amended by Directive 97/62/EC (OJ L 305, 8.11.1997, p. 42).
(3) OJ L 103, 25.4.1979, p. 1. Directive as last amended by Directive 97/49/EC (OJ L 223, 13.8.1997, p. 9).
(4) OJ L 327, 22.12.2000, p. 1.

HAVE ADOPTED THIS DIRECTIVE:

Article 1

Objectives

The objective of this Directive is to provide for a high level of protection of the environment and to contribute to the integration of environmental considerations into the preparation and adoption of plans and programmes with a view to promoting sustainable development, by ensuring that, in accordance with this Directive, an environmental assessment is carried out of certain plans and programmes which are likely to have significant effects on the environment.

Article 2

Definitions

For the purposes of this Directive:

(a) 'plans and programmes' shall mean plans and programmes, including those co-financed by the European Community, as well as any modifications to them:

— which are subject to preparation and/or adoption by an authority at national, regional or local level or which are prepared by an authority for adoption, through a legislative procedure by Parliament or Government, and

— which are required by legislative, regulatory or administrative provisions;

(b) 'environmental assessment' shall mean the preparation of an environmental report, the carrying out of consultations, the taking into account of the environmental report and the results of the consultations in decision-making and the provision of information on the decision in accordance with Articles 4 to 9;

(c) 'environmental report' shall mean the part of the plan or programme documentation containing the information required in Article 5 and Annex I;

(d) 'The public' shall mean one or more natural or legal persons and, in accordance with national legislation or practice, their associations, organisations or groups.

Article 3

Scope

1. An environmental assessment, in accordance with Articles 4 to 9, shall be carried out for plans and programmes referred to in paragraphs 2 to 4 which are likely to have significant environmental effects.

2. Subject to paragraph 3, an environmental assessment shall be carried out for all plans and programmes,

(a) which are prepared for agriculture, forestry, fisheries, energy, industry, transport, waste management, water management, telecommunications, tourism, town and country planning or land use and which set the framework for future development consent of projects listed in Annexes I and II to Directive 85/337/EEC, or

(b) which, in view of the likely effect on sites, have been determined to require an assessment pursuant to Article 6 or 7 of Directive 92/43/EEC.

3. Plans and programmes referred to in paragraph 2 which determine the use of small areas at local level and minor modifications to plans and programmes referred to in paragraph 2 shall require an environmental assessment only where the Member States determine that they are likely to have significant environmental effects.

4. Member States shall determine whether plans and programmes, other than those referred to in paragraph 2, which set the framework for future development consent of projects, are likely to have significant environmental effects.

5. Member States shall determine whether plans or programmes referred to in paragraphs 3 and 4 are likely to have significant environmental effects either through case-by-case examination or by specifying types of plans and programmes or by combining both approaches. For this purpose Member States shall in all cases take into account relevant criteria set out in Annex II, in order to ensure that plans and programmes with likely significant effects on the environment are covered by this Directive.

6. In the case-by-case examination and in specifying types of plans and programmes in accordance with paragraph 5, the authorities referred to in Article 6(3) shall be consulted.

7. Member States shall ensure that their conclusions pursuant to paragraph 5, including the reasons for not requiring an environmental assessment pursuant to Articles 4 to 9, are made available to the public.

8. The following plans and programmes are not subject to this Directive:

— plans and programmes the sole purpose of which is to serve national defence or civil emergency,

— financial or budget plans and programmes.

9. This Directive does not apply to plans and programmes co-financed under the current respective programming periods [1] for Council Regulations (EC) No 1260/1999 [2] and (EC) No 1257/1999 [3].

[1] The 2000-2006 programming period for Council Regulation (EC) No 1260/1999 and the 2000-2006 and 2000-2007 programming periods for Council Regulation (EC) No 1257/1999.

[2] Council Regulation (EC) No 1260/1999 of 21 June 1999 laying down general provisions on the Structural Funds (OJ L 161, 26.6.1999, p. 1).

[3] Council Regulation (EC) No 1257/1999 of 17 May 1999 on support for rural development from the European Agricultural Guidance and Guarantee Fund (EAGGF) and amending and repealing certain regulations (OJ L 160, 26.6.1999, p. 80).

Article 4

General obligations

1. The environmental assessment referred to in Article 3 shall be carried out during the preparation of a plan or programme and before its adoption or submission to the legislative procedure.

2. The requirements of this Directive shall either be integrated into existing procedures in Member States for the adoption of plans and programmes or incorporated in procedures established to comply with this Directive.

3. Where plans and programmes form part of a hierarchy, Member States shall, with a view to avoiding duplication of the assessment, take into account the fact that the assessment will be carried out, in accordance with this Directive, at different levels of the hierarchy. For the purpose of, *inter alia*, avoiding duplication of assessment, Member States shall apply Article 5(2) and (3).

Article 5

Environmental report

1. Where an environmental assessment is required under Article 3(1), an environmental report shall be prepared in which the likely significant effects on the environment of implementing the plan or programme, and reasonable alternatives taking into account the objectives and the geographical scope of the plan or programme, are identified, described and evaluated. The information to be given for this purpose is referred to in Annex I.

2. The environmental report prepared pursuant to paragraph 1 shall include the information that may reasonably be required taking into account current knowledge and methods of assessment, the contents and level of detail in the plan or programme, its stage in the decision-making process and the extent to which certain matters are more appropriately assessed at different levels in that process in order to avoid duplication of the assessment.

3. Relevant information available on environmental effects of the plans and programmes and obtained at other levels of decision-making or through other Community legislation may be used for providing the information referred to in Annex I.

4. The authorities referred to in Article 6(3) shall be consulted when deciding on the scope and level of detail of the information which must be included in the environmental report.

Article 6

Consultations

1. The draft plan or programme and the environmental report prepared in accordance with Article 5 shall be made available to the authorities referred to in paragraph 3 of this Article and the public.

2. The authorities referred to in paragraph 3 and the public referred to in paragraph 4 shall be given an early and effective opportunity within appropriate time frames to express their opinion on the draft plan or programme and the accompanying environmental report before the adoption of the plan or programme or its submission to the legislative procedure.

3. Member States shall designate the authorities to be consulted which, by reason of their specific environmental responsibilities, are likely to be concerned by the environmental effects of implementing plans and programmes.

4. Member States shall identify the public for the purposes of paragraph 2, including the public affected or likely to be affected by, or having an interest in, the decision-making subject to this Directive, including relevant non-governmental organisations, such as those promoting environmental protection and other organisations concerned.

5. The detailed arrangements for the information and consultation of the authorities and the public shall be determined by the Member States.

Article 7

Transboundary consultations

1. Where a Member State considers that the implementation of a plan or programme being prepared in relation to its territory is likely to have significant effects on the environment in another Member State, or where a Member State likely to be significantly affected so requests, the Member State in whose territory the plan or programme is being prepared shall, before its adoption or submission to the legislative procedure, forward a copy of the draft plan or programme and the relevant environmental report to the other Member State.

2. Where a Member State is sent a copy of a draft plan or programme and an environmental report under paragraph 1, it shall indicate to the other Member State whether it wishes to enter into consultations before the adoption of the plan or programme or its submission to the legislative procedure and, if it so indicates, the Member States concerned shall enter into consultations concerning the likely transboundary environmental effects of implementing the plan or programme and the measures envisaged to reduce or eliminate such effects.

Where such consultations take place, the Member States concerned shall agree on detailed arrangements to ensure that the authorities referred to in Article 6(3) and the public referred to in Article 6(4) in the Member State likely to be significantly affected are informed and given an opportunity to forward their opinion within a reasonable time-frame.

3. Where Member States are required under this Article to enter into consultations, they shall agree, at the beginning of such consultations, on a reasonable timeframe for the duration of the consultations.

Article 8

Decision making

The environmental report prepared pursuant to Article 5, the opinions expressed pursuant to Article 6 and the results of any transboundary consultations entered into pursuant to Article 7 shall be taken into account during the preparation of the plan or programme and before its adoption or submission to the legislative procedure.

Article 9

Information on the decision

1. Member States shall ensure that, when a plan or programme is adopted, the authorities referred to in Article 6(3), the public and any Member State consulted under Article 7 are informed and the following items are made available to those so informed:

(a) the plan or programme as adopted;

(b) a statement summarising how environmental considerations have been integrated into the plan or programme and how the environmental report prepared pursuant to Article 5, the opinions expressed pursuant to Article 6 and the results of consultations entered into pursuant to Article 7 have been taken into account in accordance with Article 8 and the reasons for choosing the plan or programme as adopted, in the light of the other reasonable alternatives dealt with, and

(c) the measures decided concerning monitoring in accordance with Article 10.

2. The detailed arrangements concerning the information referred to in paragraph 1 shall be determined by the Member States.

Article 10

Monitoring

1. Member States shall monitor the significant environmental effects of the implementation of plans and programmes in order, *inter alia*, to identify at an early stage unforeseen adverse effects, and to be able to undertake appropriate remedial action.

2. In order to comply with paragraph 1, existing monitoring arrangements may be used if appropriate, with a view to avoiding duplication of monitoring.

Article 11

Relationship with other Community legislation

1. An environmental assessment carried out under this Directive shall be without prejudice to any requirements under Directive 85/337/EEC and to any other Community law requirements.

2. For plans and programmes for which the obligation to carry out assessments of the effects on the environment arises simultaneously from this Directive and other Community legislation, Member States may provide for coordinated or joint procedures fulfilling the requirements of the relevant Community legislation in order, *inter alia*, to avoid duplication of assessment.

3. For plans and programmes co-financed by the European Community, the environmental assessment in accordance with this Directive shall be carried out in conformity with the specific provisions in relevant Community legislation.

Article 12

Information, reporting and review

1. Member States and the Commission shall exchange information on the experience gained in applying this Directive.

2. Member States shall ensure that environmental reports are of a sufficient quality to meet the requirements of this Directive and shall communicate to the Commission any measures they take concerning the quality of these reports.

3. Before 21 July 2006 the Commission shall send a first report on the application and effectiveness of this Directive to the European Parliament and to the Council.

With a view further to integrating environmental protection requirements, in accordance with Article 6 of the Treaty, and taking into account the experience acquired in the application of this Directive in the Member States, such a report will be accompanied by proposals for amendment of this Directive, if appropriate. In particular, the Commission will consider the possibility of extending the scope of this Directive to other areas/sectors and other types of plans and programmes.

A new evaluation report shall follow at seven-year intervals.

4. The Commission shall report on the relationship between this Directive and Regulations (EC) No 1260/1999 and (EC) No 1257/1999 well ahead of the expiry of the programming periods provided for in those Regulations, with a view to ensuring a coherent approach with regard to this Directive and subsequent Community Regulations.

Article 13

Implementation of the Directive

1. Member States shall bring into force the laws, regulations and administrative provisions necessary to comply with this Directive before 21 July 2004. They shall forthwith inform the Commission thereof.

21.7.2001 EN Official Journal of the European Communities L 197/35

2. When Member States adopt the measures, they shall contain a reference to this Directive or shall be accompanied by such reference on the occasion of their official publication. The methods of making such reference shall be laid down by Member States.

3. The obligation referred to in Article 4(1) shall apply to the plans and programmes of which the first formal preparatory act is subsequent to the date referred to in paragraph 1. Plans and programmes of which the first formal preparatory act is before that date and which are adopted or submitted to the legislative procedure more than 24 months thereafter, shall be made subject to the obligation referred to in Article 4(1) unless Member States decide on a case by case basis that this is not feasible and inform the public of their decision.

4. Before 21 July 2004, Member States shall communicate to the Commission, in addition to the measures referred to in paragraph 1, separate information on the types of plans and programmes which, in accordance with Article 3, would be subject to an environmental assessment pursuant to this Directive. The Commission shall make this information available to the Member States. The information will be updated on a regular basis.

Article 14

Entry into force

This Directive shall enter into force on the day of its publication in the *Official Journal of the European Communities*.

Article 15

Addressees

This Directive is addressed to the Member States.

Done at Luxembourg, 27 June 2001.

For the European Parliament	*For the Council*
The President	*The President*
N. FONTAINE	B. ROSENGREN

L 197/36 EN Official Journal of the European Communities 21.7.2001

ANNEX I

Information referred to in Article 5(1)

The information to be provided under Article 5(1), subject to Article 5(2) and (3), is the following:

(a) an outline of the contents, main objectives of the plan or programme and relationship with other relevant plans and programmes;

(b) the relevant aspects of the current state of the environment and the likely evolution thereof without implementation of the plan or programme;

(c) the environmental characteristics of areas likely to be significantly affected;

(d) any existing environmental problems which are relevant to the plan or programme including, in particular, those relating to any areas of a particular environmental importance, such as areas designated pursuant to Directives 79/409/EEC and 92/43/EEC;

(e) the environmental protection objectives, established at international, Community or Member State level, which are relevant to the plan or programme and the way those objectives and any environmental considerations have been taken into account during its preparation;

(f) the likely significant effects [1] on the environment, including on issues such as biodiversity, population, human health, fauna, flora, soil, water, air, climatic factors, material assets, cultural heritage including architectural and archaeological heritage, landscape and the interrelationship between the above factors;

(g) the measures envisaged to prevent, reduce and as fully as possible offset any significant adverse effects on the environment of implementing the plan or programme;

(h) an outline of the reasons for selecting the alternatives dealt with, and a description of how the assessment was undertaken including any difficulties (such as technical deficiencies or lack of know-how) encountered in compiling the required information;

(i) a description of the measures envisaged concerning monitoring in accordance with Article 10;

(j) a non-technical summary of the information provided under the above headings.

---

[1] These effects should include secondary, cumulative, synergistic, short, medium and long-term permanent and temporary, positive and negative effects.

ANNEX II

Criteria for determining the likely significance of effects referred to in Article 3(5)

1. The characteristics of plans and programmes, having regard, in particular, to
   - the degree to which the plan or programme sets a framework for projects and other activities, either with regard to the location, nature, size and operating conditions or by allocating resources,
   - the degree to which the plan or programme influences other plans and programmes including those in a hierarchy,
   - the relevance of the plan or programme for the integration of environmental considerations in particular with a view to promoting sustainable development,
   - environmental problems relevant to the plan or programme,
   - the relevance of the plan or programme for the implementation of Community legislation on the environment (e.g. plans and programmes linked to waste-management or water protection).
2. Characteristics of the effects and of the area likely to be affected, having regard, in particular, to
   - the probability, duration, frequency and reversibility of the effects,
   - the cumulative nature of the effects,
   - the transboundary nature of the effects,
   - the risks to human health or the environment (e.g. due to accidents),
   - the magnitude and spatial extent of the effects (geographical area and size of the population likely to be affected),
   - the value and vulnerability of the area likely to be affected due to:
     - special natural characteristics or cultural heritage,
     - exceeded environmental quality standards or limit values,
     - intensive land-use,
   - the effects on areas or landscapes which have a recognised national, Community or international protection status.

Appendix 10—Civil Procedure Rules, Rule 45 Section VII, Practice Direction 45 Section VII, and rule 52.9A

Civil Procedure Rules—Part 45, Section VII—Costs Limits in Aarhus Convention Claims

Scope and interpretation

45.41

(1) This Section provides for the costs which are to be recoverable between the parties in Aarhus Convention claims.
(2) In this Section, 'Aarhus Convention claim' means a claim for judicial review of a decision, act or omission all or part of which is subject to the provisions of the UNECE Convention on Access to Information, Public Participation in Decision-Making and Access to Justice in Environmental Matters done at Aarhus, Denmark on 25 June 1998, including a claim which proceeds on the basis that the decision, act or omission, or part of it, is so subject.

(Rule 52.9A makes provision in relation to costs of an appeal.)

Opting out

45.42

Rules 45.43 to 45.44 do not apply where the claimant—

(a) has not stated in the claim form that the claim is an Aarhus Convention claim; or
(b) has stated in the claim form that—
    (i) the claim is not an Aarhus Convention claim, or
    (ii) although the claim is an Aarhus Convention claim, the claimant does not wish those rules to apply.

Limit on costs recoverable from a party in an Aarhus Convention claim

45.43

(1) Subject to rule 45.44, a party to an Aarhus Convention claim may not be ordered to pay costs exceeding the amount prescribed in Practice Direction 45.
(2) Practice Direction 45 may prescribe a different amount for the purpose of paragraph (1) according to the nature of the claimant.

Challenging whether the claim is an Aarhus Convention claim

45.44

(1) If the claimant has stated in the claim form that the claim is an Aarhus Convention claim, rule 45.43 will apply unless—
  (a) the defendant has in the acknowledgment of service filed in accordance with rule 54.8—
    (i) denied that the claim is an Aarhus Convention claim; and
    (ii) set out the defendant's grounds for such denial; and
  (b) the court has determined that the claim is not an Aarhus Convention claim.
(2) Where the defendant argues that the claim is not an Aarhus Convention claim, the court will determine that issue at the earliest opportunity.
(3) In any proceedings to determine whether the claim is an Aarhus Convention claim –
  (a) if the court holds that the claim is not an Aarhus Convention claim, it will normally make no order for costs in relation to those proceedings;
  (b) if the court holds that the claim is an Aarhus Convention claim, it will normally order the defendant to pay the claimant's costs of those proceedings on the indemnity basis, and that order may be enforced notwithstanding that this would increase the costs payable by the defendant beyond the amount prescribed in Practice Direction 45.

Civil Procedure Rules Practice Direction 45 Section VII—Costs Limits in Aarhus Convention Claims

Limit on costs recoverable from a party in an Aarhus Convention claim: Rule 45.43

5.1

Where a claimant is ordered to pay costs, the amount specified for the purpose of rule 45.43(1) is—
(a) £5,000 where the claimant is claiming only as an individual and not as, or on behalf of, a business or other legal person;
(b) in all other cases, £10,000.

5.2

Where a defendant is ordered to pay costs, the amount specified for the purpose of rule 45.43(1) is £35,000.

Civil Procedure Rules—Part 52, rule 52.9A

Orders to limit the recoverable costs of an appeal

52.9A

(1) In any proceedings in which costs recovery is normally limited or excluded at first instance, an appeal court may make an order that the recoverable costs of an appeal will be limited to the extent which the court specifies.

(2) In making such an order the court will have regard to—
 (a) the means of both parties;
 (b) all the circumstances of the case; and
 (c) the need to facilitate access to justice.

(3) If the appeal raises an issue of principle or practice upon which substantial sums may turn, it may not be appropriate to make an order under paragraph (1).

(4) An application for such an order must be made as soon as practicable and will be determined without a hearing unless the court orders otherwise.

Appendix 11—Rules of the Court of Session, Chapter 58A

CHAPTER 58A

PROTECTIVE EXPENSES ORDERS IN ENVIRONMENTAL APPEALS AND JUDICIAL REVIEWS

Application and interpretation of this Chapter

58A.1.-(1) This Chapter applies to-

(a) applications to the supervisory jurisdiction of the court;
(b) appeals under statute,

which include a challenge to a decision, act or omission which is subject to, or said to be subject to, the public participation provisions of –

(c) Directive 2011/92/EU of 13th December 2011 on the assessment of the effects of certain public and private projects on the environment[a], or
(d) Directive 2008/1/EC of the European Parliament and of the Council of 15th January 2008 (concerning integrated pollution prevention and control)[b]

(2) In this Chapter, references to applicants who are individuals do not include persons who are acting as a representative of an unincorporated body or in a special capacity such as trustee.

(3) In this Chapter, references to a respondent's liability in expenses to the applicant or, as the case may be, an applicant's liability to the respondent means that of all the respondents in the proceedings.

(4) Nothing in this Chapter shall affect any powers of the court to make an order corresponding or similar to an order which may be made under this Chapter in any proceedings falling outwith this Chapter.

Availability of protective expenses orders

58A.2 – (1) Subject to paragraph (2), a petitioner in an application or, as the case may be, an appellant in an appeal to which this Chapter applies may apply for a protective expenses order.

(2) The applicant must be –

(a) an individual; or
(b) a non-governmental organisation promoting environmental protection.

(a) O.J. L26, 28.1.2013, p.1, which codified Council Directive 85/337/EEC (as amended), O.J. L175, 5.7.1985, p40.
(b) O.J. L24, 29.1, 2008, p.8

(3) A protective expenses order is an order which regulates the liability for expenses in the proceedings (including as to the future) of all or any of the parties to them, with the overall aim of ensuring that proceedings are not prohibitively expensive for the applicant.

(4) Subject to paragraph (6), where the court is satisfied that the proceedings are prohibitively expensive for the applicant; it must make a protective expenses order.

(5) For the purposes of this rule, proceedings are prohibitively expensive for an applicant if the applicant could not reasonably proceed with them in the absence of a protective expenses order.

(6) The court may refuse to make a protective expenses order if it considers that-

(a) the applicant has failed to demonstrate a sufficient interest in the subject matter of the proceedings; or
(b) the proceedings have no real prospect of success.

Applications for protective expenses orders

58A.3-(1) An application for a protective expenses order shall be made by motion.

(2) Subject to paragraph (3), except on cause shown, an application must be made no later than when it is reasonably practicable to do so after the applicant becomes aware that the proceedings are to be defended.

(3) An application for a protective expenses order may be made in relation to a reclaiming motion at any stage of the proceeding whether or not an application for such an order was made, or an order granted, at first instance.

(4) A motion mentioned in paragraph (1) shall –

(a) set out why the applicant is seeking the order;
(b) be accompanied by any supporting evidence, which the applicant intends to refer to in making the application.
(c) set out the terms on which the applicant is represented;
(d) be accompanied by a schedule estimating –
 (i) the expenses of the applicant in relation to the proceedings in respect of which the order is sought; and
 (ii) the expenses of each other party for which the applicant may be liable in relation to the proceedings in respect of which the order is sought;
(e) in the case of an application for liability in expenses to be limited to an amount lower or, as the case may be, higher than a sum mentioned in rule 58A.4, set out the grounds on which that lower or higher figure is applied for.

Terms of protective expenses orders

58A.4- (1) Subject to paragraph (2), a protective expenses order must contain provision limiting the applicant's liability in expenses to the respondent to the sum of £5,000.

(2) The court may, on cause shown by the applicant, lower the sum mentioned in paragraph (1).

(3) Subject to paragraph (4), a protective expenses order must also contain provision limiting the respondent's liability in expenses to the applicant to the sum of £30,000.

(4) The court may, on cause shown by the applicant, raise the sum mentioned in paragraph (3).

(5) A protective expenses order may -

(a) exclude any party's liability in expenses to any other party;
(b) limit any party's liability in expenses to any other party;
(c) provide that no party will be liable for the expenses of any other party;
(d) include provision –
    (i) as to a party's liability in expenses if the applicant is successful in the proceedings;
    (ii) as to a party's liability in expenses if the applicant is unsuccessful in the proceedings; or
    (iii) as to a party's liability in expenses regardless of the outcome of the proceedings.

Determination of terms of a protective expenses orders

58A.5-(1) In deciding the terms of a protective expenses order, the court shall (subject to rule 58A.3(1) take into account all the circumstances, including-

(a) the need to ensure that it is not prohibitively expensive for the applicant to continue with the proceedings;
(b) the extent to which the applicant would benefit (whether financially or otherwise) if successful in the proceedings to which the order would apply;
(c) the terms on which the applicant is represented;
(d) whether and to what extent the applicant is acting on behalf of another person which would have been able to bring the proceedings himself, herself or itself; and
(e) whether and to what extent the applicant is willing to limit the expenses which he or she would be able to recover from another party if successful in the proceedings to which the order would apply.

(2) The court shall not make a protective expenses order until it has given all of the parties an opportunity to be heard.

Appendix 12—The Costs Protection (Aarhus Convention) Regulations (Northern Ireland) 2013

STATUTORY RULES OF NORTHERN IRELAND

2013 No. 81

EUROPEAN COMMUNITIES

COURTS

The Costs Protection (Aarhus Convention) Regulations (Northern Ireland) 2013

Made - - - -	*25th March 2013*
Coming into operation -	*15th April 2013*

The Department of Justice, being a Northern Ireland department designated for the purposes of section 2(2) of the European Communities Act 1972(**a**) in relation to the environment(**b**), makes the following Regulations in exercise of the powers under section 2(2) of the European Communities Act 1972.

Citation and commencement

1.—(1) These Regulations may be cited as the Costs Protection (Aarhus Convention) Regulations (Northern Ireland) 2013 and shall come into operation on 15th April 2013.

(2) These Regulations only apply to proceedings commenced on or after 15th April 2013.

Interpretation

2.—(1) In these Regulations—

"the Aarhus Convention" means the United Nations Economic Commission for Europe Convention on Access to Information, Public Participation in Decision-Making and Access to Justice in Environment Matters done at Aarhus on 25 June 1998;

"an Aarhus Convention case" means an application

(a) for judicial review under section 18 of the Judicature (Northern Ireland) Act 1978(**c**) of a decision, act or omission all or part of which is subject to the provisions of the Aarhus Convention; or

(b) for review under the provisions of any statutory provision to the High Court of a decision, act or omission all or part of which is subject to the provisions of the Aarhus Convention;

"court" means the High Court;

"free of charge" means otherwise than for or in expectation of fee, gain or reward;

"indemnity basis" has the meaning assigned to it by rules of court;

(**a**) 1972 c.68. Section 2 was amended by section 27(1)(a) and (b) of the Legislative and Regulatory Reform Act 2006 (c.51) and the Schedule to the European Union (Amendment) Act 2008 (c.7).
(**b**) The European Communities (Designation) Order 2008 (S.I. 2008/301).
(**c**) 1978 c.23. Section 18 was amended by Article 170(2) of and the Schedule to the Magistrates' Courts (Northern Ireland) Order 1981 (S.I. 1981/1675) (NI 26).

"legal representative" means a person exercising a right of audience or conducting litigation in an Aarhus Convention case.

(2) The Interpretation Act (Northern Ireland) 1954(**a**) shall apply to these Regulations as it applies to an Act of the Northern Ireland Assembly.

Costs in Aarhus Convention cases

3. (1) These Regulations shall not apply where the applicant—

(a) has not stated in the application that it is an Aarhus Convention case; or

(b) has stated in the application that the applicant does not wish these Regulations to apply.

(2) Subject to paragraph (4), in an Aarhus Convention case, the court shall order that any costs recoverable from an applicant shall not exceed £5,000 where the applicant is an individual and £10,000 where the applicant is a legal person or an individual applying in the name of a legal entity or unincorporated association.

(3) In an Aarhus Convention case, the court shall order that the costs recoverable from a respondent shall not exceed £35,000 subject to regulation 4(3).

(4) Where the applicant is or was represented by a legal representative and this representation is or was provided free of charge, in whole or in part, even if the applicant is or was also represented by a legal representative not acting free of charge, the court shall order the respondent to make a payment to the Northern Ireland Lawyers Pro Bono Unit (registered charity number XR35688) in respect of such part of the recoverable costs as the court considers just.

(5) The amount payable under paragraph (4) shall not exceed the amount which an applicant would have recovered under paragraph (2) had the representation of the applicant not been provided free of charge.

(6) Where the court makes an order under paragraph (4) the applicant shall send a copy of the order to the Northern Ireland Pro Bono Unit within 7 days of receipt of the order.

(7) Upon any appeal of a decision in an Aarhus Convention case, the court hearing the appeal may make an order that the recoverable costs of the appeal will be limited to the extent which the court specifies having regard to—

(a) the means of both parties;

(b) all the circumstances of the case; and

(c) the need to facilitate access to justice.

(8) The court hearing the appeal shall have the same powers as those of the High Court under paragraph (4).

(9) The amounts specified in paragraphs (2) and (3) do not include value added tax.

Challenging whether the case is an Aarhus Convention case

4.—(1) If the applicant has stated in the application that it is an Aarhus Convention case, regulation 3 applies unless—

(a) the respondent has:

  (i) stated that the case is not an Aarhus Convention case; and

  (ii) set out the respondent's grounds for arguing that the case is not an Aarhus Convention case; and

(b) the court is satisfied that the case is not an Aarhus Convention case.

(2) Where the respondent argues that the case is not an Aarhus Convention case, the court shall determine that issue at the earliest opportunity.

(**a**) 1954 c.33 (NI).

(3) In any proceedings, including any appeal, in relation to the question whether the case is an Aarhus Convention case—

(a) if the court is satisfied that the case is not an Aarhus Convention case, it shall normally make no order for costs in relation to those proceedings;

(b) if the court is satisfied that the case is an Aarhus Convention case, it shall normally order the respondent to pay the applicant's costs of those proceedings on the indemnity basis, and those costs shall be payable notwithstanding that this would increase the costs payable by the respondent beyond those specified in regulation 3.

(4) An appeal of a decision on whether the case is an Aarhus Convention case shall lie to the Court of Appeal and the notice of appeal shall be served within 21 days from the date the decision was filed.

Injunctions

5. If in an Aarhus Convention case the court is satisfied that an injunction is necessary to prevent significant environmental damage and to preserve the factual basis of the proceedings, the court shall, in considering both whether to require an undertaking by the applicant to pay any damages which the respondent or any other person may sustain as a result and the terms of any such undertaking—

(a) have particular regard to the need for the terms of the order overall not to be such as would make continuing with the case prohibitively expensive for the applicant; and

(b) make such directions as are necessary to ensure that the case is heard at the earliest opportunity.

Sealed with the Official Seal of the Department of Justice on 25th March 2013

(L.S.)

David Ford
Minister of Justice

EXPLANATORY NOTE

(This note is not part of the Regulations)

These Regulations make provision to provide costs protection for judicial reviews and statutory reviews to the High Court of a decision, act or omission all or part of which is subject to the provisions of the United Nations Economic Commission for Europe Convention on Access to Information, Public Participation in decision-making and Access to Justice in Environmental Matters done at Aarhus on 25 June 1998.

Printed in the UK by The Stationery Office Limited under the authority and superintendence of Carol Tullo, Controller of Her Majesty's Stationery Office being the Government Printer for Northern Ireland and the Officer appointed to print Acts of the Northern Ireland Assembly.

ISBN 978-0-337-99079-3

£4.00

N5777 04/2013 435777T 19585

9 780337 990793

Appendix 13—Tabular Analysis of the Meeting of the Parties' Consideration of the Compliance Committee's Findings in Communications and Referrals Concerning the Parties' Compliance

LUKE WILCOX[1]

The following table lists every Communication on which the Compliance Committee has substantively reported, indicates whether a Meeting of Parties was convened in respect of the decision, and gives the extent of the Meeting of Parties' endorsement of the Compliance Committee's findings.[2]

Communication Reference	Country	Date of Compliance Committee Report	MoP Decision reference	MoP Outcome
ACCC/C/2004/1	Kazakhstan	18/02/2005	Decision II/5a	Fully endorsed
ACCC/S/2004/1	Ukraine	18/02/2005	Decision II/5b	Fully endorsed
ACCC/C/2004/2	Kazakhstan	14/03/2005	Decision II/5a	Fully endorsed
ACCC/C/2004/3	Ukraine	14/03/2005	Decision II/5b	Fully endorsed
ACCC/C/2004/4	Hungary	18/02/2005	N/A—Compliance Committee made no adverse findings	N/A
ACCC/C/2004/5	Turkmenistan	14/03/2005	Decision II/5c	Fully endorsed
ACCC/C/2004/6	Kazakhstan	16/06/2006	Decision III/6c	Fully endorsed
ACCC/C/2004/8	Armenia	31/03/2006	Decision III/6b	Fully endorsed
ACCC/C/2005/11	Belgium	16/06/2006	N/A—Compliance Committee made no adverse findings	N/A
ACCC/C/2005/12	Albania	31/07/2007	Decision III/6a	Fully endorsed
ACCC/C/2005/13	Hungary	10/05/2006	N/A—Compliance Committee made no adverse findings	N/A
ACCC/C/2005/15	Romania	16/04/2008	N/A—Compliance Committee made no finding of ongoing non-compliance	N/A

[1] Barrister, Landmark Chambers, London.

[2] This appendix does not address the approach of the Meetings of Parties to the Compliance Committee's recommendations in the light of adverse findings; rather, it is concerned purely with the Meetings of Parties' consideration of Compliance Committee findings.

ACCC/C/2006/16	Lithuania	04/04/2008	Decision III/6d	Fully endorsed
ACCC/C/2006/17	European Community	02/05/2008	N/A—Compliance Committee made no adverse findings	N/A
ACCC/C/2006/18	Denmark	29/04/2008	N/A—Compliance Committee made no adverse findings	N/A
ACCC/C/2007/21	European Community	03/04/2009	N/A—Compliance Committee made no adverse findings	N/A
ACCC/C/2007/22	France	03/07/2009	N/A—Compliance Committee made no adverse findings	N/A
ACCC/C/2008/23	United Kingdom	24/09/2010	Decision IV/9i	Fully endorsed
ACCC/C/2008/24	Spain	08/02/2011	Decision IV/9f	Partially endorsed
ACCC/C/2008/26	Austria	25/09/2009	N/A—Compliance Committee made no adverse findings	N/A
ACCC/C/2008/27	United Kingdom	24/09/2010	Decision IV/9i	Fully endorsed
ACCC/C/2008/29	Poland	25/09/2009	N/A—Compliance Committee made no adverse findings	N/A
ACCC/C/2008/30	Republic of Moldova	25/09/2009	Decision IV/9d	Fully endorsed
ACCC/C/2008/31	Germany	20/12/2013	Decision V/9h	Fully endorsed
ACCC/C/2008/32	European Community	14/04/2011	N/A—Compliance Committee criticised the EU case law, but did not find non-compliance	N/A
ACCC/C/2008/33	United Kingdom	24/09/2010	Decision IV/9i	Fully endorsed
ACCC/C/2008/35	Georgia	18/06/2010	N/A—the Compliance Committee noted that the legislation under consideration was unclear and complicated, but did not make a finding of non-compliance	N/A
ACCC/C/2009/36	Spain	18/06/2010	Decision IV/9f	Fully endorsed
ACCC/C/2009/37	Belarus	24/09/2010	Decision IV/9b	Fully endorsed
ACCC/C/2009/38	United Kingdom	25/02/2011	N/A—Compliance Committee made no adverse findings	N/A
ACCC/C/2009/41	Slovakia	17/12/2010	Decision IV/9e	Fully endorsed
ACCC/C/2009/43	Armenia	17/12/2010	Decision IV/9a	Fully endorsed
ACCC/C/2009/44	Belarus	28/06/2011	Decision V/9c	Fully endorsed

ACCC/C/2010/45	United Kingdom	28/06/2013	N/A—Compliance Committee made no adverse findings	N/A
ACCC/C/2010/48	Austria	16/12/2011	Decision V/9b	Fully endorsed
ACCC/C/2010/50	Czech Republic	29/06/2012	Decision V/9f	Fully endorsed
ACCC/C/2010/51	Romania	28/03/2014	Decision V/9j	Fully endorsed
ACCC/C/2010/53	United Kingdom	28/09/2012	Decision V/9n; note the Compliance Committee found a past, but not ongoing, breach of the Convention.	Fully endorsed
ACCC/C/2010/54	European Union	29/06/2012	Decision V/9g	Fully endorsed
ACCC/C/2011/57	Denmark	30/03/2012	Not yet considered by a MoP	N/A
ACCC/C/2011/58	Bulgaria	28/09/2012	Decision V/9d	Fully endorsed
ACCC/C/2011/59	Kazakhstan	28/03/2013	Decision V/9i	Fully endorsed
ACCC/C/2011/60	United Kingdom—joint communication with ACCC/C/2010/45			
ACCC/C/2011/61	United Kingdom	28/06/2013	N/A—no finding of non-compliance	N/A
ACCC/C/2011/62	Armenia	28/06/2013	Decision V/9a	Fully endorsed
ACCC/C/2011/63	Austria	27/09/2013	Decision V/9b	Fully endorsed
ACCC/C/2012/66	Croatia	27/09/2013	Decision V/9e	Fully endorsed
ACCC/C/2012/68	European Union and United Kingdom	24/09/2013	Decision V/9n	Fully endorsed
ACCC/C/2012/70	Czech Republic	20/12/2013	Decision V/9f	Partially endorsed

To date, every finding of non-compliance with the substantive articles of the Aarhus Convention itself has been endorsed by the relevant Meeting of Parties.

On only two occasions has a Meeting of Parties declined to endorse the entirety of the contents of the Compliance Committee's findings (ACCC/C/2008/24 and ACCC/C/2012/70). On both occasions, however, the non-endorsed passages did not relate to compliance with the Convention itself. Rather, they amounted to notes or recommendations included with the findings:

a. In ACCC/C/2008/24, which concerned a substantial residential development in Murcia, Spain, the Compliance Committee noted, in addition to its principal findings on Convention compliance, that Spain had failed to comply with its obligations under the Convention as related to paragraph 23 of the annex to decision I/7.

b. In ACCC/C/2012/70, which concerned the Czech Republic's application to join the EU emissions trading scheme, the Compliance Committee encouraged the EU itself, which was not a party to the Communication, to design a common implementation framework and to monitor Member State compliance with that framework.

As will be apparent, where the Compliance Committee has either found compliance with the Convention, has found past non-compliance which has since been remedied, or found conduct which does not at present but may in future amount to non-compliance, a Meeting of Parties has not usually been convened in respect of those findings.

Appendix 14—List of Useful Weblinks Relating to the Aarhus Convention

UNECE Aarhus Convention homepage
www.unece.org/env/pp/cc.html

Aarhus Convention Implementation Guide (2nd Edition, 2014)
www.unece.org/env/pp/implementation_guide.html

Travaux Préparatoires of the Aarhus Convention
www.unece.org/env/pp/adwg.html

Database of communications by members of the public to the Aarhus Convention Compliance Committee, including the Committee's findings
www.unece.org/env/pp/pubcom.html

Aarhus Convention Compliance Committee, procedural guidance and modus operandi
www.unece.org/fileadmin/DAM/env/pp/compliance/CC_GuidanceDocument.pdf

Digest of Aarhus Convention Compliance Committee case-law 2004–2011
www.unece.org/fileadmin/DAM/env/pp/Media/Publications/ACCC_Jurisprudence_Ecoforum_2011.pdf

'Aarhus clearinghouse' database of information on laws and procedures relevant to the Aarhus Convention's subject matter
http://aarhusclearinghouse.unece.org/

INDEX

Aarhus Convention
acceptance and approval, 233
access to environmental information, 2, 101–4, 221–5
see also **Access to environmental information**
access to justice, 141–66, 228–9
see also **Access to justice**
accession, 233
amendments, 229, 231
arbitration, 240–1
see also **Arbitration**
authentic texts, 234
Community institutions
see **Aarhus Convention application to Community institutions**
competence of organisations, 233
compliance mechanism, 187, 189, 232
see also **Compliance mechanism**
costs, 141, 168–75, 315–16
see also **Costs**
definitions, 220
Depository, 232
dispute settlement, 232, 250
entry into force, 233
environmental information defined, 220
environmental protection, 219
general provisions
access to wider information, 221
environmental education, 221
extensive public participation, 221
non-discrimination, 221, 261
non-persecution provision, 221
promoting Convention principles, 221
public guidance, 221
regulatory measures, 221
supporting environmental organisations, 221
voting right, 230
implementation, 1–2, 5, 41
interpretation, 7–9
NGO relationship, 181–6
see also **Non-Governmental Organisations (NGOs)**
objective, 219
party defined, 220
performance of obligations, 233
public defined, 220
public authority defined, 220
public concerned, 220
see also **Public concerned**
public participation in environmental decision-making, 2, 121–39, 221, 225–8, 235–9
see also **Public participation in environmental decision-making**
ratification, 1, 80, 233
Secretariat, 5, 230
signature, 232
specific activities, 122–3, 225, 235–9
see also **Specific activities**
status of Annexes, 231
structure, 2
Three Pillars, 2, 5, 14, 39, 42–43, 81
withdrawal, 233
Aarhus Convention application to Community institutions
access following application, 258
access to environmental information
adverse effects, 265
collection or dissemination of information, 265
cooperation, 266
guaranteed right, 261, 263
information not held by institution, 266
public interest exception, 265
quality of information, 265
refusal of access, 257, 262, 265
reports on access, 259
request for information, 264
right of access, 256–7
access to justice
acts or omissions, 263, 266
adequate remedies, 263
breaches of the law, 263
CJEU proceedings, 267
Community level, 267
effective remedies, 263
internal review, 263, 266–7
NGO standing, 263, 266–7
review procedure, 263
unsubstantiated requests, 267
accountability, 261
administrative acts, 262, 264
administrative practice, 259
applicants defined, 263

applications, 257–8, 260
Aarhus Convention implementation, 261–3
beneficiaries, 256
collection or dissemination of information, 262–3, 265
see also **Collection or dissemination of information**
Commission, 255, 261
Community institution defined, 264
confidentiality, 256
Council, 255–6, 261
direct access, 259
documents
access to documents, 255
definition, 256
registers, 256, 258–9
reproduction, 259
sensitive documents, 258
electronic access, 259
environmental information defined, 264
environmental law defined, 264
European Parliament, 255, 261
exceptions
commercial interests, 257
court proceedings, 257
economic policy, 257
international relations, 257
national defence, 257
public interest considerations, 257, 262
public security, 257
guaranteed rights, 261, 263
information on access, 259
internal consultation, 255
judicial or legislative capacity, 261
Official Journal publication, 259
omissions, 262, 264
openness, 255
personal data, 255
plan or programme defined, 264
public awareness, 261
public defined, 263
public participation in decision-making
arrangements for participation, 266
draft proposals, 266
early participation, 263, 266
effective participation, 263, 266
environmental protection, 261
information obligation, 266
opportunities for participation, 263
options still open, 263
outcome of public participation, 266
plan or programme, 262–4
public concerned, 266
sustainable development, 261
time limit for comments, 266
TEU provisions, 255
third parties, 256–7
threats to health, 262
transparency, 255, 261
Aarhus Convention Compliance Committee (ACCC)
advice and assistance, 249
case law, 189
caseload, 189–90
communications
abuse of right to communicate, 247
communications from the public, 246–7
consideration, 245, 247, 249
corroborating information, 208–9
de minimis rule, 210, 214
details of provisions breached, 252
discussion of substance, 211
domestic remedies used, 252
electronic form, 247
facts of communication, 251
format, 208
inadmissibility, 210–11
increasing number, 214
information on correspondent, 251
international procedures used, 252
length of communication, 251
manifestly unreasonable communications, 247
name of party concerned, 251
nature of non-compliance, 252
preliminary admissibility, 208–9, 211, 215
language, 209
Meeting of the Parties, 249
procedure, 246
processing, 209, 215
reasonableness, 210
remedial measures, 249–50
registration, 208
requirements, 209–10
sending the communication, 253
signature, 253
supporting documentation, 253
written explanations, 247
compliance mechanism, 187, 189, 201–4, 214, 245, 249–50, 252
see also **Compliance mechanism**
confidentiality, 248, 252–3
conflicts of interest, 190
draft decisions, 187
elections, 244
enhancement of synergies, 250
entitlement to participation, 248
establishment, 3, 243
findings, 4, 7–8, 14, 187, 189, 204–5
function, 204, 243–5
human rights protection, 206
impartiality, 187
independence, 187, 204
influence, 13–14, 39–40, 187
information gathering, 247

jurisdiction, 4
limitations, 40
meetings, 3, 188, 204, 245
membership, 3–4, 187, 204, 244–5
powers
discretionary powers, 206
international law principles, 206
limitations, 205
recommendations, 189, 205, 245, 249–50
response measures, 205
proceedings
admissibility issues, 208–11, 215
amici curiae, 211
appropriateness, 214
closed sessions, 212
communication of decision, 213
consensus-based decisions, 206
discussions as to substance, 211
draft decision, 212
due process, 215
exhaustion of domestic remedies, 210, 213
finalisation of decision, 213
flexibility, 211
formal discussions, 212
Guidance Document, 206–7
individual communications, 206
initial handling, 209–11
innovation, 214
Main Phases, 206, 208–13
Modus Operandi, 206, 211
preparation of decision, 212–13
procedural safeguards, 213–14
substantive decision-making, 206
summary of main findings, 213
summary proceedings, 214
transparency, 215
triggering phase, 208–9
understandable, 214
written submissions, 210–11
referrals, 246–7
reports, 249–50
representation, 188
structure, 243
transparency, 188
UK compliance, 189–90
website, 189

Access to environmental information
see also **Collection and dissemination of environmental information**
Aarhus Convention provisions
access rights, 101–2
active access, 101, 113
adverse effects, 108, 110222
charges for information, 113, 223
collection of information, 101
confidentiality, 222–3
copies of documentation, 102
derogation, 221
dissemination of information, 101–2
form of information, 102–3, 222
incomplete information, 104–7, 222
information not held, 104–5, 222–3
internal communications, 104, 107, 222
national law requirements, 102, 222
non-discrimination, 221
passive access, 101
promptness, 105, 222
public authority responsibility, 101–2, 222
public interest concerns, 222
publicly available information, 222
refusal of request, 104, 112, 222–3
requests for information, 101–3, 222
time-frame, 102–4, 222
unreasonable requests, 102, 104, 106, 222
commercial interests, 108, 110, 222
Community institutions
see **Aarhus Convention application to Community institutions**
course of justice, 108, 110, 222
disclosure of environmental information
see **Disclosure of information**
England and Wales
see **Access to environmental information (England and Wales)**
environment to which information relates, 108, 112–13, 223
Environmental Information Directive (EID), 99, 101
see also **Environmental Information Directive (EID)**
Environmental Information Regulations (2004), 99
European Union
see **Access to environmental information (European Union)**
fair trial, 108, 222
freedom of information, 99–100
intellectual property rights (IPRs), 108, 111, 222
international relations, 108–9, 222
legislative development, 99–101
national defence, 222
personal data, 108, 111–12, 222
pre-Aarhus initiatives
EC initiatives, 99–100
NGO initiatives, 100–1
public security, 108–9, 222
review procedure, 183
Scotland
see **Access to environmental information (Scotland)**
substantive rights, 99
third party interests, 222–3
written refusals, 223

Access to environmental information (England and Wales)
access rights, 13–15
environmental information definition, 16–17
Environmental Information Directive (EID), 15–16
see also **Environmental Information Directive (EID)**
Environmental Information Regulations (2004), 15–17
freedom of information, 15–16
Information Commissioner Guidance, 16–17
provision of information, 15–16
public authorities, 15, 17–19, 21
see also **Public authorities (England and Wales)**
public registers, 21
Access to environmental information (European Union)
biocidal products, 83
chemical substances, 82
commercial interests, 85
confidentiality, 85
court proceedings, 85
criminal matters, 86
disclosure of legal advice, 85–86
dissemination of environmental information, 82, 86
economic policy exception, 85
environmental information
EU institutions, 83–86, 95
Member State authorities, 81–83, 95
Environmental Information Directive (EID), 81–82, 95
see also **Environmental Information Directive (EID)**
commercial interests, 83
confidentiality, 83
genetically modified food, 82
legislative framework, 83–85
legitimate interest, 83
national defence exception, 85
public authorities, 82
refusal of access, 84–86
release of GMOs, 83
TEU provisions, 83
TFEU provisions, 84
transparency, 83
Access to environmental information (Scotland)
adverse effects, 44, 48
collection of environmental information, 43
commercial interests, 43
confidentiality, 44
domestic transposition, 45–48
environmental information, 43–45, 48
Environmental Information Regulations (1992), 44
Environmental Information (Scotland) Regulations (2004), 45–47
EU transposition, 44–45
exceptions, 44
failure to hold information, 44
Freedom of Information (Scotland) Act (2002), 45–47
guaranteed rights, 42–43
judicial review, 44
national defence exception, 44
procedural rules, 44
public authorities, 43–47
see also **Public authorities (Scotland)**
public interest, 44–46
refusal of request, 44–45
requests for information, 43, 45
statutory right, 46
time-frame, 43, 45
unreasonable requests, 44
Access to justice
access to Community institutions, 261, 263–3
see **Aarhus Convention application to Community institutions**
assistance mechanisms, 229
avoiding prohibitive expense, 183
see also **Prohibitive expense**
categories of challenge
breach of environmental law, 142, 229
information requests, 142–3
judicial decisions, 229
public participation, 142–3
refusal of access, 228
substantive and procedural legality, 142, 145, 165–8
CJEU case law, 198
costs, 31–37, 141, 168–75
see also **Costs**
delays, 177
derogation, 221
England and Wales
see **Access to justice (England and Wales)**
equitable behaviour, 177, 183, 229
European Union
see **Access to justice (European Union)**
interim relief, 143, 145, 175–6
see also **Interim relief**
Member State responsibility, 197
non-discrimination, 221
Non-Governmental Organisations (NGOs), 183
Northern Ireland
see **Access to justice (Northern Ireland)**
promptness, 178–9
proposed EU Directive, 197–8
protections provided
acts or omissions, 143–6, 148, 165, 228–9
adequate and effective remedies, 143, 145, 175, 229

administrative procedures, 143, 229
appeals, 143
costs protection, 148–50
environmental law, 145–7
expeditious procedure, 228
fairness, 143, 145, 177, 183, 229
fixed cost rules, 148
independent and impartial review, 142, 228
injunctive relief, 143, 145, 175, 229
judicial procedures, 143
judicial review, 148–50
national law, 142–4, 146–7, 165, 228–9
ouster clauses, 150
preliminary review procedure, 229
Protective Costs Orders (PCOs), 148
review procedure, 142, 151, 228
public concerned
maintaining impairment of right, 228
sufficient interest, 228
standing, 37–39, 151–65, 228
see also **Standing**
Scotland
see **Access to justice (Scotland)**
substantive and procedural legality, 142, 145, 165–8, 228
see also **Substantive and procedural legality**
timely remedies, 177–8, 183, 229
transparency, 183
Access to justice (England and Wales)
absence of EU legislation, 29–30
ACCC findings, 38–39
appeal provisions, 28
assistance mechanisms, 30–31
costs, 31–37
see also **Costs**
differing legal systems, 29
Environmental Information Directive (EID), 28
see also **Environmental Information Directive (EID)**
Environmental Information Regulations (2004), 28
expeditious review, 28
ICO decision notice, 28–29
impairment of a right, 29
impartiality, 28–29
judicial review cases, 31–34, 38–39
national law provisions, 29–30
overview, 28–31
planning decisions, 39
promptness, 38–39
public authority reconsideration, 28
public concerned, 29
public interest litigation, 31–32
review procedure, 28–29
standing, 37–39
see also **Standing**
subsidiarity principle, 29
Wednesbury review, 39
Access to justice (European Union)
access to EU courts
direct and individual concern, 94
fairness, 94
human rights protection, 94–95
injunctive relief, 94
internal review procedure, 93–94
Non-Governmental Organisations (NGOs), 93–95
prohibitive expense, 94
standing, 94–95
Environmental Information Directive (EID), 91
see also **Environmental Information Directive (EID)**
national level
Aarhus Convention compliance, 92–93, 95
effective access, 92–93
environmental impact assessment, 92
environmental liability, 93
lack of public participation, 92
national laws, 92
right of access, 91
refusal of access, 91
Access to justice (Northern Ireland)
costs
allocation of costs, 74
prohibitive expense, 74–76
Protective Costs Orders (PCOs), 74–76
interim injunctions, 75
legal aid, 74
public interest, 74
statutory challenges, 75
Access to justice (Scotland)
ACCC finding, 60, 62
breaches of environmental law, 58
domestic transposition, 60–71
effective remedies, 58
environmental decision-making, 58
Environmental Impact Assessment Directive, 59–60
see also **Environmental Information Directive (EID)**
Environmental Information (Scotland) Regulations (2004), 58
EU transposition, 59–60
fairness, 58–59
Freedom of Information (Scotland) Act (2002), 58
impartiality, 59
injunctive relief, 58
judicial review proceedings, 60–62
legitimate interest, 61
Non-Governmental Organisations (NGOs), 58–59
person aggrieved, 61

planning decisions, 59
private interests, 61–62
procedural rules, 59
prohibitive expense, 58–59, 63–71
proportionality principle, 60
public concerned, 58
public interest, 61–62
request for information, 58
review of procedures, 58, 60
standing, 60–62
sufficient interest, 58–59
timing of proceeding, 62–63
Wednesbury test, 60
Arbitration
appointment of arbitrator, 240
arbitral tribunal, 240–1
awards, 241
confidentiality, 240
counter-claims, 241
expenses, 241
notification, 240
third party intervention, 241

Cabinet Office Consultation Principles
CAJE submission, 197
see also **Coalition for Access to Justice for the Environment (CAJE)**
consultation period, 197
policy proposals, 197
public participation issues, 197
Civil Procedure Rules (CPR)
appeal costs, 317
costs limits (Aarhus Convention claims)
challenging a claim, 316
limits on costs recoverable, 315–17
opting out, 315
scope and interpretation, 315
Practice Direction (costs limits), 316
Coalition for Access to Justice for the Environment (CAJE)
access to justice, 191
CJEU referral, 192–3
costs
allocation of costs, 192
compatibility of costs regime, 191–3
complexity of relevant law, 193
objective or subjective analysis, 192
prohibitive expense, 191
prospects of success, 192–3
injunctive relief, 192–3
Code of Practice on Consultation
consultation period, 196
Collection and dissemination of environmental information
collection of information
ease of access, 113, 224
effective access, 113, 115–16
electronic databases, 113, 116, 224
environmental information defined, 114
lists, registers and files, 116, 224–5
mandatory systems, 114–15, 223
meta-information, 116
monitoring, 114
planning process, 115
relevant information, 114
responsibility, 101
updating of information, 114, 223
Community institutions, 262–3
see also **Aarhus Convention application to Community institutions**
dissemination of information
contact points, 224
ease of access, 113, 224
eco-auditing, 118, 225
eco-labelling, 118, 225
effective access, 113, 115–16, 224
electronic databases, 113, 116, 224
environmental information defined, 114
explanatory material, 118, 225
factual information, 118
flow of information, 114, 117, 223
official support, 224
legislative documents, 224
performance of public functions, 118
policy documents, 224–5
pollutant release and transfer registers (PRTRs), 118–19
pollution inventories, 118, 225
product information, 225
progress reports, 224
public interest concerns, 119
refusal, 225
relevant information, 114
responsibility, 101–2
strategic documents, 224
threats to human health, 114–15, 117, 119, 223
international documents, 224
international treaties, 224
national environmental reports, 117, 224
notification requirement, 117–18
performance of public functions, 225
public authorities, 101–2
publication of information, 118
specific dissemination requirements, 117
sufficiency of information, 116, 224
transparency, 115–16, 224
Community institutions
see **Aarhus Convention application to Community institutions**
Compliance mechanism
see also **Aarhus Convention Compliance Committee (ACCC)**
adoption, 202
advice to individual parties, 189
common objective, 201

communications from the public, 189, 202–4, 215
compliance committees, 202
consultative nature, 202–3
facilitative nature, 202
formation, 187
forward-looking nature, 204
function, 201–2
independent experts, 187
multilateral environmental agreements, 201
non-compliance, 201–2
non-confrontational nature, 202–3
Non-Governmental Organisations (NGOs), 183–7
optional arrangements, 202
procedures, 202–3
public international law, 201
public involvement, 202
referrals, 187, 204
review of compliance, 232
structure, 202
successful nature, 214
United Kingdom compliance, 189–90

Confidentiality
access to environmental information, 44, 83, 85, 222–3, 256, 272
disclosure of information, 19–20, 108–9
commercial interests, 19, 43, 85, 108, 110, 222, 272

Cost Protection (Aarhus Convention) Regulations (Northern Ireland) (2013)
commencement, 323
costs in Aarhus Convention cases, 324–5
injunctions, 325
interpretation, 323–4
judicial review procedure, 326
statutory review procedure, 326

Costs
ACCC decisions, 168–71
access to justice, 63, 72, 141, 148–50
adverse costs liability, 169, 193
allocation of costs, 74, 168, 192
appeals, 170–1, 173
Civil Procedure Rules (CPR), 315–17
see also **Civil Procedure Rules (CPR)**
CJEU decision, 174
compatibility of costs regime, 191–3
complexity of relevant law, 35, 67, 173–4, 193
cost cap, 76, 150, 169, 174, 193
costs follow event rule, 168
England and Wales
adverse effects, 31
complexity of relevant law, 35
costs protection regimes, 35
Environmental Justice Report, 31
frivolous claims, 35–36
importance of matter at stake, 35
interim injunctions, 34
Jackson Report, 31, 34
judicial review cases, 31–4
legal aid, 35
liability for costs, 34–35
objective or subjective analysis, 35–37
prohibitive expense, 33–35
prospects of success, 35–36
Protective Costs Orders (PCOs), 31–32, 34
Sullivan Report, 31
undertakings in damages, 34
exceptional circumstances, 168
fixed costs rule, 170
frivolous claims, 35–36, 65, 173–4
importance of matter at stake, 35, 67, 173–4
indemnity costs, 170
individual's financial position, 173
judicial influence, 194
judicial review, 193–4
legal aid, 35, 168
liability for costs, 34–35, 65, 68, 172, 174
NGO influence, 194
no private interest, 168
Northern Ireland
allocation of costs, 74
Costs Protection Regulations (Northern Ireland) (2013), 75
payment of costs, 74
prohibitive expense, 74–76
Protective Costs Orders (PCOs), 74–76
nuisance cost rules, 175
objective or subjective analysis, 35–37, 65–67, 69, 172–4, 192
previously incurred costs, 171
prohibitive costs, 169, 171–3
prohibitive expense, 33–35, 63–71, 74–76, 94, 191, 280–1, 290
see also **Prohibitive expense**
prospects of success, 35–36, 65, 67, 69–70, 174
Protective Costs Orders (PCOs), 31–32, 34, 74–76, 148, 168–70, 174
see also **Protective Costs Orders (PCOs)**
public importance, 168
public interest, 168–9, 171
Scotland
access to justice, 63, 72
complexity of relevant law, 67
frivolous claims, 65
importance of matter at stake, 67
liability for costs, 65, 68
objective or subjective analysis, 65–67, 69
prohibitive expense, 63–71
prospects of success, 65, 67, 69–70
Protective Expenses Orders (PEOs), 64, 66–71, 172
undertakings in damages, 34, 168
United Kingdom reference, 191–3
see also **Coalition for Access to Justice for the Environment (CAJE)**

Court of Session Rules
Protective Expenses Orders (PEOs), 319–21
see also **Protective Expenses Orders (PEOs)**

Disclosure of environmental information
adverse effects, 108, 110, 222
charges for information, 113, 223
customary practice, 107
England and Wales
see **Disclosure of environmental information (England and Wales)**
environment to which information relates, 108, 112–13, 223
information obligation, 105
information on emissions, 110–11
internal communications, 104, 107, 222
exemptions
commercial interests, 108, 110, 222
confidential proceedings, 108–9
course of justice exclusion, 108, 110, 222
criminal inquiries, 108, 110
discretionary powers, 104
draft documents, 106–7
fair trial concerns, 108, 222
human rights concerns, 110
information not held, 104–5, 222–3
intellectual property rights, 108, 111, 222
international relations, 108–9, 222
legitimate interest, 110
material not yet completed, 104–7, 222
national defence, 108–9, 222
natural justice, 110
personal data, 108, 111–12, 222
professional privilege, 108
public interest, 105, 107–9
public security, 108–9, 222
restrictive interpretation, 109, 223
third party interests, 108, 112
unreasonable requests, 104, 106, 222
national law requirement, 107
onward referrals, 105
promptness, 105, 222
public authorities, 104–5, 107
refusal to disclose, 104, 112, 222–3, 225
Scotland
see **Disclosure of environmental information (Scotland)**
transfer of requests, 105
Wednesbury reasonableness, 106
Disclosure of environmental information (England and Wales)
adverse effects, 19
appeals, 20
challenges to non-disclosure, 20–21, 28–29
commercial interests, 19
confidentiality, 19–20
duty of disclosure, 19, 21
Environmental Information Regulations (2004), 19
expeditious procedure, 20, 28
impartiality, 28–29
inadequate answers, 20, 28
incomplete data, 19
insufficient justification, 21
presumption in favour of disclosure, 19
public interest, 19, 21
refusal to disclose, 19–20, 28
requests for information, 19
review procedure, 20, 28–29
unreasonable requests, 19
Disclosure of environmental information (Scotland)
accuracy of information, 45
enforcement, 46
Environmental Information (Scotland) Regulations (2004), 45–47
Freedom of Information (Scotland) Act (2002), 45–47
presumption in favour of disclosure, 45, 47
public authorities, 45–46
public interest, 45–46
refusal to disclose, 45, 48
requests for information, 45–46
statutory bar, 47
time-frame, 45
Dispute settlement
Aarhus Convention provisions, 232, 250
Dissemination of environmental information
see **Collection and dissemination of environmental information**

England and Wales
Aarhus Convention influence, 13–14
access to environmental information, 13–17, 21
see also **Access to environmental information (England and Wales)**
access to justice, 28–39
see also **Access to justice (England and Wales)**
costs, 31–37
see also **Costs**
disclosure of information, 19–21, 28–29
see also **Disclosure of information (England and Wales)**
Protective Costs Orders (PCOs), 31–32, 34, 74–76, 148, 168–70, 174
public participation in environmental decision-making, 22–28
see also **Public participation in environmental decision-making (England and Wales)**
standing, 37–39
see also **Standing**

Environmental Impact Assessment Directive
access to justice, 286, 290
acts or omissions, 290
annual reports, 287
assessment of public and private projects, 285–6
availability of information, 289
comments or opinions, 289
communication with Commission, 291
competent authority, 287, 289
consultation procedure, 288
correlation table, 302–5
definitions, 287
description of project, 300
development, 287
development consent
definition 287
procedure, 285, 287–90
direct or indirect effects, 288
early participation, 288
effective participation, 289
entry into force, 291
environmental protection, 285–6
exchange of information, 291
exemptions, 286–7
fair, equitable and timely procedure, 290
form of information required, 288
harmonisation, 285
information requirement, 286, 289–90
integrated pollution control, 287
judicial review, 290
national defence, 287
national laws, 290
nature of decision, 289
personal health and well-being, 285–6
practical information, 290
precautionary principle, 285
preliminary review procedure, 290
prohibitive expense, 290
project defined, 287
projects subject to assessment, 288, 292–4, 296–9
proportionality principle, 286
provision of information, 289
public defined, 287
public concerned, 287
public participation, 286, 289
quality of life, 286
results of consultation, 290
review procedure, 290
standing
maintaining impairment of a right, 290
sufficient interest, 290
subsidiarity principle, 286
thresholds, 286, 288
time frames, 289
trans-boundary context, 286
transposition into national law, 301

Environmental Information Directive (EID)
access to environmental information
accurate information, 270
applicants defined, 271
charges for information, 270, 273
CJEU approach, 82
dissemination of information, 82, 270–1, 273–4
England and Wales, 15–16
environmental information, 269–71
European Union, 82, 95, 269, 271–2
evaluation process, 270
information not held, 272
judicial review, 270
public awareness, 270
publicly available information, 271
refusal of requests, 270–3
requests for information, 271–2
right of access, 269–70, 272
subsidiarity principle, 270
access to justice
acts or omissions, 273
England and Wales, 28
European Union, 91
impartiality, 273
independence, 273
refusal of information request, 273
review procedure, 273–4
correlation table, 275
dissemination of environmental information
electronic format, 273–4
reports, 273
threats to human health, 274
updated information, 273
entry into force, 274
environmental information
accurate information, 270
charges for information, 270
confidential information, 82
definition, 81–82, 269, 271
dissemination of information, 82, 270–1, 273–4
held by public authority, 271
quality of information, 274
implementation, 274
integration with Community policies, 269
objectives, 270
Protective Expenses Orders (PEOs), 17–18
public authorities, 81–82 , 270–1
public defined, 271
repeal, 274
requests for information
adverse effects, 272
commercial interests, 272
confidentiality, 272
course of justice, 272
environmental protection, 272
format of information, 271–2

information not held, 272
information supplied on voluntary basis, 272
intellectual property rights, 272
internal communications, 272
international relations, 272
list of criteria, 272
manifestly unreasonable requests, 272
material not yet complete, 272
Member State responsibility, 271
national defence, 272
notice of refusal, 273
overly-general requests, 271–2
personal data, 272
public interest considerations, 272
public security, 272
publicly available information, 271
refusal of requests, 270–3
restrictive approach, 272
separation of information requested, 273
specific form, 271
time-frame, 271

EU law
Aarhus Convention integration
conflicting provisions, 80
implementation, 81
legislative process, 80
ratification, 80
environmental information defined, 262
environmental law defined, 262
EU institutions, 80
see **Aarhus Convention application to Community institutions**
international agreements, 80
legislative interpretation, 80
plan or programme defined, 262

European Union
see also **EU law**
Aarhus Convention integration, 80–81
Community institutions
see **Aarhus Convention application to Community institutions**
access to environmental information, 81–86
see also **Access to environmental information (European Union)**
access to justice, 81, 91–95
see also **Access to justice (European Union)**
public participation in environmental decision-making, 87–91, 95
see also **Public participation in environmental decision-making (European Union)**

Executive regulations
public participation in environmental decision-making, 22, 48, 121, 138–9, 227

Genetically Modified Organisms (GMOs)
access to information, 83
public participation in decision-making, 26–28, 90, 137
release of GMOs, 26–28, 83, 90, 137, 184

Intellectual property rights (IPRs)
access to information, 108, 111, 222, 272

Interim relief
access to justice
England and Wales, 34
European Union, 94
Northern Ireland, 75
Scotland, 58
costs, 34
interim injunctions, 34, 58, 75

Meetings of the Parties
adoption of amendments, 229
analysis of ACCC findings, 327–30
compliance issues, 3–4, 205, 243, 327–30
see also **Aarhus Convention Compliance Committee (ACCC)**
financial arrangements, 230
function, 2–3, 5, 205, 229
information exchange, 229
intergovernmental organisations, 230
mandate, 190
NGO representation, 190, 230
policy reviews, 229
powers, 4–5
preparation of protocols, 229
procedural rules, 230
reports, 229
requirement, 2
subsidiary bodies, 229
timing, 229

Non-discrimination provision
access to environmental information, 221, 261
access to justice, 221, 261
harassment, 221
public participation in environmental decision-making, 221, 261

Non-Governmental Organisations (NGOs)
access to environmental information, 100–1, 183
access to justice, 39, 93–95, 198
Aarhus Convention
access to environmental information, 100–1, 183
access to justice, 183
accountability, 186
compliance issues, 183–7
costs issues, 194
environmental protection, 181–2, 185–6
fairness, 186

Genetically Modified Organisms (GMOs), 184
human health and safety, 186
influence, 181–2
involvement in negotiations, 182–3
judicial review, 186
lobbying, 182
Meeting of the Parties, 190, 230
minimum government standards, 186
NGO coalition, 182–4
NGO contribution, 183–5
NGO representation, 190, 230
radioactive waste, 184
sustainable development, 185
transparency, 186
unlawful actions, 186
unreasonable decision-making, 186
Working Group, 182–4, 191
Environment for Europe process, 182
exercise of rights, 181, 183
human rights protection, 185
public participation in environmental decision-making, 24, 183–4, 277
standing, 151–7, 161, 165, 263, 266–7

Northern Ireland
access to justice
costs, 74–76
interim injunctions, 75
legal aid, 74
public interest, 74
statutory challenges, 75
administration of justice, 78
Aarhus Convention
compliance, 78
implementation, 76–77
costs
allocation of costs, 74
Costs Protection Regulations (Northern Ireland) (2013), 75
payment of costs, 74
prohibitive expense, 74–76
Protective Costs Orders (PCOs), 74–76
development planning, 76
environmental assessment procedure, 75
judicial review, 73–74, 77
planning agreements, 73
planning powers, 76–77
public confidence, 78
rule of law, 77–78
Stormont Executive, 76–78

Plan or programme
Aarhus Convention compliance, 125–7
ACCC Guidance, 123
access to Community institutions, 262–3
see also **Aarhus Convention application to Community institutions**
Commission SEA Guidance, 123–5, 139
definition, 124
environmental assessment, 125
overlapping or inconsistent provisions, 125–7
public participation in environmental decision-making
England and Wales, 22–24
European Union, 87–91, 95, 266, 277–8, 282
Scotland, 48–49, 53–57, 68

Prohibitive expense
see also **Costs**
access to justice, 183
avoidance of prohibitive expense
CAJE submission, 191–3
England and Wales, 33–35
European Union, 94, 280–1, 290
Scotland, 63–71
Protective Costs Orders (PCOs), 31–32, 34, 74–76, 148, 168–70, 174
Protective Expenses Orders (PEOs), 64, 66–71

Proportionality
access to justice, 60
environmental impact assessment, 286
substantive and procedural legality, 166, 195

Protective Costs Orders (PCOs)
costs protection, 31–32, 34, 74–76, 148, 168–70, 174

Protective Expenses Orders (PEOs)
appeals under statute, 319
application procedure, 320
availability, 319–20
Court of Session Rules, 319–21
costs protection, 172
prohibitive expense, 64, 66–71
public participation provisions, 319
supervisory jurisdiction, 319
terms, 321

Public authorities
access to environmental information
Aarhus Convention provisions, 101–2
disclosure of environmental information, 104–5, 107
dissemination of information, 101–2, 222, 270–1
information held or not held, 104–5, 222–3, 266, 271–2
definition, 17–18, 43–45, 47, 81, 105, 220, 261, 271
England and Wales
see **Public authorities (England and Wales)**
European Union
see **Public authorities (European Union)**
Scotland
see **Public authorities (Scotland)**

Public authorities (England and Wales)
ACCC influence, 19
definition, 17–18

disclosure of information, 19, 21
see also **Disclosure of information (England and Wales)**
Environmental Information Directive (EID), 17–18
see also **Environmental Information Directive (EID)**
Environmental Information Regulations (2004), 17
privatised utilities, 17–18
registers of environmental information, 21
responsibility, 15
Public authorities (European Union)
access to environmental information, 81–82
definition, 81
Public authorities (Scotland)
access to environmental information, 43, 45–46
definition, 43–45, 47
disclosure of information, 45–46
see also **Disclosure of information (Scotland)**
private contractors, 47
public utilities, 47
request for information, 43
Public concerned
access to justice, 29, 58, 228
definition, 24, 129, 131, 151, 220, 279, 281
identification, 133, 137, 226, 266, 278
public participation in environmental decision-making, 24, 87, 128–9, 131, 133, 137, 225
see also **Public participation in environmental decision-making**
review procedure, 142
standing, 37–38, 151–4, 158–9, 164–5, 228
Public interest
access to Community institutions, 262
see also **Aarhus Convention application to Community institutions**
access to environmental information, 44–46, 109, 119, 222, 257
access to justice, 31–32, 61–62
costs considerations, 168–9, 171
disclosure of information, 19, 21, 45–46, 105, 107–8
Public Participation Directive
access to justice
acts or omissions, 281
fair, equitable and timely procedure, 281
impartiality, 281
independence, 281
information requirement, 283
judicial review, 281
maintaining impairment of a right, 281
national law, 281
plan or programme, 277–8, 282
practical information, 281
preliminary review procedure, 281
prohibitive expense, 280–1
review procedure, 281
sufficient interest, 281
accountability, 277
acts or omissions, 277, 280–1
amendments, 278–81
arrangements for participation, 279
availability of information, 279
comments or opinions, 278–9, 281, 283
competent authorities, 279, 283
content of decision, 281
description of project, 280
development consent, 279–80
draft decisions, 279
early participation, 278–9, 281, 283
effective participation, 278–9, 281
electronic information, 279
environmental impact procedure, 279
equitable procedure, 280
extension of projects, 280–1
fairness, 280
guaranteed rights, 277
information requirement, 278, 280
national defence exception, 278–9
nature of decision, 280
NGO participation, 277
objective, 278
opportunities for participation, 278
options still open, 279
plan or programme, 277–8, 282
see also **Plan or programme**
preliminary review procedure, 280–1
prohibitive expense, 280–1
protecting human health, 277
public concerned, 278–81
public defined, 279, 281
results of participation, 278, 283
review procedure, 280
specific activities, 277
standing
maintaining impairment of right, 280–1
sufficient interest, 280–1
subsidiarity principle, 278
substantive or procedural legality, 277
time-frame, 278–9, 283
timely procedure, 280–1
transparency, 277
Public participation in environmental decision-making
ACCC decision-making, 127
access to Community institutions, 262–3
see also **Aarhus Convention application to Community institutions**
adequate participation, 121–2
awareness of decision, 136, 227
comments or opinions, 128, 134–5, 226, 228
consenting procedures, 121

derogation, 221
early participation, 132, 137, 226
effective participation, 129–30, 132, 226
England and Wales
  see **Public participation in environmental decision-making (England and Wales)**
entry into discussions, 133
environmental impact assessment, 121–3, 226
European Union
  see **Public participation in environmental decision-making (European Union)**
examination of information, 133–4, 226
executive regulations, 121, 138–9, 227
failure of consultation, 137–8
fairness, 137
information regarding objectives, 133, 226
informing the public, 136, 225, 227
lawful consultation, 121
legally binding instruments, 121
multiple decisions, 128
national defence exception, 123, 225
national legislation, 123, 225
non-discrimination, 221
operating conditions updated, 136–7, 227
opportunities for participation, 128, 226
options still open, 132–33, 138, 226–7
outcome of participation, 227
plan or programme, 121–7, 227
  see also **Plan or programme**
proactive approach, 133
provision of information
  adequate, timely and effective manner, 128–30, 132, 137–8, 225
  comments and questions, 128
  draft decisions, 128, 226, 228
  duty to inform, 227
  early notice, 128–9
  environmental impact assessment, 128
  envisaged procedure, 128, 226
  individual notice, 128, 225
  nature of possible decision, 128
  proposed activities, 225–6
  public authority responsible for decision, 128, 226
  public concerned, 128–9, 131, 133, 137, 225–6
  public hearing, 128, 226
  public notice, 128–9, 225
  refusal of information, 134
  relevant information, 128, 134, 226–7
  time-frame, 130–1, 226
provisions for participation, 137–8
release of GMOs, 137, 227
repeated participation, 136–7
representation, 228
review procedure, 183
Scotland
  see **Public participation in environmental decision-making (Scotland)**
specific activities, 122–3, 225, 235–9
  see also **Specific activities**
strategic environmental assessment, 121
tiered decision-making, 132
transparency, 137
written submissions, 227

Public participation in environmental decision-making (England and Wales)
  environmental impact procedure, 22
  environmental policies, 22
  executive regulations, 22
  judicial decisions, 26
  national defence exception, 22
  NGO interests, 24
    see also **Non-Governmental Organisations (NGOs)**
  public concerned, 24
  planning regime, 24–26
  plan or programmes, 22–24
    see also **Plan or programme**
  procedures, 24
  Public Participation Directive, 22–23
    see also **Public Participation Directive**
  release of GMOs, 26–28
  relevant legislative areas, 23–26
  specific activities, 22–23

Public participation in environmental decision-making (European Union)
  Commission consultation procedure, 90
  effective participation, 89–90, 95
  environmental impact assessment, 88–89, 91
  EU institutions, 89–91
  exclusions, 90
  language requirements, 90, 95
  Member State level, 87–89
  plan or programmes
    effective participation, 89, 95
    environmental impact assessment, 89
    EU institutions, 90–91, 95
    intergovernmental procedure, 89
    Public Participation Directive, 88–89
    Strategic Environmental Assessment Directive, 88–89
  projects
    environmental impact assessment, 88
    EU institutions, 89
    intergovernmental assessment procedure, 87
    public concerned, 87
    reasonable alternatives,
    right of participation, 87
    trans-boundary projects, 87
  release of GMOs, 90

Public participation in environmental decision-making (Scotland)
domestic transposition, 51–52, 54–57
early participation, 49–51, 53
early release of information, 49
effective participation, 49, 51, 53, 56
environmental assessment procedure, 49, 51, 53, 55, 57
Environmental Impact Assessment Directive, 50–51, 53, 59–60, 65, 68, 71
EU transposition, 50, 52–54
executive regulations, 48
planning decisions, 53–55
plan or programmes, 48–49, 53–55, 57, 68
see also **Plan or programme**
procedures, 49
public local inquiry, 51–52
public notice, 49, 56
relevant activities, 49
specific activities, 48–49
Strategic Environmental Assessment Directive, 53–57, 68
tiered decision-making, 49–50, 52
Public registers
environmental information, 21, 44, 116, 257, 271, 273

Scotland
Aarhus Convention status
EU Directives, 41–42
implementation, 41
international obligations, 42
international treaty status, 41
Scots law, 41–42
access to environmental information, 42–43
see also **Access to environmental information (Scotland)**
access to justice, 42, 58–71
see also **Access to justice (Scotland)**
avoidance of prohibitive expense
absence of private interest, 64–65
ACCC findings, 63
access to justice, 63, 72
appeals, 71
complexity of relevant law, 67
frivolous claims, 65
importance of what is at stake, 67
liability for costs, 65, 68
limiting expenses, 63
prospect of success, 65, 67, 69–70
Protective Expenses Orders (PEOs), 64, 66–71, 172
public interest, 64, 66
objective or subjective analysis, 65–67, 69
decision-making process
accountability, 43
exercise of rights, 42
public awareness, 43
transparency, 43
disclosure of information, 45–48
see also **Disclosure of information (Scotland)**
environmental information, 43–45, 48
national defence, 44
public authorities, 43–47
public interest, 44
public participation in environmental decision-making, 42–43
see also **Public participation in environmental decision-making (Scotland)**
Secretariat
function, 5
Specific activities
ACCC Guidance, 123, 127
airports, 237, 239
chemical industry, 236–7
construction projects, 237
dams, 237
definition, 123
energy sector, 235
environmental impact, 123
Environmental Impact Assessment Directive, 122
extension of activities, 239
gas pipelines, 237
groundwater abstraction, 237
industrial plants, 237
inland waterways, 237
Integrated Pollution Prevention and Control Directive, 122
intensive farming, 237
metal production and processing, 235
mineral industry, 236
national legislation, 123
nuclear power stations, 239
oil and gas extraction, 237
overlapping activities, 122
ports and piers, 237
power lines, 237
public participation in decision-making, 121–2
quarries, 237
research projects, 239
storage installations, 238
treatment plants, 238–9
waste management, 237
waste water treatment, 237
water resources, 237
Standing
ACCC decisions, 151, 155–6, 161–2
CJEU decisions, 151–4, 158–61
England and Wales
environmental protection organisations, 38
persons aggrieved, 37

planning process, 37
public concerned, 37–38
European Union, 94–95
impairment of a right, 151, 153, 159, 165, 228, 280–1, 290
judicial review cases, 151, 158, 163–4
legitimate interest, 155–6, 158
national law, 151–2, 154, 156, 158, 160
Non-Governmental Organisations (NGOs), 39, 151–7, 161, 165, 263, 266–7
persons aggrieved, 162–3
persons requesting information, 151
public concerned, 151–4, 158–9, 164–5
restrictive approach, 159, 161
Scotland
legitimate interest, 61
person aggrieved, 61
private interests, 61–62
public interest, 61–62
substantial interest, 158
substantive interest, 162
sufficient interest, 151, 158, 162–5, 228, 280–1, 290

Strategic Environmental Assessment Directive
assessment of plan or programmes, 307–9, 313–14
biological diversity, 307
common procedural requirements, 307
consultations, 308, 310
decision-making, 311
definitions, 309
entry into force, 312
environmental assessment, 309
environmental effects, 308, 314
environmental reports, 308–11
environmental responsibilities, 308
evaluation reports, 308, 311
exceptions, 309
exchange of information, 311
future development consent, 308
general obligations, 310
implementation, 311–12
information requirements, 308, 311, 313
integrated pollution control, 311
minimum environmental assessment framework, 308
monitoring, 311
objectives, 309
plan or programme, 309
protection of human health, 307
public defined, 309
relationship with Community legislation, 311
scope, 309
sustainable development, 307
trans-boundary consultations, 307, 310
transparency, 308

Subsidiarity
access to environmental information, 270
access to justice, 29
environmental impact assessment, 286
public participation in environmental decision-making, 278

Substantive and procedural legality
ACCC Communication, 195
access to review procedure, 165–6
judicial review cases, 165–7, 195–6
proportionality principle, 166, 195
standard of review, 165–6, 195
substantive legality
acts or omissions, 194–5
breaches of national law, 194–5
review procedure, 194–5
Wednesbury reasonableness, 166, 168, 195–6

Task Forces
function, 6–7

Weblinks, 331

Working Group of the Parties
ad hoc Group, 182
compliance mechanism, 183–4
establishment, 5
function, 5, 7, 184, 191
meetings, 182–4, 197
membership, 3, 5
NGO contribution, 182–4, 191

www.ingramcontent.com/pod-product-compliance
Ingram Content Group UK Ltd.
Pitfield, Milton Keynes, MK11 3LW, UK
UKHW021036150926
475561UK00003B/138